The Global Journey of Racism

The Global Journey of Racism

Michelle Christian

Stanford University Press
Stanford, California

Stanford University Press
Stanford, California

© 2025 by Michelle Christian. All rights reserved.

No part of this book may be reproduced or transmitted in any form or by any means, electronic or mechanical, including photocopying and recording, or in any information storage or retrieval system, without the prior written permission of Stanford University Press.

Library of Congress Cataloging-in-Publication Data
Names: Christian, Michelle, author.
Title: The global journey of racism / Michelle Christian.
Description: Stanford, California : Stanford University Press, 2025. | Includes bibliographical references and index.
Identifiers: LCCN 2024047475 (print) | LCCN 2024047476 (ebook) | ISBN 9781503638259 (cloth) | ISBN 9781503642898 (paperback) | ISBN 9781503642904 (ebook)
Subjects: LCSH: Racism. | Imperialism. | White supremacy (Social structure) | Racism against Black people.
Classification: LCC HT1521 .C48 2025 (print) | LCC HT1521 (ebook) | DDC 305.8—dc23/eng/20241226

LC record available at https://lccn.loc.gov/2024047475
LC ebook record available at https://lccn.loc.gov/2024047476

Cover design: Daniel Benneworth-Gray
Cover art: Susan Wilkinson/Unsplash

The authorized representative in the EU for product safety and compliance is: Mare Nostrum Group B.V. | Mauritskade 21D | 1091 GC Amsterdam | The Netherlands | Email address: gpsr@mare-nostrum.co.uk | KVK chamber of commerce number: 96249943

Contents

	Acknowledgments	vii
	Prologue: Conceptualizing a Racist World	ix
1	Racist Modernity	1
2	Racist Empires	26
3	Traveling Racism and Deep Whiteness	54
4	Entangled Racial States	85
5	Transforming Race and Malleable Whiteness	120
6	Global Colorblindness	154
7	Fighting Global White Supremacy	190
	Afterword	205
	Notes	207
	Bibliography	257
	Index	307

Acknowledgments

I am abundantly grateful for a community and family who have taught me, uplifted me, pushed me, and cared for me. My graduate-school teachers—Joe Feagin, Wahneema Lubiano, Charles Payne, Lee Baker, Linda Burton, Mary Hovsepian, Gary Gereffi, and the Black feminist-inspired activist community in Durham—exposed me to books, ideas, movements, helped to build my confidence, and showed me the world and all its injustices. No one, though, would have as impactful of an influence than Eduardo Bonilla-Silva. Eduardo is my intellectual lighthouse and fundamentally changed the trajectory of my life. This book would not exist without the theoretical and personal foundation he made. Woody Doane, Mary Romero, and Bandana Purkayastha always supported me and the vision of what this book could be. Barbara Harris Combs models the type of academic care I hope to follow.

Kristen Lavelle, Rosalind Chou, Jennifer Mueller, Glenn Bracey, Christopher Chambers, and Jake van den Berg became the friends who really knew, saw, and inspired me. To pursue the experience of critical racial knowledge acquisition collectively together at Texas A&M and in the years that followed was a gift. Felicia Arriaga, Elizabeth Hordge-Freeman, Sarah Mayorga, Louise Seamster, Victor Ray, Trenita Brookshire Childers, Atiya Husain, Ninita Brown, and Jamaal Wright—I am so excited by the amazing work you have done since we navigated Duke and

North Carolina together. Serena Sebring's friendship, activism, and heart stays with me today.

Shaneda Destine, Althea Murphy-Price, Sherley Cruz, Chonika Coleman-King, Dorian McCoy, Lois Presser, Katy Chiles, Kristen Block, Megan Haselschwerdt, Alex Moulton, Liliana Gonzalez, Lizeth Zepeda, Michelle Commander, Deadric Williams, Robert Bland, LaToya Eaves, Tyler Wall, Michelle Brown, Kasey Henricks, Lisa East, Meghan Conley, Josh Inwood, Bertin Louis, Jessi Grieser, Aris Clemons, Jennifer Jabson Tree, Stefanie Benjamin, Dawn Duke, Shayla Nunnally, Sarah Eldridge, Stephanie Bohon, Patience Melnik, and the leaders at The Bottom —all of you made the University of Tennessee and Knoxville a better place. Your commitments to racial and social justice continue to inspire me. Above all, Jioni Lewis, I have gained so much from our friendship, ongoing collaborations, and learning when it was important to agitate. Assumpta Namaganda, our studies and friendship have taught me much about beauty, resilience, and hope.

My former and current graduate students Christopher Rogers, Nuray Karaman, Adria Ryan, Zaina Shams, Rossanna Diaz, and Elliott Howard are part of the transformative next generation of scholars, teachers, and activists. Particularly Enkeshi El-Amin, my first graduate student, who would go on to found The Bottom and revolutionize community sociology. Enkeshi, I am in awe of what you do. I am grateful for research support from Abby Tobias-Lauerman, Cameron Graham, Wyatt Smith, students from my Global Racism courses, and the intellectual community fostered in Foundations in Critical Race and Ethnic Studies.

Lastly, my family. My parents, Dale and Kathy Lake, always believed and supported my intellectual journey even as it took me further away. My in-laws, Sam and Penny Christian, my brothers Rick and Lynn Springer, and my kids Niko and Via, thank you for keeping me grounded and loved. But, mostly, Blair Christian. I became a sociologist, a mother, a traveler, a partner, and an author with you by my side. Here's to the next twenty years.

Prologue
Conceptualizing a Racist World

The story of racism is submerged. Absorbed in the voices buried in oceans, in the penetrating roots of plantations, the markings of our bordered lands, the wealth of grand cities, the poverty of scattered villages, and transfixed in our communities, on our bodies, in our daily words and actions. The story of racism is complex. Circuitous logics, changing meanings, ambiguous classifications, temporal moments, and local interpretive codes all mark racism and the elusive but definitive grip of "race." The story of racism, I argue throughout the book, is everywhere. We cannot move, breathe, love, birth, achieve, work, participate, consume, create, and just live without the story of how racism fractures, hierarchizes, and structures the possibilities for every group, every place, and everyone across the globe. We all live in a racist world, but some of us gain from its unearned abundance while others are confined within its staggering enclosures.

The Global Journey of Racism goes big. I ask readers to accompany me on an exploration to learn about the historical and contemporary global story of racism rather than how it is usually presented: as something bound within only certain geographies, impacting only certain groups; that it should be subsumed within categories of ethnicity or nation; or that it is just an idea or attitude everyone can possess against one other devoid of history, context, and power dynamics. I first began to outline the ideas I put forward in this book in an article I wrote for the *Sociology of Race and Ethnicity*, "A Global Critical Race and Racism Framework." Over the last fifteen years I conducted multiple global field research projects, traveled widely across regions, and read a lot of interdisciplinary literatures. In the process I began to see the world differently. Where some scholars argued there are only a few racial states with many differences, I saw similarities and believed that all states were racial states but not equally racist states. Where some scholars saw disjointed social processes, I saw connective points across scales and that states, groups, and geographies were relationally linked. Where some scholars analyzed white supremacist dynamics only in obvious cases, I saw its structural and symbolic impacts everywhere, all over the world, but often in subtle and less direct ways. I preliminarily fleshed these points out in the well-received *SRE* article, but I knew I needed to expand upon them. Thus, *The Global Journey of Racism* is an opportunity to magnify and develop my initial arguments with more details, examples, and geographies.

The book is also, importantly, part of a larger cohort of scholarship from inspiring thinkers and intellectuals in the Du Boisian, critical race, postcolonial, and Black Studies traditions who recenter racism in its globally determined, expansive, colonial roots.[1] For those of us sharing this perspective, racism always was a "transnational norm,"[2] pulsating through scales of global-national-local forces,[3] but for many of us, it also acted in service to global white supremacy. An analytic understanding of white supremacy as a global system is key then because, as a "multidimensional system of domination,"[4] it connected vast and diverse European imperial practices within an array of overlapping social systems to different colonial, colonially adjacent, and now postcolonial geographies. There was no region, locality, or space left untouched in what Toni Morrison describes as our "gendered, sexualized, wholly racialized world."[5] Essentially, we all contemporarily maneuver within the scars of what Charles Mills argues is "planetary" global white supremacy.[6]

This intellectual lineage and the sharpening of my critical race analytic perspective brought me to write *The Global Journey of Racism*.[7] I use the framing of "racist world" as a conceptual device not to say that every place and everyone is equally "racist," nor to diminish the "imperial guilt"[8] and responsibility of the West, but to describe how every geography is touched by European-created global racism in direct-indirect, visible-invisible ways.[9] I do not argue that racism is the same all over, that it is witnessed and has the same magnitude in every place, and/or that racism overrides other systems of domination. But I do argue that all peoples, geographies, and states are part of an interconnected global racial system and must variously contend with its deleterious effects. Therefore, the main aim of *The Global Journey of Racism* is to outline the emergence and ongoing reproduction of the global racial system of white supremacy. I attempt to show how racism travels and race transforms through the global racial system in distinct, intricate, layered, and relational ways. More succinctly, I conceptualize a global racial system framework with six analytic points.

First, the global racial system emerged in the crucible of *racist modernity and empires*. The co-constitutive forces of modernity's racial logics and empire's racist structural practice created a global racial hierarchy where most "white" racialized groups were designated for rule and nonwhite racialized groups for land appropriation, labor exploitation, scientific investigation, entertainment, even death. Liberalism, science, and spectacle imbued whiteness as the highest human taxonomic placement replete with rights, property, and capital value but also as the creators and insatiable consumers of racist commodity products, performance, and popular culture. Together, racist modernity and empires created the congealed global racial system of white supremacy that hierarchically incorporated all into its maze and "locked in [the] advantages of predominantly white countries"[10] and groups in the postcolonial, post–Civil Rights, post-Apartheid era.[11] White countries and subjectivities continue to set the global institutional rules and racial reference points the global world follows and/or contends with.[12]

Second, *racism travels* across the globe along the scaffolding built by racist modernity and empires. I draw inspiration for traveling racism's procedures from world-systems literature[13] and Eduardo Bonilla-Silva's racialized social systems approach.[14] Broadly, the global racial system,[15] interlocked through the forces of capitalism and overlapping political, social, and cultural social systems, displays how racialized distinctions and anti-Black capital, military, and cultural practices are continuously reproduced, naturalized, and mapped together across unequal geographies. Traveling racism's practices are operationalized through what I argue is a global hierarchical racialization process across multiple scales. Racialization, the application of racial meanings and categories, to bodies, groups, cultures, and geographies through praxis is fundamentally "an exercise of power" wielded across the global racial system.[16] Racialized power mechanisms "are routine, recurrent," and organizational.[17] Collectively they dis-tribute material resources and symbolic value and dictate the contours of group and individual agentic possibilities.

At the top of the scale is the historical European, and later settler colonial, geographies that created what Nadia Kim calls "imperialist" racialization processes that have contemporarily evolved into "transnational racialization," the "top-down ideological [racial practices and] processes" that global North, western actors continue to enact which still produces racist exclusions, inclusions, and hierarchical divisions.[18] Aggregated transnational racializations become a globally circulating racial assemblage of dominant global racial logics and representations[19] that come to embody "renewals, re-makings, and mash ups of older racially fashioned subjects," for a supposedly postracial, colorblind world.[20] Essentially, through the assemblage all regions and countries must engage with an "overarching white worldview"[21] even if racial ideas are adapted and applied differently or challenged across national and local geographies.[22]

Thus, the next level on the scale, "national racialization," represents the response and negotiation to transnational racialization and the circulating assemblage and how states potentially adopt and adapt racial logics and practices.[23] National racialization processes conducted by elite power groups, actors, and institutions in countries are also a reflection and interaction to where the country and groups fall within regional hierarchies.[24] Sometimes this involves complex "in-group" or "out-group" racialization procedures where some groups are designated more similar or separate from the dominant group in any given region or geography.[25] Ultimately, nations make racial claims, and structure internal racial practice, with an understanding of peripheral regional racial proximation cues and their wider placement in a global racial hierarchy dictated by transnational racialization.[26]

Third *race transforms*, evolves, shifts, calcifies, "scavenges," and disappears within and across geographies, over time, but is always linked to a shared historical global racist foundation and the contemporary global racial system.[27] "Race," the racial categories and meanings in any given geography, transforms in three ways. Transformation occurs contemporarily through how globally circulating racial practices are "locally indexed"[28] across geographic space and interact and intersect with a region and country's already colonially and historically constructed racial divisions,[29] shaping the "resonance" of certain racial constructions.[30] Because all modern states[31] are either once (and current) empire states, former colonized and/

or continuously colonized states, or noncolonized but still racialized states, the "interactive model of [racial] interpretation" geographically varies.[32]

Next, race transforms historically. At different temporal eras, across geographies racial terms, ideas, and practices changed to meet specific global-national-socio-political needs. Current racial change, however, is best understood as evolutionary rather than discretely. The roots of colonial racial description and stratification mark and regroup in postcolonial, colonially adjacent landscapes. Lastly, race transforms for geographies and groups when racialized individuals and groups cross borders through various manifestations of migration, and different bodily and cultural racial markers hierarchically place them within a national racial order.[33] Through this movement across time and space some groups may gain while others lose privileges, and a country's racial image and position may go up or down in the global hierarchy of nations.

Fourth, a *global racial hierarchy* between whiteness and anti-Blackness secures the global racial system. The global racial hierarchy is essentially a relational "architecture" that national racial hierarchies are embedded in and adaptions of.[34] Global and national racial categories only gain meaning and are analytically understood in relation to each other. Racial subordination, and the racialization of nonwhite groups under white supremacy, are understood not just in relation to whiteness but in relation to other nonwhite racial categories, especially anti-Blackness.[35] Basically, racialized groups are all part of a "shared field of racial meaning and power"[36] where hierarchical ordering structures relational racial understandings and the distribution of power within the racial structure.[37]

More specifically, many national racial formations are structured through and against the symbolism and materiality of the "global anti-Black condition"[38] that makes Blackness "the steady pole" at the base of the global hierarchy.[39] Global anti-Blackness operates regionally and nationally to define which national and local groups are placed at "the bottom."[40] A global anti-Black imaginary,[41] therefore, commonly serves as a reference point against which geographically varied groups at the bottom are judged and determined.[42] Of course, this in no way means that racial hierarchies are the same across geographies or that Blackness is experienced homogenously for corporeally but also differentially marked Black bodies and groups.[43] Here, anti-Blackness is understood foremost as a structural location, oftentimes, but not always and necessarily, literally embodied. By highlighting the operational work anti-Blackness does, I also do not seek to minimize or collapse the racist practices experienced by non-Black racialized groups.[44] Rather, within the global racial system framework, processes of racialization and racist practices experienced by different racial groups are always devised and interpreted within globally, regionally, and nationally encoded hierarchical forces and meanings.[45]

At the top of the global racial hierarchy sits global whiteness. As a transnational force of power, global whiteness ideas and practices demarcate privileged white racial structural positions across geographies in all their intersecting and layered complexities.[46] Historically through empire in regions across the globe, "colonial regimes of whiteness" formed where sociolegal, economic, cultural, and symbolic representation and categorical embodied and disembodied boundaries of whiteness developed.[47] Within current postcolonial landscapes whiteness remains to various degrees a material force of power,[48] a structural position some groups gain proximity to, a material and symbolic aspiration and status symbol, and something to manage, negotiate, or repudiate.

Fifth, *global colorblindness* ideologically supports the global racial system for a twenty-first-century cultivated nonracial palate. Global colorblindness, according to Jean Beaman and Amy Petts, attests to the "many contexts and circumstances that can produce colorblind racial ideologies" along with "the mechanisms that sustain it as a culturally hegemonic ideology."[49] Global "racial events"[50] such as the Holocaust, decolonization, global neoliberalism, the Global War on Terror, and the Black Lives Matter movement shape the contemporary global racial discourses and practices of colorblindness that intersect across versatile colorblind geographic varieties. In this context, global colorblindness praxis ensures that global racism is purged from its "historical roots,"[51] the language of "race" is expunged, and just about everything is "not racism."[52] When nothing is racist, the vilest, most "blatant racist expression[s] are renewed,"[53] and justified along with a new discursive semiotics of race, which underscore "metonymic elaborations," or "coded signifiers."[54]

As colorblind practices and logics roam and traverse the global racial system, they form connected but still distinct colorblind practices and logics.[55] Flexible "colorblind rhetoric"[56] molds with historical, national-local contexts and the much longer historical arc of global white supremacy that always included colorblind tactics with overtly racist understandings and practices.[57] Thus, global colorblindness today includes a link to the past, unlocks the discursive formations that justify seemingly race-neutral material practice, and connects disparate geographies all nested in regional and global racial hierarchies. In its wake a new "post-racial imperialism" hides contemporary forms of empire and the reproduction of the global racial system.[58]

Lastly, *collective resistance* always followed and forced change within the global racial system. Racialized Black and nonwhite groups and white accomplices fought against global white supremacy, imperialism, and colonialism, and marked new ways of being and thriving in this world. Through what Saidiya Hartman calls "the domain of practice . . . an inventory of ways of doing and a genealogy of refusal," groups challenged and resisted their everyday subordinated conditions.[59] National racial orders are therefore also always about contestation and the racial politics of "refusal" across the global racial system.[60]

Thus, my goal with *The Global Journey of Racism* is to bring typically disparate ideas and geographies about race together in one integrated synthesized analysis. I want readers to come away thinking expansively and interconnectedly. I want them to be able to see both similarities and specificities to the story of race but ultimately that our world is a woven racial tapestry connecting us all unequally. The book mostly is a conceptual rather than a primarily data-driven contribution. I place vast geographies and diverse groundbreaking terms developed in critical literatures on race, racism, empire, postcolonialism, whiteness, and colorblindness in conversation with each other and within the framework of a global racial system. Because the book's scale attempts to be "planetary," I am unable to go as in-depth as I would have liked on specific geographies, histories, and examples or to include every single locality. What I lack in detailed minutiae I hope to make up for through scale, breadth, comprehensiveness, and care.

I know, nonetheless, that the book is an ambitious project. In trying to cover our "wholly racialized world" in its entirety I know there are areas where I fall short, details I miss, language and cultural limitations I inhabit. I humbly see the text as just the beginning of scratching the surface on all the forms of global racism and its manifestations across different geographies. My biggest hope is that the book is read as an invitation. An invitation to think about racial complexity, to think about racial power, and to think about racism as an interconnected global system fueling white supremacy in direct, indirect, and not always apparent ways. Whatever limitations or absences are found in these pages, my wish is that the book will encourage and inspire others to fill my geographic, temporal, and conceptual holes.

Throughout the book I engage with language, voice, and racial representational practices with a sense of care, nuance, and an understanding and acknowledgment of the racist colonial terms that mark the modern world. I thought deeply about how and why I was engaging with specific literatures, the words I used, and the complexity, sensitivity, and caution needed when writing about global formations of race and racism in English, and as an American woman racialized white. Katherine McKittrick's contemplations on citations and knowledge production in *Dear Science* alongside Toni Morrison's *Playing in the Dark* shape my engagement. Both ask that we partake in the politics of knowledge and citational practice to, in the words of McKittrick, "trust that the works in the works cited are helping us understand and talk about and theorize how to know the world differently," even as we may not agree.[61] Through this we practice "citations as learning, as counsel, as sharing."[62]

In *The Global Journey of Racism* I read, cited, and engaged with foundational racist texts to highlight how racist knowledge made what Morrison calls "intellectual domination possible" while simultaneously uplifting the Black, nonwhite, and critical scholars who documented these histories and theorized racism's production.[63] As both McKittrick and Morrison thought about and "wrestled with" the implications of this work from their subject positionalities as Black women in North America, I have done so as a white American woman.[64] My subject positionality engendered a constant process of questioning, reckoning, and sitting in humility with an awareness of what I know, do not know, and cannot know: how whiteness benefitted, shaped, and shapes my life. This process never ends.

Writing about global racism is particularly fraught and overflowing with the words and labels of racist colonial knowledge and cartographies. Dionne Brand poetically espouses, "no language is neutral" when it is born from definitive assault.[65] It is astonishing how much of the global norm today operates within an everyday semiotics that reify colonial and imperially informed terms like "Middle East," "sub-Saharan Africa," "West Indies," "America," and so many more, even as decolonization brought forth acts of renaming and reclaiming. As Sabelo Ndlovu-Gatsheni reminds us, "most present-day social identities [and national borders] are traceable to the dawn of" conquest,[66] when Europe created what Sylvia Wynter calls the "rules of representation" and "categorical models" of identification,[67] while alternative languages and words were torn from newly racially embodied peoples deemed threatening or lacking in cultural worth.[68]

Throughout the text I struggle with how I use these labels and therefore reify their everyday use. My intentions when I use terms—in particular, commonly used geographic designations—are to bring attention to these histories and the ongoing contemporary racial representations they continue to reflect. I do not, however, use specific racist expletives of harm in recounting racism's elaboration. I also write in English, but, when possible, I use the local language terms that regional scholars argue to express a national and local racial meaning. Identifying "reliable, contextualized translation" is nonetheless challenging as debates exist about specific meanings of terms.[69] I chose to rely on interpretations from regional and national critical race scholars. With this lens and focus, I engage with scholars who sometimes challenge local interpretations that obfuscate away from race to spotlight how racism reproduces.

I also chose not to capitalize "white," but I capitalize all other racialized group categories unless not originally capitalized in direct quotations. The history of nonwhite racial capitalization is widely connected to racial justice activism, and cultural group formation prior and after racialization, but I also know individuals, and diverse groups in different geographies, make capitalization choices based on personal choice and complex racial geographic histories.[70] In the United States, some scholars have begun to capitalize "white,"[71] as many mainstream news organizations do, to ensure that whiteness is emphasized and that those racialized as white cannot fall into its universalizing, nonlabeled norm. I find these rationales compelling, but I also worry about the unintended implications for capitalizing "white" in the contemporary moment when some white individuals and groups claim racial marginalization as victims of racism. As racism evolves, meanings and terms evolve, yet they are always linked in different capacities to their historical, global foundational roots. We will necessarily always need to contend with the politics, complexities, and ramifications of racial signification in its global and national forms.

Ultimately, *The Global Journey of Racism* asks readers to grapple with racism's discomfiting realities. Empires may be technically gone but the global racial system of white supremacy remains. Racism is everywhere, but racism is commonly perceived through colorblindness to be nowhere. Racism is structural and material but also ideological and personal. Racism is constituted through a global hierarchy between whiteness and anti-Blackness, but different groups and geographies can embody "white" and "Black" structural locations alongside other racial categories in-between. Racism is found in all geographies, but not all geographies, and the dominant groups in those geographies, are equally culpable or benefit from the production of racism. Again, it would be a misreading to interpret this book as arguing that all geographies are "racist." Racism at its most basic definition is a global system of power rooted in white supremacy. Regional and country racial replications emanating from former colonized geographies are not equivalent to former western imperial and white settler spaces who benefit the most from the global racial system and continue to set the global racial standards others must follow or negotiate.[72] Today's global white supremacy may have new rhythms, beats, and turns, but the racial architecture and beneficiaries of its original design remain.

In this book, I attempt to bring the global processes of our racist world to life. The first two chapters historically situate the emergence of a global racial system. Chapter 1, "Racist Modernity," focuses on the ideas, logics, and representational practices of race that arose in Europe at the dawn of a new global epoch—modernity. Liberal ideas, scientific knowledge, and cultural performance and display created essentialized hierarchical understandings of race that spread throughout the globe and across empires. Chapter 2, "Racist Empires," is a companion to chapter 1. Racist empires were the global material racial engines that connected disparate and vast colonial geographies to each other and metropole centers. Traveling racist practices like genocide and dispossession, enslavement and forced labor, fear-based exclusions and containments, and the creation of racial categorical divisions and control were pursued throughout overseas western empires just as empires were knotted together in dialogue, confrontation, and collaboration and collectively policed who could engage in imperial projects.

Chapter 3, "Traveling Racism and Deep Whiteness," outlines the contemporary forms of traveling racism after the supposed fall of empires through the forces and articulations of global racial capitalism, militarism, and culture. Traveling racism resembles a domino effect where the nested process of global hierarchical racialization proceeds from the foundation of racist modernity and empires but often under the veil of perceived colorblind practice. The deep whiteness at the base of traveling racism's mechanisms structures and informs its globally, regionally, and nationally dispersed pathways. The disclosed procedures of current global racial capitalism highlighted in the chapter particularly unlock the ensnarled, overlapping, and intersecting racial forces that maintain a dramatically unequal economic, militaristic, and cultural world.

Chapter 4, "Entangled Racial States," explores how modern states are all embedded in entangled colonial histories and entangled racial zones of power and influence. Four zones— United States' Track-Laying Dominance; Western European, Russian "Empire[s] Strike Back"–Postcolonial Claims; Australia Holds On–China Maneuvers; and Israel Separation, Gulf Eminence, and Black Africa Exclusion—demonstrate how specific states, or a cluster of states, act as racial power players, wannabe regional power players, or serve as a racial contrast state within zones. The historical institutionalization of race in regional, national, and local social systems, and its layered racialization articulations today, showcase how significantly, limitedly, and/or distinctively race organizes local realities.[73]

Chapter 5, "Transforming Race and Malleable Whiteness," delves into the complex history of how some groups and countries captured a form of white material and symbolic status, while others lost whiteness, but most languished outside its margins. The transformation of race through malleable constructions of "whiteness" particularly exposes the intricate and nuanced ways global whitening occurred in the global racial system to reproduce global white supremacy even while most whitening negotiations were illusory at best.

Chapter 6, "Global Colorblindness," details six overlapping "politicultures," using Vilna Bashi Treitler's term[74]: anti/postracialism, multiculturalism, *mestizaje* and racial democracy, ethnic dominance, "the predicament of Blackness," and the conservative right that collectively embodies the ideological production of global colorblindness. The variations in forms of global colorblindness highlight the "nimble"[75] ways racism is "conceal[ed]"[76] to propel the global racial system forward. Global colorblindness requires the active engendering of "structured blindness"[77] and the centering of white racial knowledge.

The concluding chapter 7, "Fighting Global White Supremacy," anchors the long history of counterknowledges and antiracist provocations alongside the current urgency to fight against global white supremacy. The hope and challenges to racial consciousness cultivation, racial literacy development, and racial solidarity commitments, all while daring to build and practice new worlds, remind us that agency, resistance, care, and "refusal" were always present in the global racial system and guide our future.

One
Racist Modernity

In 1605, Anne of Denmark, the Queen of England and wife to King James I, performed with her ladies-in-waiting *The Masque of Blackness*. As the queen and her ladies sauntered through Court as "blackamoors" with painted black faces and arms, they enacted some of the earliest documented English performances of blackface racist spectacle.[1] Prior to King James's ascension, Elizabethan England (1558–1603) underwent profound changes due to a burgeoning Renaissance art and visual culture, coupled with a desire to build vast overseas riches. European Renaissance cultural production adapted and advanced the medieval moral binary aesthetic of white and black symbolism.[2] "Binarism" laid the foundation for what Kim Hall calls the "tropes of blackness."[3] These tropes played with and embodied nascent racial meanings arising across visual and literary schematics that would help the English make sense and interpret the new world around them. In this early modern era, Shakespeare would create a character in Hamlet that became "a universal [white] paradigm of humanity,"[4] while the English merchant Hawkins family enshrined their newfound wealth with a coat of arms visually chronicling African capture and enslavement.[5]

Of course, Queen Anne's portrayal of anti-Blackness and England's cultural rendering of difference come out of the European medieval legacy that created the "Muslim Saracen" and "the Moor." For almost 800 years a Muslim dynasty ruled a religiously and ethnically multicultural *Al-Andalus* (Andalusia), a part of modern Spain, and simultaneously stirred fear, envy, and rage among European Christian monarchies and the Catholic Church. Being defined as a "Moor" concealed a broad heterogeneous group of Arab, Berber, Arab-Berber, and West and North African groupings and took on varied significations across European geographies.[6] The "Blackamoor figure," a "hybrid" of constructions on "Black Africans" and "Muslim Moors," condensed representations reflective of European anxiety about its burgeoning "Others."[7] Early on, "the Moor" elicited fascination and repulsion from Christian Europeans with multiple derisive meanings and cultural representations attached to the label to denote "the ethnically, culturally, and religiously 'strange.'"[8] Throughout the Middle Ages the pejorative term "Saracen" similarly highlighted perceived ungodly ways of being but also was a "fluid embodiment" where salvation and assimilation were rendered possible for "familiar Saracens," those more culturally and phenotypically European, vis-à-vis "foreign Saracens," those "black, strange, horrific."[9]

While ongoing battles against Muslim rule were waged, anti-Jewish praxis also rose, and the obsession to identify Catholic "good lineage" and "purity" was heightened.[10] Although religious movement was possible through conversions, the benefits for *conversos* (Jewish converts) or *moriscos* (Muslim converts) in Spain were limited by *limpieza de sangre* (blood purity) certificates issued by the Church. Such certificates guaranteed the "pure" genealogy of noble Catholic families. Soon, different cities began enacting blood purity laws, and after the *Reconquista* in 1492, when the fall of Grenada brought an end to Muslim rule in Spain, the speed of mandated Jewish and Muslim expulsions in Spain and England accelerated.[11]

Inventing "the Moor" produced a language, a visual iconography, and controlling legal technologies that bled into, but ultimately would be surpassed by, the creation of the "African slave" and the beginning of the transatlantic slave trade. By 1444, when Portugal brought 240 enslaved African captives to Lagos, in a grotesque scene of Portuguese jubilee and African suffering,[12] the country had already fought Spain for control over the wealth to be gained by controlling the Eastern Atlantic islands off the west coast of continental Africa. Portugal claimed the island of Madeira and operated "the first sugar mill of the Atlantic world."[13] The 1479 Catholic Church–brokered Treaty of Alcáçovas maintained Spanish rule of the Canary Islands but granted Portugal "church-sanctioned control of all of sub-Saharan Africa."[14] The occupation of the Canary Islands and Madeira, the 1482 Portuguese-built fort of Elmina in Ghana, and starting in 1485, the Portuguese colonization of the island of São Tomé collectively symbolized the "staging area" for what the future of modernity would represent.[15] Over the next hundred years the importation of enslaved Africans to Europe drastically increased,[16] enslaved African labor would produce a new form of industrialized consumer-based sugar, and São Tomé would go on to become ground zero for the nascent transatlantic slave trade.[17]

While the Portuguese were developing new techniques of imperial governance, and glowing in the profits accrued from the trade and exploitation of African gold and enslaved African labor, Spain, not wanting to be outdone, sought out new trading wealth. In preparation for his western voyage, Christopher Columbus visited Portugal's fort in Elmina to learn about the "habitability of that torrid zone" and had an extended stay in the Canary Islands.[18] After Columbus's landing, claiming, and naming the islands of the contemporary Caribbean in 1492 and in later visits, and establishing the colony *La Isla Española* (Hispaniola) for Spain, the challenge of managing a new overseas empire became urgent. Hitherto Spanish and Portuguese imperial moves were justified with religious proclamations and papal bulls granting them authority over "infidel lands" through "just wars."[19] By and large, divisions and inequities across Europe were viewed through the prism of "theological categories" where "the savage man" was a "wild man within sin or lack of reason, [and displayed] the absence of discipline, culture, [and] civilization."[20] Medieval Christian Kings spent centuries fighting Crusades against Muslim "Saracen" and "infidels," sharpening anti-Jewish sentiment and persecution, and imbuing cultural connotations to lightness and darkness symbolism—but within a framework of religion.[21] In the name of Christ, and with *encomienda* politics, indigenous Arawaks, and other groups in Hispaniola, were forced to labor under horrendous conditions and pay tribute to the Spanish Crown. Hundreds of thousands of indigenous peoples died. When Spaniard Bartolomé de las Casas began protesting the experiences indigenous communities faced, culminating in the 1542 New Laws of the Indies for the Good Treatment and Preservation of Indians, enslaved Africans were recommended as a replacement source of labor.[22] Fortuitous for Spain, by the mid-sixteenth century, Portugal already had one hundred years of advancing the ruthless practices of African enslavement and traffic.

Queen Anne's extravaganza of blackface performance, inferior representations and oppressive practices against religious "Others," the repulsion and allure of "the Moor," imperial Christian conquest, ascendent capitalism and the withering of western European feudal relations, and above all, the beginning of the global trade of enslaved African peoples were the necessary foundational bricks to global white supremacy. These historical junctures and episodic formations are best seen as an emergent racial cauldron that created the material conditions and ideological inflection points to support a forming global racial system and a language of racial categorical difference.[23] Prior to modernity "race" was not a "worldview."[24] Granted, ancient civilizations in antiquity and rulers of the medieval era practiced ruthless imperial forms of violence, enslavement,[25] and group bias.[26] They were "saturated with prejudices and chauvinism,"[27] but a global system of interconnected "material structures of racial domination"[28] cojoined with an "independent set of [racial] logics"[29] was not organizing it or justifying it.

Essentially, there is no one object or concept, one event, or one year that shows us that we have arrived at a global racial system. Rather, we find that during the modern era, particularly by the seventeenth century, a constellation and convergence of thoughts, narratives, and material contexts ushered in white global racial power dynamics in relation to nonwhite racialized bodies and spaces. The world became "knit[ted] together" as a single interconnected global racial system propelling white supremacy.[30]

In this chapter I outline the historical emergence of "racist modernity" and its most defining components. First, racist modernity, what I characterize as the engine of knowledge and culture that created racial political liberalism, science, and representational spectacle, helped Europeans make sense of the modern world, and most importantly, who should rule it. Racialized subjectivities and racialized spaces were created and told a global story of supposed racial fact that nonetheless did not exist without racial power. Ascribing racial subjectivities determined one's rightful place in the world, the conditions of one's lived reality, and the potential and possibility of racial movement, rigidity, or marginalization.

Second, racist modernity was globally situated. Racist practices circulated across, between, and through connected imperially pursued and governed geographies. The in-motion, traveling, adopted, and adapted ideas of race created the assumed givenness, essentialization, and naturalness of "race" despite divergent racialized spaces and histories. Tellingly, the political and scientific ideas, logics, and cultural aesthetic production of racist modernity left practically no geography untouched, even if only indirectly felt and seen.

Third, group and geographic transnational racialization through liberalism, science, and spectacle forced elites, intellectuals, and everyday people in many inferiorly racialized geographies to negotiate the stamp of race by often reproducing its very same debilitating logics. All told, the advent of racist modernity and its inescapable milieu became the discursive and representational racial scaffolding to our contemporary racist world. Below I highlight the connecting forces of liberalism, science, and crowning spectacle to the onset of global racial positionalities and the domain of racial power.

Emergence of Racialized Subjectivities and Racialized Geographies

For race to become a defining, organizing, and commonsense category of difference, the cosmology of supernatural belief and the religious fundamental arc of human identity had to change. The newly forming modern world needed to be "secularized" while still incorporating and validating Christian religious sentiment.[31] Christianity would augment and support the understanding of natural human relations, but new tools and ideas surrounding rationality, progress, governance, science, and the pursuit of personal material enrichment were necessary. In this changing sociopolitical world, what we would call "modernity," change and progress was wrapped in budding capitalism, secularism, rule of law, and men committed to rationality, "self-reliance and self-assurance."[32] Yet, at its core, as Barnor Hesse writes, "modernity is racial."[33]

Racial modernity, above all, "generated a particular kind of subjectivity,"[34] a "mode of subjective understanding,"[35] according to Sylvia Wynter, that classified, ranked, and categorized human difference with the precision and rigor from the subject understanding of the modern, rational, European learned man. These men were living through an "epochal shift."[36] Fascinating stories that chronicled the wondrous and treacherous sites of faraway lands and peoples were reaching their shores, a budding merchant class was disrupting rigid feudal distinctions, and philosophical ideas about liberty, property, and self-identity were emerging. These men ultimately created a new "defining logic of race," where "the codified organization of knowledges" determined a new racial paradigm of human value and worth.[37]

Importantly, the pursuit and facilitation of new knowledges and material social relations through racial modernity, as articulated by such scholars as W.E.B. Du Bois, Barnor Hesse, José Itzigsohn and Karida Brown, Achille Mbembe, and Howard Winant, was a worldwide racial phenomenon.[38] All peoples, geographies, and proper modes of societal organization became racialized and globally organized by race. Classifications went beyond physical and phenotypical markers. They conjured an objective reality of "differential [racial] essences" that hierarchically placed groups and geographies across a continuum of progress, beauty, and value.[39] Modern Europeans marked their "essences" as displaying a natural commitment "to political, social, cultural, and moral progress," a reflection of their own believed "superior condition," according to Zygmunt Bauman.[40] Concretely, therefore, the racial logics and knowledges that developed were racial evaluations made by Europeans who decided who was significant, who was a part of human history, and who held capacity for rationality and advancement.[41]

Within this evaluative brew, the hierarchy between categorical whiteness and Blackness began to take shape. All categories, particularly those in the middle, were "always in flux, sometimes changed rapidly, and [were] produced and reproduced" in specific ideological, geopolitical, and material contexts, but the global hierarchy between whiteness and Blackness remained.[42] "Africa" of note would come to represent a particular imaginary, and its inhabitants and descendants were turned into "bodies of extraction and subjects of race,"[43] beyond history or civilization,[44] a subjectivity labeled "deficient and lacking essence or ontology."[45] Connected in relation and opposition, whiteness became a new transnational material and discursive force, an embodied geographically territorialized subject in Europe, but also linked to historical migratory movements in and outside of Europe. Still, just who and which geographic space held the highest position within whiteness, and exactly where was it found, was also hotly debated across European intellectual currents.[46]

Mostly, the belief that we know something about racialized groups because they are rooted in the racial logics that also describe specific geographies was without question.[47] Geographic racial knowledge came to life through the visualizations of modern maps that outlined the boundaries of the global color line. European cartographic practices imagined, framed, defined, and produced racialized geographies—continents, borders, group spatial boundaries and characteristics, hospitable and inhospitable zones. Examples go all the way back to proto-racial forms in the famed Catalan Atlas of 1375, to the new colonial maps and surveys marking the "New World."[48] In these "categorical models of the earth's geography and people" everyone had a race and every space was racialized.[49] Maps provided a schematic for racial knowing where the contours of the modern world were traced with "fictions" that masqueraded as mastery of place.[50] Altogether then, racial modernity was predicated on what Alexander Barder describes as the "global racial imaginary" radiated through the lens of whiteness.[51] Those who racialized themselves as "white," or even beyond race, naturally defined the rules and contours of this new modern world and utilized a vast machinery of adaptable, liberal, scientific, and popular culture mechanisms within modernity's trappings to do so. Forming global white racial domination set the silhouette of discovery, knowledge, representation, wealth capture, personal enrichment, and entertainment.

Liberalism

Liberalism in modernity is commonly described as embodying a "central paradox."[52] As the rights of the rational, universal man were developed and deployed for emancipatory potential in political liberal thought, racism flourished. Yet, as Charles Mills, Lisa Lowe, David Theo Goldberg, Saidiya Hartman, and others argue, liberalism was constitutive of racial domination. Race, as Charles Mills writes, "historically penetrate[d] into liberalism's descriptive and normative apparatus so as to produce a more or less consistent racialized ideology."[53] Liberalism could only emancipate man with reason and bring about societal progress if it demarcated and policed who were actual liberal subjects. Seventeen-, eighteenth-, and nineteenth-century political thinkers "enshrined" "white personhood" while marking the boundaries of "non-white sub-personhood," according to Mills.[54] White personhood underscored individual capacity for rationality, autonomy, and moral principle, traits denied to nonwhite subpersons.[55] The "modern," "individual," "western man" "possesse[d] interiority of person" that granted them the privilege of "property" over one's rational self and through personal freedoms attained through labor, ownership, and transformation.[56] "Liberal discourses of freedom [basically] enable forms of subjection," nonetheless.[57] Thus, there never really was a contradiction within political liberalism because its formation and applicability was only made historically available with the possession of whiteness.

Through liberalism, the intellectual foundation for racist governing and economic practices was built. From David Hume to Immanuel Kant, John Locke, and John Stuart Mill, the racialized lack of interiority of nonwhites was largely a given and the political legal strategies devised and/or influenced by such thinkers reflected such. Locke's *Second Treatise on Government* (1689) specified the conditions of slavery in just war and legitimized African enslavement. David Hume, influential to later polygenists (see "Science" next), attached a note in his 1753 edition of his essay *Of National Characters* that declared a defined Black inferiority in all custom, manner, and form.[58] Hume's moral framework posited "national differences were social, racial differences were inherent," limiting the scope of moral subjectivity for a constructed denigrated Blackness.[59] James and John Stuart Mill outlined a utilitarian perspective of race where the benefits to capitalism and good governance reflected and justified white racial cultural advancement and rule and dictated the possibility for progress for those "unfit for liberty."[60] Within these varying liberal perspectives, racial identity became the cudgel to understand the function of the state and organized evolving governance regimes for the various needs of imperial management.

In consequence, the subsequent legal framework codified what Aileen Moreton-Robinson describes as the "white possessive"[61] of property and identity that dictated who was fit or unfit for liberty, whose lands could be possessed, which groups could be exterminated, and who was chattel and who was free.[62] Critical race theorist Cheryl Harris's towering treatise, "Whiteness as Property," underscores how the property of whiteness was more than the ability to be granted ownership over space and control of one's labor, as it also included all manners of "liberties, powers, and immunities that are important for human well-being."[63] The possessors of whiteness not only had a "particular type of subjectivity" but also set the epistemological and material rules for human existence and the rights attainment for others. Crucially, the appeal and expansive application of liberal tenets, such as individualism, freedom, liberty, property, and equality, produced innovative, flexible forms of racial subjugation across time and space.[64] The "chameleonic"[65] nature and pliant adaptability of liberal concepts guaranteed their evolution from overt racist liberalism to their always-present colorblind applications along with rapid acceleration in the late twentieth and twenty-first centuries. A "*white* universalism," nonetheless, continues to anchor the interpretation of laws and dictate the possibilities for redress (emphasis in original).[66] Also connected, despite ideological appeals to the contrary, "violence" always stood at the center of "liberalism's reformism, its claims to modernity, its promises of freedom, and its notions of the law."[67]

Science

The racial ideas forming through political liberalism corresponded with the larger pursuit to first philosophically, then scientifically, uncover and unlock the secrets of human variety. Beginning in the mid–late seventeenth century, racial taxonomies opened the epistemological door to essentializing human difference in the language of race. By this time, the tentacles of European empires were churning out enslaver, merchant, sailor, missionary, and colonial administrator accounts of the visual, physical, moral, and spiritual details about the vast peoples who inhabit the world.[68] From the beginning, classifying always exhibited fraught, dubious distinctions. Historian Nell Painter declares that "anarchy had dogged human taxonomy" attempts.[69] Philosophers, writers, scientists, and artists were, nonetheless, guided by similar assumptions: It was possible to categorize human populations, categories are more or less discrete, variation is physical and metaphysical, and difference is rooted in hierarchy.[70] Where they varied was in explaining why and how there were such distinctions, how many there were, the specific terms deployed, and the groups and geographies included. Table 1.1 outlines some of the most prominent racial science works and the classifications devised. My aim in the table is to underscore the messiness and imprecision of human classification, and the loaded racial derision apparent in terms, rather than make any definitive claim regarding the exact divisions the writers intended, as I am aware that interpretive debates, particularly on translations, exist.

Initially, taxonomies were more like sketches, ideas linking "race," or a similar term that corresponded to race, to the Great Chain of Being and a single human source—*monogenesis*. A climate theory of degeneration was widely assumed to cause human variation.[71] Later, multiple sources of human origins—*polygenesis*—dominated. The geopolitics of race among empires, the demands of specific colonial geographies, and the confluence

TABLE 1.1. **Racial Science Prominent Works**

Scholar	Year	Published Work(s)	Racial Divisions	Racial Ideology
François Bernier	1684	A New Division of the Earth According to the Different Species or Races of Men	Europe, Africa, Asia, Lapps*	Monogenesis
Carl Linnaeus	1735, 1758/1759	Systema Naturae, tenth edition	Europaeus albus (white), Americanus rubescens (reddish), Asiaticus fuscus (tawny), Africanus niger (black)	Monogenesis
Georges-Louis Leclerc, Comte de Buffon	1749–1767	Histoire Naturelle	Lapp Polar, Tartar, South Asian, European, Ethiopian, American^	Monogenesis
Edward Long	1774	History of Jamaica	Negroes (Creole Black, Maroons, free, enslaved), Mulattoes, Indians, Whites (Creole White, servants), Jews	Polygenesis
Immanuel Kant	1777	Of the Different Human Races	White Race, Negro Race, Hun Race (Mongol or Kanuck), Hindu or Hindustani Race	Monogenesis
Johann Friedrich Blumenbach	1795	On the Natural Variety of Mankind, third edition	Caucasian Variety, Mongolian Variety, Ethiopian Variety, American Variety, Malay Variety	Monogenesis
Thomas Jefferson	1787	Notes on the State of Virginia	Whites, Blacks, Slaves, Tribes of Indians (Red men)	"Difference is fixed in nature."
Dr. Charles White	1799	An Account of the Regular Gradation in Man	European, Negro, Hottentot, American Savage, Asiatic	Polygenesis
Dr. Samuel Morton	1839, 1844	Crania Americana; Crania Aegyptiaca	Caucasian Race (Caucasian, Germanic, Celtic, Arabian, Libyan, Nilotic, and Indostanic Families); Mongolian Race (Mongol-Tartar, Turkish, Chinese, Indo-Chinese, Polar Families); Malay Race (Malay and Polynesian Families); American Race (American and Toltecan Families); Ethiopian Race (Negro, Caffrarian, Hottentot, Oceanic-Negro, Australian, Alforian Families)	Polygenesis

Author	Dates	Work	Races	Concept
Joseph-Arthur de Gobineau	1853–1855	Essay on the Inequality of Human Races	White Race (Caucasian, Semitic, or Japhetic); Black Race (Hamites); Yellow Race (Altaic, Mongol, Finnish, and Tartar)#	"Existing races constitute separate branches of one or many primitive stocks."
Louis Agassiz	1854 (1845)~	Sketch of the Natural Provinces of the Animal World and Their Relation to the Different Types of Man in Types of Mankind by Josiah Nott and George Gliddon	Hyperborean Race (Arctic Realm); Mongolian Race (Asiatic Realm); White Race (European Realm); American Indian Race (American Realm); Nubian, Abyssinian, Foolah, Negro, Hottentot, and Bosjesman Races (African Realm); Telingan, Malay, and Negrillo Races (Malayan Realm); Papuan and Australian Races (Australian Realm); South Sea Islander Race (Polynesian Realm)	Polygenesis
Herbert Spencer	1864 1873–1934	Principles of Biology; Descriptive Sociology	English, Negritto Race, Malay-Polynesian Races, African Races, Asiatic Races, North and South American Races, Hebrews and Phoenicians, French	Social Darwinism
Francis Galton	1869; 1853	Hereditary Genius; The Narrative of an Explorer in Tropical South Africa	White, European, Native, Negroes (Black), Hottentot (Yellow)	Eugenics

* Bernier did not use single terms to define what he called "four or five species or races," except for "The Lapps." He mostly imprecisely aggregated geographies and specific "kingdoms" together.

^ There are debates on exactly how many divisions Buffon made, often a product of diverse translations. He likely believed there were multiple "races" embedded in these categories. Nevertheless, the perceived five-to-six classification schema would travel, be applied by others, and take on larger implications for racial governance in specific geographies.

Gobineau documented mixtures and hierarchies within and between what he termed "the three primitive elements of mankind" that produced "tertiary" and "quaternary" types.

~ Agassiz first published these ideas in French in *Revue Suisse*.

with gender and sexual norms underscored classification determinants. A "science of aesthetics"[72] exposed how gender, notably African women's bodies in relation to white women's, organized evaluations with a language of beauty, sexuality, and morality to code racial distinctions.[73] Of note, the term "race" took time to develop into its modern conceptualization. Within classical and medieval literatures, "*gens*—a Latin word that is usually translated as 'people' or 'nation' . . . linked by origin" is seen.[74] Various etymological concepts and meanings for race first emerge between 1200 and 1500 with numerous significations. Some definitions connected to familial lineages, especially nobility. Others signified some form of origin or kind or movement. The Spanish *raza* was about horse breeding; the Italian *razza* conferred sorts, breeds, and descent; the French *race* designated "a group of individuals who conspire"; and *ras* from Middle English was about "speed, swift course, current."[75]

The French were pivotal in getting us to our modern understanding and subsequent English language adoption. In the fifteenth century, the French *race* "signified 'origin' [*extraction*],' 'ancestry' [*lignée*], 'lineage,' or 'breeding,' of both people and animals" (emphasis in original).[76] French scientist François Bernier (1684) is credited with "radically expand[ing]"[77] original constructions of race with his categorization of "*Especes ou Races d'hommes*," which racially homogenized groups, granted "pride of place to Europe,"[78] and chronicled the phenotypical aesthetics among women. Swedish naturalist Carl von Linné, better known as Carl Linneaus (1735), divided the species "Homo" into four "*varietate*" (*Europaeus, Americanus, Asiaticus, Africanus*) along a line of physical and mental traits, granting us the "durable,"[79] "one massive hierarchy of races"[80] we negotiate today. But it would be French Georges-Louis Leclerc, Comte de Buffon (1749), who is most credited with widely deploying *race*, preferring it over Linneaus's *varietate*.[81] Buffon thought *race* better reflected a "'history' of traits passed down through generations in innumerable different forms . . . [and exhibited] a constant state of variation."[82] His interest lay with "explaining varieties of humankind"[83] but he nonetheless utilized "highly inexact" "general impressions" to demarcate human classification, and like his contemporaries, naturalized the ranking of all types of physical and intellectual representations.[84] According to Sabrina Strings, Buffon also "articulated a new physical identity for *black* Africans" (emphasis in original) centered on "dark skin," and "enormity" of size he argued was caused by "idleness" that rendered them deficient in mental capacities.[85]

The writings of these new "race experts" on the whole were marked by the inconsistent usage and conflation of the terms *species, variety, type, nation*, and *race*. German philosopher Immanuel Kant (1777), however, stood out during this early period for his "systematic biologisation of the idea of race," strengthening the claim of "permanent inherited characteristics signified by skin color, and its formal differentiation from the terms 'variety' or 'species.'"[86] Kant was one of the early thinkers, along with Linneaus's tenth edition of *Systema Naturae*, to use colors specifically to categorize whiteness and blackness: e.g., *die Race der Weissen* (the white race) or *Hochblonde* (noble blond or very fair), and *Schwarze* (black).[87] His climate theory of degeneration "solved an [urgent] puzzle" in the time of empire.[88] Those constructed as white did not need to worry about degeneration if they left Europe because their race had already developed out of the "numerous seeds and natural predispositions" within human beings. Aesthetic beauty for Kant was also notably connected to moral maturation.[89] Johann Friedrich Blumenbach was inspired by Kant's ideas of both race and beauty and by Linnaeus's, but particularly, Buffon's division of humankind, but added a more detailed methodological analysis of skulls. His revised third edition to *On the Natural Variety of Mankind* (1795) outlined five "varieties" and introduced the term "Caucasian." Blumenbach praised the beauty of the "Caucasian variety" with his "Georgian female" skull in contrast to the "Ethiopian" and "Mongolian."[90]

Blumenbach ushered in a new era to the science of race. The seventeenth- and eighteenth-century impressions would become the concrete human biological essentialism of the nineteenth and early twentieth centuries.[91] The new human physical anthropological "data" analyzed and gathered by British, Portuguese, Dutch, French, and other colonial scientists and administrators "on the ground" and "in the field" heightened the perception of objective scientific inquiry in the name of human progress.[92] Proto-anthropological, ethnologist techniques were already seen in the eighteenth-century writings of enslavers, planters, and folk intellectuals, such as Edward Long and Thomas Jefferson. Long's *History of Jamaica* (1774) and Jefferson's *Notes on the State of Virginia* (1787) were in dialogue with the budding racial analyses of the day and Enlightenment thought, but their perspectives were firsthand accounts gleaned from the hard truths of the colonial frontiers. Jefferson found a way to maintain his Enlightenment disposition with the reality of racial enslavement and indigenous dispossession by "helping to invent" "a biological category of race" "for political reasons."[93] Long wrote his historiography from a new subject position of "white creole consciousness."[94] His colonial planter expertise in support of constructed Black inferiority, evoking the language of separate "species" taken from the words of David Hume, legitimized Black enslavement for colonial growth and metropole consumption. Both Jefferson and Long helped to create a new popular, commonsense biological perception of race, beyond official naturalist classification schemas and categories. Their perceptions were equally imbued with traveling global racial thought and the local racial meanings and insights forming from colonial and newly independent white settler racial regimes.

Within the headwind of the abolition debate, and with the growth of nineteenth-century polygenism, and later Darwinian evolutionary theory, a new intensified racial scientific language emerged. Medical surgeons and physicians led this new cohort of polygenist "race specialists." The English Dr. Charles White and Americans Dr. Samuel Morton and disciple Dr. Josiah Nott were notable for their application of cranial and skeleton measurements, vivid illustrations of skulls and faces of racial categories, often including sculpture from Greek and Roman antiquity and Egyptian monuments, and the overlaying of human physiology in correspondence to animal representations. These studies were a mix of engagement with past naturalist "race literature," e.g., Buffon, Blumenbach, Curvier, and Linneaus, physical anthropology measurements, and ethnological reports coming from the European outposts of empire. White's *An Account of the Regular Gradation in Man* (1799), an early polygenist text, cites Jefferson's *Notes* and Long's *Jamaica*, Dutch physicians' chronicles of the peoples off the Cape of Good Hope, and the miscegenation practices within the West Indies and Americas. The most infamous, and widely circulated, was Nott and "Egyptologist" George Gliddon's *Types of Mankind* (1854). "Designed as a compendium of all anthropological evidence" of polygenist data,[95] and dedicated to the memory and work of Samuel Morton, the volume also included a chapter by famed Harvard-based Swiss naturalist Louis Agassiz, who outlined sixteen races, with further divisions, embedded in eight geographic and topographical realms.

Scientific racism made its next move after the emancipation of slavery across much of the globe in the mid–late nineteenth century. By then, the assumed link between race and biology was mostly unequivocal. Charles Darwin's groundbreaking principles of natural selection and evolutionary theory outlined in his publication *On the Origin of Species* (1859) were applied by Herbert Spencer, and the emerging school of thought, Social Darwinism, to explain "contemporary social processes."[96] For Social Darwinists, the laws of nature guarantee that white populations "represented the latest and highest form of evolutionary progress"[97] and that only "the [racially] fittest would survive."[98] Black American scholar Ralph Bunche wrote in 1936 that Herbert Spencer's racial explanations "tickled the egopalates of many people."[99]

Social Darwinism complemented the budding "science of eugenics," founded by Darwin's cousin, Francis Galton, and used mathematical statistics to show how "the more suitable races" can be strengthened by controlling reproduction and through the promotion of the most important heritable genetic traits, such as intelligence.[100] Social Darwinism and eugenics shook up global racial scientific knowledge by accentuating that white populations were in a "global racial struggle" for their survival if they did not fend off the biological threat from the weaker races.[101] These scientific race developments complemented the mid-nineteenth-century "fruitful remarriage of race and nation"[102] when racism and nationalism cojoined.[103] The application of racial essences to individual nations allowed for the latent hierarchical types built into discrete naturalist racial categories to be heightened. Racial differences between "white" types such as the British, Irish, Saxons, and Aryans found new traction in popular ideas of evolutionary theory.[104] Robert Knox's *Races of Man* (1850) and William Ripley's *The Races of Europe* (1899) argued for the superiority of the Anglo-Saxons and measured white European groups by their proximity to or distance from features associated with Blackness.[105]

The racial arc and changing conception of "Aryan" is an instructive example of traveling and changing racial categorization to accentuate hierarchies of whiteness and serve geopolitical purposes. The term was coined in 1768 by the Frenchman Abraham Hyacinthe Anquetil-Duperron, the first European to transcribe the Avesta, the primary collection of Zoroastrian sacred texts, and who decided "Aryan" was the traditional name of the ancient peoples of Iran.[106] Ancient Persians were said to have migrated to Europe, creating the foundation of Indo-European languages like Greek, German, and Sanskrit, and, hence, a common race.[107] From the start, "the fundamentals of the Aryan myth were conspicuously romantic in nature" while also clinging to science.[108] National ideas about *volk* and peoples connected to character and cultural traits were already forming across Europe and began to bleed into biological racial terms. As Aryanism transformed, it became detached from Asia, was abstractly identified as the "master race" or "highest race" within and between racial classifications, and eventually became synonymous as a "Nordic" or "German" race and "non-Jewish."[109] Aryans essentially had to be racially elevated within whiteness to manage various perceived threats from white racially classified groups, especially Jewish and Slavic.[110] Superior qualities and characteristics about Aryans were thus frequently applied by nationalist writers and race theorists,[111] and across Europe groups and scholars, such as in Italy, Sweden, and the Independent State of Croatia, claimed a national Aryan racial ancestry.[112]

As racist science traveled throughout the globe, many geographies outside of western Europe and its vast colonial possessions found themselves racially coded. In response, several developed their own language of racial science within the racial parameters constructed by European race scientists. Some Russian, Japanese, Chinese, Korean, Turkish, Indian, and Iranian intellectuals, along with thinkers in the formerly Spanish-colonized territories in Central and South America, sought to position themselves within whiteness, closer to whiteness, or in competition with whiteness, and away from Blackness. Late imperial Russia found itself being inferiorly racialized as Slavic by western Europe, but it also relied on classifications to control its vast, geographically contiguous empire.[113] Russian anthropologists "followed Linnaeus's general"[114] divisions but essentially racialized its massive population by "employing a category of ethnicity, *narodnost,* to define difference."[115] Dividing the empire along ethnic classifications engaged with racial physical differences, but "the human diversity of the Russian Empire proved highly complex and often confound[ing]"[116] except for the belief in a "unified Jewish type."[117] Creating classifications, nonetheless, "provided scientific credibility to" negative perceptions of groups within the empire, such as Polish, Jewish, Chinese, and other "yellow races,"[118] and naturalized differences in contrast to Slavic Russians. Despite deploying ethnic terms, the ascription process of "race," and the use of scientific racial logics, according to Marina Mogilner, was the "language of [Russian] imperial modernity."[119]

Japanese elites, reeling from humiliation and anger at being racialized as "Homo Asiaticus" and "Mongolian," at being forced to sign unfair treaties with the West in the mid-nineteenth century, and whose citizens experienced racism when they traveled to Europe and America during the Meiji period, adopted, for a Japanese context, western knowledge of race to both emulate and challenge white global power.[120] Meiji intellectual Fukuzawa Yukichi's 1869 *Shōchū bankoku ichiran* (Pocket Guides to the

Countries of the World) followed Blumenbach's division and specifically evoked color for racial classification, placing white on top, yellow in the middle, and Black on the bottom. By the end of the nineteenth century, Japan's fate was tied to improving its racial standing through imperial ambitions and the term *minzoku* "played a role in building Japan as an imperial nation-state," intensifying the self-racialization of the Japanese as different from its future imperial subjects.[121]

China, similarly, was alarmed by its negative transnational racialization, but intellectuals found they could repurpose the racialized meaning of "Yellow" and link it to a positive struggle against white domination. Chinese reform intellectuals Yan Fu (1854–1921), Liang Qichao (1873–1929), and Huang Zunxian (1848–1905) adopted global racial hierarchies, Social Darwinist beliefs, and sounded the alarm for Chinese racial survival, according to Frank Dikötter.[122] Liang linked white and yellow races in superiority, policed which groups could be "Yellow," and "declared Han race and Yellow race" as synonymous.[123] The twin forces of anti-Manchu political sentiment and global racial science and hierarchies combined to animate Chinese racial discourse.[124] Japanese and Chinese interpretations of race then influenced Korea and were published in the "first modern Korean newspaper, *Hanseongsubo*," and seen later in the "widely popular and influential *Observations on a Journey to the West* (1895)," then in the privately owned paper *Dongnipsinmum*.[125]

By adopting the premise of racial hierarchy through engagement with racial science, non-western European countries naturalized racial difference as a means to challenge transnational racial inferiorization. Each country operated within a constrained framework of possibilities and within specific forms of "colonial vulnerab[ilities]."[126] They were only able to make racial claims within a supposed scientifically determined global racial architecture and the local/regional racial power dynamics and racial reference points available. The wide global embrace of eugenics underscores the hegemony of the global racial hierarchy and the hope and possibility for racial "improvement" for countries and groups deemed racially unfit by racialized white countries and scholars. "Positive eugenics," the cultivation of reproduction of individuals with beneficial traits, and "negative eugenics," the restriction of reproduction of those with less desirable traits, influenced the policies pursued by countries to thwart feared racial decline, as reputedly had already occurred in places like ancient Greece, Egypt, and Spain.[127] This policy range encompassed drastic measures, like sterilization, but also more indirect means, such as immigration controls and encouragement, along with education, health, and sanitation improvements. Many countries, particularly in Latin America, were influenced more by neo-Lamarckian theories of hereditary that emphasized the effects of the environment but not for all groups.

Regardless of distinct country approaches to eugenics, the international eugenics movement represented an "interconnected international network of scientific academies . . . who shared common terms and similar sources" steered by the domineering influence of the United States, Germany, and wider Europe.[128] International groups such as the International Federation of Eugenics Organizations (IFEO) and the Pan American Eugenics Organization held meetings, shared findings and strategies, and ensured eugenic knowledge traveled far and wide. At its peak between the two World Wars, more than thirty countries had active eugenics programs and there were thirty-six international conferences with participants from fifty-six countries.[129] The United States implemented some of the largest and harshest eugenics programs under the steerage of Charles Davenport. Davenport, a Harvard-trained biologist at the Carnegie Institute, established the Cold Springs Harbor Center, published the periodical *Eugenical News*, and trained hundreds of field workers. After the U.S. Supreme Court upheld sterilization in the 1927 case of *Buck v. Bell*, twenty states passed sterilization laws[130] with North Carolina sterilizing until the 1970s,[131] and parts of Canada, Sweden, Mexico, Switzerland, Norway, and Germany followed with their own sterilization programs. Geographies ranging from Australia, Bermuda, China, England, France, Hungary, New Zealand, Poland, Russia, and South Africa debated sterilization. Nazi Germany brought eugenics to its most deadly manifestation with the Holocaust when Jewish populations were feared and blamed for the nation's supposed racial degeneracy.[132]

Spectacle

The third component to racist modernity is racist spectacle. Race needed to be translated into popular culture for it to fully cement its grasp on the imagination of everyday people; that is, when "the average man in the street . . . demonstrate[s] an ability to expound at length on the term at the slightest provocation," according to Ralph Bunche.[133] Racist spectacle is the racial cultural production that facilitated white subjectivity through the debasement and denigration of People of Color, most unabashedly those racialized as Black. As Saidiya Hartman writes, "The emphasis on blackness, subjection, and spectacle is intended to denaturalize race and underline its givenness."[134] From the beginning, as Enlightenment thinkers were expounding on the rules of governance, rationality, and morality, and scientists were creating the racial taxonomies of humanity, these ideas and principles were being communicated through the growth of popular press, museum exhibitions and international expositions, theatrical performances, modern art, and new consumer products particularly by the nineteenth century. These mediums were easily digestible, widely consumed, and, most importantly, considered universally entertaining or useful to newly racialized white audiences with new middle-class needs. The act of creating entertainment out of racist knowledge cemented its allure, its common sense, its extensive embrace across geographies. In the process, a globally expansive white racial subjectivity coalesced in white imperial metropoles, in white settler geographies, in contested racial landscapes, and throughout the perimeters of racist empires.

From the mid-nineteenth century onward, printed materials of all kinds, from sensationalist "muckraking" to social commentaries, juvenile adventure stories, and the latest scientific advancement of the day, told stories of racial difference in newspapers, magazines, low-priced books, and highbrow literary and scientific outlets.[135] Race was communicated to white audiences, or new immigrant audiences in hopes for whiteness, through an array of outlandish visual and descriptive representations, overtly racist epithets, and with sterile scientific appraisals. In the United States, *Harper's*, *Atlantic Monthly*, and *Dial* catered to a new middle-class readership eager to learn about foreign affairs, the "race question," and unfolding immigration.[136] Victorian England media depicted the details of empire and British identity in outlets like *Punch* magazine, and Australia's *Bulletin* heralded nationalist white Australian sentiment.[137] *Punch*, from its first issue in 1841, is considered one of the "most successful magazines of the English-speaking world," due to its global influence and longevity.[138] Abridged, serialized portions of influential Social Darwinist books and racial policy commentaries also found a home in mass media as did its fictional translation into popular dime-novel storylines. The dime novel, and its basic formula that depicted the American western frontier as populated by "lawless" and "savage" "Indians" in need of redemption from white society, was hugely popular in the U.S. and Europe.[139] From the

1890s onward, authors of natural history popularized descriptive scientific racial typologies through serials and introduced photography's visual human objectification, most dramatically in Augustus Keane's work in *Living Races of Mankind* (1901).[140]

Media also commented on and advertised the new museum shows and international expositions, curated by American and European powers who made imperial glory and national technological progress must-see global attractions. The 1851 Great Exhibition conceived by Britain's Prince Albert and Henry Cole served as a global "prototype for a nascent mode of spectating . . . Spectators entered into a . . . 'ideologically loaded space' that helped construct and reinforce a visual [racial] rhetoric . . . that sold 'difference' . . . whether in material products or in people—as spectacle: a commodity to be gazed or gawked at along with other objects of art and industry."[141] Not to be outdone by the British, the *Exposition Universelle* in 1855 and again in 1867, 1878, 1889, 1900 declared France's cultural and imperial superiority.[142] As the French empire expanded, colonial exhibits became grander, louder, and included "indigenous villages" from Indochina, West Africa, Equatorial Africa, and the Southern Pacific Territories.[143]

Other European examples were the 1883 Amsterdam International colonial and export trade exhibition, the 1898 Exhibition of Women's Work in the Hague, the Danish colonial exhibition in Copenhagen in 1905, the first Portuguese colonial exhibition in 1934 and again in 1940, and in 1958, Brussels World's Fair. In the U.S., the 1893 Chicago World's Fair and the 1904 Louisiana Purchase Exposition in St. Louis trumpeted America's ascendency, its nascent empire, and communicated white racial evolutionary progress with anthropological displays of skulls and measurements, and in St. Louis, renditions of genteel southern plantation life prior to the emancipation of those enslaved.[144] Expositions were connected to the incipient museum shows and "human zoos" that traveled throughout western European metropoles and the imperial adjacent geographies like Russia, Switzerland, and the Nordic countries that accentuated racial barbarity, perceived grotesque physiology, and ethnological curiosity.[145]

Racist gendered spectacle saw its apex in the devastating treatment of Saartjie "Sara" Baartman. Sara was an enslaved Khoikhoi, who the Dutch derisively labeled "Hottentot" when they settled in the Cape of Good Hope in the seventeenth century. Since early Cape colonialism, the Khoikhoi were chronicled with a mixture of disdain, fascination, and allure by

European travelers, physicians, and naturalists—and often racialized in opposition to Black Africans.[146] When Sara was put on extravagant display in the Cape, London, and Paris in the early nineteenth century as "an erotic scientific curiosity," "the Hottentot Venus," her journey chronicled the erasure of Khoikhoi difference and the consolidation of Black women subjugation as a single object of derision and bodily mockery.[147] Her lived experience combined all aspects of the emerged global racial system: scientific knowledge, imperial crossings, and the manufacture and profit from transnational gendered-racist presentation found in print, mass media, and the museum.[148] By the time Sara died in Paris in 1815, Georges Cuvier, zoologist, mentor of Agassiz, and correspondent with Jefferson, had already turned her into a scientific demonstration, but in death rendered her a subject of violated anatomical study.[149] Museums throughout Europe and the U.S. intimately displayed the violence and death of racist voyeuristic practice.[150]

Beyond the brutalities of museum-curated collections, racist violence practiced as terror entertainment saw its most horrific unimaginable form in lynching. Many lynchings in the U.S. became communal white entertainment and were commemorated with souvenirs and photographic postcards and glorified in the new emerging motion picture technology.[151] D.W. Griffith's celebrated movie about the rise of the Ku Klux Klan, 1915's *The Birth of a Nation,* was widely watched in the U.S., including at the White House and across Europe, and shaped the nascent film industry, and the production of racism on screen for the next century, including the colonially charged genre of "jungle films."[152]

Racist voyeurism and performance reached its broadest appeal through the global travel and enthusiastic consumption of minstrel shows. From Queen Anne's production of "blackamoors" in the early seventeenth century to its height in the mid-nineteenth century and throughout the early to mid-twentieth century, blackface minstrel shows were the "transcolonial cultural imaginary" linking whiteness across the globe through the performance of manufactured anti-Blackness.[153] "The ability to put on blackness" with theatrical production, music, and language translated for a popular audience the cultural codes of scientific racial classifications, chattel slavery, and imperial racialized labor and societal division on a transnational scale.[154] These "transnational transmissions" of minstrel production were found throughout the U.S., Hawaii, Europe, Canada, the Caribbean, South America, Australia, India, South Africa, and South

America and reached Singapore, Indonesia, Hong Kong, Egypt, Greece, and Turkey, among many other locals.[155] Minstrel shows cultivated a common global knowledge of anti-Black archetypes, like "Jim Crow," supercharged the proliferation of anti-Black racist slurs and imagery, and was highly adaptable to local sociocultural contexts. Local adaptions and national forms included the production of *Kaatje Kekkelbek* (Life among the Hottentots) in South Africa,[156] *Bengalee Baboo* (Bengali Babu) in India,[157] *Haji Firuz* in Iran,[158] and *Osman 'Abd al-Basit* in Egypt.[159] Essentially, throughout the globe in specific geographies, we find what Chinua Thelwell calls "burnt cork nationalism"—the denigration, commodification, and "pillaging" of constructed global anti-Blackness and its local group associations to secure whiteness, or at least become closer to or compete with whiteness, and to naturalize global white supremacy.[160]

Non-Black racialized groups were also perceived through a lens of minstrel spectacle and/or performed blackface to maneuver away from inferior racialization, such as with Irish immigrants and in Egyptian nationalist theatre performance.[161] Anti-Chinese caricatures were performed in San Francisco and Australia, and the Wild West Shows of "playing cowboys and Indians" were popular in Europe, as were the performative appropriations of American indigenous symbolism and perceived virility in fraternal organizations and private clubs.[162] Blackface and its adjacent cultural productions became common global entertainment, inspired countless cultural aesthetic fields—such as print media, event posters, satirical drawings, advertisement, animation, comedy shows, circus and trapeze, radio, movies, and music—and intersected with local aesthetic performance traditions. Carnival culture with the Klopse Carnival Troupes in South Africa, Carnival in Argentina and Uruguay,[163] and clowneries in France, most noticeably with the *Footit* and *Chocolate* clown team,[164] all applied minstrel aesthetics. The global currency and influence of blackface was profound.

Most demonstrative of the pervasive minstrel appeal is seen in how minstrel aesthetic repertoires were also turned into what Anne McClintock calls the "imperial kitsch of consumer spectacle" and "commodity racism."[165] Not only was imperial racial capitalism creating the conditions for white wealth and middle-class consumption, but race also informed the creation of new commodity products, how products were advertised and marketed, and how products were appropriated for white tastes. "Popular culture and consumer goods reinforced a collective sense of imperial greatness and power."[166] Children's books and toys based on minstrel imagery, such as the anti-Black "Golliwog" doll and character that first appeared in Florence Kate Upton's 1895 book *The Adventures of Two Dutch Dolls and a Golliwog*[167] and "Globi" the blue parrot, created by Swiss department store Globus, who ferried children off to "exotic, faraway" colonial geographies, were ubiquitous and beloved by white children and families.[168]

Characters were also used as advertising mascots. Advertising leaned hard into racist representations and language with different iterations of, for example, the "*blackamoor* washed white" (emphasis in original) or the reverse, to sell soap, chocolate, and household items and in the visual depictions of colonized subjects in commodity trademarks and print signage.[169] Products were exported to new emerging markets such as in East Asia, where the "Golly" doll, "mammy" representations, and other racial illustrations found an audience in Japan and Korea[170] and local companies adopted and created their own minstrel-influenced advertisements for Asian regional export.[171] Japan's first direct exposure to western anti-Black cultural performance was courtesy of the blackface minstrel performances performed by white American sailors to entice trade negotiations with the Tokugawa shogunate in its three-year voyage from 1852–54.[172] "Minstrel diplomacy" occurred in other regions such as in Mexico and in the Pacific.[173] Geographies in Latin America produced and widely popularized the minstrel-inspired children's characters of *Memín Pinguín* in Mexico and *Cocorí* in Costa Rica.

Racist products and advertisement dovetailed with imperial cultural appropriation. Lisa Lowe documents how British manufacturers copied Indian "chintz" patterns displacing Indian imports and subsequently removing any non-British identity.[174] Across Europe teahouses, coffee shops, diamond cutting and polishing became quintessentially English, French, Austrian, or Belgian, detached from the enslaved and forced labor cultivating sugar, tea, coffee, and mining precious gems. The "white gold" of sugar, particularly, unlocked the possibilities of "whole new industries": French patisserie, English deserts, and Belgium chocolates.[175] These new products, performances, and anthropological expositions all made available by empire shaped and creeped into all facets of modern cultural life, obliterating the line between high and low aesthetic tastes. The traditional European "culture of taste," as seen in the Dutch and English Golden Ages of Art[176] and later French Impressionism, depicted imperial fantasies and aesthetic aversion along with modern bourgeois life, supported by empire.[177] Most clearly, whether racialized nonwhiteness in art and beauty and through commodity fetishism was made hypervisible or invisible, constructed as objects of desire, servitude, or difference, "whiteness [always was the] assumed normative condition" and ideal.[178]

Foundational and Counterknowledges

Outlining the beginning and propagation of racist modernity is important because it provides the foundation to the racial knowledge still with us today. This racial knowledge built the epistemological domination emergent from the global material-connected power plays of western empires, their colonial claims, and their cultural performances and creations of racial difference. The new language, ideas, and enaction of racial liberalism, science, and cultural production crisscrossed, collided, and exploded in metropole, colonial, and in-between spaces alike. Thus, the "change" of what modernity represented had its most profound repercussions in the change seen in the creation of white racial global processes and the newly formed white global racial selves. This is important to emphasize because it demanded that all ascribed racial groups and geographies concede to its power and operate within its designated boundaries of discursive and material possibilities.

Still, despite the demand to acquiesce to the production and performance of racist modernity, there always were voices, people, and bold and subtle acts that challenged its contaminated knowledge and cultural carnage. Hence, at the heart of modernity is also the core of rupture, defiance, and renouncement. I address more in the book's conclusion these counterknowledges, resistance moves, and solidarity formations, but a few examples include how by the nineteenth and early twentieth centuries, transnational Black intellectuals such as Robert Alexander Young, Frederick Douglass, Anna Julia Cooper, Maria W. Stewart, David Walker, Quobna Ottobah Cugoano, W.E.B. Du Bois, Ida B. Wells-Barnett, Pauline Hopkins, and C.L.R. James challenged racist terror, enslavement, and scientific racism, and unlocked our understanding to the societal formations of devastating racist domination.[179] Tukufu Zuberi describes how the scholars in this era who arose "in resistance to the racialized self ... established an analytic foundation for the creative critical counter response to social oppression ... enslavement and white supremacy."[180]

Global Black and nonwhite radical presses and Black abolitionist newspapers throughout colonial and independent territories published stories to counter white narratives. Black aesthetics, words, storytelling, and art also interpreted the lived experiences of subjugation and movement with tenderness, beauty, rage, and transcendence. Regardless of the "normative negative conceptions of blackness," as Katherine McKittrick writes, Black knowledge and cultural praxis always sought "liberation and reinvent[ion]" and remade "the terms of Black life" outside the parameters of racist liberalism, science, and spectacle.[181]

To further situate these resistant proclamations, we need to outline the specifics of material imperial racial formations. In the following chapter, therefore, I turn to racist empires, the globally interconnected material force of racist modernity. The co-constitutive emergence of modern western empires and racial logics each relationally informed the other. Inter- and intra-imperial needs dictated colonial racial formations and the diverse mechanisms devised to manage, control, and extract value from racialized bodies and landscapes.

Two
Racist Empires

Racist modernity was the visual, descriptive, psychological, ontological tapestry overlaying the expansive, interconnected global structure of racist empires. The ideas, science, spectacle, and logics of race were consolidated through the material practices of racialized social systems within, across, and between racist empires.[1] Simply put, racism organized every aspect of modern overseas empires and the relationship between empires, culminating in one global system. Lisa Lowe's conceptualization of "intimacies" foregrounds the connections, strategies, policies, and often contradictory rationales that structure political economic hierarchical relations between the metropole and across continental colonies, and the variously raced and gendered bodies produced by imperial divisions.[2] Similarly, Patrick Wolfe frames multiple "racial regimes" within empires to showcase how a "far-flung network of unequal social relations" is brought to life by distinctive and "concurrent racialisations" to meet ongoing and evolving imperial needs.[3]

"Intimacies," however, were equally constituted across empires and "concurrent racialisations" were layered, embedded in different markers, and interconnected and hierarchized across the global field. There is undoubtedly a heterogeneity and malleability to imperial racial formations that tell us something about the complexity and disorder of racialization. Different historical moments, geopolitical economic needs, varying local logics, and how differences were perceived prior to colonialism interacted with global racial representations, and specific imperial racial ideologies, to generate divergent colonial racial orders and modes of governance that were specific and discrete to any given colonial space.[4] Yet, for all the divergent racial colonial forms, all were incorporated in and structured by a global racial system. As Jean-Paul Sartre succinctly wrote in 1957, "racism is built into the system" of the "colonial *apparatus*" (emphasis in original).[5]

First, all racist empires shared common inter-imperial features. For example, they developed their own national racial identities through imperial practice.[6] They cultivated inter-imperial transnational racial knowledge. And they engaged with and perpetuated the same global racial hierarchy and classification scheme between whiteness and anti-Blackness. Tellingly, all racist empires shared the same repertoire of transnational political economic practices like conquest, enslavement (acutely in earlier eras), dispossession, population controls, and domination through colonial state governance modalities, even if they chose and implemented different forms.[7] Pointedly, all deployed what Partha Chatterjee,[8] and adopted by George Steinmetz and other theorists of colonialism, refer to as the "rule of colonial difference" where conquest and subjugation of local populations was unambiguously defended through the lens of "racial dualism": European whiteness in contrast to all else.[9]

Second, interconnected racist imperial practices unfolded across a shared changing historical timeline of geopolitical and capital expansion demands, global and national crises, evolving racial ideological rational across geographic contexts, and imperial state competitions and collaborations. There are broadly four eras to modernity's racial imperial formations: (1) the 1500–1800s are characterized by early Spanish, Portuguese, English, French, and Dutch colonialism in the Caribbean and "Americas," European state mercantile charter companies and colonial rule in parts of Asia, and the transatlantic trade of African enslaved bodies; (2) 1807–1917 represents mid–late colonialism, the mostly abolishment of the transatlantic slave trade, the slow end to national forms of slavery and Spanish colonialism in Latin America, the rise in the rhetoric of "free trade" and the use of new labor regimes, and the Berlin Conference of 1884–85; (3) 1918–44 typifies the late colonialism of Africa, Asia, and parts of the "Middle East," what is commonly considered the global imperial peak, and the colonial fallout of World War I and advent and protraction of World War

II; (4) 1945 to the present encompasses formal decolonization following World War II with continued, often hidden forms of imperial rule.

Across each period, racist colonial management and imperial connective points were equally rationalized with a combination of what David Theo Goldberg describes as naturalist (biologically racially inferior) or historicist (culturally racially inferior) justifications[10] and were governed by varying modes of colonial rule: formal direct or informal indirect rule, departments, mandates, and protectorates, and embedded within various types of settler colonial patterns, plantation and/or extractive exploitative economies, and/or combined heterogeneous forms.[11] Imperial rule, as Ann Stoler positions, was always an amalgam of "blurred genres," in constant "movement and oscillation" to shore up control.[12] "A difference of degree, not of kind."[13]

Importantly, it took time for imperial racial orders to coalesce. Early colonialism was marked by the transition from religious imperial pursuit, somewhat malleable and forming racial categories, to a more concrete racial worldview of white supremacy by the 1700s with direct overtures to the phrasing "white supremacy" by the mid-1800s.[14] At each subsequent historic pivot point of empire—geopolitical, territorial, labor, and alliance need—race helped to organize the options made available and pursued.

Third, racist empires understood racial distinction, and their national racial subjectivities and colonial management forms, in contrast or comparison, and in alliance and competition with other empires, creating a global racial hierarchy of empires. All racial empire states "[were] drawn into racial frames of reference," within the "rings of racial globalities" and jockeyed, competed, and fought for placement along a racial imperial plane.[15] Competition notably for colonial wealth, status, and prestige was fierce. Who had the imperial upper hand—what Sampie Terreblanche labels the "trendsetting" and "track-laying" countries others chased and followed—evolved over time.[16] Whiteness became a form of economic and symbolic capital gathered and deployed by imperial powers to pursue "track-laying" status, and negotiate inter-imperial racialization, across the imperial racial hierarchical field.[17] Hierarchical placement was dynamic, complex, and multifaceted; but as empires went up and down the hierarchy they always attempted to coalesce around or jockey for supremacy within whiteness.

Early on, Spain and Portugal, flush with racial economic capital from African Gold Coast exploitations and labor extraction from American geographies, set the racial template. But soon Spain's leading status was challenged on racial terms. Its European rivals, the Netherlands, England, and France, constructed the *La Leyenda Negra* (The Black Legend) as racial propaganda to render Spain unworthy of its colonies ironically because of the "atrocities [committed] against the indigenous" and distanced Spain from European civilization and imperial whiteness.[18] On the opposite end, Italy justified its late play for colonial glory with "the idea of *italiani brava gente* (Italians are good people)" whose Latin, Mediterranean racial roots supposedly made them "nicer" colonizers.[19]

Fourth, non-European empires were transnationally racialized outside of whiteness by European powers. The Ottoman empire, which originally ruled outside racial organizing logics,[20] was racialized apart from European whiteness and considered a threat to Christian Europe during the first two periods of overseas colonialism.[21] After slowly losing its territories from the early nineteenth century until its disintegration following World War I, many of its former territories were recolonized and racially managed first under more traditional colonial arrangements, then later under the new imperially informed League of Nations Mandate System or by the late European imperial player, Italy.[22] Like the Ottoman empire, the late imperial ambitions of Japan were perceived as one of the greatest challenges to European powers. Japan's empire simultaneously confronted global white supremacy as an "Asian" imperial actor but also adopted western global racial ordering with Japanese cultural codes.[23] Thus, the global racial hierarchy of modern empires exposes how western European empires maintained and policed racial civilizational standards among themselves and challenged the imperial aspirations and statuses of racialized nonwhite states.[24] Pursuing a modern "colonial empire" was a pursuit for global structural whiteness,[25] and/or a "reorientation" toward whiteness for racially suspect imperial powers,[26] but whiteness was unsteady and subject to challenge.

Lastly, no geography or space was left untouched and unaffected by the practices of racist empires. White racial geographies in Europe that had no colonies still benefited from white supremacy or had access to liminal whiteness as seen in the Russia empire, across eastern Europe, and Iceland.[27] Nonwhite racialized landscapes that were never "formerly" colonized, like Thailand or Nepal, were nevertheless "semicolonial/crypto-colonial/auto-colonial."[28] Even non-people-inhabited Antarctica,[29] which was fought over in a series of rival expeditions by European and former white settler then independent geographies, became an environment where whiteness was literally and figuratively projected to procure imperial national greatness.[30]

In the rest of the chapter, I highlight specific interconnected and shared imperial practices that affirmed the global racial hierarchy, left colonized geographies grappling with racial subjugated status, and defined the racial material and representational inequities that shape us today. The imperial practices of genocide and dispossession, enslavement and forced labor, materializing racial panics, and actualizing racial categorical divides and control were the transnational assemblage no geography or peoples could bypass. The global racial system captured everyone and every place in its wake.

Genocide and Dispossession

Violence stood as the foundation of modern colonialism.[31] Violence of exploitation, violence of expropriation, violence of removal, violence of stripping identities, violence of enslavement and death.[32] Patrick Wolfe declared "elimination" as the motivating factor in predominantly settler colonial geographies who operated under the constitutional claims and crown authority of the Doctrine of Discovery and Right of Conquest to forcibly take and declare colonial possessions.[33] Thus, the first period of imperial expansion and colonialism is defined by what Robbie Ethridge describes as contact "shatter zone(s)"[34] where the tactics of warfare, massacres, capitalist labor exploitation, the facilitation of disease, and the destabilization of indigenous communities culminated in indigenous genocide across the broad "Americas."[35] Prior to American colonization, the Canary Islands served as the first proto-genocidal example.[36] There were over six hundred indigenous groups across North America before colonization. By the twentieth century "up to 99% of the Continent's indigenous population were eradicated."[37]

Indigenous racialization evolved in different colonial periods, across geographies and racial hierarchical landscapes. Upon first colonial "discovery" of the "New World," groups were framed as ungodly "idolators."[38] Initially, these communities were forced into enslavement. Historian Gerald Horne estimates that from Columbus's voyages to the end of the nineteenth century as many as five million indigenous individuals in the Americas were enslaved.[39] With the introduction of African enslavement, and when Blackness became associated and codified with permanent hereditary enslaved status, the racial logics applied to indigenous communities in the Americas shifted. They could achieve crown protections, engage in trade and treaty negotiations, but were never constructed as racially equal to whiteness. Broadly, all were racially homogenized as "Indian," what racial science in Linnaeus categorized as "Americanus" or what Charles White determined to be the "American savage." Yet, specific groups also held different "civilized" statuses in white European's determination and sometimes held alliances with one European imperial power to challenge another. Thomas Jefferson praised some indigenous qualities (and contrasted those qualities to Blackness), and the Cherokees, Creeks, Chickasaws, Choctaws, and Seminoles became constructed as the "The Five Civilized Tribes" closer to perceived white attributes. Spain distinguished between colonizable "civilized Indians" and "barbarous Indians."[40]

Racialization and colonial governance depended on the political economic needs of specific empires, and demands for land and settlement quickly became the guiding force. The extractive colonies of early Spanish, French, English, and Dutch colonialism, which produced American and Caribbean indigenous group decimation, quickly gave way to increased African enslavement, plantation sugar and cotton economies, and white settlement and expansion in the Americas. In North America, regardless, if some groups were deemed more civilized, a binary racial division separated them outside of whiteness and justified racist practices. By the nineteenth century, addressing "the so-called Indian problem" was paramount to settler success. With a combination of naturalist and historicist racial assertions, the framing of indigenous "assimilation" to achieve a higher standard of "civilization" became "shorthand" for a disparate set of interconnected institutions and policy interventions across scales and geographies—land removal, creation of reservations, deceptive treaty practices, residential schools, and forced adoptions—to culturally "kill" what remained of indigenous identities and sovereignty claims after the initial decimation.[41] Canada, which had one of the most extensive and brutal systems of residential schools, took around 150,000 First Nation Inuit and *Métis* children from their families and placed them in the Canadian Indian Residential Schools system, where 6,000 children died.[42]

Importantly, the racial ideological production of "Indigenous" or "Native" is both place-specific, connected to broadly defined local geographies across the world and the original peoples who inhabit them, and an idea; a racial subject positionality situated in relation to either Blackness or whiteness or combined forms of racialization. Thus, depending on geography, imperial power, and colonial governance, "Indigenous" represented overdetermined racial meanings. England made the *"Indian,"* Spain the *"Indio,"* and France the *"Indigène,"* but also simultaneously created the "Native" (*Eingeborene* for Germany), "Aborigine," and "Autochthone" categories. Indeed, these categories mostly originated from imposed Latin and Greek constructions. Most definitively, then, these terms represented different racial distinctions, layered racialization, and/or were considered racially interchangeable across different racial colonial, white settler independent geographies.[43]

For example, the "Native" designation was legally codified in most colonial rule governance as "subjects" separate from "citizen" rights. During late colonialism in East Africa, all "natives" were socially racialized as "Black" but groups like the Maasai were additionally racialized as more "noble," more like some American indigenous groups, in comparison to other African "native" groups, such as the "reviled" Kikuyu.[44] Correspondingly, the Khoikhoi across South and Southwest Africa held different racial layered subject statuses. They were constructed as "Native," but sometimes separated from Blackness (some Europeans referred to them as "Yellow," sometimes they were compared to "American Indians") and other times, as with their global reputation as studied subjects of racial science or when rebellions rose, they personified "Blackness."[45] Thus, many European imperial powers made racial claims about "their" "native" groups in relation or contrast to ascribed indigeneity in the Americas, the racially created and geographically mislabeled term "Indian," which globally came to embody the originally "conquered [native] populations" of racist empires.[46]

In the United States, "Indian" and "Native" were racialized the same, separate from Blackness, even though new multiracial bands formed in response to white settler colonialism. Oceania was a mix. In the Pacific, being "Native" or "Aborigine" was ambiguously defined between "Malay" (Asian) and "Melanesian" (Black)[47] across the disparately imperially governed islands, but all colonial racial rankings placed Malay above Melanesian.[48] Australia's First Nation Aboriginal and Torres Strait Islanders communities' Black-embodied indigeneity shaped how they experienced the shared global anti-Indigenous colonial practices of genocide, land confiscation, child removal, and reservations but as Black-embodied subjects.[49] Essentially, either away from or through Blackness, these complexly racially categorized processes forming indigeneity and nativeness mattered for colonial labor, land, and marriage policies and how groups responded to each other and to competing colonial forces.

Racial Enslavement and Forced Labor

With the decimation of American indigenous populations, and their changed subject status, the transatlantic trade in enslaved Africans was globally harnessed, and voraciously fought over by imperial powers to meet pressing labor demands, particularly in agriculture commodity production across the Americas. In the sixteenth century, 277,000 Africans were sent to the Americas, with close to 90 percent going to Spanish territories—New Spain, Cartagena, and Veracruz.[50] In the seventeenth century, Brazil's enslaved population drastically increased, a trend that would continue for the next three hundred years, with the Caribbean islands and North America quickly following suit. By 1815 there were three million enslaved in the U.S., Brazil, and the Caribbean; in 1860 there were six million in the U.S., Brazil, and Cuba.[51] A vast imperial system linked Caribbean and colonial commodities to backward- and forward-connected metropole industries, such as shipbuilding and commodity manufacturing, artisan support services, banking, insurance, accounting, and finance—all to the sale and embodied expropriation of racialized Black bodies.[52]

The transatlantic trade was begun and led by Portugal until 1640, then Portugal was displaced by Britain until 1807, when the British ended the trade, and Portugal took over again until 1865.[53] Others such as the Dutch, French, Spanish, Danish, and the U.S. all appear as players, with the Dutch making the largest effort to expand its global reach. The Netherlands, with support from its newly risen banking class, merchant elites, and flush from the conquered Portuguese East Indies trade by the Dutch East India Company (VOC), dominated seventeenth-century European imperial rivals. The VOC gained a notorious reputation for violence when it established trading posts in the "Malay Archipelago" and enslaved indigenous groups.[54] When the Dutch West India Company (WIC) launched in 1621, it quickly became deeply involved in the trade of enslaved Africans and colonization, first in Brazil, then the Caribbean. The WIC was also considered "a model of collaboration between European powers."[55]

Control of the transatlantic trade was sought because of the explosive profits gained from the twin forces of sugar and African enslavement from the sixteenth to nineteenth centuries. "By 1660 the value of sugar on world markets exceeded the value of all other tropical commodities combined."[56] Sugar plantation cultivation, from its height in Brazil, Barbados, and across the Caribbean, was "grueling and [extremely] dangerous" with tremendously high mortality rates.[57] In Suriname, a WIC monopoly ensured that a continuous supply of enslaved Africans was available for the endlessly brutal techniques deployed by planters to increase sugar, coffee, cocoa, and timber production.[58] Every stage of sugar's commodity cycle—capture of people to enslave, the Middle Passage, clearing, cultivation, processing, shipment, and European consumption—was produced through unfathomable violence. All told, thirteen million Africans were "brutally snatched from their homelands";[59] likely another six million were killed in or close to their homelands "during the hunt for slaves"; and an additional 10 percent died during the passage.[60] When the trade mostly ended in 1807, enslavement would last another eighty-plus years in the Americas with Big Cotton from the Mississippi River Valley displacing sugar as the global commodity king fueling the Industrial Revolution.[61] "More than the cotton gin," cotton production skyrocketed due to the "systematic increase in violent methods [used] in supervision and punishment" of the enslaved who were trafficked in the lucrative internal U.S. slave trade.[62]

Above all else the traffic of African men, women, and children was the bedrock to the global racial system and instilled the distinct subject positions of anti-Blackness and whiteness.[63] A process, according to W.E.B. Du Bois, where "labor was degraded, humanity was despised, [and] the theory of 'race' arose."[64] Diverse African cultures, peoples, and languages became "Black" in a "uniform system of debasement,"[65] and through enslavement "the transnationalization of the Black condition"[66] touched every corner of the world. Blackness became a "social fact and epiphenomenon," according to Marcus Hunter,[67] but was also not a "monolith or invariable production of race/racism," writes Saidiya Hartman.[68] Across the colonies throughout the seventeenth century, slave codes codified Blackness, with Barbados acting as an early adopter influencing other English colonies,[69] and wealth and status creation became a total racialized process in the service of whiteness.[70] There was not one law, or one act, that fused enslavement and the lowest racial hierarchical status with Blackness, but a series of laws, practices, and ideas about race across empires that encompassed the assemblage.

Essentially, the practices and views of Black enslavement and Black subject status became a global "social institution,"[71] a "reciprocal articulation" between varied anti-Black global practices,[72] causing overlapping ripple effects: in the trans-Saharan enslavement traffic, in regions with different groups enslaved but where Blackness would nonetheless become associated with enslavement (e.g., Iran and North Africa), in reactivating premodern proto anti-Blackness across specific regions, in geographies where non-Black but dark-skinned enslavement was also practiced (e.g., in the Cape Colony and East Indies), in locales without Black bodies, and in post-enslavement global labor practices. Local populations were compared, placed along a hierarchy, and accorded statuses in relation to constructions of anti-Blackness and their local interpretive divisions. As such, the "varied and contested articulations of (anti) blackness" defined colonial domination and in the afterlives of what Hartman describes as a "travestied emancipation."[73]

The slow dissolution of Black enslavement throughout the mid–late nineteenth century quickly gave way to a global indenture labor pool from empires' outposts of mostly Chinese and South Asian workers, but also Portuguese, Indonesian, Vietnamese, and Melanesian workers. To satisfy liberalism's call for "free labor," enslavement was merely repackaged through new models of racialized forced labor.[74] The racially derisive terms "coolie" and "yellow trade"[75] came "to define and obscure [the] boundary between enslavement and freedom"[76] but also embodied a complex structural racial middle location between Blackness and whiteness and in relation to local racial population designations throughout the Caribbean, South America, the U.S., Australia, South Africa, the Pacific, India, and Southeast Asia.[77] The term "coolie"—initially "originated from the Tamil word for wages '*kuli*,'" representing "low-level workers in the Indian Ocean labour market"—would take on an even more specific racial meaning in the context of India where the British invented "tribal" designations separate from caste, and transformed "tribal" groups, notably the Chotanagpur, into the British empire's racial labor reserve while also relying on them to cultivate a new agro-industrial tea in Assam for global consumption.[78]

Thus, the racial middle positioning of indentured labor took on various meanings across the global racial hierarchy embedded in regional and national hierarchies in specific colonial/postcolonial geographies. Even with middle positioning, however, the practice of "blackbirding" in Oceania, the kidnapping of Melanesian men and women for forced labor in Australia, Fiji, and New Caledonia,[79] maintained debased labor subjectivity with embodied Blackness alongside its symbolic representations attached to specific groups across locales. Forms of Black enslavement also continued in parts of North Africa beyond abolition.[80] Hence, after the predominantly global formal end of racial enslavement, a dense and shifting racial labor hierarchical system formed across empires, within a single colony, and in independent geographies with workers sometimes gaining access to whiteness (Portuguese), situated in the middle (East and South Asian), and maintained at the bottom (Melanesian, Black African). Moreover, unfree labor practices continued across the globe with Black formerly enslaved populations across diverse landscapes experiencing new techniques of racial labor domination. After the backlash to Reconstruction, the four million formerly enslaved Black Americans found themselves bound to the rules of sharecropping, debt peonage, incarceration and the placement on chain gangs, and repressive Black Codes.[81]

Racist Fears

Across empires, manufactured fears of uprisings, fears of interracial alliances, fears of interracial intimacies, fears of any crack in global white imperial domination, were met with "the logics of violence" and the oppressive power of the law.[82] My use of "fears" is not to suggest any legitimacy to the fear-induced racist procedures pursued, but to expose the severe acts and social controls enacted by white imperialists and colonialists to temper their anxieties about losing any form of racial power. Specifically, throughout imperial geographies we find an assortment of racist fear-based laws, mandates, and de facto social codes to ensure white racial spatial control. Examples include segregation, pass, antimiscegenation, and racial blood quantum laws, as well as citizenship and anti-immigration laws, with public health orders, emergency orders, and law enforcement mechanisms following suit.

Global white fears were so acute because those enslaved, those forced to labor, those whose lands were taken, fought back and made their own worlds and communities. From the beginning, enslaved Africans revolted on ships, ran away from Western Hemispheric bondage, formed communities with indigenous groups, and led resistance campaigns throughout the Caribbean.[83] Indigenous communities across the Americas fought against colonization, white settler expansion, and joined with free and runaway enslaved to challenge early Spanish, Portuguese, Dutch, French, and English imperial powers. Spaniards referred to "fugitive" enslaved runaway communities as *cimarrones*, what the English would adapt as *maroon*, the term applied throughout the region, and in Brazil represented the African phrasing *quilombo*.[84] Maroon settlements were found in Florida, Virginia, the Carolinas, Louisiana, and in the Caribbean, notably Jamaica and Haiti. The great *quilombos* of Brazil were numerous, wide-ranging, and defied colonial forces.

The social controls enacted from enslaved revolt ushered in colonial violence, deeper segregation, and the sharpening of racial distinction. Under attack white supremacy also produced new disparate imperial management, labor, and territorial conquest strategies. The fundamental and globally impactful racial resistance event of the Haitian Revolution (1791–1804) is also notable in how global white supremacy regrouped after this blow to its dominance. The revolution, led by maroons, enslaved, and Free Black men, was white imperialists' worst fear: an example that showcased the racial fault line to Enlightenment ideals, the power of Black communal rebellion, and the global popularity of its profound symbolism.[85] Black American abolitionists like David Walker, James Theodore Holly, and Fredrick Douglass turned Haiti's success into a transnational rallying cry for Black freedom.[86] The global white racist backlash was swift and hard. Haiti became a pariah nation, was not initially internationally recognized, and was eventually required to pay 150 million francs in reparations to the French for "lost property."[87] As other European-sanctioned racial enslavement slowly ended in the revolution's fallout, European enslavers (British, Danish, Dutch, Spanish) also demanded and received "reparations" for their "lost wealth."[88] Global colonial imperial policies also notably regrouped and adapted to maintain white ascendancy. Black enslavement continued in the U.S. and Brazil and combined with the turn to global imperial migrations of racialized forced and voluntary labor regimes. The U.S. became a new imperial power with the Louisiana Purchase in 1803 and France turned to Asia and Africa to reclaim its stature.[89]

Walter Rodney details how continental Africa, ravaged and unstable from centuries of pillaging and cultivating group strife to procure African bodies for bondage, became the epicenter of late nineteenth- and early twentieth-century colonial frontier battles,[90] with Germany and Belgium entering the European overseas imperial mix, initiating the eponymous "Scramble for Africa" with the Berlin Conference of 1884–85. Global white imperial practice thus sought to mute the Black rebellion of Haiti and its global demand for racial equality by colonizing all of Africa. Moreover, the "Black Peril" of constructed Black male sexuality was continuously stoked and condemned via white terror inflicted across territories through beatings, lynchings, and colonial state executions.[91] As C.L.R. James candidly wrote, white fears always "bred a savage cruelty."[92]

The emergent imperial racial labor chains post–Haitian Revolution also became part of the new jumbled and multidirectional "Yellow Peril" global racist panic in the mid–late nineteenth and early twentieth centuries.[93] Yellow Peril was a "free floating" geographically wide concept connected to both specific groups, notably the Chinese, and to all racialized as "Asian."[94] The racist caricature and vilification of Asians as "pollutants," "deviant," and as "coolies" bent on Western Hemispheric takeover, stoked white labor and political elite fears and mob violence.[95] Japan's imperial ambitions and "victories [achieved] over Qing China in 1894–95 and then tsarist Russia in 1904–5" quickly embodied the quintessential racial menace to European imperial power's white global dominance.[96] After Japan's victory over China, Germany's Kaiser Wilhelm II (1859–1941) warned of the "danger looming from the East" in a commissioned picture entitled "Against the Yellow Peril" that was sent to monarchs across Europe and reprinted in *Harper's Weekly* in 1898.[97] American Lothrop Stoddard's *Rising Tide of Color* boldly asserted "the white man towered [as] the indisputable master of the planet."[98] Coming off the European destructive heels of World War I, Stoddard warned of the threats to "white supremacy," notably the Japanese, who "methodically [adhered] to the white man's school" and produced "a body-blow to white ascendancy."[99] To counter the "rising tide," white "solidarity" and the cultivation of the "sacred [white geographic] bond" was crucial.[100]

Yellow Peril discourse harnessed a "transnational anti-Asian racism" in the form of specific international, regional, and national anti-Asian policies.[101] In turn, "hemispheric Orientalism," a term Erica Lee deploys to describe the expansive array of anti-Asian laws and practices across the Americas and beyond, flourished.[102] A roster of the most impactful policies, which coalesced with the broader global Social Darwinist and eugenics policy zeal, included: in the U.S., the 1875 Page Law prohibiting

Chinese female immigration, the 1882 Chinese Exclusion Act, the 1907–8 Gentleman's Agreement limiting Japanese immigration in the U.S. and Canada, the 1913 Alien Land Law, and the 1924 U.S. Immigration Act excluding all Asians (and setting national quotas for other groups); in Canada, the 1885 Chinese Head Tax, the 1908 Journey Law indirectly prohibiting South Asian and other immigration, and the 1923 Chinese Immigration Act barring most Chinese immigration. Mexico, Brazil, and Peru also passed a series of national or municipal laws that sought to limit or ban Chinese and Japanese immigration.[103] The Immigration Restriction Act of 1901 in Australia, known as part of the White Australia Policy, limited non-British immigration. Russia, fresh from Japanese defeat, attempted to control the movement of Chinese, Korean, and Japanese workers across its borders.[104] During World War II, 2,118 Japanese from Peru, Bolivia, Paraguay, Uruguay, and Venezuela were deported and interned in the U.S., joining the over 120,000 Japanese Americans interned.[105]

Yellow Peril stood in relation to Black Peril and a deeper, more profound fear of white retribution and interracial alliance. The interwar period, awash with alarmist calls from missionaries, colonial administrators, the media, eugenicists, and scholars in the new field of "race relations," was a time of whiteness on edge.[106] White anxious geographies and actors, informed by an ascendent Japan,[107] Black internationalism and resistance, and anticolonial insurgencies, were certain that a "race war" was looming. Even "racial pragmatism," an interwar discourse and strategy that sought to minimize direct overtures to white supremacy by advocating for in-direct colonial rule and separate development practices, did not represent a shift in views of white superiority but rather an urge to temper colonial "race consciousness" and ensure continued European colonial might.[108] All told, the consistency and urgency of racist fears shaped the multifaceted tenor and maneuvering of white imperial and white independent geographies' praxis to minimize the perceived vulnerability of global white supremacy.

Racial Categories, Divisions, and Control

Racial enslavement, removal, dispossession, and labor divisions along with immigration and spatial-familial management mechanisms produced a versatile, flexible, and sometimes contradictory array of racial hierarchical categories as part of European imperial racial formations.[109] The global racial categorical hierarchy between whiteness and Blackness was mostly secure but just who was "white" and who was "Black," who was "citizen" and who was "Native," and all the categories in-between, was dependent on temporality, geography, social relations prior to colonialism, imperial power, form of colonial rule, the dominant racial ideology circulating at the time, and the discretion of colonial administrators.[110] Racial categories were processual,[111] simultaneously opaque, porous, and ever-changing[112] depending on political and economic rational, but rigid in the maintenance of the racial hierarchy in protection of whiteness on top, especially as resistance occurred and when mixed-race populations formed. Thus, the material structures of the global racial system produced "race-thinking and racist-thinking define[d] populations in racialized categories," in the words of Stephen Small.[113] Interestingly, European imperial powers often differed in racial categorical fluidity (Spain), eras of strictness (British, Dutch, German, Italian), and false universalist constructions (French and later Portugal). Many colonial geographies also changed imperial hands, displaying the overlapping effects of multiple and interlaced regimes of racial formations.

There was additionally much racial categorical variety and logic within the same imperial system, with imperial powers tasked with controlling vast and geographically expansive empires diversely colonially managed and populated. Moreover, racialization categories and presumptions changed over time, often beginning as loose constructions before becoming more restrictive, while the hierarchy remained. Racial categories were altogether multipurpose, overdetermined, and intersectional, e.g., cross-cutting at different historical moments with enslaved status, regional/national origin, religion, caste, gender, and diverse local ethnic/community groupings and geographies to produce meaning. Classifications were codified in law, notably in colonial codes, censuses, surveys, colonial reports, company reports, and legal mandates dictating material livelihoods, notoriously free/unfree statutes, and spatial/institutional arrangements.

Often, legal designation for whiteness was merely "citizen," and/or "European," and the multifaceted racial meanings of "Native" or "Indigène" were commonly "indeterminate," providing possibility for categorical movement and flexibility for colonial needs that in turn produced diverse racial subject statuses of natives and foreigners alike but all in relation to white imperial citizenship.[114] The multiple terms that directly and indirectly signified whiteness expose the power of whiteness's always malleable formation, and its simultaneous overt and colorblind roots, with assumed top racial standard-bearer authority and status. Therefore, through the everyday vocabulary of racism that produced the language of racial hierarchies, meanings, and categories, we see the "highest expression of the colonial system," in the words of Albert Memmi.[115] "Racism [was] not . . . an incidental detail but . . . a consubstantial part of colonialism."[116] What Aimé Césaire equates as "colonization = 'thingification,'" where "the relations of domination and submission" placed racial meaning behind all the terms, discourses, and representations that reflected one's colonial placement, worth, and circumstance.[117]

Moreover, racial meaning was also expressed in small daily practices, micro-exchanges, physical space, visual representations, and subtle social cues and mores.[118] Thus, from the beginning there was a combination of both official categorizations, like in censuses and statutes, and the colloquial terms and norms used to represent difference and determine hierarchical arrangements and expected social behavior. In essence, colonially divided groups were racialized in multiple, overlapping forms and placed within multiple embedded hierarchies with meanings changing temporally, when material needs arose, and across geographic boundaries. One's racial categorical location was simultaneously embedded in a single racial category hierarchy, a national/intra-imperial racial hierarchy, a regional racial hierarchy, and a global western imperial racial hierarchy—together the global racial system. Table 2.1 highlights a nonexhaustive mix of different imperial legal categories and everyday terms.

SPAIN AND PORTUGAL

Spain and Portugal were the imperial forerunners to racial categorization. This early era marked the gradual transition from religious to racial markers. Initially *gente de razón* (people of reason) and *gente sin razón* (people without reason) demarcated bifurcated colonial governance between the *república de españoles* (Republic of Spaniards) and *república de indíos* (Republic of Indians).[119] Quickly, the religious identity-policing tools and social stratification formations practiced in medieval Spain were adopted and adapted to handle and contain the challenge of new racial mixtures and maintain Spanish dominance. At first, when applied to Spaniard-indigenous sexual relations, the gendered racial dynamics to intimate racial crossings was viewed by the Crown more banally. If a Spanish

TABLE 2.1. Colonial Racial Categories, Terms

Spain	Portugal	Netherlands	England
Nueva España: *Españoles, Peninsulares, Criollos, Indios, Mestizos, Castizos, Mulattoes, Moriscos, Albino, Torna Atrás, Lobo, Zambaigo, Cambujo, Albarazado, Barcino, Coyote, Chamizo, Coyote Mestizo, Ahí te Estás, Negroes, Zambos, Chinos*	**Brazil:** *Branco, Peninsular, Creole, Pardo, Preto, Mulatto, Crioulo, Negro, Indio*	**East Indies:** *Europeanen* (Europeans), *Inlanders* (Natives), *Inheemsche*, (Indigenous), *Vreemde Oosterlingen* (Foreign Oriental), Chinese, Indo-European	**India:** Turk-Iranian, Indo-Aryan, Scytho-Dravidian, Dravidian, Aryo-Dravidian, Mongolo-Dravidian, Mongoloid^
Philippines: *Peninsulares* (European White), *Filipinos, Indios, Moro, Chino-Sangley, Mestizos, Mestizong Intsik* (Chinese Mestizos), *Inquilinos*	**Angola:** *Branco, Indigenas, Amarelo, Negro Abronzeado, Negro Quasi Retinto*	**Suriname:** *Blanken* (White), Free Mulattos/ Coloureds and Negroes, Slaves*; Indian, Maroon, Creole, Foreign Oriental (from East Indies, Java)	**Jamaica:** White Protestant, Enslaved Black, Free (Jews, Mulattos, Negroes, and Indians)
1860 Spanish Colonial Standard Census: *Blanco* (White), *Libre* (Free), *Esclavo* (Slave)	**East Timor:** Papuan, Malayan, *Negrito*		**East African Protectorate:** European, Asiatic, Anglo-Indian, Native (including Kikuyu, Maasai, Ulu, Kikumbuli, and Kitui #)

Sources: Carrera 2003; Laforteza 2015; Emigh, Ahmed, and Riley 2021; Mattos 2006; Luttikhuis 2013; Vink 2008; Rai 2022; Milner-Thornton 2020; Newman 2018; Garraway 2005; Collins and Nam 2022; Davis 2021; Rouighi 2019; Steinmetz 2007; El-Tayeb 1999; Pergher 2021; De Napoli 2021; Fusari 2021.

* 1738 Colonial Registration

^ 1901 Census racial types; Risley, *The People of India*

Five Native Reserves

France	Germany	Italy
St. Domingue: *Grands Blancs* (Grand Whites), *Petits Blancs* (Small Whites), *Esclave Nègre* (Black Slave), *Gens de Couleur Libres* (Free People of Color), *Mulâtre, Mulâtresse, Quarteron, Métis, Mestif, Mamelouque, Nègres Quarteronné, Sang-mêlé*	**South West Africa:** *Reichsangehörigen* (Citizen of the Reich), *Europäer* (European), *Weiß* (White), *Ausländer/in* (Foreigner), *Eingeborene* (Native) (including Ovaherero, Khokhoi, Witbooi/ Nama, Bondelswart), *Rehoboth, Mischling, Farbige Deutsche* (Colored German)	**Eritrea:** *Cittadino Italiano* (Italian Citizen), *Indigeni* (Indigenous) (including Tigrinya, Saho, Afar, and Bilin, Kunama, Nara), *Suddito Coloniale* (Colonial Subject), Habasha, Black, *Meticci*
Indochina: European, *Citoyens* (French Citizen), *Asiatiques etrangers* (Asian Aliens, Chinese), *Asiatiques Assimilable* (Asian Japanese), *indigène* (including Ammonite, Khmer), *Eurasiatique* (Euroasian), *Métis, Outres Gens de Couleur* (Other People of Color)	**Samoa:** Polynesian Somoan	**Libya:** Italian Citizen, Metropolitan Citizen, Italian Subject, *Italiana in Tripolitania e Cirenaica* (Italian Citizenship in Tripolitania and Cyrenaica), Libyan Italian Citizen, *Indigeni* (Indigenous peoples), Muslim, Israelites, Foreign non-Muslim, Arab race
Algeria: *Colons, Pieds Noir* (European Algerian), Oriental Semites (Arab), *Indigènes Autochtones* (Berber)		

father chose to recognize his child with an indigenous woman, the child was socialized as Spanish.[120] Soon, racist fears, particular with the growth of enslaved Africans joining indigenous rebellions, predicated stricter boundary protocols, and the Spanish Royal Pragmatic decree regulated "unequal marriages" in an overt racialized form by 1805.[121] The *sociedad de castas*, or *sistema de castas*, was an amalgamation of governing laws and practices that allocated opportunities, rights, and entitlements among "*españoles*" (Spanish), who were placed outside of casta designations, "*indios*" (Indian), "*mestizos*" (Spanish and Indian), "*negroes*" (Black), and "*mulattoes*" (Black and white). *Limpieza de sangre* (blood purity) was no longer solely about pure Catholic nobility but the "overriding superiority of the *español* category" and the need to maintain familial honor through the blood purity of emergent whiteness.[122]

Casta categories rapidly grew, marking multiple types of lineage combinations that could change across geographies and were also influenced by how *calidad* (quality) was signified, such as by occupation, language, and dress (see Table 2.1).[123] The proliferation of *casta* designations introduced an elite weighty unease with mixed-race peoples "often described as being of '*color quebrado*'" (broken color).[124] Eventually, *casta* became *raza* to interpret complex social relations and secure overseas Spanish imperial order.[125] Portugal, similarly, governed their early post-seventeenth-century colonies with *Estatutos de Pureza de Sangue* (Purity of Blood Statutes) but rather than solely claiming purity of "Old Christian" descent, in Portugal and in its Brazilian colony, the highest category was to be without race or *raça*, comparable to placing "*Español*" beyond *casta* designations.[126] "The formulation 'with no race of Moor, Jew or Mulato' became common" while Blackness was associated with slavery and lineage regardless of actual free status with terms such as *pardo, preto, mulato, crioulo,* and *cabra* sometimes referenced synonymously.[127] Brazil, like Spanish-governed colonies, embodied a wide range of color-emphasized lineage designations.[128] By the late nineteenth and early to mid-twentieth centuries in Portuguese colonial geographies ranging from Goa in India, to East Timor in Indonesia, to Angola in southwest Africa, racial anthropological categories were created and locally used but also embedded within the binary legal distinctions between "citizens and aborigines."

THE NETHERLANDS AND ENGLAND

The Netherlands was another early imperial racial category trendsetter. Gerald Horne argues that the Dutch were "pioneers" in "developing overarching racial identities in order to facilitate colonialism," notably global constructions of whiteness across its empire.[129] The first colonial endeavors of the Netherlands occurred with the Dutch East India Company (VOC) (1602–1799) and the Dutch West India Company (WIC) (1621–1792). The racial landscape forming in the Cape Colony waystation for the VOC was used as evidence for seventeenth-century European racial theorists and offered a template for colonial rule mixed with monopolistic commercial and economic interests.[130] The legal categories "company employees, free burghers, Khoisan, slaves and free Blacks" remained and hardened with the British takeover in 1806.[131] Determining the "Khoisan" (a combined term of Khoikhoi and San groups) as an insufficient labor source, the Cape had a multiracial nonwhite "alien" enslaved population from Southeast Asia and East Africa, along with Chinese workers.[132] A 1776 ordinance of the Dutch parliament abolished the distinction between "free humans and enslaved" except for "'negroe- and other slave' from the colonies that travelled to the Netherlands."[133]

In Suriname, the WIC held a monopoly to supply enslaved Africans and categories developed between white Europeans, including Portuguese, German, and Jewish settlers; enslaved African, Indian, and Carib; maroon; and indentured South Asian and Indonesian workers from the Dutch East Indies post-1870. Eighteenth-century colonial divisions saw a broad swath of mixed-race categories form: *carboeger, mulatto, mestice, castice,* and *poestice* that developed into a generic designation of *coloured* or *couleurling* in the nineteenth century.[134] In the late nineteenth century, the Netherlands introduced an assimilation "Dutchification" policy where Suriname "was seen as a *Nederlandse volksplanting* (a planting/making of Dutch people)," and early twentieth-century "Indification" supported light-skinned creoles, and later "Hindustani" groups.[135] In contrast, in the Dutch East Indies, legal pluralism, *Regeeringsreglement,* was institutionalized in 1854 with the categorization article 109RR further explicitly demarcated in 1906. Europeans were subject to European law, with "Natives," customary law, and "Foreign Orientals" (mostly Chinese) placed in the middle, which in turn structured different material conditions, rights, taxes, and militia conscription obligations.[136] Legal designations remained with the 1901 Ethical Policy, *Ethische Politiek,* which sought to raise living standards, educate, and outline limited political participation for "Natives" while Dutch rule and territory expanded.[137] The mixed racial category *"Indisch"* or *"Indo"* also developed and changed over time but entailed European rights if the child was recognized by Dutch fathers.[138]

The British, in constant early battle with Spain and the Netherlands for territory, had the most expansive overseas empire by the nineteenth and early twentieth centuries, representing "a chaotic pluralism of British interests at home and of their agents and allies abroad."[139] A racial kaleidoscope of designations was overlayed to produce complex racial formations in the Americas, Asia, Africa, the Middle East, and the Pacific. Former British white settler territories of the United States, Canada, Australia, and New Zealand also became imperial practitioners of race-based categorization upon their independence. Early colonialism in the Caribbean saw racial labels applied to small white planter elites, European Christians, and non-Christian settlers, enslaved, free, and mixed-race Black, and "Indian" and "Carib" populations. Jamaica, the most important Atlantic holding in the midcentury with the largest enslaved community, was influenced by former Spanish rule, Protestantism, and the threat of European demographic precarity to produce codified racial distinctions between "white Protestant subjects and categories of free people ('Jews, mulattos, negroes, and Indians')."[140] The determination of who was a "white subject" was paramount for legal and social rights[141] and became the foundation of naturalization and citizenship throughout British (and at least indirectly all) colonial geographies. By 1844, divisions had crystalized along White, Brown (or Colored), and Black classifications enumerated in the West Indies census of that year and would remain until WWII, with some local variety, such as in St. Vincent, where in 1861, categories were divided by complexion (White, Coloured, Black) and race (European, African, Asiatic, Carib, and Mixed) in census tables.[142]

Next to the Atlantic region, "greater India," which encompassed Burma to the whole of areas east of Suez, was popularly framed as the "jewel in the crown" of British imperial lore and reflective of evolved colonial management and complex overlapping racial categorical divisions.[143] At first, the wealthiest region, Bengal, was governed by the East India Company since 1757 until it was taken over by the British Crown in 1858 and further territories were added. Throughout British reign several racial theories traveled and coalesced at certain moments and exposed the amalgamation of religion, region, race, and caste. The stadial theory of human development, Aryan race theory, martial race theory, and the depot labor migratory system all provided distinct racial meanings to forming categories.[144] After the 1857 Indian Mutiny, which brought the end to Company rule and increased anxiety about the "mutinous" high-caste Hindu leaders from northern India, martial race theory grew. Punjabi Sikhs and Nepalese Gurkhas were recruited for military service because they were "natural" soldiers "predisposed to the arts of war" and subsequently sent to police and maintain order throughout the empire.[145] Historically overlapping at this time was "the depot system" that determined which groups were suitable for certain types of work to fill the empire's (and other empires') indentured labor needs after the end of formal enslavement,[146] and the larger belief that India could achieve civilizational standards under British tutelage.[147] The evolving census divisions added another layer. The 1864 census "covering the Island of Bombay arrived at fourteenfold overlapping classifications of race, religion and caste," but the later 1872 Bengal census was whittled down to nine categories.[148] By the time the 1901 census occurred, headed by Census Commissioner of British India, Sir Herbert Risley, the racialization of caste assumptions to phenotypical traits in support of Aryan race theory and budding scientific racism was complete.[149] Seven racial types were determined, with high-caste Hindu Aryans placed atop and "tribal" groups separated from caste formations.[150]

Late British colonialism, particularly apparent in African colonial possessions and mandates gained after World War I, saw a push toward more informal indirect rule and bifurcated legal and racial divisions. Mahmood Mamdani describes African colonies as structured with two groups: "races" and "tribes." Mamdani conceptualizes "races" as those considered not native to Africa (e.g., Europeans and Asians) or indigenous (e.g., Arabs, Colored, etc.), and "tribes" as the divisions between "native" African groups. Races were governed by civil law with a hierarchy between the "master race," Europeans, and "subject races"; and "tribes" were mandated by a customary legal system.[151] The creation of "tribes" heightened perceived ethnological groupings and what was thought to be "original and pure tradition." Hence, "the designation of . . . 'tribe' performed" specific "racialized meanings" for differentiated groups and served as a collective debased racial category.[152] Not all African censuses split up "tribes," with some merely enumerating "African" as a racial category but deploying "tribal" categories in colonial reports.[153] Thus, "lumping and splitting" was the basis of all colonial orders but took on specific features between forms of colonial governance.[154] "Europeans" were lumped together, then split in degrees of whiteness; "foreign races" were lumped, then divided outside of whiteness and Blackness; and "Africans" were lumped, then split by "tribal" Blackness categorical divisions. Regardless of the exact descriptive term used by colonial regimes, "race" or "tribe," race was organizing the discursive landscape and associative meanings.[155] Mapping European whiteness, and comparing all else to its formation, was always the underlining project.

FRANCE

Of all the empires, the late French empire during the nineteenth-century Third Republic "was one that put the greatest stress on its civilizing mission—the *mission civilisatrice*," which facilitated the colonial racial policies of economic, political, and cultural assimilation of perceived "inferior races" governed by a centralized administrative state in Paris.[156] Early French colonialism and enslavement was ruled from 1685–1848 by the *Code Noir* (Black Code) (with a reprieve from 1794–1802 when slavery was briefly abolished, only to be reinstated by Napoleon Bonaparte). Enslavement brought "economic transformation" to seventeenth–eighteenth century France on the cusp of political revolution.[157] Race, nonetheless, exposed the limits to the revolutionary ideals of equality circulating throughout France when the 1802 decree reestablished slavery and "restricted citizenship to whites."[158] France's most valued possession, St. Domingue (Haiti), was powered by the Black enslaved and included a hierarchical white anxiety-inducing range of *métissage* (mixture) categories[159] including the influential "*gens de couleur libres*" (Free People of Color) who were subject to increased repression throughout the eighteenth century.[160] After the Haitian revolution France regrouped with new formulated Republican ideas of assimilation while continuing racial difference. Assimilation, in the later colonies, commonly gave way to "association," a lighter version of indirect rule.

Assimilation and association took on different forms across French settler colonies, colonies of exploitation and extraction, and embedded within the "civilizational hierarchy" of the empire: Europeans on top, then the Vietnamese, next Algerians, then sub-Saharan Africans, and at the bottom, Kanak peoples in New Caledonia.[161] All were divided between "citizen" and "subject" designations that made most Europeans automatic citizens, but with citizenship only available for *indigénate* populations "when conditions and qualifications were met." The *code de l'indigénat,* first implemented in Algeria and then traveling throughout the colonies, was the separate system and series of laws that dictated noncitizen, *indigène,* possibilities. Racial categorization and divisions between *indigène* groups and *estrangers* (nonwhite foreigners) determined by colonial administrators "differed greatly across the variegated ethnic, political cultural and social spaces . . . across the French empire."[162] The "catch-all" *indigène* was an effective colonial tool of hierarchical difference.[163] In Indochina, *indigène* was an Annamite (ethnic Kinh, Khmer, and Chinese), while at other times Khmer was separated.[164] In Algeria, *indigène* aggregated the entire local population with Islam, but also constructed "the bad Arab versus good Berber" fissure, and placed Berber closer to whiteness and historically Christian, with both in comparison to the over one million European settler Algerians, *colons* (French, Italian, Spanish, Maltese, Jewish) who had emigrated by 1900.[165] In New Caledonia *indigène* came to represent a French colonized subject positionality "where colonized status [anywhere in the empire was] the key criterion" while also maintaining racial divisional beliefs between mainland Kanak Melanesians and Polynesian Loyalty Islanders.[166]

GERMANY AND ITALY

Late German (1884–1920) and Italian colonialism (1885–1947, with the end of the Somalia trusteeship in 1960) saw divergent colonial rule practices and racialized constructions within German African, Oceania, and Chinese colonial geographies, and for Italy, between North African and the Horn of Africa groups, and after the rise of fascist race laws. Both powers enacted deadly colonial racial repression. Although late to the overseas colonial machine, German intellectuals played crucial roles in facilitating the global racial knowledge of scientific and cultural difference and advancing Social Darwinism.[167] These engagements were brought to acquired territories. Samoans were seen as Polynesian "noble savages" and governed with a German belief in "cultural salvage" but German rule, according to George Steinmetz.[168] In Southwest Africa the Khoikhoi moved up and down the racial continuum as supposedly "mimics," "noble" then "ignoble" "savages."[169] The *Rehobothers,* mixed race but sometimes distanced from mixed-race *Michling*, were turned into a "wedge" group between Khoikhoi and the Ovaherero.[170] The latter's culture was perceived irredeemable and only useful for labor or to be destroyed.[171] When the 1904 *Vernichtungsbefehl* (order of annihilation) against the Ovaherero was unleashed, a brutal repression was also in place against the Witbooi (part of Khoikhoi, Nama) rebellion.

All told, the racist genocidal practices inflicted upon the Ovaherero and Nama—the first German concentration camp, death marches, deceased bodies violated for racial science, and forced camp labor—laid the groundwork for the Holocaust thirty years later.[172] After the carnage, Germany implemented the repressive 1907 Native Ordinances with regulations ranging from pass and ID tags, residency requirements, and land and cattle ownership prohibitions.[173] In Germany, the *Reichstag* debated and obsessively agonized over laws to control racial purity and ban interracial marriage by extolling *Rassengefühl* (racial feeling) in protection of German whiteness and against the perceived imminent "concrete threat to the German nation."[174]

Most Italians, scholars, art historians, and the Catholic Church saw colonization as the path to strengthen the post-1861 unified Italian state, to equally position Italy in the league of European powers, and as a reclamation of the classical cultural heritage of ancient Roman territories.[175] Ancient regions supposedly needed to be "liberated" from constructed barbaric and backward Ottoman and Ethiopian rule and returned to the "rightful inheritor of the classic Roman Empire."[176] From the beginning race and *italianità* were linked, propelling imperial ambition and disparate colonial management.[177] Italians negotiated regional European racialization as somewhat less white, particularly southern Italian, by first claiming "Latinity," a shared Latin race with France, and/or as leaders of the Roman "Mediterranean race," but later aligned with Aryanism in fascist rule.[178] Citizenship, defined through blood and origin with *jus sanguinis*, became the vehicle to reinforce Italian racial lineage in the metropole and colonies. The over seven million Italians who emigrated to the U.S. and Latin America between 1861 and 1910[179] were also viewed as an arm of indirect Italian colonial power[180] even as they negotiated different racialization processes in receiving countries, for example, through whiteness in Brazil or originally distanced from whiteness then accepted as such in the U.S.

The politics of race evolved, somewhat fluidly, in the beginning of colonial rule particularly in Tripolitania and Cyrenaica, combined as Libya in 1934, then became more restrictive.[181] Olindo De Napoli argues that the colonial "politics of indeterminacy" between *cittadino* (citizen) and *suddito* (subject) blurred direct distinctions but still demarcated racial difference.[182] Native Libyans acquired Italian subject status in 1912 under separate judicial authority as Muslim and Jewish *indigeni* (indigenous people),[183] "colonial citizenship" in 1919, and "Libyan Italian citizens" in the late 1930s.[184] Intra-imperial racial hierarchy and anti-Blackness dictated the liminal "subject" status of the groups in the Horn of Africa (Eritrea, Somalia, and later Ethiopia) who had been under Italian rule in some form since the late 1880s.[185] A further hierarchy formed with the "*Habasha*," Orthodox Christians, above other Black, non-Christian groups, and with the multiracial "*meticci*."[186] The Declaration of the Empire of *Africa Orientale Italiana* (AOI) (which combined Eritrea, Italian Somaliland and Ethiopia) began new fascist thinking on race.[187] A series of fascist race laws inspired by the 1938 publication *Il fascismo e i problemi della razza* (Fascism and the Problem of Race) or *Il Manifesto degli scienziati razzisti* (Racist Scientists' Manifesto) ensued.[188] In 1937 "'relations of a conjugal nature' between a citizen and colonial subject of AOI" was criminalized and punishable by up to five years of imprisonment, and the 1939 *The Penal Sanctions for the Defense of Racial Prestige against the Natives of Italian Africa* increased punishments in the Penal Code and outlined a "comprehensive framework for racial segregation."[189] Consolidated fascist rule was policed with street violence and performed by the dreaded "blackshirts." Massacres, "concentration camps, public executions, [and] forced marches," in what Ian Law calls "genocidal fascist colonialism," were all implemented.[190]

Knowing and Defying Racist Imperial Practice

Distilling the material practices of racist empires is fundamental because it underscores the traversing, interlaced, connected, collaborative, and competitive ways western European empires pursued overseas wealth, governed and controlled their colonies, and made the new modern world with the cudgel, precision, and force of global racism. The global figure and practice of race emerged within the compass, the slave ship, the whip, the sugar barrel, the picking bag, the traders' ledgers, and the Crown's law. Still, as addressed in the ending of the last chapter, these tangible and intangible encasings of racism are also allegories of rejection. Although racist empires defined the language and material modality of how race was created and experienced, it did not stop the individual and collective ways racism was challenged and how new threads of life and knowledge were woven.

Achille Mbembe reminds us that those enslaved "continued to create world[s]. Through gesture and speech, they wove relationships and a universe of meaning, inventing languages, religions, dances, and rituals and creat[ed] community . . . [that] constantly tore at the veil of [racial] hypocrisy and lies."[191] Slave uprisings and everyday freedom practices, as addressed above, arose alongside the advent of maroon communities. Adam Bledsoe writes, "Marronage was perhaps one of the most creative and emergent methods of life-building found in the modern world,"[192] where multiracial and all-Black societies formed in confrontation and negotiation with white supremacy but always in protection and value for Black life.[193] Tukufu Zuberi reminds us that "liberation narratives of the enslaved and the Appeals from 'free' individuals of African descent" radically indicted racial enslavement, oppression, and the false liberties that excluded all but those who were racialized white.[194] Saidiya Hartman draws our attention to how the everyday thoughts and actions of those most marginalized radically claimed space, chose families, and curated knowledge.[195] They created what Marcus Hunter and Zandria Robinson describe as "villages," "the intricate, tight networks and strategies Black communities developed behind the veil . . . to survive and thrive."[196] Collectively, indigenous knowledge practices, cultural movement, and generative life was sustained by all communities racialized outside of whiteness in various ways.

Moreover, during the historical period of racist empires, Black scholars particularly were also the first to outline the operation and ubiquity of global white supremacy. Du Bois lamented the global color line, the production of anti-Blackness and violent whiteness, and Anna Julia Cooper "saw an intimate link between internal and external colonization, between domestic racial oppression and imperialism."[197] Eric Williams and C.L.R. James outlined the frames of racial capitalism and revolt; and the Howard School of International Relations, including Alain Locke, Ralph Bunche, and Merze Tate among others, "wrote about white world supremacy from the standpoint of its victims."[198] Writer, activist, organizer, and anticolonial intellectual leader George Padmore "interrogated the white world system and zeroed in on European imperialism" with race and labor as its engine,[199] and Claudia Jones placed Black women's work at the center of exploitative racial capitalism.[200] In the throes of World War II, Merze Tate defiantly declared, "In the coming global order there must be freedom for all or freedom for none."[201]

These foundational knowledges against racist empires outline how to understand the contemporary reproduction of our racist world in the chapters ahead. The remaining chapters wade into the deep caverns of the global racial system to determine exactly who today is laboriously treading water, who is gliding atop, and who is drowning below. Specifically in the next chapter I mark how racism continues to travel throughout the globe supported by centuries of racist modernity and empires' deep intertwined capitalist, militaristic, and cultural roots while also appearing contemporarily as colorblind.

Three
Traveling Racism and Deep Whiteness

The World Inequality Lab presented sobering findings in its 2022 report. Not only did the richest 10 percent of the global population take 52 percent of all global income, and the poorest half earned just 8.5 percent, but the richest 10 percent held 76 percent of all global wealth and the bottom 50 percent just 2 percent.[1] While staggering global wealth inequality flourished, the International Labour Organization documented the global rise of nonstandard forms of employment, temporary and part-time jobs, informal and own-account work, and heightened wage gaps between top and bottom earners.[2] The World Inequality report authors state bluntly, "Contemporary global inequalities are close to early 20th century levels, at the peak of Western imperialism."[3]

This presumably shocking statement is not so shocking at all when we look at the geographic distribution of inequality. Within the United Nations' racially veiled designations of "developed countries" and "developing countries," with the latter further demarcated by "least developed countries," we see the steady maintenance of concentrated wealth in once imperial global white cartographies and profound material and spatial global anti-Blackness.[4] Of the forty-seven least developed countries, thirty-three are in continental Africa outside of North Africa, five are broadly in Oceania (Melanesia), three in South Asia, three in Southeast Asia, one in the Gulf (Yemen), one in the Caribbean (Haiti), and one in

Central Asia (Afghanistan).⁵ Countries within the European Union and North America have eleven and sixteen times higher per capita income from those in "sub-Saharan" Africa.⁶ We also see dramatic inequities within regional entangled racial zones (e.g., Australia and New Zealand versus the rest of Oceania).

E. Tandayi Achiume, the U.N. Special Rapporteur on Contemporary Forms of Racism and critical race theorist, vividly underscores that the "distinction between 'high-income' and 'low-income' countries is directly related to the racist economic extraction and exploitation that occurred during the colonial era," essentially because of racist empires.⁷ Sampie Terreblanche's 1997 testimony to South Africa's Truth and Reconciliation Commission and his wider writings on western empires took this position a step further.⁸ Global historical structural racism and racial capitalism specifically directly "enriched" those racialized white⁹ and the distributive effects continue to be manifold. Sociologists and other scholars describe this phenomenon as "unjust enrichment" and "unjust impoverishment" accrued from global white "cumulative advantages" and particularly Black "cumulative disadvantages."¹⁰

Succinctly, the emergence of a racist world "locked in"¹¹ and enshrined global racial inequities in notably capitalism, militarism, and culture today.¹² Sara Ahmed reminds us that "whiteness is . . . a matter of what is behind, a form of inheritance . . . an effect of past accumulations" that organizes our world.¹³ White communities and spaces continue to accumulate more and remain constructed as possessors of "value": capital skills, worthy of safety, and embodying advanced cultural aesthetics. All the while those groups and spaces racialized low on the global racial hierarchy still struggle for advanced material livelihoods, safety from state violence, and control over their cultural innovations and imagery. This global "white racist sedimentation" structures ongoing and evolved traveling racist practices today.¹⁴

Therefore, with this foundation serving as an anchor, contemporary traveling racism exemplifies a global racial domino effect. The current global arrangements of white-governed racial capitalism; ongoing, white-led global and national security military actions; and globally white-constructed racial cultural production are the first domino drops that trickle across the globe. Contemporary global racist practices represent the shifting terrain of white global political economic needs, white global security threats, and white global racial representations. When regional, then national, and finally local social systems engage, negotiate, and coercively and indirectly follow the white global lead, the next dominoes fall, eventually ensnarling the world entirely.

Second, these practices and scaled forms of racialization are typically viewed as race neutral or colorblind, personifying natural neoliberal "market" forces, "logical," "commonsense," "necessary" national security choices, and "cultural," supposedly nonracial representations. Traveling racial practices, from global and national economic procedures, war and military engagements, and racial imagery production posit neutrality but enshrine racial inequities and foreclose the possibilities for racial acknowledgment. In essence, through beliefs in race-neutral procedures and worldviews, the racist foundation to the global racial system, and the myriad ways it perpetuates global racism today, is rendered mute, nonexistent, and, therefore, current global racial inequalities become mere reflections of natural, expected inequities. I delve more specifically into the global discourses and national adaptions to global colorblindness in chapter 6.

Third, these collective global structural forces ensure the continuation of a global "possessive investment in whiteness" and the ossification of a globally deep whiteness.[15] The contemporary global racial order basically mirrors the deep whiteness at its base. Deep whiteness drives contemporary traveling racism's many interconnective forces forward and ensures its replication. Specifically, deep whiteness anchors the economic pathways possible; labels who and what is a military threat and who is to be protected; and is the pleasure, spectacle, commodification, and presentation of racial allure, fetishization, and manufactured difference. Deep whiteness exposes as well, according to john powell, how those racialized white can benefit from the "spoils of a racist system without being personally racist."[16]

Throughout the chapter I showcase traveling racism's ubiquitous presence most acutely seen in global racial capitalism, militarism, and cultural production. Significantly, the crushing waves of traveling racism map the connections, disjunctures, and pathways of the global racial system.

Global Racial Capitalism

Contemporary global racial capitalism spreads through modern global production networks. Global production networks are the "fragmented" capital components of commodity input-output structures—design, inputs, harvesting, processing, manufacture, packaging, transportation, distribution, marketing, retail, consumption—that are "dispersed" across unequal racialized geographies and upheld by global-national institutional policy apparatuses.[17] All global production networks are governed by different transnational "lead firms," some with inceptions that began during colonialism, who typically represent the highest "value" segments of the chains (e.g., research and development, design, and branding) and set the standards and price points supplier firms must negotiate.[18] These pressure points subsequently structure disparate labor regimes down the chain. Different industries, whether it is apparel, manufacturing, tourism, agriculture, or natural resources, represent different input-output firm power arrangements, geographic incorporations, and specific industry demands that taken together tell us something about how race organizes production networks through what Chantal Thomas describes as a "technology of economic allocation, . . . production" and value.[19]

These production networks emerged out of the path-dependent processes of the still burning flames of racist empires, as products of the unjust enrichment white geographies and firms amassed, the global "development project" to "modernize" former colonies, and the neoliberal "globalization project" since the 1980s.[20] At each historical juncture, as Stuart Hall declares, global capital embodied a complex articulated structure, rooted in material, racial, and social relations of difference.[21] Articulation, however, is as much about (dis)articulation, what Jennifer Bair and Marion Werner highlight as the changing racial economic politics of chain exclusion, inclusion, and stratification that reproduces uneven racialized geographies and stratified racial labor formations.[22] In effect, articulation and disarticulation global chain practices reflect traveling racism through how (1) exploitation, (2) expropriation, (3) replication, and (4) legal protections encode a rotating prism of racial value allocation that continuously preserves the property of global whiteness.[23] These forces are all collectively "systemically imbricated" rather than singularly produced.[24]

LABOR EXPLOITATION

First, racism travels across each node of the commodity input-out structure in a constantly moving international division of labor. Transnational lead firm corporations choose supplier firms and geographies in search of flexibility, profits, ease of product movement, markets, and cost savings.²⁵ Depending on the industry, consolidated "first-tier suppliers" have emerged, notably in electronics, automobile manufacturing, and apparel, who then outsource parts of production to subcontractors and sometimes offshore to additional external geographies.²⁶ Outsourcing logics are racial logics. Racial labor exploitation is justified in a cacophony of "development," "entrepreneurial," and "modernizing" work discourses that ensure the maintenance of a constant devalued global racialized labor source.²⁷ Intersectional racial labor exploitation also forms as other markers of racial difference are embedded in, and specific to, local geographies. Markers such as gender, caste, ethnic, and migrant status intersect with race to create intricate, overlapping, and layered hierarchical racial divisions of labor across chain actors and stages of production.²⁸

Gender particularly intersects with race, producing further undervalued feminized racialized labor. Over 190 million women work in global production networks, 42 percent of total chain employment, most in apparel and agriculture.²⁹ Racialized feminized reproductive labor is also at the base of chains where household care and subsistent livelihood maintenance are least valued and commonly erased as components to global production.³⁰ Racialized women's work is more concentrated in categories of employment that are seasonal, precarious, and informal. Cotton pickers in Africa, home-based garment piecework in India, and tourism sex workers in the Caribbean all demonstrate the consequences to the global forces to structural intersectionality.³¹ The latter tourism example accentuates how racialized bodies are also sexually commodified in exploitative global chain exchange.³² Lastly, at the top of the chain, racialized white women's entry into higher work positions in the global North, along with the easing of care responsibilities and ready access to cheap clothes, food, and household goods, is directly subsidized by nonwhite women's exploited racial reproductive and productive labor from the global South and North.³³ Structurally, white adjacent women, or elite women in middle, triangulated racial geographies (see chapter 5) like those in Gulf states and parts of East Asia such as Singapore, Hong Kong, and Taiwan, also benefit from racialized migrant global domestic workers from the Philippines and East Africa who are embedded in layered and unequally regulated global labor chains.³⁴

Racism further travels between the geographies where global production nodes are placed. Geographies represent different forms of racial capital value and transnational racialization processes. Keeping to the anti-Black foundation of global capital accumulation, Black geographies, as Adam Bledsoe and Jamaal Wright argue, are commonly constructed as vacant and left to the "rational agendas" of global capital actors.[35] Exploited racial labor also comes from racialized geographies that have their own national and regional racial hierarchies. Groups from these divisions represent the various ways transnational-national group racialization shapes production network placement, stratification form, and expulsion in relation to each other. Indigenous tomato pickers are exploited in Mexico, migrate to Florida, and work alongside further marginalized Haitian migrants.[36] Indigenous Mexican workers who migrate to the U.S. are also placed lower in the field-harvesting hierarchy compared to *mestizo* Mexican migrant workers.[37] Local Mauritanian workers compete with contract Chinese and Indian apparel migrant workers in export processing zones.[38] Papuan workers were historically excluded and had limited work opportunities in mining in West Papua, Indonesia.[39] Centrally, traveling racism across national geographies, and the movement of racial bodies across regional and national borders, reflects local and proximal racial understandings of difference, informed by colonial racial histories, and contemporary circulating racial discourse about those who inhabit specific spaces. Therefore, racial rational discourses across geographies influence who is constructed as fitting specific skilled, de-skilled, or expendable labor needs that production networks rely on to meet global tastes, price concerns, and just-in-time demands.

EXPROPRIATED SPACE

Exploited racialized labor rooted in discrete space is deeply connected to the varied practices of racist expropriation in service to global production. Nancy Fraser argues that "expropriation works [as an 'ongoing confiscatory process' that] confiscate[s] capacities and resources and conscript[s] them into capital's circuits of self-expansion."[40] Expropriation includes the privatization of space and land for resource extraction and commodification, along with the removal of racialized bodies from space. These are the ongoing forces of what David Harvey describes as "accumulation by dispossession" in service to capital needs and in response to budding capital crises.[41] All global production networks rely on expropriation, but extractive and tourism chains are pronounced.

The exploration, extraction, refining, and distribution of different extractive products—energy (e.g., coal, gas, uranium, oil), metallic minerals (e.g., iron ore, titanium, bauxite/aluminum, copper, gold, platinum, silver), and nonmetallic minerals (e.g., brick, salt, sand, diamonds, gems)—deploy environmentally destructive removal techniques, alter sustainable land usage practices, and remove communities who stand in the way of extraction. Many of the largest consolidated transnational energy corporations, ExxonMobil (US), Shell (UK), Chevron (US), BP (UK), Total (France), Gazprom (Russia), and PetroChina (China), seek vast resource supplies from racially marginalized geographies across the globe while employing comparatively few workers relative to their size.[42] Most national governments of resource-heavy geographies were formerly colonized and find themselves forced to negotiate highly uneven and inequitable contract concession agreements. In the process, local communities become the most affected but least rewarded. To secure more favorable terms local governments hope to renegotiate new contracts after years of extraction but commonly experience steep pushback and limited successes.

Accordingly, labor exploitation and community expropriation operate in congruence as ongoing global racial capitalism processes.[43] While energy extraction relies on less labor, mineral extraction is labor intensive and ripe with abuses down the chain. Examples include Freeport McMoran Copper and Gold Inc., a U.S.-based company that owns and operates through its subsidiary, PTFreeport Indonesia, the largest gold mine and most profitable copper mine in resource-rich West Papua. The company has operated with relative free range and limited regulations since the U.S.-backed Indonesian New Order government arranged the original contract in the late 1960s.[44] Freeport has concessions encompassing over 2.6 million hectares in West Papua where local Papuan indigenous populations, the Amungme and Kamoro, are directly affected by displacement, state security violence, and polluted natural resources.[45] In 2017, 20,000 contract and 12,000 permanent mine workers were laid off in a furlough program and an additional 8,300 workers were fired for participating in a strike against the program.[46]

Another example is seen in the eastern part of the Democratic Republic of Congo, where the largest global deposit and production of coltan is found. The Congo was always a colonial target of racial fascination, repression, and violence to gain access to the region's rich reserves of precious minerals and natural resources. Contemporarily, anywhere from 200,000 to 550,000 Congolese mineworkers work in extraction.[47] Coltan is a key component in the manufacture of capacitors integrated into circuit boards by electronics and chip producers that go into cellphones, laptops, and other electronic manufacturer assemblies.[48] Coltan mining in 2013 occurred in around 200 small artisanal mines where *creuseurs* (miners), many of them children, earned around $1 and $5 a day.[49] The major mines were originally controlled by rival armed factions who sold to traders, who were in turn financially backed by European commercial houses and coltan processors.[50] The foundation of racist expropriation and exploitation of Congolese minerals is rooted in destructive Belgium colonialism and liberalization within the 2000s Mining Law that "favored multinational large-scale extraction" and cooperative establishments for *creuseurs*.[51] Reform attempts over the years to eradicate "conflict minerals" have created what Claude Wakenge terms "reform conflicts"[52] where *creuseurs* continue to be exploited, the mines continue to be expropriated, and global insatiable demand for electronics proliferates. All the while the high consumer price points for electronic products never trickle down to the base of the chain.

Expropriation is also found in the panorama of tourism geographies where tourism production networks rely on the cordoning and enclosing of pristine, natural spaces in global South geographies, and the commodification and packaging of cultural "heritage" for dominant white tourist consumers. Racialized indigenous groups' communal lands along beaches, in forest territories, savannahs, and mountain ranges were colonially ravaged and are continuously at risk of losing the limited land they possess to various forms of "land grabbing." Contemporary land grabbing extends the colonial project Sharlene Mollett describes as the racial framing of land as "empty," "uninhabited," or "neglected" by "irrational" "native" land usage techniques.[53]

Land confiscation dynamics specific to tourism include conservation initiatives, global firms who build hotels and resorts, infrastructure and excursion activities in coveted, typically legally protected locations, and expatriate white amenity migrants and newly initiated tourism providers who relocate to tourist destinations.[54] East African "safari" tourism is particularly revealing since British colonialism created and fostered global tourism as an exportable service commodity. White settler "white hunters" began the tour operator industry in Kenya, initiated the National Park system, and privatized, particularly Maasai, communal lands and created "ethnic reserves."[55] Many of the biggest and elite national tour operators today are descendants of this white settler group who now coordinate and own many of the tourism chain components that take and accommodate tourists in national parks and reserves or on land just outside of parks they have leases for.[56]

Private, widely foreign or white-elite managed, exclusive conservancies across Africa have risen as a tool for global tourism expansion packaged as "pro-poor" development.[57] In private conservancies land is shielded from different forms of community use, tourists get access to vast wildlife and ecological sites under the "protection" of foreign stewards, and local communities are supposedly supported by camps and tour operators who build schools, boreholes, and provide bed and monthly usage fees. Yet, communities often find that fees are weakly distributed and unevenly rewarded, they are excluded from jobs or steered toward work that accentuates racist constructions, and their lack of materiality is packaged and sold to arouse feel-good tourist emotions.

Thus, we find broadly traveling racism moves throughout tourism chains via the mechanisms that expose how destinations are marketed and described, which suppliers are chosen by lead tour operators and hotel firms to be part of the chain, how national and local workers and communities are incorporated, the visual representations of their commodification, and the privatization of public racial indigenous space. Tourism particularly exposes how racist expropriation is a group-embodied and symbolically racially violent phenomenon. The global commodification of perceived racial difference extracts the symbols, environmental landscapes, and cultural modes of being groups engage with and determine themselves. Through racist extraction, the constructed embodied cultural value and visual, environmental spatial history of groups are stolen, repackaged, and turned into manufactured racial products for global consumption.[58] These same cultural practices are simultaneously fetishized as examples of exotic attraction and calcified in constructed authentic states of nature to further justify land expropriation.

Altogether, extraction procedures anchored upstream to global production networks initiate the domino effect of racist practices down the chain. The uprooting and displacement of communities; the manipulation, racialization, and global presentation of communities' cultural images; the privatization, degradation, and segregating of land through concession agreements; the unequal arrangement of various firm economic actors; the stratification of different forms of labor—all are influenced by the racist practices that occur one step ahead in the chain. Racism necessarily travels through these chains in overt ways: in how space and labor are racially conceptualized at each stage, and how lead firm and first tier supplier firms decide which businesses further down the chain to establish linkages with. But also indirectly: the global forces of white unjust enrichment and cumulative advantages expose the hidden racial foundation of firm and geographic success. The firms and states that have the most economic and political power in the chains, those that have transnational and nationally embedded networks, and those that can dictate the terms and standards of global economic incorporation for everyone and everywhere else, tell an ongoing story about race and the deep whiteness at its core.

REPLICATING RACIAL CAPITALISM

Despite what some argue,[59] the economic rise of semi-peripheral economic state actors in global production networks, like Brazil, Russia, India, China, and South Africa, who are collectively labeled the BRICS, does not represent a disruption to global racial capitalism and the role of global white supremacy.[60] Instead of being disrupters, these geographies should be viewed as examples of the complex interplay between the ongoing forces of cumulated global white economic control and transnational racialization,[61] and the adoption and adaption of global racial logics that are then applied to groups and countries racialized even lower on the global racial hierarchy. Essentially, these countries exhibit what Wangui Kimari and Henrik Ernston, evoking Stoler, call the nexus between "imperial durabilities" and "imperial invitations." Imperial durabilities and invitations speak to the ways BRICS geographies are enticed to replicate racial capital accumulation across global South chain configurations and must compete with global North economic firms.[62]

We must also remember that the economic elite-firm actors in these geographies are often representative of their own racial colonial histories and can embody the highest positions in their national racial architectures (e.g., white Brazilians, white Slavic Russians, high-caste Indians, Han Chinese, and white South Africans). These racialized top statuses, however, do not override the transnational racialization of these geographies and firms as "nonwhite" (or "off-white" in Russia's case), that they are racially placed lower than the U.S. and western Europe in the global hierarchy of nations, and that they react to transnational racialization in complex ways. Moreover, in a Black geography like South Africa, Black national political power has not overridden white South African national and global economic dominance that structures the country's engagement with global economic possibilities.

Complex responses to racialization as seen through racial replicating, what Manuela Boatcă further describes as the "mirroring, and disseminat[ion] [of] racialized mechanisms" across scales and geographies of the chain, are notably viewed through the lens of China's economic presence in Africa.[63] Fundamentally, China's engagement in Africa simply follows and represents the racial domino effect where China looks further down the global racial hierarchy for investment and influence. Donald Nonini and Aiwha Ong argue that "Chinese transnationalism" is a new way of "being Chinese [that is] inseparable from far-flung capitalist projects."[64] A key component of China's narrative in Africa distinguishes its actions as "based on mutual respect and friendship among equal sovereigns" in contrast to the West.[65] This narrative, nonetheless, ultimately works to obscure new patterns of "colonial racialism."[66] Chinese chain practices, notably in large-scale infrastructure projects, are marked by the "massive compulsory acquisition" of land, large concessional loan debt, and the "unequal treatment" and higher placement of Chinese over African workers.[67] Roberto Castillo argues that as China seeks to be a "technosaviour" in Africa it can reproduce and remake global anti-Blackness,[68] an anti-Blackness that has also become reactivated across China in debates about the African presence in its borders.[69]

China undoubtedly, and East Asia by and large, still continue to represent a "racialized, Orientalist construct"[70] that regenerates the historic Yellow Peril discourse, particularly against China, due to its dominance built from over forty years in export production, as a home for, and now practitioner of, foreign direct investment (FDI), and because it is a communist state.[71] Indeed, the U.S.'s Cold War strategy secretly supported Taiwanese engagement with Africa against China both to harness an exploitable racialized technological labor source and to downplay its own machinations in the Continent.[72] Therefore, Castillo's framing of "multiple triangulations"[73] (see chapter 5) is a useful way to see how Taiwan, China, and other countries more generally are racially triangulated between whiteness and anti-Blackness within global racial capitalism and the global racial hierarchy of nations broadly. They are both recipients of racist articulation practices and able to remold and reproduce those very same practices down the hierarchy.

WHITE CAPITAL PROTECTION

Finally, the legal protections of whiteness encoded in global governance and its influence on national legal frameworks ensure the smooth functioning of global racial capitalism in a presumably race-neutral fashion, which ultimately "intensifies . . . [the institutional organizational practices of global] racial erasure."[74] The post-WWII Bretton Woods economic world order, managed by the World Bank, the International Monetary Fund, and later the World Trade Organization (WTO), reflects and reproduces the racialized power inequities born from colonialism in an evolved form of global "[white] law."[75] Multilateral organizations govern and structure global policy to which national governments must adhere in a manner that erases the global white unjust enrichment that marks racial fault lines between former empire states and colonies.

In the late twentieth-century decolonizing global political economic landscape, former colonies simply became "developing countries" that merely needed to "catch up" and "modernize." Colonial racial civilizational discourses now turned into racial modernizing and empowerment through capitalism narratives.[76] After an initial postcolonial period of state-centered development, global actors spurred a debt crisis and brought on multilateral institutional–led neoliberal globalization by the 1980s. Racial neoliberalism hit Latin American and other postcolonial landscapes with a pronounced traumatic force. States were required through a series of loan agreements to implement structural adjustment policies (SAPs) that opened their economies to FDI, export-led manufacturing, currency devaluations, and labor deregulation, and were asked to limit social protections and welfare, including food subsidies.[77] Philip McMichael reports: "From 1978 to 1992, more than 70 countries undertook 566 stabilization programs and SAPs to manage their debt."[78]

Other policy tools in the global legal protection of whiteness arsenal include Export Processing Zones (EPZs) and Special Economic Zones; WTO trade provisions like Trade-Related Investment Measures (TRIMs), Trade-Related Intellectual Property Rights (TRIPs), and the General Agreement on Trade in Services (GATS); and unequally negotiated individual country bilateral and regional free trade agreements.[79] Over the last thirty years EPZs have grown exponentially worldwide—3,500 by 2006. EPZs lure FDI with lower taxes, weak-to-nonexistent labor standards, and minimum custom controls.[80] China employs 40 million of the 66 total million global EPZ workers.[81] TRIMs limit "local content requirements" and technology transfers for foreign investors and TRIPs make global biopiracy of indigenous knowledges and resources legally possible.[82]

Globalization legal frameworks also supported the dominant emergence of private global NGO development actors. These mostly foreign, commonly white-led and -run agencies, operate across the globe, and receive funding from global multilateral organizations and global North countries directly to perform functions typically conducted by states. Global NGOification, therefore, further privatizes access to public goods and racializes which groups and countries are constructed as worthy of aid and/or can be potential "agents" in their own development.[83] The ripple effects to the "normative whiteness of development" also constrain nonwhite aid actors' ability to challenge global white-led development practices, according to Rhea Rhaman. "White adjacent groups" then can reproduce hierarchical racial dynamics in local settings.[84] All told, the global governance regime, and the pressures and limitations it places on national economic and social protection laws, and nonwhite development groups in hierarchically racialized former colonies, reflect the deep whiteness marinating throughout the global economy.

Global Racial Militarism

Global racial capitalism is also entwined with global racial militarism, and reflected in Dr. Martin Luther King's "giant triplets of racism, materialism, and militarism."[85] Imperial "war-making"—through conquest and removal, in the search for bodies to enslave, and for colonial security maintenance—along with the quotidian violence to discipline subjects and secure colonial order, was intimately wrapped in "race-making."[86] The interconnections between racial capitalism, war, and colonialism are in sharp focus with the example of the production and use of atomic weapons during World War II and the aftereffects of Cold War maneuvers.

The United States supported extractive Belgium colonialism to ensure ongoing export of Congolese ore that produced uranium, an essential component in atomic weapons manufacture.[87] The U.S. then tested atomic weapons in the racialized zones of New Mexico, dropped two atomic bombs in 1945 in Hiroshima and Nagasaki, Japan killing 200,000 people, and continued atomic bomb testing in the Marshall Islands until 1958. After the war, in decolonizing, postcolonial Democratic Republic of Congo, the U.S. destabilized and impeded democratic development by covertly supporting the 1960 assassination of Patrice Lumumba and the thirty-year authoritarian rule of Mobutu Sese Seko.[88] In this one example we see the dense web of U.S.-driven capital, military, and colonially facilitated interconnections that engulfed "Black" Belgium Congo, "Indigenous-Mestizo-Mexican" New Mexico, "Polynesian" Marshall Islands, and "Asian" Japan in the deadly economic and military weaponry of the global racial system. Other would-be nuclear powers followed suit with their own testing in racially marginalized colonies and zones. The Soviet Union tested in Kazakhstan; France tested in its colonies in Africa and the Pacific; China in Xinjiang; and Britain in Australia.[89]

We also see the historical discursive antecedents to the racialized terrorist subject in how anticolonial resistance movements, and colonial racial groups' rights claims, were criminalized and liberation fighters were turned into "insurrectionists" and "terrorists" who needed to be "pacified."[90] These racial labels determined what was then ostensibly legal, legitimate colonial state violence against the constructed "barbarian" "brutality" of "uncivilized" peoples, which further justified seemingly "necessary" repressive colonial tactics and strategies, such as martial law, emergency orders, curfews, and detention camps.[91] By the time decolonial movements gained momentum after WWII, many colonial powers were in full battle against "rebels" and "terrorists." For example, the British and the French engaged in brutal practices in their campaigns against the Land and Freedom Movement in Kenya (called "Mau Mau" by the British) and the Algerian National Liberation Front fighters in Algeria.[92]

These colonial histories necessarily situate and contextualize contemporary global racial militarism as enacted through the Global War on Terror.[93] Thus, the current "racial logic governing" who is a "terrorist" and where are they found, according to Atiya Husain, has its beginning in "anticolonial politics" and the long arc of racist colonial securitization practices.[94] Most acutely, we see the legacy of unraveled colonial militarism and violence in (1) the global spread and adoption of racial "terror" discourses and practices across vast geographies; (2) the racial outsourcing of specific military practices and support services along with the ongoing use of colonial "sacrifice zone" geographies for military activities;[95] and (3) the racial outsourcing and externalization of migrant and refugee containment in the name of "national security."

"TERRORIST" CONTAINMENT

The current material and discursive manifestation of the Global War on Terror is centered on what Sohail Daulatzai and Junaid Rana call the "global figure of the racialized Muslim,"[96] and Saher Selod, Inaash Islam, and Steve Garner identify as the process of *"global Muslim racialization"* (emphasis in original).[97] Since the 1980s, only to be intensely accelerated in the post–September 11 milieu of reactionary wars in Iraq and Afghanistan, and massive global surveillance operations, the target of the terrorist threat has been the amorphous "Muslim terrorist." The racial construct both collapses disparate nationalities and geographies and leaves room for specific temporal and spatial renderings and adoptions. "Terrorism," as a "social and political[y]" ascribed framework,[98] supports the traveling machinery of a global "counterterrorism apparatus"[99] that enacts and legitimizes military action; produces "racialized surveillance"[100] in legal statutes, for example, at airports, in mosques, and other locals; and displays extraordinary legal maneuvers only applied to "terror suspects."[101] Moreover, terrorism is used as a discursive "excuse" for a range of policies and practices that concentrates white and national elite political-economic control, and creates new geographic external and internal binary designations of ally or threat.[102] These practices travel throughout the globe to implement antiterror state goals and then bounce back to the U.S. and Europe to profile, police, and enact state violence on mostly Black and Brown bodies and geographies, and in moments of antiracist uprisings.

The Global War on Terror first domino drops[103] proceed from the U.S., British, Australian, French, and E.U. antiterrorist discourses and security efforts to "remove" "fanatical" terrorists from the global panorama. The global counterterrorism apparatus connects global North and global South geographies in a manifold interplay between unequal global military and economic forces and the mirroring and synergy of "counterterrorist" state-directed logics in local sociopolitical landscapes. For example, after Israel, Egypt is the second-largest beneficiary of U.S. military aid, "receiving 1.3 billion every year since 1987," and implements a security regime of "forced disappearance" in the name of "counterterrorism."[104] Mali, with French, British, and U.S. support, launched "Operation Serval" in 2013 to "free" the north of Mali from "Islamists" that spread to Burkina Faso and Niger, becoming "Operation Barkhane."[105] France stayed in Mali until 2022, only to be replaced by Russian mercenaries from the Wagner Group. China launched in 2014 the "Strike Hard Campaign against Violent Terrorism" against Uyghur and other Turkic Muslims. According to a 2021 Human Rights Watch report, "as many as a million people have been arbitrarily detained in 300 to 400 [Chinese] facilities, which include political education camps, pre-trial detention centers, and prisons."[106]

The U.S. and Europe's criticism of China's anti-Muslim campaign discursively reinscribes a form of global whiteness where the U.S. and European powers see themselves as the only moral and legitimate authority of the Global War on Terror and proper adjudicator of which states can commit and be militarily supported in acts of violence.[107] We see this in the U.S. and U.K.'s relationship with Saudi Arabia. U.S. and U.K. arms sales in the billions of dollars powered the Saudi Arabia–led regional coalition against Houthi rebels in Yemen. A 2023 Oxfam report documented tens of thousands of civilian deaths, with over four million displaced, and 1,727 incidents that caused civilian causalities in 2021–22.[108] Many civilians, particularly Black Yemeni *Muhamasheen*, were blocked by "coalition-imposed restrictions on access to humanitarian relief, food, water, medicine, and other essential items."[109]

Another example includes the U.S. and Europe's steadfast support of Israel's decades-long antiterrorism policies. The harrowing, contentious nationalisms in the region since the establishment of the state of Israel and the subsequent cycles of war have facilitated a devastating dynamic between Israel and Arab states, who with various degrees were all separated out of whiteness, but now represent complex hierarchical global racial formations and regional power configurations. In this context, Palestinians became the constructed "Palestinian/Arab/ Muslim terrorist" subject,[110] according to Andy Clarno, where the normalization of a "permanent emergency regime"[111] contained, enclosed, and policed Palestinians with advanced security technologies that are then packaged and sold in the global counterterrorism marketplace.[112] After the brutal November 7, 2023 Hamas attack against Israel that killed over 1,200 people and where some 250 hostages were taken, Israel responded with a massive bombing campaign and an on-the-ground troop assault in Gaza. The ongoing violence has killed over 40,000 Palestinians, leveled communities and civic social institutions, and displaced over a million people.

The counterterrorism efforts in Mali, Egypt, and Yemen particularly expose the scales of racialization at play and the layered markers that render some Muslim identities hierarchically above others in the global racial assemblage but still subjects to anti-Muslim global racial logics. Global North support of Saudi Arabia, the wider Gulf, and Pakistan, for example, is predicated on these geographies performing as counterterrorism allies, and the sharing of a common "enemy," such as Iran since the 1979 Iranian Revolution. In the case of Pakistan, and a country like Jordan, their national political elites' cultivation of the relationship is pursued to offset unequal regional economic deprivation. Although the Aryan myth discourses historically fueled Arab, Persian, and South Asian negotiation with global white supremacy, relational hierarchies between these categories today channel regional and national racial logics and counterstrategies to engagements with U.S. global hegemony.

These hierarchies reflect Gulf ascendency in regional "Arab" landscapes, Indian positioning over Muslim South Asia, and Persian dominance in multi-ethnic Iranian fault lines that also distances from Arab histories and spaces. "Arab," "Middle East," and "Muslim" still operate as colonially informed and modified racial concepts for the Global War on Terror, but they also cascade and collide with other colonially influenced regional and local notions of difference, which are reflected in disparate Global War on Terror consequences. As a regional whole, nonetheless, the collective consequences are steep. The Cost of War project estimates 4.5 million people have died due to the "Post-9/11 Wars" in Afghanistan, Iraq, Pakistan, Syria, Yemen, Libya, and Somalia.[113] Drastically, global racial militarism "reverberates" through the traveling racist practices that produce more death in the shadow of war through "economic collapse," the "destruction" of social public goods, "environmental contamination," and "the trauma and violence" that racialized geographies and specific racial groups in those geographies were disproportionately forced to endure.[114]

MILITARY CONTRACTORS AND SACRIFICE ZONES

In many ways, the Global War on Terror and other military actions reveal the new racial economics of war. The outsourcing of military practices and support services, and the use of ongoing racialized colonial states and geographies as "sacrifice zone" sites of defense preparation and base proliferation, define roving global racial militarism in the late twentieth and early twenty-first centuries. Around a third of the $115 billion spent on Private Military Contractors (PMCs) between 2001 and 2013 in the U.S. was dominated by just ten global companies, including Halliburton,

Brown and Root, and DynCorp.[115] These companies arrange, coordinate, and package military services and hire and train a "flexible coercive workforce" of workers/soldiers spread across the global racial labor hierarchy.[116] There is a distinct division between what Amanda Chisholm describes as the "ideal white contractor" and its racially separated counterparts.[117] "Racialized contractor" practices that mark the conditions and stratification of work are determined by the racial capitalism forces of value application, extraction, and exploitation.[118] The racial construction of soldiering goes back to the British racial theory of martial races, addressed in chapter 2, where certain groups were constructed as good, obedient soldiers with natural "martial attributes."[119] Chisholm's study of Gurkha soldiers in Afghanistan exposes how these past historical colonial racial logics are reinscribed for the Global War on Terror in the name of national security defense.[120]

Russia's ongoing war aggressions across multiple regions have notably relied heavily on PMCs. In 2015 Russian PMCs were operating in four countries but by 2021 they were found in twenty-seven, engaging in a range of activities from combat operations to intelligence collection, disinformation campaigns, and protective services.[121] President Putin's military endeavors, what Rafia Zakaria labels his "imperial racist agenda," have essentially two tracks.[122] One is waged through war to solidify and unify white Russian Slavic populations (e.g., his annexation of Crimea in 2014 and invasion of Ukraine in 2022), and the other is to exert influence and extract natural resource concessions in Syria and throughout Africa. Russia supports Syrian president Bashar al-Assad's merciless assault to hold onto power with Russian PMCs participating in combat operations in key Syrian cities.[123] Russia is also found in "at least 16 countries in sub-Saharan Africa," including Sudan, the Central African Republic, Madagascar, and Mozambique with the specific aims to sever those nations' relationships with their former European colonial authorities and to gain access to lucrative mining extraction rights.[124] The U.N. found that in the Central African Republic Russian PMCs were involved in "excessive use of force, indiscriminate killings, the occupation of schools, and looting on a large scale."[125] The PMC Wagner's once unimaginable June 2023 rebellion against Russian military command exposes the reach of PMCs' growing power and their initial ability to dodge accountability.[126]

Within the U.S., PMCs are most pronounced in their relationship to global base construction, operations, and staffing. The U.S. has by far the largest number of foreign bases with "around 800 U.S. bases," "in more than 70 countries," while Britain and France together have only around thirteen in "mostly former colonies," Russia has around nine in once Soviet republic geographies, and a few countries have one foreign base.[127] The U.S. Cold War "forward strategy" to thwart Soviet expansion propelled the acceleration of base construction that continued apace and took on new resonance in the Global War on Terror.[128] The U.S.'s colonial expansion and ongoing colonial relationship with its territories—beginning with Hawaii, Puerto Rico, and the Philippines, then later through "trusteeship" over the Trust Territory of the Pacific Islands (Marshall Islands, Palau, and Federated States of Micronesia) beginning in 1947 that turned into "compacts of free association"—ensured relatively free reign for base placement, hazardous weapons testing, and indigenous displacement.[129]

According to David Vine there were eighteen global cases of various racial groups' displacement to accommodate U.S. military base demands.[130] Bikinians, from Bikini Atoll in the Marshall Islands, were forcibly removed in 1946 and placed in dire living conditions to accommodate what would be sixty-eight atomic and hydrogen bomb tests that utterly destroyed and contaminated Bikini Atoll and other atolls.[131] The islands are still used today as the Ronald Reagan Ballistic Missile Defense test site. The U.S. Navy additionally controlled part of Culebra Island in Puerto Rico as a bombing range site for over fifty years, only to leave after a hard-fought local civil disobedience campaign.[132]

The U.S also worked in collaboration with the British to gain strategic base access to the Indian Ocean through the British-controlled British Indian Ocean Territory (BIOT), which consists of the seven atolls of the Chagos Archipelago. The British severed the archipelago from its original status as part of the colony of Mauritius during decolonization to maintain a colonial presence in the region and expelled the 2,000 Chagossian inhabitants to Mauritius and the Seychelles, where they continue to live in poverty.[133] The Chagossians are a group of once enslaved African and indentured Indian plantation workers who created their own distinct culture. The atoll of Diego Garcia in BIOT is described as a "black hole [legal] strategy" exempt "from some national laws and international treaties."[134] The area would go on to serve as a launching stage for the U.S. invasions of "Iraq and Afghanistan from 1990 to 2006,"[135] and the British invasion of Iraq in 2003, along with air strikes on Syria in 2015 and 2018.[136] Diego Garcia was also a "destination of several CIA 'rendition flights.'"[137]

The wide global expansive reach of U.S. bases, and its partnerships with former imperial powers, directly replicate and maintain racist colonial structures through legalized state violence, land confiscation, racial divisions of base employment labor, and the severe deterioration of environmental ecologies and community social relations. The needs of foreign soldiers on bases are also catered to by outsourced and privatized racialized support staff,[138] and off base by racially marginalized communities, spaces, and bodies, most dramatically seen in the sexual exploitation and intimacies pursued with local sexually racialized women.[139]

EXTERNALIZATION OF BORDER MANAGEMENT

Lastly, global racial militarism travels through unequal geopolitical arrangements where global North countries outsource managing migrant and asylum attempts with neighboring or proximal racialized nonwhite countries or territories to stop and contain migrants and asylees outside their borders. "Third country" agreements between the U.S. and Mexico; Australia and Nauru and Papua New Guinea; the U.K. and Rwanda; Israel and Ethiopia, Rwanda, and Uganda; and the E.U.'s FRONTEX relationships with Morocco, Libya, and Tunisia, to name just a few, represent the externalization of racial "threat" management and the racial criminalization of asylum seekers and "irregular" migrants.[140] In the process, new twenty-first-century "racialized security regimes" form, reminiscent of the creation and use of imperial colonial racial police and military forces.[141] Contemporarily, white states rely on nonwhite states and bodies to police, control, and contain outside its border other nonwhite groups further down the global racial hierarchy, a process not unlike how the U.S. recruits nonwhite U.S. soldiers to enact U.S. foreign military state policy.

Australia's externalization policy operates through "Operation Sovereign Borders." The policy came out of an infamous 2001 incident where the then Howard government refused to allow a Norwegian freighter that rescued 400 Afghan refugees from entering Australian waters. The policy in effect since 2013 states that anyone who arrives by boat is sent to desolate Nauru or Papua New Guinea's Manus Island for "offshore processing" and "offshore detention."[142] Australia also operates a detention center on its Christmas Island territory that for a decade saw detainee hunger strikes and riots before temporarily closing in 2018 only to technically reopen in 2019. Asylum seekers, many from Africa, who attempt to enter Israel's borders are governed by the "Prevention of Infiltration Law" and are labeled "infiltrators," immense "threats" to national security.[143] In the late 2000s the government entered in secret third-country agreements with Eritrea, Rwanda, and Uganda to use these countries as sites of deportation without prior assessing of asylum applications. A reported 4,000 Eritrean and Sudanese asylum seekers were sent to Rwanda and Uganda between 2013 and 2018 before the program was forced to shut down.[144] The most recent third-country agreements were signed in 2023 between the U.K. and Rwanda and U.S. and Mexico. In a revised agreement after an initial Supreme Court blockade, the U.K. sought to send some asylum seekers to Rwanda to claim asylum, but the Labour Party aimed to terminate the program upon its election in 2024. Similarly, the U.S will deport thousands of non-Mexican migrants to Mexico to apply for Mexican asylum.

Since the E.U.'s establishment of the Polish-based border agency FRONTEX in 2004, part of its directive was to seek "co-operations" with third countries regarding "expertise and information-sharing," and "some detention and application-processing functions."[145] Early pilot programs included establishing migrant processing centers in Libya and the Great Lake region of Africa and in arrangements with Morocco over protection of the Spanish territories of Ceuta and Melilla, located at the northern tip of Morocco.[146] In 2005, thousands of African migrants attempted to cross into Ceuta and Melilla and were attacked by Moroccan and Spanish forces. Ten were killed and hundreds injured.[147] Twenty-three mostly Sudanese migrants were killed in 2022 after trying to enter the border control area of Melilla.[148] Since 2017, Italian funding for the Libyan Coast Guard to patrol the Mediterranean Sea and forcibly return migrants has been in effect and has caused an increase in the number of attempted migrant departures from Tunisia and subsequent deaths at sea. In 2022, Tunisia recovered more than 800 bodies of people who perished at sea and more than 300 had been found by the beginning of 2023.[149] Overall, the *Washington Post* estimates that the E.U. has provided more than 400 million euros, with additional funding for specific antimigrant projects, through the E.U. Emergency Trust Fund for Africa, alongside individual country agreements, to countries such as Tunisia, Morocco, and Mauritania between 2015 and 2021.[150]

Racial border externalization enforcements lead to cascading racial practices in third-country "partner" nations. Mexico increased militarized enforcement at their southern border and deportees from the U.S. joined a background of marginalized nonwhite mestizo and indigenous Mexicans seeking jobs, housing, and safety in Mexican cities. Thousands of deportees from the U.S. in Mexico were also targets of vicious attacks. Across the Maghreb region of North Africa, African migrants from outside Maghreb experience the overlapping forces of anti-Blackness that emanate from Europe and unravel and intersect with distinct histories and discourses in the region.[151] In 2023, Tunisian president Kais Saied claimed Black "irregular migration" was "part of an international plot to change Tunisia's character," the Tunisian version of the "Great Replacement Theory," that led to asylum seekers being evicted from homes and neighborhoods being raided.[152] In 2013, Morocco announced major reforms to its migration policy to "reject[] the moniker of 'Europe's policeman'" but "violence in Morocco's northern frontier has continued unabated."[153] Most acutely, third-country nations embedded in recent racial colonial legacies and continued forms of colonial arrangements must navigate and negotiate white global states' racist procedures and narratives in ways that reinscribe new racial practices in their borders. Most profoundly, migrants and asylum seekers who end up in the array of global externalized detention centers—from bleak Nauru to the outskirts of Tripoli, and across the vast northern border of Mexico—experience a calamitous form of racist disappearance. They are physically removed from global white geographies and figuratively removed from the global white collective conscious.

Global Racial Cultural Production

Global racial capitalism and militarism are informed by the global racial logics always in motion throughout the global racial system. The global racial assemblage of essentialized racist group tropes, burnished and saturated with racist modernity and empires, and made legible and enticing through popular culture consumption, continues to globally travel today as compact global reference points countries and firms draw from, repurpose, and reenact in their own racial image needs and material discursive landscapes. The foundational archive for racial "Otherness" built from racist imperial divisions, science, and spectacle, what Stuart Hall calls the "repertoires or regimes of representation,"[154] has evolved for a twenty-first-century global colorblind palette that nonetheless recycles and reinscribes original archetypical representations around what being "Black," "Native," "Muslim," "Latino/a/x," and "Asian" express. Within these categories are a range of globally resonate racial "sub-archetypes" that conjure specific images, perceptions, expressions, and aesthetics of racial reduction that ultimately still naturalizes, and practically biologizes, racial difference.[155] In many ways the global circulation of racial understandings through the assemblage now finds power in how it "does not need to be actively named,"[156] how it operates alongside racial magnetism and desire, and through the complete absorption, appropriation, and ultimate expulsion of racial groups' own form of cultural racial meaning-making and contestation.

The media and popular culture, via imagery, taste cultivation, aesthetics, music, movies, television, and the internet, particularly, still serve as a key social system through which cultural production moves worldwide and is understood within local representational practices and logics. Basically, they are our modern forms of twenty-first-century racist spectacle. Local media players absorb the racist messaging of the global assemblage in a process of remake and adaption for regional and local audiences. Specific regional and nationally produced racial representations that intersect with global constructions are then packaged into national media products and regionally, and sometimes globally, reexported. This process at times is described as a flattened "cultural hybridization" of the global cultural economy. But media interventions should always be read from the vantage of global power dynamics and global racial hierarchies within the global racial system. Representational practices are always embedded in, informed by, and respond to racial cultural and visual hierarchies of global sociopolitical power. The continuation of anti-Black and culturally appropriative practices, alongside the creation of new regional cultural racial products, reveals interacting, layered global-regional-national racial cultural processes.

ANTI-BLACK REPRESENTATION AND CULTURAL THEFT

The manufacture, traveling, and consumption of anti-Black cultural representations during racist modernity has remained in the contemporary globalized "supranational circuitry of anti-Blackness"[157] despite the current simultaneous global proliferation of Black hip-hop style and form, Black sports idolization, and cultural resistance moves by Black artists.[158] In its most direct manifestation, we still find current examples of blackface and broad anti-Black representational iconography as seen in traditional holiday celebrations, television shows, commodity advertisements and commercial promotions, collectibles, and across posts on social media platforms. European examples of holiday commemoration include overt forms as in *Zwarte Piet* (Black Pete) in the Netherlands, who comes out each year for *Sinterklass* (Feast of St. Nicholas holiday)[159] to reenactment battles between "Moors" and "Christians" to mark the Reconquest of Spain, and in Spanish Catholic holiday parades.[160] Outside of Europe, Iran still celebrates the Nwruz, the Persian New Year, with the appearance of *Haji Firuz,* and the Ecuadorian troupe, *Sambos Illimani con Sentimiento y Devoción,* dance as *"Sambos"* in the annual *La Fiesta de la Virgen de la Candelaria.*[161]

Blackface caricatures continue to be visualized with outlandish racist bodily displays and performed with behaviors associated with defining anti-Black sub-archetypes (e.g., servility, vulgarity, criminality, primitiveness, and simplicity).[162] These acts are consumed today with a deracialized claim that extols tradition or culture while still producing racist debasement. Outside of holiday festivals, blackface sketches were seen in television programs in the U.S., U.K., Poland, Australia, Philippines, Japan, South Korea, China, and Lebanon. In 2018, China's CCTV staged a blackface skit marking Chinese-African relations that evoked quintessential anti-Black and gendered anti-African essentialism but was labeled not racist by the Chinese embassy.[163] Likewise, in 2023, two contestants on the Polish version of *Your Face Sounds Familiar* international show impersonated Beyoncé and Kendrick Lamar in blackface. The production company claimed "surprise" about the backlash.[164]

The embrace of manufactured anti-Black racial performance always historically sat alongside desire, pleasure, and consumption of Black art, what Saidiya Hartman explains as subjugation through "desire and revulsion, terror and pleasure."[165] Contemporary fetishization operates from what Wesley Morris calls "secondhand blackness": appreciation and allure from the comfort of a privileged racial standpoint.[166] Poignantly, Lauren Michele Jackson writes, "Everybody wants the insurgency of Blackness with the wealth of whiteness . . . they want blackness only as a suggestion . . . [in a manner that] keeps centuries of subjection and violence at bay."[167] Coveting, partaking, and seeking pleasure in the beats, sounds, styles, and propulsive declarations of Black cultural production and exuberance but mostly from the safety, gaze, and assuredness of non-Blackness marks the global cultural landscape.

Moreover, the "vampiric" "theft" of Black expression, aesthetics, and innovation, borne from both what Danyel Smith describes as the "transmogrification of Black oppression to fleeting and inclusive Black joy," and the everyday cultural acts of world-building beyond and outside of domination, always followed white attraction.[168] American popular culture, that in many aspects became global popular culture, is replete with what musicologist Matthew Morrison describes as the "scripting, commodification, and embodiment" of "sonic performances" of "Blacksound" and style in service to white racial capitalism.[169] From ragtime to jazz, and the blues to soul, rock, and hip-hop, white capitalists and white artists put on the figurative suit of "Blacksound" that defined the racial parameters and racial economics to what Stoever, adopted by Morrison, describes as "the sonic color line."[170]

The racialization of sound with its visual cues on bodies, dress, culture, and geographies places boundaries around manufactured cultural racial authenticity that simultaneously devalues and freezes its original creators while spawning countless valued imitations, alterations, and presentations for white and non-Black sensibilities. As rock music represented before it, when white artists re-recorded, and repackaged with a white sheen, the songs of what was then labeled as "race music,"[171] nowhere is this seen more than in the global spread and adoption of hip-hop sound, aesthetics, and speech. Global hip-hop adulation and replication is both a powerful vehicle for the making of "Black Diasporic subjects" where African-descendant youth harness the "performative contours of hip hop" to understand and express their own racial marginalization, often in locales that typically deny racism and seek to produce colorblind subjects,[172] and is ripe with appropriative racial cosplay.

For example, hip-hop appropriation in East Asia is connected to the history and ongoing militarism of anti-Asian U.S. racial dominance in the region, the introduction of anti-Black minstrel performance and commodity advertisements, along with the post–Korean War presence of Black American soldiers. Contemporary hip-hop cultural desires and presentations of self through perceived Black and/or hip-hop aesthetics often serve as a way for youth culture in the region to subvert rigid expected racial homogeneity and gender propriety but also can reinscribe transnationally circulating essentialist beliefs on Blackness.[173] When national artists and businesses manipulate those sounds and performances to create and market their own national cultural products, the original racial context and current unequal racial dynamics that structures how hip-hop is created, distributed, marketed, and received is erased.

K-Pop is an illustrative case. An industry initially partially borne from the more organic "authentic connections" between Black American soldiers and South Korean patrons at a nightclub that catered to Black soldiers in the 1990s[174] gave way to tightly managed and produced "idols" who often claimed Black style, speech, and beats but were mostly detached from Black life. Some acts even performed in blackface.[175] Joyhanna Yoo Garza argues that many K-Pop idols appropriate what she calls "chronotopic capital," the "fragmented, decontextualized [racial] styles" of a "different time and place" that can "reproduce reductive scrips of racialized and gendered U.S. Black and Brown histories in a global context."[176] The global exportation of mainstream K-Pop videos, personas, and dance moves then profits from the "notion that racialized depictions become everyone's property,"[177] and specific K-Pop idols come to embody, according to Chuyun Oh, "post-Asian-ness as non-racialization."[178]

Still, it is important to understand K-Pop's complex racial formation, which Michelle Cho calls "palimpsestic."[179] The industry and its stars are embedded in layered colonial histories, transnational racialization, and globally ubiquitous Black appropriative practices that dictated the ways in which it emerged, has evolved, and how groups are racially seen and consumed across geographic boundaries. When idols come to the U.S. and Europe, anti-Asian tropes can mark them, just as Korean Americans and other diaspora communities seek solace from anti-Asian racism in their music.[180] The global *reggaetón* phenomenon has a similar arc. Reggaetón hails from Panama and the segregated migratory-informed Black geographies of *los caseríos* (public housing) in Puerto Rico that were historically racialized as places of violence and hypersexuality by white Puerto Ricans.[181] Reggaetón's current global mainstream success, however, speaks to how the "whitening of reggaeton" made it a more digestible global product.[182] Whitening, nonetheless, still involved the essentialization of a "Latin look," basically a "tropicalized Latina/o," according to Petra Rivera-Rideau and Jericko Torres-Leschnik, that met white global aesthetic pleasure appeals while still placing the artists and sound outside of whiteness.[183] Even the Puerto Rican mainstreaming of Black reggaetón artist Tego Calderón, Rivera-Rideau argues, involved placing his Blackness within a safe, less threatening presentation more connected to Puerto Rican "symbols of folkloric blackness" than "foreign rap" that worked to accentuate the ideology of Puerto Rican *mestizaje* (see chapter 6), even as Calderón himself highlighted and challenged anti-Blackness in Puerto Rico.[184]

With the K-Pop and reggaetón examples we see how the practices of traveling racism embedded in regimes of representations crisscross, interact, and produce overlapping racial representational meaning. "Blacksound" both constructed essentialized notions of Blackness and also underscored how the ingenuity and self-expression of Black artistry was globally desirable but filtered through national racial repertoires of representation that coded those local performing bodies as nonwhite and "Other," but more approachable, sellable, and universal. This process is seen in the beauty and wider culture industries as well where white beauty influencers take the inventive style, cultural tools, and performance of Black women and adapt them for self-promotion and more "likes" on social media platforms, while Black women are made obsolete and their bodies are globally policed and stigmatized.[185]

Shirley Tate argues that brands seek out "racially ambiguous" ambassadors, where Blackness is made "palatable for audiences globally," but the "monetary value of lighter skinned, loosely curled hair aesthetics" remains.[186] "Exotic (but not too dark)" is packaged and sold.[187] The global juggernaut of the reality TV Kardashian brand is emblematic,[188] as is the performance appropriation of the "twerk" and other dance movements by white pop stars and Tik Tok personalities,[189] and the linguistic appropriation of Black American language and slang for corporate advertisements.[190] In what hip-hop scholar and artist A.D. Carson describes as "rap wash," corporations and American foreign policy institutions use the art of hip-hop to burnish credibility for capitalism, American global dominance,[191] and even support for the War on Terror.[192] These selective racial manipulations and articulations fit alongside more overt ongoing anti-Black cultural practices found in the massive global appeal of skin bleaching products[193] and the use of "digital Blackface" in GIFs, memes, video games, and AI-generated rap artists.[194]

REGIONAL CULTURAL PRODUCTS

National cultural production of racial meaning and presentation collides with and responds to these transnationally circulating racial tropes and globally white-led culture industry practices. In its aftermath we find select nonwhite geographies emerging as important multimedia, film, and television creators, such as, Japan, South Korea, Hong Kong, India, Nigeria, Brazil, and Turkey, who then export their cultural products to regional and global audiences. In various ways, many of these countries' media industries both challenge and reproduce static racial assumptions that adhere to global norms, and the idea of a white universalized consumer, but in a fashion that caters to local racial representational regimes informed by regional and national racial politics and hierarchies. For example, the internationalization of Japanese anime underscores what Amy Shirong Lu considers a form of "depoliticized" Japanese representation where "any typical Japanese physiognomy from [anime] characters" is hard to detect while features of whiteness are heightened and the symbolic disparagement of non-Japanese Asian and Black representations historically found prominence in storylines.[195] With a global market value over $22 billion boosted by internet streaming platforms, anime's de-racialized characters "neutralize" any hint of Japanese "Asian" specificity while leaning into an indirect global white universalism even while being wildly popular with nonwhite youth consumers.[196]

Hong Kong's "martial arts cinema," in contrast, amplified globally circulating East Asian tropes connected to Kung Fu[197] while "Huallywood" in mainland China created cinema centered on Han Chinese ethnic national themes while also pursuing co-productions with global partners that present action-based storylines of multicultural colorblind landscapes.[198] Outside of East Asia, India's Hindi language–centered Bollywood industry has a devoted global following throughout the Indian diaspora with its "all-inclusive risk free and formulaic" genres, but has yet to fully cross into a white universalized globally consumable product.[199] Representations of whiteness in Bollywood films take on layered meanings as "something to both embody and repudiate" in its relation to notions of Indianness,[200] and/or something the Indian diaspora should strive for.[201] India is one of the largest global markets for skin-bleaching brands and several Bollywood stars have endorsement deals.[202] Moreover, Hindu nationalist film performances can "facilitat[e] the production of both devoted Bollywood spectators and Hindu Right supporters" vis-à-vis other Indian national racialized groups.[203]

Of all the global regional film hubs, the rise of Nollywood, or Nigerian cinema, over the last thirty years calls our attention to the power of countering anti-African representations and the tensions that amount when stereotypical tropes are also presented. Nollywood was borne from the ingenuity needed to negotiate the material hardships of extreme structural adjustment mandates. Producers "rejected the prohibitive costs as well as the European high art associated with celluloid film in favor of video technologies."[204] Thousands of series and movies are produced each year with most distributed via satellite, on digital platforms, in YouTube channels, and global streaming services like Netflix. Noah Tsika argues that Nollywood stars "maintain an emphatically anti-essentialist, self-pluralizing approach to Africa and Africans" and "Nollywood films tend to unveil a multidimensional heterogeneous landscape of Africa away from the Hollywood model."[205] Foundational racial essentialist presentations are reversed and altered when Nollywood producers and artists evoke an "oppositional gaze" against the suffocating boxes in which African subjectivity is commonly placed.[206] Even so, some representations straddle a difficult line between agentic reclamation and what Ekwenchi describes as the "domesticat[ion], reinforce[ment], and legitim[ation] of racist images of Africa and African people circulating in western popular culture" in some films.[207]

Lastly, next to cinema, the regional and global consumption of national television soap operas, from Brazilian and Mexican telenovelas to Turkish melodramas, actively engage with national-regional racial hierarchies and global racial circulations. Telenovelas are perhaps one of the most successful non–global North media products, next to Japanese anime, with Brazilian telenovelas, for example, being dubbed and aired in prime time viewing hours in more than 130 countries.[208] Brazil's "TV Globo has produced more than 300 telenovelas" over a thirty-year period, with most sold to international markets.[209] Products are exported across South America, the U.S., some European locales, and even in a few Asian and Middle East territories.

The racial representational politics of telenovelas is stark. Most series notoriously only showed major characters that have "light skin," and "Black and indigenous people, clearly defined as such, are seldom seen."[210] If they are presented, the characters typically fall into sub-archetype characters of servility and hypersexuality. The hypersexualization of Black women built into media depictions in Brazil is also notably filtered through the TV export of the "*Mulata Globeleza*," who introduces Carnival each year entirely naked except for colorful body paint.[211] Black Brazilian artists and producers push back against these mainstream racist depictions in a manner that contributes to what Reighan Gillam defines as an "antiracist visual politics,"[212] as Black American and European film and television artists historically and contemporarily have as well. They must, however, contend with the cultural forms of traveling racism's spider web reach and popular hegemonic consumption. Black American Hollywood artists are still told that Black stories "don't translate overseas."[213]

Turkish soap operas have also amassed a regional and sometimes global consumer audience but mostly across Arab geographies, the Balkans, and in Turkic-language-speaking countries in Asia. An interesting interplay is at work between the representations depicted and the Arab regional dispersal and consumption of Turkish soap operas. As a regional cultural exporter Turkey maintains its geopolitical intermediary position between the West and the "Middle East" and unifies Muslims across the region in protest to global anti-Muslim policies, military engagements, and media representations. Marwan Kraidy and Omar Al-Ghazzi call this phenomenon a "Neo-Ottoman Cool."[214] "Chromatic" whiteness[215] is still at play, however, as Turkish actors are represented with fair features, and one of its most popular global male actors, Kıvanç Tatlıtuğ, is called the "Middle East's Brad Pitt." Tatlıtuğ became an international sensation in multiple Arab countries with the widely popular soap opera *Noor* and can be seen today across global media platforms. Therefore, whiteness is unevenly representationally maintained in Turkey and the Middle East even as cultural production seeks to challenge global anti-Muslim, anti-Turkish, and anti-Arab representations. Ultimately, the representational politics of deep whiteness in global racial culture makes it difficult for national and regional media players to disrupt global circulatory racial tropes, images, and white figurative and literal aesthetics.

Global Superhighway of Racism

Global racial capitalism, militarism, and culture are intimately collectively connected, exemplifying the varied and interwoven mechanisms of traveling racism. Traveling racism proceeds from the branded manufacturer to the *maquiladora* shop floor, to the home-based sewer, to the cotton harvester, and back to the retail store and global consumer. Traveling racism journeys to sacrifice geographies of military rule and proliferation, to the military divisions between soldiers and private workers, and on to the racialized bodies across regions and zones deemed a threat. And traveling racism advances globally resonate racial archetypes to national geographies for absorption, adaption, and cultural media consumption. Ultimately, our blue jeans, our borders, and our favorite music genre tell us something about concentrated racial economic power, legitimized racial state violence, and who benefits from desired racial aesthetics, sites, and sounds. Deep whiteness basically marks the lanes which the global superhighway of traveling racism operates within. We are all forced to drive on its roads even as many try to exit.

As we see through racial capitalism, militarism, and representations, the global possessive investment of whiteness's power lies in its perceived natural order, its justifiable inequities, and its regionalized applications. In the next chapter I turn to the entangled racial state formations traveling racism touches down in. Entangled state practices tell the story of entangled racial zones, proximal racial understandings, and the continued story of layered national, regional, and global racialization forces shaping national social systems.

Four
Entangled Racial States

When Nelson Mandela walked out of his prison of twenty-seven years, South Africa's barren Robben Island, on February 11, 1990, and became the first Black president of South Africa four years later, the last link in the chain to white supremacy was supposedly broken. The prior forty-plus years, following World War II, was marked by global decolonization of the major imperial powers and Civil Rights legislative successes in the U.S. For many the moment embodied a realization that the scourges of Nazi horrors and Apartheid policies were finally swept into the dustbin of history and the problem of racism was fixed once and for all. Yet, the narrative of racial triumphalism of the postwar era hides the more pernicious reality of continued global and national racisms within the global racial system.

The history of purported racial progress from colonial racial domination and practiced national white supremacy is better understood as a product of what critical race theorists analyze as "interest convergence." Derrick Bell's pioneering analyses on Civil Rights legislative changes, after decades spent fighting litigation battles, claimed that Black Americans "gained social justice when their interests converged with the interests of the white majority."[1] The hypocritical image of fighting fascism while allowing colonial and national racisms to flourish, the double V campaign of Black World War II soldiers,[2] and the budding Cold War with the Soviet Union pushed American legislative action and influenced imperial Allied strategies. Gerald Horne argues that World War geopolitics and Cold War machinations made imperial powers' acceptance of avowed white supremacy increasingly tenuous.[3] Essentially, maintaining "separate but equal" mandates and European overseas colonies became financially and politically untenable post–World War II as decolonization movements and "the specter of national liberation"[4] intensified, Europe had to rebuild after the war, and when the Soviet Union, with its antiracist communist propaganda proclamations, started lurking at the gates of global power. Therefore, through a constellation of forces, after over four hundred years, the costs to overt global white supremacy became too great and antiracist, decolonial pressure too strong.

"Progress," however, could not and did not disrupt global racial power. As Derrick Bell reminds us, change only occurs when the remedy sought does not "threaten" or "alter the status of whites."[5] The postwar, decolonial racial order, particularly dominated by the U.S., found "new technologies of racial domination."[6] These technologies fused racial modernity's discursive investment in liberal freedoms with the evolved racial imperial techniques of global racial capitalism and militarism addressed in chapter 3. For example, in the early postwar years, despite global narratives in support of freedom and democracy, the U.S. and decolonizing European imperial powers continued to support "good anti-Communist"[7] Portuguese and Belgium colonial projects in Africa,[8] and propped up antidemocratic repressive dictators across the global South.[9] Former empire states and the U.S. also sought to reframe "race" as a theory of "race relations" where natural group "conflict" was emphasized and the global project of racism, empire, and white supremacy, and its multiple and disjointed impacts across geographies, was erased. This logic underscored a belief that the "West should not be singled out because everyone was also racist."[10]

Indeed, since its initial emergence, as I have addressed in the preceding chapters, the global racial system always relied on flexible, malleable, and unstable "white supremacist ascriptions"[11] that interacted in complex ways across geographies' local social organizations, creating distinct racial orders, *but was always a western-dominated and initiated project*. National racial orders today are products of global colonial formations, international relational interstate hierarchies, and the process where embedded global racial logics and national forms intersect to produce inequities. The new global racial order is still mostly dictated by white global state actors whose position at the top of the racial hierarchy is "so deeply woven into the fabric of [global] social life that it appear[s] natural, effectively conditioning the design and enforcement of an international legal, [social and economic] order."[12] Thus, rather than a full "break" from white supremacy's past, we can best describe the last fifty-plus years as chiseled cracks that sit alongside newly evolved, pernicious racist praxis and entangled racial states. Michelle Commander keenly reminds us that "freedom remains elusive as racism is persistently renovated."[13]

In this chapter I show how the current state formation within the global racial system is reproduced by a hierarchy of entangled racial state practices. Following broad decolonization, the world is still populated by unequally situated nation-state dynamics with power configurations closely mirroring earlier colonial arrangements. These inequities spotlight how the rise of the "nation-state" during colonialism, along with the colonially crafted boundaries, racial controls, and procedures of statecraft, became the model that structured postcolonial racial negotiations.[14] Therefore, the lingering, haunting effects of racist empires remain in the postcolonial landscape, as seen in how the "coloniality of power" is imbued in institutions, economies, quotidian language, and collective psyches that reproduce unequal racial realities.[15] The parameters of the state continue to be deeply and intimately bound to global and regional racial processes and the forceful and subtle material and discursive power-laden pressure points that constrain and outline national racial categorical meanings, possibilities, and national racial material well-being.

Situating entangled racial states in the contemporary decolonized moment needs to be further qualified, however, because empire states, in many ways, continue to be empire states in the direct sense, where they control what the U.N. labels, harkening back to its 1945 charter, "Non-Self-Governing Territories."[16] While most geographies across Latin America, Africa, and Asia operate as politically independent sovereignties, many island states, particularly in the Caribbean, Oceania, within the Indian Ocean, and in the polar regions, continue to be under the authority of either the United Kingdom, France, Netherlands, United States, or Australia. The contemporary "window-dressing"[17] of the language of colonialism includes the terms "Overseas Territory" (U.K), "Overseas Department" (France), "Constituent Country of Kingdom of Netherlands" (Netherlands), "Unincorporated Organized Territory" (U.S.), and "Non-Self-Governing Overseas Territory" (Australia).[18] Regardless of current imperial calls of support for self-determination, there is much "structural continuity" that showcases the "persistence of colonial" governance[19] along with the vast and varied self-interests of imperial powers to maintain their "territories," as already addressed in chapter 3, through contemporary placement of military installments and detention centers. Thus, we still have an interconnected "Global Racial Empire," as pronounced by Olúfẹ́mi Táíwò, even if hidden and a bit more subtle.[20]

Largely, contemporary entangled racial states are found in two ways. First, the racist divides and controls of imperial racial formation processes that created racial categories have evolved and been reconstituted through a multilayered form of Frank Dikötter's "interactive model of interpretation."[21] The contemporary interactive model highlights how the facilitation of national racial orders occurs from scaled racialization and the interaction of global, regional, and national racialization projects and its intersection with local stratification forms. The racial "circulatory system"[22] of current transnational racial meanings and identities travels into local spaces and crashes into a country's historical transnational-national racialization and political economy in ways that are contemporarily absorbed, negotiated, added upon, or pushed away from. Layered racialization, as during colonialism, highlights the power configurations of global (somewhat) formerly imperial state actors that continue to have the ability to racialize and dictate material racial realities, and how regions and states respond to being racialized, often with further racialization.

We find, regardless of the postcolonial moment, as Andrew Delatolla argues, "State making . . . and global relations continue to be embedded in racist structures of [colonial] civilizational hierarchies."[23] Hence, contemporary state racial formations are "structured by [their colonial] legacy" and new racial relational material dynamics.[24] Thus, we cannot understand contemporary racial categorical divisions in states outside of their entangled colonial/historical, regional, and present global racial formation forces. Most clearly, therefore, postempire racist states structure the dynamics of postcolonial state racial formations. Even while some postcolonial states produce new racial inequities, they must always be viewed in response to and negotiation with the foundation of global white supremacy.

Second, national racial categorical hierarchies embody the culmination of national racialized social systems producing structural, systemic racism. National racial structures are the multilevel economic, political, social, and institutional social systems borne from the remnants of racist modernity and empire.[25] National racial social systems transformed through traveling racism, global and national "racial events,"[26] and global capital and racial representational evolutions that reconstituted racial inequalities in the local vicissitudes. Each social system is riddled with racial practices and mechanisms that produce structural racial inequality without the need of overt racist sentiment or appeal. National racialized social systems are entangled together and entangled with regional and global material pressures.

Therefore, across regions and in specific states we find how the global racial system is maintained directly and indirectly, subtly and loudly, and often through coerced, limited options, particularly in Black racialized geographies. Most adeptly, nationally entangled structural racism continues to secure global "institutional [and symbolic] white power and privilege" with or without white bodies in the direct mix.[27] In this chapter, I highlight how these dynamics play out across four entangled racial zones: (1) United States' Track-Laying Dominance; (2) Western European, Russian "Empire[s] Strike Back"—Postcolonial Claims; (3) Australia Holds On, China Maneuvers; and (4) Israel Separation, Gulf Eminence, and Black Africa Exclusion.

Entangled Racial Zones

Nation-states are embedded and entangled in contact zones of racial power and influence. For me, "entanglement" is a helpful heuristic concept that captures contemporary layered racial state power configurations. My use draws inspiration from Ramón Grosfoguel's application of Frantz Fanon's zones of being and nonbeing,[28] but I elaborate further by designating explicit zones and their specific racial dynamics. With this approach we find that racial states are essentially entangled in three layers: their colonial/imperial histories, current global racial hierarchies, and regional state racial forces. National social systems and local interpretive racial meaning and divisions are then subsequently embedded within those three scales. In Figure 4.1 I designate four broad entangled racial geographic zones. Each zone is hierarchically structured with global/regional racial power state(s) that racialize and influence the region and are visually depicted as the largest circles with dark gray shading: United States/Canada, Australian/New Zealand, Western Europe, and Israel. These racial power states embody former/current imperial metropoles and former white settler states but also must contend and respond to specific states in the regions, highlighted as the next biggest circles with medium-gray diagonal shading, that attempt to wield influence. A step below the latter are states represented by somewhat smaller circles and light gray horizontal shading that also try to exert regional pressure. Nonshaded circles are broad regional categories that scales of state power, or lack thereof, are embedded within. At the bottom are the smallest black circles, such as Cuba, Haiti, parts of the Caribbean, Syria, Palestine, Melanesia, and sub-Saharan Africa, that rather than exhibit power, act as zone racial representational flash points from which the regional hierarchical composition of the racial bottom is mapped.

The four zones I highlight are not concrete, static, or completely globally comprehensive. The U.S., in Zone 1 for example, not only racializes Latin America but also all other zones, as does western Europe. Israel is also globally racialized complexly and does not hold the same weight as the top dominant states in other zones. States can also be positioned simultaneously in multiple zones. This nonexhaustive typology of zones reflects zone designations that are based on an amalgamation of neighboring geographic connections, once imperial-colonial linkages, and current migratory processes. They are imprecise, but I find roughly visualizing racial hierarchies of power and spheres of influence allows us to pinpoint

FIGURE 4.1. **Entangled Racial Zones**

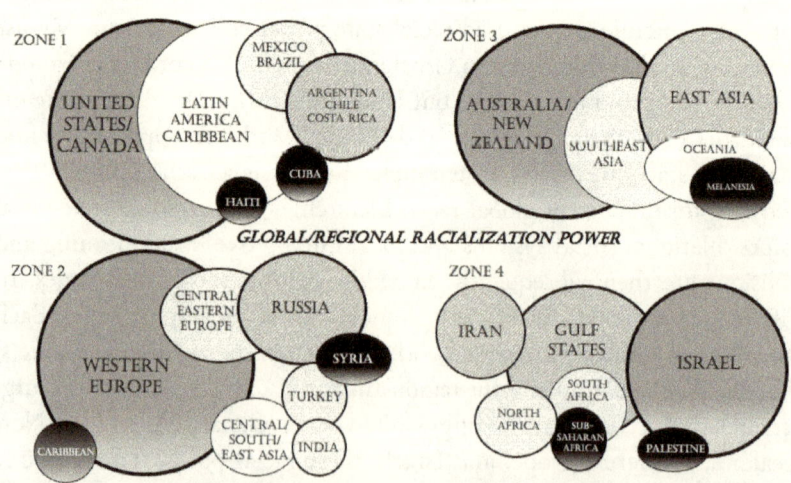

which regions/states have the greatest ability to make authoritative racialization moves, which states are trying to make new racialization moves, and which states carry the consequential brunt of other countries' racialization moves. These are the messy, entangled geopolitical multitudes that undergird state race-making, racial ideological responses, and structural racial inequities.

ZONE 1: UNITED STATES' TRACK-LAYING DOMINANCE

The United States acts as the current leading global track-laying role that former racist empires vied for. As a white settler turned imperial state its racial practices are globally felt and always negotiated. There is a robust and fundamental scholarship on U.S. racial formations and structural racism within its borders.[29] Racial formation analyses uncover the historical legal process of state litigation in protection of whiteness[30] alongside the evolution of racial categories.[31] Groups are racialized within the parameters of the legacy of Black enslavement and Jim Crow; indigenous dispossession and genocide; Mexican, Hawaii, Alaska, and Puerto Rican territorial conquest; anti-Asian immigration repression; and the War on Terror targeting of Muslims. U.S. white supremacy divided groups and fomented "ethnic projects" in the cultivation of anti-Blackness while structural racism flourished.[32] Current racial segregation in housing and schooling in many cities are at pre–Civil Rights integration levels,[33] and the criminalization, hyperpolicing, and carceral violence inflicted upon Black and Brown bodies are relentless.[34] Wealth inequities connected to the cumulative and ongoing forces of racist practices in housing, education, labor stratification, banking, and white flight grow and persist.[35]

The U.S. therefore excludes and marginalizes specific groups in its borders outside of whiteness and adjudicates racial value of those beyond its borders. The immigration enforcement machine that lends itself to racist securitization highlighted in chapter 3 works throughout the zone. So does the ongoing effects of U.S. foreign policy, going back to the 1823 Monroe Doctrine, American corporation dominance with the United Fruit Company, and contemporary socioeconomic racial inequities produced through the North American and Central American Free Trade Agreements. Those nationally racialized in the U.S. as "Latino" or "Hispanic" are products of both Spanish and U.S. colonization.[36] These two global layers of historical racialization structure current U.S. transnational racialization, contemporary racial phenomena inside national Latin American borders, and racial acceptance or rejection when groups migrate and move throughout the region.[37] Each Latin American country represents different historical-political-economic racial divisions, and the national legacies of immense *casta* designations, but broadly, mostly still conform to a hierarchy of Spanish-descendent white elites on top, or those considered "white presenting"[38] mestizos, and the multiple multiracial categories in the middle, followed by indigenous groupings and Blackness on the bottom.[39] Racist state practices are produced by "rules of racial exclusion," according to Tanya Hernández, that become the "equivalent of [the] law."[40]

National categorical racial divisions often become further collapsed through geographic racialization. Specific states like Bolivia and Guatemala are transnationally racialized and nationally present as primarily "indigenous"; Argentina, Chile, and Costa Rica as "white"; and Mexico, Venezuela, and Colombia as "mestizo." These transnational racial perceptions evolved from global forces and postcolonial state-making dynamics in the mid–late nineteenth century where national elites cultivated specific national racial ideologies such as *mestizaje, indigenismo,* or white exceptionalism to confront and negotiate global white supremacy (see chapters 5 and 6). Singular national racial identities, however, obscure national racial inequities and the racial politics of global geopolitical support, as in the case of the mainly white Cubans, the "golden exiles," who fled Cuba following the 1959 revolution for the U.S. and received political and economic support, unlike the racially constructed nonwhite Cuban "*marielitos*" of the 1980s.[41] Or as seen more recently in the U.S. platform, white-European-descendent Venezuelans who hold dual nationality are given to "criticize the [Venezuelan] government, advocate the removal of current President of Venezuela, Nicolás Maduro, or even encourage invasion from the U.S."[42]

Cuban "communism" in many ways adds another layer to the transnational racialization of contemporary Cuba as a nonwhite geography and acts as a U.S. foil, with Venezuela, shaping policy in the region. The denial of structural racism and anti-Blackness in socialist Cuba is embedded in the larger regional geopolitical racial formation and speaks to the complex realities of Caribbean racial formations where geographies are caught between Spanish and the very recent French, Dutch, Danish and British colonial legacies, current U.S. dominance, and the reality that colonialism never died in many of the islands. The British were still handing over Caribbean colonies into the 1980s and continue to control Turks and Caicos, British Virgin Islands, the Caymen Islands, Montserrat, and Anguilla as Overseas Territories while France and the Netherlands each control four islands, and the United States three. Cumulative structural racial inequalities in housing, labor markets, health, politics, and segregated landscapes, borne from once-massive Black enslavement, imperial indentured labor, and white settler elite patterns continue, as does anti-Black media and beauty practices.[43]

The disastrous legacies of indigenous genocide and violent plantation-based Black enslavement that created "plantation pigmentocrac[ies]"[44] are impossible to "overstate," as "race, class, and color hierarchies" from that era reproduce across current social systems.[45] White American and other foreign capital interests, notably, circulate in postindependence and colonial-dependent relations. Islands had to accept, first, "industrialization-by-invitation" (1940s–1980s) programs to buttress extraction and tourism industries, then neoliberal global financialization schemas (1980s–present), and, lastly, ongoing cycles of disaster capitalism exploits. Disaster capitalism facilitated public service privatization and foreign fiscal oversight and is seen most recently in the fallout of the 2010 Haitian earthquake, and subsequent U.N.-introduced cholera outbreak, and after hurricanes Irma and Maria in Puerto Rico.[46]

Thus, current U.S. dominance, and European imperial entangled relations, continue and solidify what Lorgia Garciá-Peña describes as "symbolic border[s]" that demarcate race, value, and materiality between countries throughout the region.[47] These racialized symbolic borders police belonging and rank racialized nationality groups, determining economic, symbolic, and political worth. Within the Caribbean, Puerto Ricans once positioned themselves as the "whitest people of the Caribbean,"[48] with over 80 percent of people over the last twenty years self-selecting the single race "white" Census box,[49] but now compete with colonial "white" islands like Dutch Aruba, or those with sizable white and expatriate populations such as the British Cayman Islands and Bermuda.

Racial geographic border lines are particularly felt between the created and contested division of the Dominican Republic and Haiti. Anti-Haitian practices in the Dominican Republic that limit citizenship possibilities while relying on Haitian workers[50] are connected to the U.S. occupation of the island (1914–34) and the fomenting and facilitation of anti-Blackness and Dominican political racial responses.[51] Haiti stands as the racial bellwether against which other countries within the region judge and position themselves. Despite its storied history as the home of Black revolt and freedom, Haitians languish in penetrating structural anti-Black precarity: debt bondage, incessant waves of U.S. and global intervention, environmental and social disasters, the NGOization of goods, and free trade exploitative industrial development.[52]

Similar symbolic national distancing dynamics that also demand material racialized divisions of labor play out across greater Latin American geographies as well. Costa Rica positions, and is transnationally positioned as, a beacon of peace, stability, and development, apart from racialized nonwhite countries in Central America, but relies on Nicaraguan agriculture and construction workers.[53] Chile and Argentina distance from South American nonwhiteness, and the regional migrant groups from Colombia, Venezuela, Peru, and Haiti who work in commercial, service, and domestic sectors.[54] The over four million estimated Venezuelan migrants who have left Venezuela since 2015 experience varying regional country receptions and racial perceptions, but new entry bans and discriminatory practices against Venezuelans are now the norm.[55]

Brazil's symbolic racial boundaries are mostly internal between regional Black racialized zones in the North, white zones in the South, and indigenous zones in the Amazon, all of which correspond to national racial economic and social development inequities.[56] Even with these internal regional demarcations, Black zones in the North, notably in Bahia, although marketed and commodified as nonwhite tourist products, and where the presence of Blackness is "everywhere," the landscape is still governed by strict segregated public space norms.[57] Political power and economic opportunities remain in the hands of Brazilian *brancos* (whites) and foreigners. In indigenous Amazonian areas[58] ongoing illegal mining operations flourish and pave the way for the potential passage of PL191/2020, which would allow for legal mining and the construction of hydroelectric dams on indigenous lands,[59] but Brazil's president, Luiz Inácio Lula da Silva, asked to withdraw the bill in 2023.

Brazil is commonly hailed by global actors and some academics as the antithesis to racism because of its racial democracy ideology (see chapter 6). Yet critical scholars over the last thirty-plus years have challenged such pronouncements and documented the deep forms of structural, systemic racism produced through anti-Black exclusion.[60] Anti-Black practices are found in labor market and education discriminatory mechanisms that limit employment and schooling possibilities, all of which sustain Afro-Brazilian poverty.[61] The long-standing practice of *criação* ("informal paperless adoption")[62] of young Afro-Brazilian girls, *filhas de criação,* to care and provide unpaid domestic work for white Brazilian families continues as a form of modern racial slavery.[63] Persistent police violence and killings abound and are reflective of what Keisha-Khan Perry, engaging the work of Denise Ferreira da Silva, writes as historically endemic and a product of the "material consequences of gendered racial subjection."[64] Astonishingly, "between 1980 and 2014 a record one million Black people [in Brazil] were killed."[65]

Other South American geographies that have large Afro-descendent populations have similarly stark divides and ubiquitous anti-Black colloquial expressions, representations, and racist structural practices.[66] In Colombia, which has the largest Afro-descendent population in the Spanish-speaking Americas, most Afro-Colombians are saddled with extreme poverty, lack basic utilities and social goods, and experience limited upward mobility pathways. The Pacific, where most Afro-descendent communities are located, suffers as "an acute and lasting antiblack zone of social abandonment,"[67] according to Jaime Alves and Tathagatan Ravindran. Global capital circulates in the region supported by national policies that render Black space "empty" and/or "criminalized" and measures Afro-Colombian value contingent on the "precaritization of their labor."[68]

Beyond Black Latin American geographies, anti-indigenous racist practices and forms of structural racism are notable in the Andes and Central America and even when indigenous representation is present in politics. Ravindran's scholarship on "enduring racism" despite "indigenous resurgence" in Bolivia is revealing.[69] He documents labor market stratification based on "good appearance," which is code for white-mestizo presenting (a practice found throughout the entangled zone),[70] supposed antiracist white-mestizo elites who support the de facto maintenance of their privileges, and the painful internalized racism that is acutely experienced by "*cholitos*," rural Indigenous women whose bodily and presenting markers of diminutive difference are patronized and denigrated.[71]

Canada sits with the U.S. as the other major white racial power state within the zone but positions itself as the benign, fair, even antiracist paragon to the United States' extreme racism. This perspective of "stupefying innocence,"[72] according to Dionne Brand, runs afoul of the long history of how "racism so permeated Canadian society"[73]: from Black slavery, segregation, and erasure,[74] anti-Asian immigration bans, and First Nations genocide. Yet the mythology and celebrated imagery of the "peaceful frontier,"[75] one of "benevolent Mounties" and vast wildernesses, remains.[76] These representational trappings of white settler pasts rewashed as colorblind patriotism but wrapped in modern Canadian multiculturalism hide the reality of ongoing structural racism. Black and First Nations Canadians are "overwhelmingly overrepresented in police-involved deaths," experience disproportionate rates of poverty and neglect in Canadian health services, and First Nations children make up over 50 percent of children taken into child welfare services but represent just 7 percent of children in the country.[77] The 2022 Ottawa "Freedom Convoy" truck protests further demonstrated latent Canadian white nationalism and the racial privilege awarded the truckers by a lenient Canadian police force.[78]

ZONE 2: WESTERN EUROPEAN, RUSSIAN "EMPIRE[S] STRIKE BACK"—POSTCOLONIAL CLAIMS

Zone 2 is perhaps the starkest in its state racial entanglements because of its historical racial power foundation as the geographic home to racist modernity and empires. There are multiple layers to unravel. First, there is the regional relationship pole between western Europe and Russia, which structures a power tug-of-war where Russia attempts to exert influence in the countries once part of the Soviet Union and beyond, and western Europe endeavors to keep a lockdown on its borders while accepting racialized workers, Russian resources, and elite nonwhite capital. In many ways, this dynamic is a fight over who controls the borders and representations of European whiteness. Russia contemporarily positions a true "white" identity and continental power base while western Europe expands and retracts who receives symbolic and material whiteness at its discretion.[79] The racial maneuvering by Russians is an extraordinary discursive power play that seeks to snatch whiteness from the boundaries of western Europe and make Russia its natural home. I address in chapter 5 how the geopolitics of E.U. expansion exposes the regional politics of European whiteness.

Within European state race-making processes, however, there are further divisions between Western, Northern, Central, and Eastern zones. Historical continental racial events over the last thirty years, like the breakup of the Soviet Union, the disintegration of Yugoslavia, the end of Greek, Spanish, and Portuguese dictatorships, and the manufactured "migrant crisis" over the last decade influence regional racialization dynamics and how states manage, control, regulate, and represent longstanding and newer racialized nonwhite populations within the zone. Nonwhite racialized Europeans are mostly the multiple generations of descendants of former colonial subjects who left former colonial geographies for metropoles, alongside the newer former colonial arrivals, in addition to the latest immigrant groups from the region and asylum seekers from Africa and the Middle East. Essentially, three layers of racialization are negotiated by nonwhite Europeans and Europeans on the peripheral end of whiteness. They negotiate history; in other words, their personal understanding of their colonial (or regional) geographies' racialization processes and colonial divisions; different racialization dynamics when they cross different European borders; and racialization within their national homes in Europe. All racialization processes are interacting, shaping structural racism practices within political, economic, institutional social systems, geopolitical plays, and ongoing national crises, all of which shape state racial inequalities. Commonalities, particularly for those racialized as "Black," still construct similar "constituent elements," nonetheless, to produce what Stephen Small calls a "Black Europe."[80]

These layered racialization processes are also fueling how groups understand their own racial marginalization. Some groups arrived in metropoles with relative racial privileges based on specific colonial racial formations and hierarchies only to experience new racialization and maneuvering vis-à-vis other groups from empires' wide colonial geographies. This colonial history along with East/West historical nation-making remnants, and continued regional country comparisons and distancing, contextualizes how racial domination plays out in former empire and European empire–adjacent geographies in the zone, producing specific contemporary racial orders. Substantially, the "Empire[s] [have been] strik[ing] back"[81] for the last fifty years to maintain their dominant global material positions and national white European racial identities. Striking back, however, is now produced through the ideological technologies of global colorblindness that correspond across the region as either forms of post/antiracialism or ethnic dominance politicultures (see chapter 6). A further strike entails what Olivia Harrison describes as "linguistic *détournement*," which turns once colonial "'natives' and their descendants (*indigènes*) into immigrants (*immigrés*) and the emigrants of old (*colons*, settlers) into 'natives.'"[82] "Native" constructions for the zone now are thus applied to consolidate and sustain "native" white European cartographies. Some of the dominant European country examples of the zone are the following.

Spain and Portugal were the first oversees modern European empires, but their imperial trajectories drastically diverged when Spain was forced to relinquish some of its last territories to the U.S. in 1898, while Portugal held on to its colonies (including Angola, Mozambique, Cape Verde, Guinea-Bissau, São Tomé e Príncipe, and East Timor) until 1975, the last European power to "officially" decolonize.[83] Separate imperial trajectories but related European forms of regional peripheral racialization negotiations and mid-twentieth-century dictatorships, along with employment crises in the 1980s and 1990s, produced connected but distinct contemporary racial orders. The racial implications to Portugal's bitter hold over its colonies, pursued by the regime of the *Estado Novo* dictatorship (late 1920s–74), most pronouncedly under the rule of António de Oliveira Salazar (1932–68), unwind across the Portuguese landscape today. Salazar encouraged Portuguese settlement across its renamed African "provinces" and an estimated 800,000 Portuguese left. Over 500,000 returned, the "*retornados*," to Portugal following African independence and most renounced their settler identities.[84] Nonwhite *retornados*, specifically the biracial children of white Portuguese, were ostracized. Former colonial African subjects also came to Portugal, as white Portuguese were emigrating to more prosperous European geographies, but most were pushed into what Celeste Curington describes as "gendered *antiblackness*" low-skill work, and segregated to the outskirts of Lisbon.[85] Members of these PALOP (*Países Africanos de Língua Oficial Portuguesa*) communities are "vulnerable to unemployment, two times less likely to get into university... and fifteen times more likely to be incarcerated."[86]

Spain's late twentieth-century immigration following Francisco Franco's dictatorship (1939–75) and its admission to the European Union (1986) was marked by North African (mostly Muslim Moroccan), South American (Ecuador), and middle and southern African arrivals.[87] These groups, along with Roma populations, remain outside of a Spanish-constructed whiteness that minimizes its medieval, multiethnic Muslim-rule era. Roma are perceived and marketed to tourists as inherently "Spanish" but criminalized and lack constitutional recognition.[88] Immigration procedures, historically in the early years after the dictatorship, provided pathways toward legalization for some undocumented groups, but "such openness [was] fragile" as economic crises and political racial discourses influenced policy.[89] Racist violence against Moroccan immigrant agriculture workers and their homes broke out in El Ejido in 2000, eight years after the 1992 murder of Black Dominican Lucrecia Pérez. The less overt racist practices found in housing and employment access, in political representation, along with racial police profiling, notably of those racialized as Black and Muslim, are the more insidious ways Spain's racial order is sustained.[90] Spain's long-contested regional identity fissures between Old Castile, Basque Country, and southern and eastern Spain are also remade with new regional racial projects.[91]

As two of the oldest, most expansive, and continued imperial practitioners, France and the Netherlands share similar racial orders based on racial denial, assimilation demands with constructed cultural homogeneity, and stark racial divisions between the descendants of its formerly colonized citizens, new immigrant groups, and white racialized French and Dutch. In the immediate decades following decolonization, Algerians (600,000), Moroccans (140,000), and Tunisians (90,000) from the Maghreb arrived in France[92] and Indonesians (300,000),[93] Surinamese, and Dutch Antilleans came to the Netherlands, later joined by Turkish and Moroccan guest workers.[94] France's ongoing colonial connection to its Caribbean overseas Departments and Collectivities (Martinique, Guadeloupe, Saint Barthelemy, Saint Martin) re-creates former colonial group hierarchies between those racialized as Arab and Black, and divisions within, in relation to "*français-français*" ("French-French").[95] Segregation and isolation in deteriorating *banlieues* (public housing),[96] an education system that inflicts "symbolic violence"[97] by erasing nonwhite French culture, and vigilantly policing non-Christian religious practice and any acknowledgment of race mark the French racial order.

In the Netherlands, Gloria Wekker and Philomena Essed's work exposes the insidious ways racism shapes Dutch white national identity and structures material racial realities from immigration policies to education tracking along with the language and visual iconography deployed and positioned, notably in how globally renowned Dutch art is honored.[98] The introduction of new racial binary language in the 1980s, as white Dutch descendent–driven Apartheid was ending in South Africa, marked a new era of race-making.[99] The term "*autochtoon*" represented indigenous, authentic "Dutch," while "*allochtoon*" indicated being from somewhere else, "not-quite-Dutch" regardless of generations in the country. Furthermore, a colonial hierarchy was remade within the *allochtoon* category as western civilizational standards determined a group's hierarchical placement. For example, as Essed and Trienekens argue, immigrants, many biracial, from the formerly Dutch Indies "count as western *allochtonen*" along with "Japanese, who under Apartheid qualified as [a limited form of] 'honorary white'" status.[100] The government stopped using the designations in 2016, but the new phrasing of "inhabitants with a Dutch or a migration background" has a similarly coded meaning.

German racial formations proceed in the long shadow of the 1913 Nationality Act, where the "national essence" was confirmed in "blood,"[101] fascist race laws and the Holocaust, current Black German and German Turkish inequities, and in the aftermath of the country accepting hundreds of thousands of Syrian refugees in 2015. Connected is the colonial racial legacy of citizenship laws across Europe, notably the continuation of *jus sanguini* (right of blood) and the conditions placed on *jus soli* (birthright), felt throughout the zone. No country offers unconditional *jus soli*, and parts of Central, Northern, and Mediterranean Europe have no *jus soli* options.[102]

Italy and Greece over the last decade particularly show what Camilla Hawthorne describes for Italy as the intimate connection between *jus sanguini* citizenship battles, European colorblind post/antiracial practices, and the "resurgence of overt nationalism" that more or less demands national whiteness.[103] The expression "*Una facia, una razza* (One face one race)" links Italy and Greece to a constructed shared ancient "Mediterranean race" that guides contemporary citizenship exclusions.[104] Greece, particularly, politically operates within a continuous historical racial formation loop of Ottoman rule and Turkish disassociation, Greek antiquity exaltation, and affirmations of biological sameness connected to ancient European pasts. We saw these ideas forming during the Ioannis Metaxas era (1936–41) and the Junta (1967–74), then on into neoliberal austerity in the 2000s that also saw the rise of the neofascist Golden Dawn political party.[105] Basically, Greece and Italy's western European peripheral status, like Portugal and Spain, as suspect white states, shaped racial formation crises responses and structural inequity. Migrant groups are vilified, and racialized nonwhite subjects' citizenship is constantly contested. The 900,000 children born and raised in Italy whose parents came from the outskirts of Italy's African colonial geographies among other diverse regions find themselves "unrecognized and disenfranchised,"[106] as do the "Lost Antetokounmpos" generation of Greece.[107] Dramatically, Golden Dawn was "declared a criminal organization" with numerous leaders jailed in 2020, but many of the practices within social systems that produce racist exclusion persist.[108]

Much of Central Europe, the Balkans, and Eastern Europe find themselves navigating an even more entrenched suspect white state status across the zone but within the orbit, machinations, and racial ideological influence of Russia and the fallout from state socialism.[109] Within this wide geographic scope each state negotiates, according to József Böröcz, "nested Orientalism" a term he adopts from Milica Bakic'-Hayden, reminiscent of postcolonial writings on Orientalism,[110] to describe how states within this part of the European landscape are regionally hierarchically positioned and judged based on their European attributes.[111] Complex racial negotiations do not necessarily show fealty to the "West"; rather, some states deride the West, particularly Hungary and Poland, for its supposed liberalism and multiculturalism that undermines the sanctity of European whiteness.[112] According to Ivan Kalmar, when these states perform as "white" protectors and become the "last holdout[s] of genuine white European civilization," they challenge their peripheral white status.[113]

National boundary-making, regional alliance building (such as when the Czech Republic, Slovakia, Romania, and Hungary aligned to refuse E.U.-decreed refugee quotas), and common anti-Roma, anti-Jewish, and anti-Muslim racisms are structurally activated to take oxygen away from East/West power vacuums. Western chastisement and eastern appeals, nonetheless, do not override foreign capital's economic grip in these states, and the overall desire to stay within or become part of the E.U. For most, their historic transnational racialization as inferior "Slavic" whites always lurks in the mesh of geopolitical plays, western European reception of Central and Eastern European migrants, and the countries' mechanisms of racial exclusions or inclusions within national social systems.[114]

Divisions within "Slavic" whiteness also undergird regional Slavic hierarchies. Embedded within Woodrow Wilson's racial science–informed decision that there needed to be separate Slavic states following the breakup of the Austro-Hungarian empire after World War I was the assumption that race and nationality fused and that there were racial divisions between Slavic peoples.[115] Within this part of the zone, the Yugoslav region, or the wider "Balkans," acutely represents multiple layers to the Slavic racial project. As documented in the revelatory analysis of Catherine Baker, at different historical moments, various transnational-national-local levels of racial formations collided. In the interwar period different adaptations of scientific racism were pursued to unite or separate groups. Anthropologist Vladimir Dvornikovic introduced the "Dinaric race" to unite all South Slavs together, but Serbian nationalist projects sought to separate their Slavic identities from Bosnians and place Croatians outside of Slavic identity altogether.[116] During Yugoslavian state socialism, and with President Tito's (1953–80) allegiance to the Non-Aligned Movement,[117] a colorblind path was presented only for biological racial discourses by Serbians against Bosnian Muslims to come roaring back during the war in Yugoslavia (1991–99).

The war was a pivotal entangled racial event. Transnational racialization narratives from western Europe and the U.S utilized racial discourses of either racially separating the Balkans as a region torn by "ancient 'ethnic' or even (with direct colonial overtones) 'tribal' hatreds" (harkening back to an Ottoman-rule past) or in need of saving because of their whiteness.[118] Serbian nationalists also reestablished historic Serbian racial identity claims aligned with Orthodox Christianity. In the postconflict decades, all the new states that emerged sought to distance themselves from any correlation with a racially perceived "Third World" conflict and defended their racial status as white Europeans.

In the debris of the Cold War, the Russian Federation continues to be an oppositional axis point in the zone, shaping national racial orders in Eastern Europe and Central Asia, and cultivating regional alliances, but now, basically, with direct racial appeals. Despite the recent heyday of socialist internationalism that delighted in producing antiracist propaganda to call out the racism of the West,[119] racial distinctions, racial language, and racial hierarchies have been a part of Russian rule since Tsarist imperial pursuits and the adoption of scientific racism. Under the leadership of Vladimir Putin (1999–present) we find a racial order where the state racializes migrants, polices perceived non-Russianness, and cultivates racial academic knowledge, and where multiple social systems practice overt discrimination with "Slavs only" advertisements[120] or "outlawing" certain Caucasian names.[121] Structural racism is further wrapped in the deep landscape of racist violence that is fomented and sporadically unleashed over the last twenty years.

Contemporary Russian racial classifications are rooted in the imperial, then Soviet, practice of an internal passport system that identified populations and regulated movement based on "nationality."[122] Creating nationalities was an ascriptive process and "limited populations' rights and resources." Eugene Avrutim writes that "the state's classification system primed people to see the world in unambiguous racial terms."[123] Much of the racist vitriol and structural domination found today in work, housing, and politics is experienced by Roma, Chechens, and Caucasians, and the millions of former Soviet citizens from Central Asia.[124] This collides with the long simmering history of anti-Jewish racist pogroms and praxis. In the Russian racial formation, Caucasians are *not* white and Turkmen, Kazakh, and Uzbek did not exist as meaningful singular ethnic/nation, now racial categories, until the Soviet regime created "national republics, each named for a single ethnic group"[125] carved out from complex, heterogeneous, multiethnic landscapes.[126]

Therefore, Central/Eastern European and former Soviet states navigate across the West-East white power divide and situate their own racial reactions and practices within this backdrop. Central Asia, racially framed as "barbaric Mohammedans" in nineteenth-century imperial Russia and historically "backward" during Soviet times,[127] still find lineage and kinship ties outside Soviet-defined maps but must operate in a nation-state order and regional anti-Asian and anti-Muslim civilizational hierarchy. Finland, part of the Russian empire until 1917, distances itself against Russian regional maneuvers and the history of being racialized outside of whiteness in racist science, and subsequently marginalizes Russian migrants who in turn begrudge being compared to "asylum seekers" and treated as if they were "not white."[128] Inuit Greenland, still under Danish rule, must negotiate being used as a strategic geographic pawn in the long-standing Danish-U.S. military alliances against Russia,[129] all while seeking an autonomous economy and independence.[130]

Lastly, the Caucasus region, Georgia, Armenia, and Azerbaijan, deluged with violent racist attacks against their citizens in post-Soviet Russian cities, must navigate continued dependence on Russia and its potential wrath when deciding how to challenge Russia's racist practices.[131] The estimate of as many as one million Russians fleeing conscription into Putin's war in Ukraine for haven in Central Asia and the Caucuses will add to the already-present Russian hegemonic racial influence even if their presence is presumed to be an act of Russian dissent.

On the opposite end of the zone, the United Kingdom, specifically its political head England, acts as one of the most powerful countries within the western European imaginary, but also serves as an albatross in Europe's collective union. Its domineering acts against Europe, not unsimilar to Russia, are also in protestation over maintaining a national construction of whiteness, but in this case England's distinctive Anglo-Saxon British racial identity. After WWII, beginning with the 1948 Windrush generation from Jamaica, Britain's globally vast colonial subjects, now imperial citizens after the passage of the 1948 British Nationality Act, came to Britain and almost immediately subsequent governments enacted barriers to their acceptance as full British citizens. The 1968 Commonwealth Immigrants Act was in response to South Asian East African migration, and the 1971 Immigration Act introduced and institutionalized the term *"patrial"* (code for "white") to represent citizenship based on lineage to British ancestral lands.[132] Evolved formations of racial citizenship and immigration, along with fears of E.U. migrant crossings, continued with then Home Secretary Theresa May's "hostile environment" (2012) anti-immigrant policies that culminated in Brexit politics.

Thus, Black British, Asian British, and later Chinese and African British identities were always in negotiation, structurally determined and marginalized in social systems, and placed in constant contrast with white racial Britishness. Colonial-defined racial hierarchies across the empire and between groups now play out in the imperial "heartland," creating fissures and new racist representations, along with new solidarities. England's long arm of fomenting white racial belonging, and regionally and transnationally racializing non-Britishness—be its protohistory in Ireland, to its imperial height, to the contemporary Commonwealth and continued colonial dependencies—is constantly in motion and influencing reactions, competitions, and power plays within the zone and throughout other zones.

ZONE 3: AUSTRALIA HOLDS ON—CHINA MANEUVERS

Zone 3 is broadly regionally marked by Australia's, and to a lesser extent New Zealand's, continued power hold as former "white dominion" colonial states in a region mostly transnationally racialized as "Asian," with all the historical racial colonial divisions embedded within that designation. As Australia attempts to shape the region, East Asia—China, Japan, and South Korea—vie for influence, with China rising above the others, while negotiating the global historical legacy and new forces of anti-Asian racism, the weight of Japanese colonial harms, U.S. military aggression and capital interests, and continuous internal racial fault lines. The literal and symbolic middle of the zone, Southeast Asia, is strikingly scarred by intense Dutch, French, Portuguese, and British racial colonial foundations, American-led anticommunist wars, and ongoing regional racial maneuvering and negotiations with a dominant China. All the while Oceanic islands in the zone struggle for full independence, development, and inter-island solidarity as colonially crafted racial hierarchical divisions produced between the islands and regional forms of global anti-Blackness collide. Thus, knotty racialization abounds but global white supremacy continues to shape global "Asian" and indigenous subjectivities and regional and national racial responses.

Contemporary Australia and New Zealand's racial orders, born from the complete domination of white settler political praxis of the last two hundred years, nonetheless produced similar and different racial-embodied indigeneity and response. Australian Aboriginal and Torres Strait Islanders were historically racialized as "Black" and often placed at the bottom of a transnational Black hierarchy while being connected to larger regional Black indigenous identities across the Pacific islands that skirt Australia's east coast.[133] The Māori in New Zealand/Aotearoa were racialized "Polynesian" and placed higher within the wider Oceanic islands' racial hierarchy. A British civil servant even went so far as to claim a Māori ancient Aryan ancestral linkage in the book *Aryan Maori* (1885),[134] an idea further developed in some racial science constructions that Polynesians were "Caucasian."[135]

Both racialization schemes placed the groups below European-descendent whiteness, but the Treaty of Waitangi (1840) "guaranteed undisturbed possession [for the Māori] of all their lands, fishers, and other valued 'assets.'"[136] The politics and violence of white settlers, the Pākehā in New Zealand, and their demands, nevertheless, assured massive Māori land dispossession and racist structural marginalization, but the treaty also created late twentieth-century openings for Māori activist sovereignty claims.[137] Māori have reasserted their rights and gained greater political representation through Mixed Member Proportional representation (MMP) and Māori electorate roll systems,[138] but the promise of "biculturalism" is weakened by some Pākehā grievances against reparations and material distributive practices, and continued structural racial inequality in housing, jobs, health, and education.[139]

Aboriginal and Torres Strait Islanders Black-embodied Australian indigeneity was always symbolically and violently condemned, and groups today face massive forms of structural subordination in criminal justice, health, and education and find their communities continuously pathologized or rendered static.[140] They also disappear in the backdrop of Australia's strained multicultural maneuvers and the resurgence of anti-Chinese posturing in the wake of Chinese capital investment moves in the Pacific and paranoia over "foreign interference."[141] Within the zone, we find reformed "Yellow Peril" frames emanating from Australia but also complexly in geographies like Singapore. In Singapore, home to a long-dominant colonially informed Chinese descendent racial hierarchy, we find a specific form of "co-ethnic racialization."[142] Newly arrived Chinese are seen as unwanted and threats by Singaporean Chinese.[143] Co-ethnic racialization addresses how other sociocultural markers of difference are used by similarly constructed racial groups to hierarchically differentiate among each other. The practice is connected to the broader process of how disparate ethnic and sociopolitical groups were transnationally, racially, and categorically lumped together during the era of scientific racism and through colonial practices, and the navigation schemas these groups deployed often produced regional and internal racial hierarchies of value and worth.

Japan pioneered local adoptions of this process during the height of scientific racism. Japan produced a regional Asian hierarchical scale during Japanese colonialism while attempting to offset the height of global Yellow Peril racist fear. Contemporary Japan continues this history with its attempts to reconcile and assign racial designations from what Manami Matsuoka, adapting from Tanabe, describes as *"seikou toutei."*[144] Internal indigenous groups such as the Ainu and Okinawans, historical colonially created Korean *"Zainichi* (residing in Japan),*"* and Chinese *"Sangokujin"* communities, along with foreign Brazilian Japanese workers and western English workers, all hierarchically map along global, regional, and national racial designation scales.[145] Basically, *gaikujin,* non-Japanese nationals, are weighted by their perceived closeness to modernity and constructions of Japaneseness. South Korea, similarly, navigates a context of national historic "shame" from Japanese colonialism and later American occupation, but sees America more favorably[146] and as an ally in challenging communist North Korean threats and Chinese regional advances.

Thus, the wide encompassing racialized "China threat" plays out in complex, layered praxis in the zone, and has dramatically increased in the fallout from Covid-19, where China is somewhat conceived as the sole regional "Yellow Peril," whose diasporic nationals and financial capital travel throughout. But outside the zone, all geographies, except for Australia and New Zealand, also become one potential "flexible amalgamation of racialized, feminized menace."[147] China's transnational racialization, cosigned with later communist rule and capitalist pursuits, facilitated a contemporary dense racial order. Originally drawn from Stalin's "nation" characteristics, but also influenced by Chinese Confucius ideas, Mao introduced "minority nationalities" (*shaoshu minzu*), originally forty-two, now fifty-six, but Han superiority presumptions were a given and *minzu* groups were viewed in need of civilizing.[148] Despite policies to mitigate ethnic regional inequalities,[149] Han are beneficiaries of state support in ethnic autonomous zones, and, as seen in actions against the Uyghurs, enact repressive acts. Likewise, Han Chinese/Taiwanese in the island of Formosa, now Taiwan, impinge on the sovereignties of indigenous peoples, like the Sediq and Truku. African migrants in Guanzhou have also animated anti-Black rhetoric and fears.[150] Like in the historic reformer period of scientific racism negotiations, assimilation to Han superiority in different forms continues to be the ultimate nation-building ideal, what Yinghong Cheng calls an "emerging Han racial nationalism," to exert global influence in a global racial system still dominated by white supremacy.

Southeast Asian racial orders from Vietnam, Cambodia, and Laos to Myanmar and Indonesia operate out of the historically dense web of colonially mandated divides of group privileges or exclusions, social and economic instability from years of American military actions that brought regional devastation, and ongoing western development influences and intertwined global capital insertions and inequities. Vietnam, Cambodia, and Laos were governed by France as the *L'Union Indochinoise* (Indochine Union). A long-fought battle for independence was waged but evolved into an American-led war against communism with devastating racial consequences across the global racial system. Black American soldiers were brought to the front lines[151] as Vietnamese, Cambodians, Hmong fought for self-determination, but had to navigate within a milieux of foreign powers' entreaties and violence, and colonially accentuated regional divisions. In the fallout from colonial fissures and U.S. military bombardment, sociopolitical havoc ensued: Pol Pot and the Khmer Rouge came to power in Cambodia and remained in part until 1999, millions died, ethnic groups were forced to flee, and immense environmental degradation and the bodily toll of war marked the landscape.[152]

During French colonial rule, Cambodia was especially externally "mummified" with support given to a "traditional monarchy social structure,"[153] while the Vietnamese were chosen over Cambodians by the French to work in colonial administration because they were framed as more "technically rational."[154] Contemporary anti-Vietnamese discourse and propaganda in Cambodia harken back to Vietnamese expansionist practices prior to French rule, direct French racialization and divisions sowed between the groups, and the national heightening of a distinct Khmer identity. Yet, both countries, with Laos, globally compete as cheap, transnationally racialized labor and as sites of foreign-led export-based global economic participation. Cambodia's perception of a neighboring Vietnamese "existential threat," however, drives the country into a strategic regional alliance with China.[155]

Myanmar most greatly navigates the colonial legacy of racial divisions, isolation, and militarism but within the ruins of the British imperial system that invented "Burma." Myanmar was first governed by the British Raj in India until several Anglo-Burmese wars and pacification practices brought about a series of racial governance reforms with long-lasting implications.[156] British colonially carved borders and racialization processes brought once-disparate groups together under one colonial supervision but divided groups by "national ethnic races."[157] Ministerial Burma, the central area where most of the Burman majority reside, was ruled directly while the smaller ethnic groups in the peripheral areas, the Frontier Areas or Excluded Areas, were ruled indirectly. Non-Burman groups had less contentious relations with the British and were rewarded. Ethnic groups "like the Karen and Kachin were favoured by the colonial administration" with low-level military and bureaucratic placements and opportunities for education in England.

These policies and colonial racial fictions had a "disastrous effect" on the postcolonial racial order.[158] For most of the rule of General Ne Win (1962–88) an isolated Myanmar implemented the forced assimilation process of "Myanmification" that accentuated Buddhist Burman dominance within the British-constructed "national ethnic races."[159] The 1982 Citizenship Law created three categories of citizenship eligibility but only for "national ethnic races."[160] The Rohingya were not included. State violence has followed for the predominantly Muslim group in the western province of Arakan who experience "travel restrictions, forced evictions, demolitions, and closed IDP camps."[161] Karen are also internally displaced and have been in armed struggle for autonomy since 1949.

Indonesia, one of the most populous states in the zone with China and India, is shaped by Dutch imperialism, U.S. and Australian spheres of influence, and changing racial national identity pursuits since independence was achieved in 1949. In the postindependence years, notably under the U.S.-backed violent overthrow of the government by General Suharto (1967–98), the New Order's policy of assimilation was linked to the ideology of *Pancasila*, "the belief in one supreme God, humanism, nationalism, popular sovereignty and social justice."[162] To go against *Pancasila* as a homogenous national identity force was to go against stability and western-backed economic development and any discussion of "ethnicity (*suku*), religion (*agama*), race (*ras*), and interclass (*antar golongan*)," the acronym SARA, was prohibited.[163] Indonesian citizenship was influenced by Dutch colonial racial constructions between "natives" (*pribumi*) and "non-natives" (*non-pribumi*). The framing of a "*Masalah Cina*" (China problem), and with Chinese Indonesians being seen as "non-natives," the Chinese were separated from national belonging as during colonialism.[164]

Then and now, Indonesia is home to one of the most diverse geographies with over a thousand ethnic and subethnic groups, but Javanese are the largest group with over 40 percent of the population, and they dominate Suharto and post-Suharto era politics. The divisions between native groups of the archipelago, and U.S. and Australian transnational racialization influences, are further exposed when Indonesia gained control of West Papua from the Dutch in 1962; and later in 1975, when Indonesia invaded, occupied, and violently battled the Timorese in East Timor for twenty-four years once Portugal ceded the territory. West Papuan and Timorese populations were both racialized under Dutch and Portuguese colonialism as "Papuan," thought to be part of the "Melanesian Black race types," but Timorese were also said to be a vexing mix of "Malay" and "Papuan", "yellow and Black."[165] Accordingly, Papuans and Timorese were considered "too primitive" to warrant self-determination.[166] After Suharto's fall, and regardless of the rise of Indonesian multiculturalism, Papuans experience racist taunting and abuse, and spatial segregation produced by the originally colonial policy of *transmigrasi* and later continued with resettled Javanese in peripheral outer islands.[167] Within the wider zone,

Australian geopolitics in support of or against specific Indonesian policies was always connected to the more immediate geographic racial threat Indonesia posed to Australia's borders, and subsequent governments continuously accentuated a manufactured fear of the "vast, densely populated Muslim archipelago."[168]

The islands strewn throughout the Pacific Ocean are literally and symbolically marked by the still-in-use racist cartography of Jules-Sébastien-César Dumont d'Urville, competing European colonialists, and eager anthropologists who geographically and racially reified Polynesian and Melanesian divisions. Polynesia, the "many islands" including Samoa, Tonga, Easter Island, Hawaii, and New Zealand, navigate the legacy of the romanticized white gaze and internalized anti-Blackness against Melanesians in their islands and in Papua New Guinea, Solomon Islands, Vanuatu, New Caledonia, Fiji, and Australia.[169] As during the height of colonial racial science, and as seen in Portuguese and Dutch constructions in Timor and then New Guinea, racially creating and disentangling constructions of Blackness in the Pacific included comparisons to "Malays" in the East and "Polynesians" in the West.[170] Relational comparisons and hierarchical placement continue today as impoverished islands contemporarily compete for economic development and political positioning, while China enters the mix pushing trade, construction initiatives, concessionaire loans in the hundreds of million,[171] and initiating security partnerships,[172] causing new racial paranoia from Australia, New Zealand, and the United States. The U.S. territorial holdings in Micronesia and American Samoa ensure that the new global racial power plays among Australia, U.S., and China will dictate the predicaments and material well-being for these racially divided and colonially marked island states.

ZONE 4: ISRAEL SEPARATION, GULF EMINENCE, BLACK AFRICA EXCLUSION

Zone 4, broadly including the contested geographic terms "Middle East," "North Africa," and "sub-Saharan Africa," unfurls across one of the most richly diverse and complicated racial entanglements of all the zones. A long history of migratory movement, Muslim dynasties prior to European colonialism, together with late European colonial arrangements with the British, French, Italian, Belgium, German, Portuguese, and later ongoing American influence, reveals manifold and compounded racial divisions across the region and in specific geographies. This is a zone where religion, ancestral lineage, geographic and nationality affiliation, and bodily encoded markers all complexly distinguish racial meaning and structural placement. Racial maneuvers and contemporary ascription processes are in reaction and interaction with colonial and transnational racialization that marked "Jewish," "Arab," "Muslim," and "African" outside of whiteness in many ways, but meanings at different scales also shift and take on knotted power dynamics within regional and national borders.

Thus, zone categories are globally placed within a hierarchy below whiteness, but different categorical groupings can achieve connections to an unstable form of structural whiteness (see chapter 5). Some Jewish Israeli identities sit above Muslim and Arab in the global racial hierarchy and Black African is consistently placed at the bottom of all regional hierarchies. However, "Black" is also a fluid category within the zone. When Blackness intersects with other markers of difference, like perceived ancestry or lineage, religion, or nation distinction, those identities may be elevated in a way that mitigates or accentuates the forces of global, regional, national, and local anti-Blackness.

The 1917 British Balfour Declaration; the 1967 Israel occupation of the West Bank, Gaza Strip, and Golan Heights; the Cold War's impact on destabilizing decolonized African geographies and the introduction of structural adjustment measures; the end of South African apartheid and the Rwandan genocide both occurring in 1994; the September 11, 2001 attack and the launching of the global "War on Terror"; the Arab Spring that began in 2010 and the Syrian civil war that followed; and South Sudan becoming the latest nation-state in 2011—all represent seismic racial events that reverberate throughout the zone. The racial consequences produced in the zone from these events are products of colonial racial orders and the struggles of postcolonial state-making that teeter within the scaffolding of European global dominance and artificial national outlines.

The establishment of Israel in 1948 in the fall of the British mandate is marked by seventy-five-plus years of Palestinian dispossession, regional military attacks, and anti-Israel blowback that has re-entrenched divisions among groups, all of which originally suffered under global white supremacy. The constant "suppression of Palestinian rights"[173] is entangled in the western powers' support of Israel as a malleable but unstable transnationally racialized western state ally in the region,[174] and in ongoing practices of stratification among nonwhite Israeli racialized positionalities.[175] In this heady and "emotionally charged atmosphere"[176] that situates state policy, Israel has implemented practices that have tremendous consequences for Palestinians and created new racial hierarchies within Jewish and Israeli identities. Palestinian treatment varies depending on Israel's "territorial jurisdiction": West Bank (martial and administrative law), East Jerusalem (mix of martial and administrative law), Gaza Strip (counterinsurgency), and within Israel (civil law).[177] The 5.9 million Palestinian refugees originally created from what Palestinians call their *Nakba* (catastrophe), and Israelis the War of Independence, who live in Jordan, Lebanon, Syria, the Gaza Strip, and the West Bank, seek unlikely pathways back to their former homes while navigating statelessness and inequalities in refugee host states.

The Right of Return (1950), the Law of Absentees' Property (1950), the Jewish Nation Fund Law (1953), an "endless permit [and checkpoint] regime," the power of the Israel Defense Forces (IDF), and the state-sanction of over 700,000 Israeli settlers in around 250 settlements in the occupied West Bank and East Jerusalem, are racial projects that infuse materiality into Israel racial formations.[178] Arab Jewishness, the constructed *"Mizrahi,"* and African (mostly Ethiopian) Jewish identities also experience unique racial positioning outside of European-descendent Jewish communities but are also positioned in relation to African asylum seekers, migrant workers from the global South (like Filipino and Thai workers and now increasingly Indian workers),[179] Arab Israeli citizens, and Palestinians. Thus, multiple racial markers collide, underscoring intersectional divisions within Jewish and non-Jewish identities alike.

The larger transnational racial assemblage, nonetheless, still works to place Jewish identities outside of whiteness, or not quite white, with anti-Jewish sentiment present, informed by long-standing anti-Jewish racial history, across Europe, the U.S., and other geographies. The devastation of the October 7, 2023, Hamas attack and kidnappings, and the subsequent mass violence against Palestinians in the Gaza Strip (and settler violence in the West Bank), has unleashed an uncertain monumental new stage to the conflict born from the fault lines of historical western empires, colonial carvings, and postcolonial state devastations.

"Arab," an identity connected to language, land, and later to a specific position within Islam,[180] was transnationally ascribed as a racial category during racist modernity and empires to define a region but also a religion outside of white European Christianity. Local constructions of "Arabness," and later Arab nationalism, and subsequent Arab hierarchies, were a response to dynamics at the fall of the Ottoman empire when the League of Nations denied the right of immediate self-determination to the Arab region and granted Britain mandate status of Palestine, Jordan, and Iraq (Britain already exerted wide control and influence in the Gulf through a series of treaties) while the French held the mandate for Syria/Lebanon, and when both European powers solidified essential racial constructions and divisions.

Historically, the Gulf and "Middle East" regional geographies had long embodied a "complex group of [peoples and spatial arrangements] with a long history of border crossing,"[181] ethnic movement, and group affiliations tied to lineage collectives and familial lines, all of which crossed our notion of modern borders. When the British took over, however, they "insisted on pure . . . lineages" and privileged specific lineage groups over others, creating a hierarchy within the Arab racial designation.[182] British produced local knowledge and understandings with the *Gazetteer of the Persian Gulf, Oman, and Central Arabia* manual. The manual became an "instrument of rule" and "symbolic register of prestige of Gulf Arabs."[183] The British empowerment of certain sheikhdoms and ruling families "territorialized power"[184] within newly emerged nation states that continued when the Americans became the dominant influence in the Gulf through oil exploration. American corporate racism accentuated Arab inferiority with the introduction of strict racial protocols that discriminated against Arabs and other nonwhite racialized groups in oil production jobs and in racially segregated and vastly unequal work camps.[185] Texaco, Chevron, Exxon and Mobil, the collective owners of ARAMCO's racist operations in Saudi Arabia, along with British-constructed regional divisions, laid the groundwork for a consolidated contemporary Arab Gulf racial identity and the current production of racialized inequities.[186]

Intricately, a Gulf Arab positionality sits atop a regional Arab hierarchy. Gulf states regionally recognize which "Arab" identities can make "claim[s] to authenticity" as "people of the Gulf."[187] Arab groups outside the Gulf Cooperation Council (Kuwait, Saudi Arabia, Bahrain, Qatar, United Arab Emirates, and Oman) find other markers racialize them beyond the "romantic tropes of Arab Bedouin ancestry," which works to purify a region historically defined by "multicultural, multilingual, and multiracial pasts."[188] Arab-Muslim identities exterior to the Gulf, such as Egyptians and Palestinians, measure lower in the hierarchy and were part of the first wave of "foreign" workers to fill labor needs. Syrians and Lebanese embody different racial Arab positioning. Christian Arab Lebanese were historically elevated over Muslim Arab Syrians by the French, but Muslim Syrian Arab refugees have not received favorable placement in the Gulf just like Palestinian refugees have not. Rather, Gulf countries financially outsource humanitarian care through economically weakened Jordan and Lebanon, which house many Palestinians and Syrians.

Widely, therefore, Gulf states, and states throughout Southwest Asia and the Middle East, negotiate indirect colonial legacies and transnational anti-Muslim racism in complex ways. The European racial knowledge inspired "Arab-hatred" still "permeates popular sentiment and scholarly production" in parts of modern Iran, for example.[189] At the same time Saudi Arabia and other Gulf states act as "counterterrorism allies" with the West and protect an imagined Gulf dynastic citizenship regime that relies on exploited global racialized labor to sustain it and valorized white western labor to give it prestige.[190] Over 40 percent of the working population in the Gulf are migrant labor,[191] most governed by the *kafala* employer-sponsorship system.[192] The racial categorical amalgamation of the prevalent Gulf "Indian" migrant worker embodies broad subjectivities of South Asian descent and beyond, with all the associative pejorative attributes given, despite long settlement ties to the Gulf.[193] On the opposite end resides foreign "expatriates," the American and European "cosmopolitans" whose passports and symbolic white capital make them elevated "experts" in the regional racial field, notably in Dubai.[194]

Blackness further demarcates and muddles divisions with "Arabness" and shapes explicit experiences of regional and national forms of anti-Blackness. Anti-Black sentiment echoes the slow linking (but not mandating) of slavery and Blackness across many Arab regions after the European racial marking of the transatlantic trade, and when global-colonial, anti-Black racial epistemologies interacted with local understandings to "mark[], stigmatize[], and reproduce[]" a disparaged Black body.[195] Blackness was historically constructed as "external" regardless if it was always internally present.

Yemen particularly embodies a delicate context of multilayered scaled regional racialization and internal anti-Blackness. Yemen is separated outside Gulf cooperation, and thus much of the Gulf racial project, but operates a strict Arab lineage hierarchy that determines discrete social positions.[196] Those categorized outside those lineages are "foreign" descendants or "without origin."[197] Those racialized as "Black" are the *"akhdam"* (servants) or the *"Muhamasheen"* (the marginalized) who are constructed as the descendants of the "foreign" "Ethiopians" who invaded pre-Islamic Yemen and were ousted by "indigenous" Yemenis and subsequently enslaved.[198] This "origin myth" of the *Muhamasheen* relegates them to permanent outsider status as "'Black' and 'African' as opposed to Yemeni and Arab."[199] Their Blackness is also not about phenotype, as some non-*Muhamasheen* do not phenotypically differ from other groups. Rather their Black subjectivity serves as an archetype the transnationally and regionally "racialized Yemeni figure" distances from,[200] including the highest Arab elites to the low status, *"beny al-khumus"* (service providers).[201] Subsequently, they experience the worst forms of degradation, exclusion, and vulnerability, especially in the mayhem of the ongoing government war, with Saudi support, against the Houthis.

Blackness in North Africa is even further layered, yet many states still enact anti-Blackness accentuated by colonial racial knowledge and rule. The erasure of the once European enslaved, the historical capture and increased enslavement of adjacent groups from areas corresponding to modern Niger, Mali, Chad, Sudan, Nigeria, and Benin,[202] and the present lives of slavery in Mauritania[203] expose the insidious continued essentialization of servility with Blackness and the symbolic and material violence inflicted on those categorized through what Afifa Ltifi describes as "social blackness."[204] Social Blackness in North Africa is both beyond and imbued through "chromatic blackness," evoking supposed "universal meanings" and truths.[205] These reified truths coalesce around constructed "natural divisions" between North/South Africa, that the "Sahara constitutes a natural border," and, therefore, as Leila Tayeb writes, creates the reality that "racial whiteness [is] indigenous to North Africa, racial Arabness contribut[es] to the maintenance of that whiteness, and racial blackness [is] non-indigenous."[206] The French, British, and Italian colonial demarcations ensured that the fluid, and anything but pristine and stable, ethnolinguistic social groups would become "Berber," "Arab," "African."[207] In her study of Egypt, Eve Troutt Powell argues that European imperial race categories were "either accepted, denied, translated or redirected" in complex negotiations to transnational anti-Arab and anti-Muslim racialization that produced both locally conflated terms for Blackness and nationalist movements toward whiteness.[208]

More specifically, Egypt's racial architecture dances within the parameters of the fallout from its participation in the colonization of Sudan with Britain, the literal drownings of Nubian territory and subsequent group displacement, and positioning Egyptian Arab modernity in proximity to whiteness to deflect its geographic closeness to perceived African "barbarism."[209] Blackness in Egypt was placed upon Nubian and Sudanese identities but ascriptions were not so clear-cut,[210] and some Nubians distance themselves from Blackness.[211] There is also a more recent revival of "neo-Pharaonism," which "claims that contemporary Egyptians share the same genetic makeup as ancient Egyptians" and challenges perceived Afrocentric perspectives placed upon Egypt.[212]

Other North African designations and ascriptions of Blackness expose overdetermined factors of perceived enslaved descent, phenotype, nationality, labor position, and border demarcations, all colliding.[213] We also find new nationally pursued colonial maneuvers, re-creating and solidifying the composition of the current racial bottom. For example, Morocco, and initially Mauritania, gained control of the region of Western Sahara after Spain relinquished its colony in 1975, then known as Spanish Sahara. The Saharawis, originally nomadic groups of Berber, Arab, and Black African descent, fought for territorial independence, with many refugees ending up in Tindouf, Algeria. Those who remained in the contested occupied territory were contained by a 1,700-mile defensive wall, the Berm, military crackdowns, and a subsidized settler Moroccan population.[214]

In Tunisia, and other locales, descent from enslaved status is often marked by the label *"atig,"* meaning "'liberated by,' and is followed by the last name of the person who liberated the person's enslaved ancestors" until the practice was challenged in court in 2019.[215] Similarly, in Morocco and elsewhere, the label *"Haratin,"* plural for *"Hartani,"* a derisive term that connotes "free Black person, and/or formerly enslaved persons," sits alongside other derogatory terms for "Black and/or descendants of slaves."[216] Blackness is further blurred for the two separate Tuareg groups in Algeria, *Kel Ahaggar* and *Kel Adagh*, originally Malian refugees. The *Kel Adagh* "consider themselves superior to Blacks" and take issue with the "Blackness of the Malian government."[217]

Broadly, the fluidity and flexibility of Black ascription in North Africa, however, does not negate the reality of global-local embodiments of anti-Black epistemologies and structural subordination that apportions Blackness and Africanness away from Arabness and North African indigeneity.[218] Black activists brought festering, normalized anti-Blackness to the surface during the Arab Spring, and Tunisia became the first country in the "'Middle East' and North Africa to pass a law that criminalizes racial discrimination in 2018," followed by Egypt in 2019 and Algeria in 2020.[219] Still, fighting structural racism was not included in the laws, and overt degradations persist as do new exclusions and violence against racialized Black students and migrant workers from the wider continent.[220]

Within the remainder of the African continent, contemporary postcolonial states struggle to fulfill promises of material well-being for their citizens and communities while negotiating manufactured identities, borders, and global anti-Blackness. The ravages from centuries of racialized Black enslavement, European colonialism, Apartheid, and postcolonial state rules not of the states' making, with continued exploitative global capital and development practices, take an immense toll on states' ability to mitigate global structural racism and the deep wounds of national fissures accentuated by European powers. Sabelo Ndlovu-Gatsheni writes, "The achievement of political independence did not result in full realization of the dream of transcending the distortions cascading from colonialism."[221] Contemporary global racial formations repackage but maintain calcified anti-Black racist tropes on the construction of "Africa" and "African identities." Independent geographies were unable to deracialize the racial social systems, and the categories of colonialism created in the production of white supremacy are still in place.[222] Now, as during colonialism, Europeans or non-Africans are "agents of development and Africans [are] subject to it." These dynamics muzzle the capacity of states and structure the parameters African state leaders maneuver within while trying to pursue development as a "national project."[223] Internal migration between rural/urban geographies, out-migration for economic pursuits in other countries in the zone, along with pursuing paths to the Gulf, and for some, Europe, are long-utilized practices of survival that are locally racially enacted and globally, regionally, and nationally racially received.

Overlapping racial markings that historically unfolded—the transnational racialization of anti-Blackness; regional North/South divides; and the ever-present impact of colonially derived "native tribes" that hierarchized African native groups and placed them in relation to each other, whiteness, white settlers, and "non-native races"—continue to reverberate. Across West, East, Central, South African geographies this pattern repeats. Racial colonized groupings also now intersect with the new fault lines of Black Diaspora communities searching for a symbolic home and belonging and new white settlers searching for economic opportunity and/or selfhood through performances of white saviorism. In

West Africa, once dotted with dozens of castles, forts, and lodges that propelled the transatlantic trade of African enslavement, the Elmina fort remains as a site of what Michelle Commander calls "diasporan mourning" and "Afro-Atlantic speculation."[224] Diasporan communities yearn and create imaginings of Africa and local communities grapple with the "pressing realities" of African underdevelopment and the prospects and hopes of global Black solidarities.[225] White colonial subjectivities are also "returning" to multiple African geographies but as new "development" and "skilled" experts.[226] They live in segregated spaces, receive higher pay, extract racialized care, and embody contemporary forms of white authority. Connected are the thousands of Americans and Europeans running, opening, and volunteering with charities and nonprofits, many religious and/or education-based, who receive public and private global funding. These dynamics directly re-create colonial missionary civilizing practices that propagate and benefit from the global racial system.[227]

Global Racial Hierarchy of States

Entangled racial states bring to the surface four necessary ways to understand national racial orders embedded within the global racial system. First, all entangled racial states are products of entangled colonial pasts (whether colonizer, colonized, or adjacent), where overt white supremacy was the global structural and symbolic norm and national and local geographies and peoples were racialized by racist empires in distinct forms across a global racial hierarchy. Second, these global sociohistorical processes took hold in regional, national ethnic-socio-political logics and zones of influence, shaping how nation-states were able to negotiate, respond, and experience transnational racialization in similar and distinct ways. Third, the national racial formations that arose expose the malleability of racial categorization and the rigidity of the global racial hierarchy. Whiteness and anti-Blackness remain the axiom pole all racial orders negotiate within even while distinct racial orders emerged without white or Black bodies present. Fourth, and most important, entangled racial states are not all equally racist states. Racism is present everywhere in all entangled states but understood across a scale where some states are the originators of the racist system, some states are both recipients of racism and reproducers of the racial system, and, lastly, some states are mainly recipients of racism. Former colonized geographies' negotiation of racism by reproducing racism is not the same as the racism still dictated by former empire states.

Sudan and South Sudan are an instructive example. Northern Sudan's decolonization Arabization policy toward South Sudan is reflective of British-Egyptian conquest and British racial colonial policy. British policy favored elite, "self-defined Arabs," who were bolstered by the "authentic Sudanese Arab genealogies" constructed by the British. The British also steered those ascribed as being of "slave descent" into the military and manual work.[228] Privileged northern Arab elites, however, were also marked by the racialized construction of "Sudan," which by then had globally rendered "Sudan" an equivalent to Blackness and enslavement even if its ancient rendering had a broader signification. Subsequently, Sudanese Arabs were relegated to inferior placement within the Gulf Arab racial hierarchy.[229] In response, Northern Arab nationalists attempted to reappropriate and apply "a new plural form for the Arabic adjective *sudani* . . . to describe themselves . . . and a new plural form *sudaniyyun*, to mean Sudanese nationals,"[230] to contest regional inferiorization while still maintaining presumptions to Arab authority.

Accordingly, the best avenue for successful postcolonial state building and racial negotiation determined by Northern Sudanese Arab elites was the assimilation of non-Arabs and non-Muslims in the country. Thus, Northern Sudanese's dominating policies and violence against the South, followed by unnuanced global media analyses and white saviorism reactions, with the continued devastation and marginalization of South Sudan even after statehood, are enveloped in multiple entangled scales of racialization and entangled racial state power inequities. Global and regional anti-Blackness shaped all of Sudan (as is seen contemporarily in 2024 in how the world mostly ignores the ravages of the war in Sudan), but the Southern Sudanese became structurally "Black," and experience national anti-Black policies, in a geography where everyone was transnationally racialized as "Black."[231]

As we can see, global white supremacy is everywhere but hides in the typical fixation on discrete national racial boundaries and easy but often false national racial group assumptions that are detached from the historical reality of traveling, transforming, and the constant repurposing of racism within the global racial system. Nowhere is the recycling and calcification of white supremacy more evident than in the politics, practices, and, for most, the mirage of whitening. I turn to the uneasy history of global whitening, with all the intricate complexities and nuanced understandings, in the next chapter.

Five
Transforming Race and Malleable Whiteness

In 1895 Costa Rican diplomat Richard Villafranca published *Costa Rica: The Gem of American Republics*. With effusive praise, charm, and persuasion, Villafranca made the case for why Europeans and white Americans should emigrate to Costa Rica. For one, Costa Rica's government was modeled on the United States, where special care was given to ensure the protection of liberties, civil rights, and the rights of private property holders. Second, Costa Rican people were unique within a "riotous" region. According to Villafranca, "The natives of Costa Rica are principally the descendants of the early Spanish settlers and conquerors . . . they are somewhat above their neighboring nations in the arts of civilization."[1] Simply put, Costa Rica was unique, regionally advanced, and "white." Arguably, the position of elites at the turn of the twentieth century was that all Costa Rica needed to be an even stronger, bolder, model nation-state was more foreign investment, more European and American bodies, basically, more whiteness. To ensure this goal, the country implemented policies that supported Italian and Spanish *colonias*, legally excluded the settlement of people of Chinese and African ancestry,[2] and cultivated, through Villafranca and others, a country image that shared the European and American global investment in democracy, capitalism, and above all else, whiteness.[3]

The *Leyenda Blanca* (White Legend) of Costa Rica exposes the contradictory nature of *blanqueamiento* (whitening) appeals then and now. Countries and groups already needed to be symbolically white to become more materially white. The exceptional, civilizational qualities of whiteness naturally applied to specific groups and spaces during racist modernity and empires could be captured, packaged, and presented for those suspect countries and groups who fell outside the traditional domain of "white." But just how far outside of whiteness a country fell mattered, as well as if a country could distance itself from other groups and countries even lower on the global racial hierarchy. Essentially, in tandem, countries had to fertilize symbolic whiteness to produce more structural whiteness. The endeavor for whiteness, nonetheless, was always fraught, always embedded in colonially racialized processes and contemporary entangled racial zone manifestations that produced disparate corporeal, cultural, and geographically situated racialized bodies, groups, regions, and cartographies. Soliciting whiteness, once historically hailed, now more illusively drawn, was simultaneously a survival tactic, a coercive response, a hegemonic reality, and now acts as a potent contemporary mechanism in the reproduction of the global racial system.

As addressed in chapter 3 the global racial system today is tended to and propelled forward by the deep whiteness pulsating through global racial capitalism, militarism, and culture, shaping everything, everywhere, everyone, and its interaction in regional-national-local racial forms. The well of whiteness is so deep and structurally sound that everyone must contend with it. Thus, the system ensures that the easiest way to negotiate whiteness is to acquiesce to its governing logics, its material rewards, its commonsense, now supposedly colorblind worldview that renders whiteness apparently invisible. As Sara Ahmed, in engagement with Frantz Fanon, reminds us, "If the world is made 'white' . . . a world that is inherited [from colonialism] . . . then the body at home is one that can inhabit whiteness."[4] Thus, both consciously and unconsciously, directly and indirectly, groups and countries historically and contemporarily are forced to navigate how whiteness "governs the future."[5] By governing the future, according to Riyad Shahjahan and Kirsten Edwards, whiteness influences aspirations, ensures the conditions that make "it economically and culturally harmful to not invest" in, and most astutely, is malleable enough to seduce and liminally reward.[6] Necessarily, malleable whiteness, a "disembodied"[7] whiteness, an "elastic[]"[8] whiteness, creates a mirage of movement, "an orientation that puts certain things within reach"[9] while denying full membership and benefits to most countries and groups outside its original construction.

Therefore, in this chapter, I explore global whitening, the history of how different groups and countries captured whiteness, how some lost whiteness, and how others teetered unstably within and outside its margins. Whitening as a historical and geographic contingent formation changed over time, was insecurely captured, and created disparate advantages. To fully understand global whitening as a transnational form with regional and national fault lines we must, first, conceptualize whiteness across a global racial field. Figure 5.1 is a visualization of the global field of whiteness.[10] I draw some visual inspiration from Claire Jean Kim's "Racial Triangulation" figure[11] and expand her "field of racial positions"[12] broadly to the entirety of the global racial system. This expansion allows me to accentuate how racist modernity and empires racially placed all countries and groups across a global plane between whiteness and anti-Blackness. Countries and groups outside of traditional whiteness must navigate their historically determined racial "standpoint"[13] in a process Leila Tayeb calls a "geopolitically grounded [understanding of] whiteness."[14] This includes positioning specific national racial identity presentations within and as a reflection of "globally circulating formations of racial hierarch[ies]."[15]

The field of global whiteness positions demonstrates the hierarchical ordering of countries and groups determined by the historical and ongoing transnational racist constructions of white superiority and anti-Black inferiority. Hierarchical ranking is dictated by the racial inclusion or exclusion of global symbolic and material resources and the global racial perceptions of value. For countries and regions, the United States and western Europe are placed at the top, with South Asia and continental Africa outside of North Africa at the bottom. The middle, visualized in Figure 5.1 with a blurred gray circle under the plane rather than a triangle point as in Kim's diagram, represents the various countries and regions that are transnationally racialized "in-between," and maneuver along the plane depending on changing transnational racialization practices and/or how well they can step and move within the field, capture forms of white capital, and potentially racially separate from lower-placed countries. "Middleness" is a nuanced, complex, and intricate racial position. Middle countries and groups more commonly reflect certain embodied features and perceived inherent sociocultural traits.[16] Yet, middle countries and groups must negotiate their "triangulation(s)" within the gaze and motivations of global

FIGURE 5.1. **Global Field of Whiteness and Anti-Blackness**

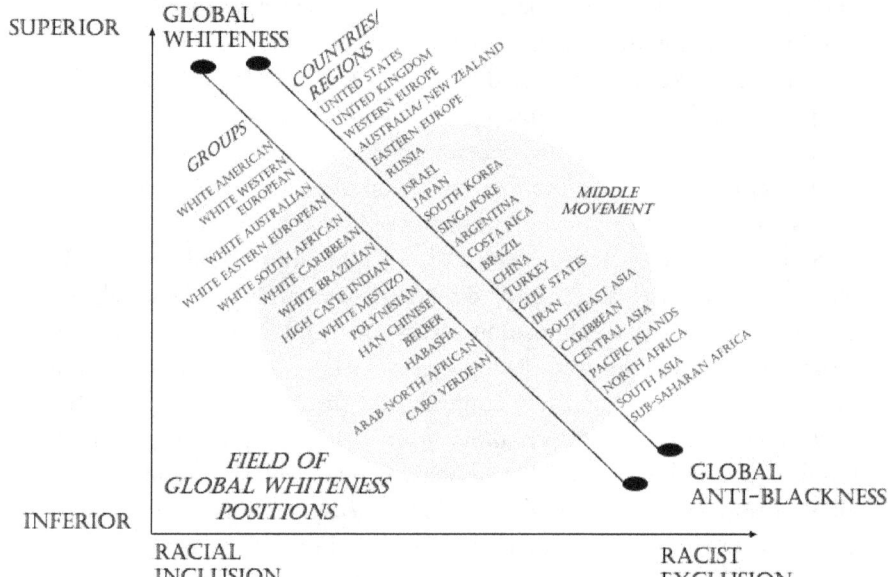

Source: Michelle Christian, "A Global Critical Race and Racism Framework: Racial Entanglements and Deep and Malleable Whiteness," *Sociology of Race and Ethnicity* 5, no. 2 (2019): 169–85. Copyright @ [2019] (Sage). [https://doi.org/10.1177/2332649218783220].

and national white favor that can be pulled at any minute. In the end, inhabiting the absolute property interests of whiteness, as Cheryl Harris notes, was always about the "absolute right to exclude."[17] The global field of whiteness is, therefore, a global "field of power"[18] that operates as an unequal force, an untenable desire, and in the global context of the cold reality of material racist devastation ensures many entangled racial states are coerced to participate to receive reprieve.

Groups within low-positioned countries can also find higher placement across the field. Racialized country group divisions, first manufactured through the colonial knowledge of racist empires, emboldened white colonists and settlers, and turned specific local groups (and imported groups) into test cases for disembodied white adjacency. National racial divisions thus emerged as "complementary-contradictory and tension laden" responses to intimate national negotiations with transnational racialization of both a country and discrete groups.[19] Many of these groups, as addressed in chapters 3 and 4, became the elite power players in their country's insertion in global capital circulations, transnational military relations, and as racial image makers. Therefore, all individuals, groups, and countries "attempt" to racially "locate themselves" at "national and international [field] levels."[20] Through this process, depending on their position, countries and groups try to either hold on to their racial ranking, shape the placement of others, or delicately maneuver within their placement.

Second, we must analyze how global whitening possibilities were in play when countries and groups captured material "white" capital and gained a higher structural position across the racial field. Capturing material white capital operated through several sometimes connected but at other times disjointed discrete contexts and mechanisms. Such mechanisms included: (1) *Categorical adjustable whiteness.* Specifically, the malleability of imperial, colonial, and state "white" categories and statures allowed some "nonwhite" and racial "intermediary" individuals, groups, and countries to wholly change their legal and/or social racial label and gain access to specific white material advantages. (2) *"White" body movements.* The imperially and historically state-supported transnational movement of white-perceived groups to new and forming national racial orders to fill specific socioeconomic roles made higher racial placement possible for groups who were adjacent to whiteness or questionably white and supported some countries' pursuit of national population whitening. (3) *White racialized skills.* Gaining access to imperially and colonially constructed advanced "civilizational" skills and credentials, such as western education standards,[21] language fluency,[22] and cultural norms, allowed some groups and countries to also gain socioeconomic opportunities and structural racial movement.

Third, we must examine how material "white" capital was transformed by countries into symbolic "white" value that was then presented and transnationally racially evaluated for global hierarchical placement along the plane.[23] The acquisition and communication of white material and symbolic capital is always a dialectic process. The presentation of symbolic whiteness works through revealing how a country or group shares in the "cultural codes"[24] of global whiteness that amount to the "modern values,"[25] which Jemima Pierre describes as "civilization, modernization, progress, and development" that also encode "moral" superiority.[26] In effect, through "social performances of [white] value," some countries package what Nina Bandelj and Frederick Wherry describe as a specific form of a "nation's cultural wealth."[27] Intrinsic to this production is also distancing away from groups and countries racialized lower in the racial field while also commonly economically relying on those racialized groups. Countries symbolically racially positioning "whiteness" further entailed the historic and contemporary enactment and enforcement of racial immigration and *de jure* and *de facto* spatial segregation policies. As countries, and dominant racialized groups in those countries, decide who can immigrate, who can naturalize, who are citizens, and which bodies can traverse across social boundaries, white material and symbolic geographies can form and reproduce.[28]

Lastly, we must always acknowledge whiteness's unsteady rewards. Any structural or symbolic gains garnered from maneuvering upward across the racial field was always unstable, always precarious, and always contingent on a multitude of embodied, structural, geographical, and temporal factors. White advantages achieved by a group in one geolocational standpoint may disappear in another. A country's hierarchical placement goes up or down depending on global geopolitical forces, transnational racial events, and the constantly evolving tactics and logics of global whiteness. Neda Maghbouleh's conceptualization of "racial hinges" and "racial loopholes" is helpful here. The concept of a racial hinge highlights how specific groups or countries may find, through a constellation of processes and with the tactics addressed above, that the door to whiteness may open but just as quickly close. In addition, even when some measure of whiteness is achieved, such as a higher country ranking, legal categorization, education status, or even aesthetic visual appeals, a "racial loophole" is present: racism is still experienced in different social systems and across scales and alternative geographies. The racial loophole ensures that achieving whiteness in one indicator does not necessarily translate to others.[29] Hence, liminal white groups and countries may achieve an elevated structural racial status in specific contexts and temporal moments, but most will never amount to a form of peak whiteness, a whiteness that is never questioned and always assumed.

In the remaining chapter I document the historical accordion movement of malleable whiteness for groups and countries. The properties and logics of whiteness changed depending on the needs of specific imperial goals and colonial geographies, globally circulating discourses of the day, and the geopolitical racial context of independent state formations and global power dynamics and competitions. White fungibility for groups and countries, and the varying ways groups and countries bought or fell into unstable whiteness, kept global white supremacy alive even when the perceived racial tapestry of whiteness expanded. I end the chapter with a contemporary example of country whitening through European Union expansion. The racial politics of expansion exposes how all potential country candidates are required to project and protect European whiteness.

Who, What, Where, Was *White?* A History of Unstable Racial Movement

Within the over four hundred years of racist modernity and empires the journey of whiteness was always in flux, always in contestation, but its elevated prominence was absolute. European imperial machinations, in competition and in partnership, constantly sought new grammars, new procedures, new "sorting techniques" to maintain control and justify rule.[30] When race became the ultimate organizational logic, and "white" racialization was placed atop the global racial hierarchy, who was white, what was white, and where was whiteness found were perpetually, desperately muddled. As addressed in chapter 1, racist science struggled to demarcate the categories of whiteness fixating and vacillating among broad categories, subcategories, and groupings and rankings within categories. The terms "Aryan," "Teutonic," "Nordic," "Alpine," "Caucasian," and "Anglo Saxon," jostled as broad white signifiers, with "Celt," "Mediterranean," "Hebrew," "Slavic," "Iberic," "Latin" more often referenced as a form of supposed "Orientalist whiteness"[31] that had lost some of its purity.[32] "White" was also typically not used as a "scientific" category but more as a descriptive adjective of phenotype within these racial essentialized terms.

Overlaying the geographic boundaries of whiteness was similarly jumbled. Europe became the ultimate definitive border, sealed most prominently in Linnaeus's tenth edition of *Systema Naturae* (1758) with "white" "Homo Europaeus." But where Europe began and ended was in dispute, as were the exceptions to the rule, and how to demarcate and define groups who supposedly descended from the historical movement of "white" bodies in and out of Europe. Blumenbach's "Caucasian variety" "included all inhabitants of Europe (except for Lapps and the remaining descendants of the Finns)" and "those of Eastern Asia . . . and Northern Africa."[33] Samuel Morton, who adopted Blumenbach's division in *Crania Americana* (1839), divided the "Caucasian Race" into "Caucasian," "Germanic," "Celtic," "Arabian," "Libyan," "Nilotic," and "Indostanic" "families" that were further divided into specific regional branches.[34] The geographic expanse of Morton's "Caucasian Race" encapsulated western and eastern Europe, the Gulf, North and Middle Africa, and South Asia. Augustus Keane's *The World's Peoples* (1908), whose ideas were cited in U.S. white legal petition cases, divided the "Caucasic or White Division" group between "Hamites," "Semites," "Aryans," and "Polynesian" who were spread out in "North Africa; most of Europe; parts of southwest and Central Asia; South Africa; parts of Siberia, Irania, India, Indo-china and Malaysia; Polynesia; Australia; New Zealand; [and] North and South America."[35] In addition to a lack of fixed spatial guideposts to racist science, the colonial cultural codes of whiteness interwove with "constructs identified as 'peoples,' 'nations,' 'cultures,'" and "citizens" where whiteness was often presumed in relation to nonwhiteness if not fully codified as such.[36]

Therefore, historical white ambiguity left room for white maneuverability. Maneuverability, nonetheless, could only go so far. Not all groups or regions could glide into whiteness, even if argued through "science" or "culture," because whiteness was never about science, geography, or virtue. It was always about power and ascription. European elites, Crown authorities, and later, European settlers in colonial then independent settler nations shaped and changed the parameters and axis points to whiteness as they saw fit. When white expansion occurred, however, it was typically anxiety-inducing for white colonial elites, allowed for only because of political or military necessity and vigorously fought against by colonialists when the Crown overrode their racial desires. Insecurity almost always followed for those who received new white privileges. Any discerned threat to white supremacy could provoke loss of newly acquired white advantages.

Colonial law, Crown and imperial legal statutes, and later white settler state formations were integral to how whiteness became endowed with its multilayered properties and how diverse legal categories that represented whiteness were carved, solidified, and challenged.[37] "White" began to enter the legal lexicon in the American colonies and in the Caribbean in the seventeenth and eighteenth centuries,[38] most prominently seen in slavery statutes and in determining who could vote, who could marry whom, and who could participate in militias. We also find various references to "white" in colonial documentation. Often, however, across diverse geographies, "white" was also obscured under the designation of "European," or nationality titles that dictated who was subject to European laws. Some non-Europeans labels, such as "Foreign Orientals," received access to some privileges under European laws.[39] Of consequence, legally petitioning for whiteness emerged in some eighteenth- and nineteenth-century Spanish, British, and French colonial geographies as an avenue for individual petitioners to make a legal case for white status.

PETITIONING FOR WHITENESS

Much of colonial Spanish Americas operated under *limpieza ordinances*, rules and legal provisions that gave alleged pure blood categories, "Spaniards and white creoles full civil rights and privileges," and barred nonenslaved mixed-race "*pardo*" and "*mulatto*" categories access to high-ranking professions, university studies, the priesthood, and from holding political office.[40] To receive these privileges some *castas* could pay a fee and request a *cédula de gracias al sacar*,[41] a royal decree that gave the petitioner permission to legally change an aspect of their racial condition, or change their racial title outright.[42] As addressed, medieval Spain already understood the possibility of individual social movement through the history of religious conversions and/or buying blood purity certificates. Historian Ann Twinam painstakingly documented forty petitions for whiteness in the last decades of the eighteenth century to the Council of the Indies, the supreme governing, legislative, and judicial authority over the Spanish Empire in the Americas.[43] There were multiple cases from Venezuela (13), Panama (9), Cuba (8), Guatemala (4), and Columbia (2), while Honduras, Mexico, Argentina, and Peru each had one.[44] Initial requests (seventeen of forty) were made without overt legislative guidelines dictating the procedure and only six asked for "total whiteness," or a legal change in racial identity.[45] Most petitions were requests for exemptions to receive a racial privilege typically only granted for whites.[46] Throughout the early decades of the eighteenth century a proto form of petitioning had already emerged when *castas* requested a "royal 'favor (*merced*)" to bypass a specific racist edict.[47] By 1795 the "new price list for the *gracias al sacar* petitions . . . included for the first time the option to buy whiteness."[48] "A *pardo* could become a Spaniard . . . for 500 *reales*."[49]

Petitioning took years and included letters of support, entreaties of service given to the Crown, and assertions of *naturaleza*, or a racially clean past. Looking at the case of Córdoba in Argentina, historian Erika Denise Edwards highlights "four hundred ecclesiastical and civil court courses" where African-descendent women sought strategies to "socially ascend"[50] by "declaring themselves Spanish or Indian"[51] to marry Spanish fiancés or "relied on an Indian identity"[52] to gain their and their children's freedom from bondage. Other examples of appeals to an imperial Crown for categorical whiteness include the Danish West Indies. In 1831 King Frederick VI issued a decree that some members of the "free colored class" should be able to become white in political standing after an in-person delegation of the free Black community traveled to Copenhagen to "air their grievances against Danish colonial society."[53]

In contrast to the direct appeals made to the Spanish or Danish Crowns, in the British Caribbean, notably Jamaica, petitioning for whiteness was "highly localized and ad hoc."[54] Because free people of African descent had limited ability to inherit money and/or property and held few rights in judicial proceedings, "private act" petitioning became one of the only legal options to change one's racial standing. Claimants made individual requests invariably highlighting their elite status, Christian upbringing, prominent connections, and "reputed" historical racial lineage[55] to the "colonial legislature for a private act" that would be "submitted to the Privy Council in Britain for confirmation."[56] Historian Brooke Newman found hundreds of people who solicited for whiteness with "twenty-five private acts [passed] between 1733 and 1760, granting 91 mixed race individuals some legal provisions of whiteness."[57] Samuel and Edith Hurwitz documented 128 bills passed throughout the entirety of the eighteenth century.[58] Whiteness was initially based on if a petitioner could prove they were at least three generations removed from African ancestry but later changed to four generations after Tacky's Slave Revolt in 1760.[59] If successful, privileges granted almost always carried "restrictions" and some individuals filed multiple petitions for additional rights.

Petitioning for whiteness was less practiced in French Saint-Domingue (Haiti), as many, particularly elite, light-skinned "Free People of Color" over generations, held some of the same property statuses of white French creoles. After French losses in the Seven Years' War (1756–63), however, historian John Garrigus argues, "French [colonists in] Saint Domingue refused to acknowledge the social and political 'whiteness'" of the once-accepted wealthy elite families.[60] Many of these families were reclassified as "*affranchis*," meaning "freemen" or "ex-slaves," throughout the 1770s and 1780s and lost the use of the respectable titles "*Sieur*" and "*Demoiselle*."⁶¹ Some petitioned locally to reclaim their social white status back, and pleaded their case directly to the French Crown, but the constructed threat they presented to traditionally white French creole elites and working-class French accelerated the hardening of racial divisions and the racial policing of public space. The treatment of Haiti's Free People of Color underscores the frailty of gaining some forms of white prestige. Across European colonies, as more people sought to "become white," or receive some privileges of whiteness, many white settlers, elite and nonelite alike, fought against whitening practices. In Venezuela, the political establishment issued an "*Obedesco pero no cumplo* (I obey but I won't comply)" against Spanish imperial whitening policy and "temporarily banned publication of the whitening clauses."⁶²

In the late nineteenth- and early twentieth-century United States, and the newly united Australia, nonwhite and non-Black racialized immigrants brought individual civil cases to challenge their exclusion from legal naturalization based on whiteness. Fifty-two cases, two going all the way to the Supreme Court, made it through the U.S. court system. The inexact moving target of whiteness was apparent as "applicants from Hawaii, China, Burma, and the Philippines . . . [and] all mixed race" individuals failed to become "white" whereas "applicants from Mexico and Armenia" were legally determined to be "white."⁶³ The courts vacillated in uncertainty on "petitioners from Syria, India, and Arabia."⁶⁴ In these cases, racist science, "common sense,"⁶⁵ and "humanistic race" (i.e., historical knowledge on culture and civilization)⁶⁶ interpretations of race were contradictorily deployed by both applicants and judges to shakily define the lines of whiteness.

Australian authorities looked to the court cases in the U.S. for guidance on its mainly Syrian/Lebanese applicants and determined the judgment on their whiteness was "inconclusive."⁶⁷ Inconclusivity, however, leaned toward acceptance. Discretionary provisions were added to the Australian Nationality Act of 1920 to accommodate Syrians, but not other racial groups, after a collective petition on behalf of the Syrian community was sent to the Australian government in 1909. As late as the 1960s, an individual white petition case was filed in South Africa. Chinese merchant Daniel Song petitioned the South African Population Registration Appeal Board in 1961 to be reclassified as "white" because he argued he fit the law's description of "generally accepted as a white person."⁶⁸ After winning his appeal, the Population Registration Amendment Act of 1962 added additional language to accentuate that a person is white only if they are "*not* generally accepted as a coloured person . . . or not in appearance *obviously* not a white person" (emphasis added).[69]

The U.S. and Australian white legal petition cases expose how whiteness was determined through an unsteady global alchemic mix of white scientific and quotidian logics, understood in contrast to global geopolitical nonwhite political foes, such as the Ottoman empire, and by extension Iran, and made socioreligious markers, like Christianity, a measure of global whiteness.[70] These cases, along with the eighteenth-century individual petitions for whiteness in Spanish, British, and French imperial geographies, and the mid-twentieth-century South African case, underscore how whiteness was understood through a global racial relational logic. Just what was a legally white racialized condition was almost always an unattainable moving target. Even with some insecure "successes" racial movement was repeatedly challenged and precarious.

Historical Group Racial Movement

Outside of individual legal petitioning to change one's racial status, it was more common for some varieties of historical group whitening to occur because of established imperial socio-political-economic racial processes that facilitated the possibility of three types of groups to change their racial stature, if not always their nonwhite racial identity. First, for some labor-economic designated groups positioned in European imperial divisions of labor, racial movement was a possibility. Second, some "Native" groups who achieved, in white colonialists' view, "civilization" capacity could potentially gain a higher racial status. Lastly, for different multiracial groups, some imperial and colonial legislative practices made achieving limited "white" rights possible, but forms of whiteness were also forcibly imposed. Consequently, group racial movement toward whiteness was made available because of specific structural conditions within the global racial system and its unfolding in specific colonial geographies. Sometimes groups actively participated in whitening, other times racial change reflected evolving global racialization dynamics in national racial architectures, and for others, aspects of whiteness were made "compulsory" and were devastating.[71]

IRISH, PORTUGUESE, JEWISH, SYRIAN/LEBANESE— AMBIGUOUS WHITENESS

Irish, Portuguese, Jewish, and Syrian/Lebanese groups traveled throughout European empires occupying distinct labor, economic, and military positions. Many, depending on geography and political context, were able to capture varying degrees of white standing. The Irish and Portuguese were traditionally closest to whiteness, as being Christian (but Catholic) Europeans, and of all the groups, ultimately became unmistakably white, but historical racial scientific designations of "Celtic" and "Iberian" Caucasian varieties labeled them as lesser whites and, in some nineteenth-century discourse, even separate races. Initially, the Irish were widely used as indentured laborers (but not enslaved) and/or were political prisoners in the Caribbean in the seventeenth century.[72] By the end of the seventeenth century, as Black enslavement and sugar cultivation increased, "ambiguous whiteness" turned into what Shirley Tate and Ian Law argue as "fully white within creole societies."[73] In contrast, Portuguese Catholics did not arrive in the Caribbean until the nineteenth century after the abolition of slavery. Although they had an empire, the Portuguese were somewhat racially distanced from other white European imperial powers. Portuguese emigrants came from the Portuguese-claimed islands of the Azores, Cabo Verde, and Spanish Madeira. Also indentured and contract workers, they labored in Guyana, Cuba, Trinidad and Tobago, and Hawaii. In Hawaii, 20,000 Portuguese arrived between 1878 and 1913.[74] Their status as "*lunas*" on plantations, intermediaries between Northern European supervisors, "*Haolo*" (white European descent) plantation owners, and East Asian and native Hawaiian laborers, placed them in a probationary white condition.[75] They were not "officially" white (they had a separate category in the census), but they became legally white, and were constructed as "good white citizen" candidates by the 1940 census and during the wider postwar era.[76]

Different Jewish groups also left the wider Iberian Peninsula, but as originally forcibly removed populations. Virtually all Jewish communities were expelled from western Europe by the end of the fifteenth century. By the end of the sixteenth century, however, a Jewish community formed in Amsterdam presumably because the Dutch assumed a shared "hostility toward a common [Spanish] enemy."[77] Ironically, expulsion created the possibility for "emancipation" and the potential for "full equality of citizenship"—but in the "New World."[78] Thus, in the new European overseas colonies, as whiteness was being developed, Jewish groups found they could gain rights not available in Europe.[79] The rise of the Netherlands as a maritime power, in competition with England and Spain, motivated new imperial settlement strategies. The Dutch West India Company (WIC) issued a "pledge of religious toleration" and the first Jewish community in the Americas was settled in then controlled Dutch Recife, Brazil, by 1637.[80] It would be Jewish settlement in Curaçao, with material support from WIC beginning in 1659, however, that became permanent and affluent. Jewish colonialist rights included "complete freedom of conscience, communal self-government . . . and acceptance as burghers."[81] Curaçaoan Jewish communities went on to become merchants and international traders and some participated in the trade and regional economy based on Black enslavement.[82]

Therefore, through economic and political structures in seventeenth- and eighteenth-century Dutch Caribbean, Jewish communities were able to gain a form of "whiteness."[83] "Jewishness," however, separated the group from elite Protestant whiteness and whiteness somewhat, if at all, for poor Jewish communities. Moreover, in Suriname, Jewish plantation owners became a global pro-abolitionist propaganda symbol of the "cruel planter"—as if distinct from white Protestant enslavers—and poor Jewish communities were depicted away from whiteness in the drawings by the famous Antwerp painter P.J. Benoit.[84] Across other European imperial geographies, Jewish rights were more mixed. Most imperial powers in the Caribbean colonies, nonetheless, racialized them more frequently as white or white-adjacent by the nineteenth century and many Jewish communities saw themselves as white as well.[85] The French view on Jewish rights shifted across time and colonial geographies. Most Jewish communities were expelled from the French Caribbean after 1685, but by the nineteenth century, within the white European settler political colonial landscape of Algeria, local Jewish groups received collective *"en bloc"* French citizenship in 1870 in contrast to Muslims.[86]

Where to draw the racial line or not between Jewish and Muslim designations was never clear for white colonialists and in the imperial metropoles. Jewish and Muslim identities were often collapsed as racially "Semitic" through scientific racism, but they were also variously separated as either a "Hebrew," "Jewish," or a "Mohammedan" race that meant something different depending on time, colonial power, and geographic context. Sephardic expelled Jewish groups versus Jewish groups present in Arab and Ottoman geographies, and later Ashkenazic Jewish communities fleeing Eastern European persecution—all could be racially constructed differently. The movement of Syrian/Lebanese[87] immigrants from the Ottoman empire during the late nineteenth and early twentieth century highlights the complex positioning of Arab whiteness and the role of Christian, Muslim, or Jewish affiliation. Although Syrian/Lebanese emigration from the Ottoman empire was "technically illegal," emigrants found ways to circumvent the ban, and by 1898 those in the Lebanon region could "travel freely" if they retained Ottoman citizenship.[88] Most who emigrated came from the Mount Lebanon area of what is now in the state of Lebanon and were Arab Christians. Landing in Latin America or the Caribbean, versus the U.S. or Australia, as the white petitioning cases attest, determined if Syrian/Lebanese were automatically racialized as white.

The almost 100,000 Syrian/Lebanese who entered Brazil, with Jewish groups, were white on arrival.[89] Although their emigration was not financially subsidized like European groups, they gained "unrestricted access to commercial resources and spaces available" to white Brazilians.[90] In contrast, Syrian whiteness had to be proven in the U.S. and Australia. Sarah Gualtieri argues that the diasporic Syrian community engaged in a transnational dialogue with each other and in the wider global Arab press to make sense of their global racialization, personal racial identities, and how it was disparately perceived across different geographies.[91] More often than not, appealing to whiteness—either through Christianity, the scientific Caucasian classification, evoking the Phoenician myth (see Country Racial Movement), or distancing from Asian and Black groups—was actively pursued within the diaspora. Moreover, broadly, Arab Christians were racialized differently from Arab and Turkish Muslims. Whiteness was accentuated in the former while an "Oriental" designation was more likely applied in the latter. Christianity became a white wedge to separate groups from suspect white regions. Jewish constructions were mixed. Jewish identities' connection to whiteness was more contingent on whether the emigrant group originated in European or Ottoman territories. As the strained U.S. and Australian acceptance of Syrian whiteness exposed, in Brazil it also its had limits. Following global eugenic immigration policy trends, by the 1930s Brazil's racial acceptance hardened and "Middle Eastern Catholics or European Catholic non-Aryans . . . were denied entrance to Brazil."[92]

Japanese groups never received the "white status" attributed to Irish, Portuguese, Jewish, and Syrian groups when they emigrated, but Japan's growing stature as a twentieth-century imperial power and modernizing economic powerhouse created distinct pathways for racial maneuvering. In Brazil, after being denied access to the U.S. because of anti-Asian laws, with Japanese government financial backing, large Japanese immigrant colonies were supported in São Paulo and Paraná by 1917.[93] Brazil would eventually become home to the largest Japanese diaspora community, the *Nikkei*. To spur trade with Japan, the small Japanese community in South Africa under the Apartheid regime received limited "honorary white" privileges vis-à-vis other "Asiatic groups" as it pertained to specific policies like the Group Areas Act.[94] Correspondingly, in French Indochina the Japanese were labeled *"Asiatiques assimilable,"* which gave them access to property ownership, in contrast to Chinese who were *"Asiatiques etrangers."*[95] Global Yellow Peril discourses, however, weakened Japanese advantages and by the mid-1930s Japanese immigration to Brazil[96] was limited, and debates on Japanese legal racial status in South Africa never really placed the Japanese on par with legal whiteness.

DUBIOUS COLONIAL CATEGORICAL PRESTIGE

The limits to gaining some features of white materiality for specific groups are particularly clear when we look at the improbable pathways of racial mobility within colonial racial architectures. As highlighted in chapter 2, creating hierarchical racial categorical orders in colonial geographies was paramount to white European imperial domination. Some groups were racialized closer to whiteness if the group was believed to be useful in the enforcement of colonial policy and rule. In Black African geographies, such as northern Nigeria, globally constructed Black inferiority was mitigated if the British determined the group in question, like the Fulani or Kanuri, had a "ruling race" ancestry connected to an ancient Aryan tie.[97] Similarly, the *Habasha*, the combined Amhara and Tigrayan speaking groups who were Orthodox Christian and from the Ethiopian highlands, now Eritrea, were uplifted by European colonial powers, particularly Italian, and constructed as embodying "Semitic origins" with European bodily features.[98] These "favorable" white proximal racialization perceptions were varyingly adopted by the groups and used to retain positions of power and resources; but these groups were never globally accepted as "white." Furthermore, anti-Blackness was weaponized against them at will to justify evolving colonial economic and military priorities. Thus, white European racial esteem and higher colonial racial placement were always contingent on white supremacist imperial beliefs and geopolitical interests.

The development of the colonial categories of "*assimilado*" (Portuguese) and "*évolué*" (French and Belgium) underscores how the colonial straitjacket of white standards ensured that "*indigène*" or "native" movement to a constructed assimilated and civilized condition was always unsettled and never quite racially available. These terms gained traction in the period of late colonialism when the Portuguese and French were adamant to build and retain their colonies by declaring their practices were civilizing forces of good. The formal recognition of *assimilado* status in the Portuguese Colonial Act of 1930 was based on the attainment of specific education and financial abilities and Portuguese cultural adoptions.[99] Elite, light-skinned Cabo Verdeans, "*Brancos de terra*, or whites of the land," were widely considered *assimilado*, and used "as the colonial administration's *lançados*, or middlemen in imperial trade"[100] throughout Portuguese African territories, but most Black indigenous groups in Guinea, Angola, and Mozambique remained officially "uncivilized."[101] Goans, Christianized Hindu elites or self-proclaimed Portuguese descendants from Portuguese-controlled Goa in southwest India, like Cabo Verdeans, similarly filled colonial roles in Portuguese African territories.[102] Goans were also recruited by the British colonial government in East Africa to occupy clerical roles above Black East Africans and "Indians."[103] Many Goan traveling elites fully identified with Portugal, and in particular ways a specific form of Goan whiteness, but they were always placed outside a traditional Portuguese white identity and later British white identity. When Goans in East Africa sought British subject status after the inclusion of Goa in the Indian Union in 1961,[104] they found a British passport would not protect them from white British racism when they immigrated to the United Kingdom in the 1970s.

The *évolué* title in French and Belgium colonial geographies demarcated those colonial subjects who through education and cultural adoption of European values could potentially achieve citizenship status, colonial administrative positions, and special privileges only white Europeans had access to, like white-only café patronage and skilled work. The category was applied in French Caribbean colonies and West and Equatorial African colonized geographies but took on specific resonance in the Belgium

Congo. The calamitous human atrocities of King Leopold's Congo Free State (1885–1908), where ten million Africans were killed in pursuit of ivory and rubber, forced the Belgium government when they took over colonial authority to globally project an image of a "model colony" with "model subjects."[105] During the Free State period the term "*immatriculé*" had been established to separate "traditional" Africans from those who practiced a "Christian and Western lifestyle."[106] *Immatriculés* were governed by the Belgium civil code and received more rights. Acquiring *évolué* status, and the imperial white rights it provided, nonetheless, was always "inherently incomplete" and "deeply humiliating," according to Patrice Lumumba's daughter, as racist maxims guaranteed a continuous moving target of who, and what combination of tests and criteria, represented an *évolué*.[107]

MULTIRACIAL UNCERTAINTIES

Some colonial mixed-race populations gained strained racial movement toward white-protected rights, but racist fear of miscegenation and racial degeneracy, together with the horrific role of white patriarchal sexual violence across geographies, rendered most multiracial groupings firmly outside the boundaries of whiteness. In the early period of colonialism, when company mercantilism dominated, the Dutch, British, French, and Portuguese had looser positions on cross-racial intimacies, even marriage, if it could help secure local power and allegiances.[108] In early Spanish territories, the Crown allowed some marriages with indigenous women if "it secured Spanish settlement."[109] But racial stigma and shaky rights followed for the children from many of these relationships.

"Anglo-Indians" in British East India Company territories petitioned the British parliament and different jurisdictions of the Company state to challenge the restrictions placed on their status, and argued for the use of the category (and have the rights) of "colonial Britons."[110] The "Indo-Dutch" in Indonesia were able get the legal status of *Indische Nederlanders* (Indies Dutchmen), and in postindependence Indonesia after immigration to the Netherlands, many were able to move outside the construction of "*allochtonen.*"[111] In early Spanish colonies, as cross-racial *casta* designations multiplied, so did unease about the ambiguity of categorization and the spread of "*mala sangre*" (tainted blood).[112] The "*mestizo*" label took on different meanings, and represented divergent access to privileges, across Spanish colonial spaces. In the Spanish-governed Philippines, Elaine Laforteza documents how the term "*ilustrados* (meaning 'the enlightened ones')" was an amalgamation of *mestizos* who favored "Castilian ways" while exerting "sovereignty in colonial society."[113] Filipino *mestizos* included Chinese and Spanish variants, but as Spanish mestizos gained "ascendency within colonial society" a performance of mestizo whiteness was required to advance Filipino national identity.[114]

With the rise of scientific racism during late colonialism in the nineteenth century, and particularly in the interwar periods of the twentieth century, mixed-race populations came to embody a white purity biological threat. Yet, depending on the empire, and whether cultural European adoption and the whiteness of the father was emphasized, forced assimilation created new colonial placements. Throughout the French empire "*Métis*" groups held different colonial roles where markers including "class, racial characteristics, and fluency (or lack thereof) in French language and culture" impacted colonial French attitudes and positions in colonial society.[115] The practice of coercively or forcibly removing *Métis* children in French Indochina under the guise of "protection societies," modeled on Dutch "Eurasian welfare" practices, brutally enforced whiteness.[116] In the Belgium Congo and Ruanda-Urundi, around 20,000 mixed-race children were kidnapped and raised in Catholic missionary orphanages "to guarantee complete assimilation to European culture"[117] and after 1959 taken to Belgium where many remained stateless.[118] These colonial practices in Africa and Asia echo the violent devastation wrought by indigenous child removals in Australia, Canada, and the U.S.

Moreover, anti-Blackness was closely affiliated with the treatment of mixed-race children. Historically, the fusion of enslavement with Blackness established that the children born from sexual violence and rape committed against enslaved women would follow the status of their mothers. For varying multiracial free Black men and women, as the individual petition cases show, attainment of any white resource was constantly mitigated by white proclamations of perceived debased African ancestry. After the global abolishment of slavery, anti-Blackness persisted through the global "afterli[ves] of slavery," with one of its effects seen in the experiences of Black mixed-race colonial subjects.[119] *Métis* mixed-race children in Vietnam whose fathers were Indian and African French colonial soldiers were not considered to hold the same possibility of becoming "racially French" as "Eurasian children" during the interwar period.[120] After the rise of the Vietnamese Revolution in the mid-1940s, France tried to challenge colonial independence movements by symbolically positioning a constructed colorblind French imperial community where all mixed-race children, regardless of the race of the father, could be united in a common French culture, but anti-Blackness persisted.[121]

When Germany entered the African imperial project, fixing the supposed problem of generations of African mixed-race unions was paramount. The *Rehobothers,* descendants of Dutch Boer settlers and Nama groups, had already adopted European practices—spoke Cape Dutch, practiced the Dutch Reform faith, and emphasized their European ancestry—before Germans claimed South West Africa.[122] The *Rehobothers*, and the further mixed unions that came from their descendants, along with other mixed-race populations, were too African to gain any German rights in colonial rule. Marriages once accepted, where the wife and children were, for example, priorly classified as British and/or legally or socially known as "white," were now reclassified as "native" by the Germans.[123] Some German husbands wrote letters proclaiming the white virtues and white physical features of their families to demand that their German patriarchal citizenship rights be restored.[124] Broadly, we find in German and Italian late colonial orders an obsession with embodied whiteness, where to get citizenship rights if you were mixed race meant you had to be one "who looks the character someone qualified as 'white'" for Germans,[125] and "show on their body" the presence of biological whiteness through "craniometrical tests" for Italians.[126]

Thus, the adjudication and dispersion of any white rights, privileges, or legal statutes for any group was most always ascertained by how far one was perceived to be physically or culturally removed from Blackness. Consequently, the selective group expansion to some of the material opportunities of whiteness always protected and maintained the global racial hierarchy.

Historical Country Racial Movement

Historically within the global racial system most transnationally racialized nonwhite geographies were either colonized, targets for colonization, or fended off colonization by embracing the uneasy logics of global whiteness. Whiteness was the determinant through which imperial greatness was measured and cordoned off which countries had the "right to assume statehood," self-government, and join the family of nations.[127] Thus, all countries from the mid-eighteenth to mid-twentieth centuries, at the peak of racist science and global European imperial dominance, in one way or the other, had to pursue a relationship with whiteness to justify their independence and separate from those countries at the racial bottom to gain upward traction across the global racial plane. This new global era of "institutionalized whitening," described by Erika Denise Edwards, was informed by historic ongoing imperial formations and the individual practices described above.[128] Without a doubt, the whitening strategies pursued by the new independent states run by Anglo white settler elites, like in the U.S., set the global template and also had the power to transnationally racialize other countries out of whiteness.

WHITE SETTLER STATES' CONSOLIDATION OF WHITENESS

Former European colonial white settler spaces, where white settlement was a tool of colonial management, implemented a series of imperial, immigration, citizenship, and labor measures to retain and further whiten their landscape and shore up new white national identities when they became independent. Quickly after the ratification of the U.S. Constitution, where Black enslavement was allowed to continue, and the infamous 3/5 comprise was reached, the 1790 Naturalization Law codified "free white person" as a requirement for naturalization.[129] Moreover, to fulfill its "manifest destiny" of regional white rule, the U.S. purchased western territory from France in 1803, went to war with Mexico and Spain and gained half of Mexico's territory in 1848 and most of Spain's remaining colonies in 1898, and overthrew Hawaii's monarchy in 1893 and annexed its territories in 1898.[130]

This imperial performance of whiteness, however, came with new nonwhite populations that needed to be managed and controlled and produced hotly contested debates over who could be "white," and how to whiten these areas most quickly. With the 1848 Treaty of Guadalupe Hidalgo Mexicans received citizenship at the federal level, a form of "legal whiteness," but were socially considered "not white," or what Laura Gómez refers to as "off-white," and their federal racial status was challenged in states.[131] In fact, Gómez argues that whether if and how quickly a new U.S. territory was able to change its racial demography through new white settlement determined if the territory was considered worthy of statehood.[132] Therefore, the U.S. pursued a broad encompassing whitening project through subsidized internal white migration, confining indigenous groups to reservations or marked nonwhite racialized space, and by limiting the movement and/or rights of nonwhite groups in the territories and states, and excluding them from the wider United States.

Like the U.S., rendering full citizenship a privilege of whiteness was one of the chosen necessary paths to whiten in Australia and New Zealand as well. Avowed global white supremacist and eugenics advocates like Madison Grant and Lothrop Stoddard believed that "all the white regions of the new world won by white expansion over the previous four centuries" were in jeopardy unless they stopped the "color migration peril."[133] As addressed in chapter 2, Yellow Peril fears helped spur broad transnational anti-Asian policies, but these policies also simultaneously facilitated national whitening. When the Commonwealth of Australia was created in 1901, unifying the Australian colonies, the new country immediately embarked on a series of policies that sought to restrict immigration from non-European countries and "build a strong prosperous society founded upon the principle of [white] racial and cultural homogeneity."[134] The Immigration Restriction Act, the Post and Telegraph Act, and the Pacific Island Labourers Act, all in 1901, with the 1903 Naturalization Act, collectively became the "White Australia Policy" that would last in various capacities until the 1970s.[135] The Australian "white nation fantasy," according to Ghassan Hage,[136] made it possible that by 1947, "99 percent of Australians were white, and 90 percent were of Anglo-Celtic origin."[137]

Less acknowledged is New Zealand's more "flexible," and what P.S. O'Connor describes as a "cleverer," "White New Zealand" policy that mostly evaded scrutiny by being "carefully designed" through discreet mechanisms to prevent the settlement of Asians, particularly South Asians fleeing Fiji after their period of indenture. These policies, along with similar ones in Canada and the Johnson-Reed Act of 1924 in the U.S., globally represented the will and power former white settler British colonial states yielded to build prosperous white independent geographies and ascend in the global racial hierarchy of nations.

Of course, these countries were never really white, and continued to rely on exploited nonwhite labor and resources from once indigenous lands to industrialize and grow, but the policy web of white supremacy maintained almost complete subordination of Black, indigenous, and First Nations' rights even if those groups were technically able to be "citizens."[138] Furthermore, the ideological work, along with drastically increasing the white racial demography of these geographies, effortlessly made whiteness symbolically naturalized with these national identities. Even for suspect white groups particularly in the U.S., roughly a million had already entered the U.S. as initially constructed "free white persons" before they were targeted with restrictions in the 1924 Act, and by the second half of the twentieth century were structurally incorporated into the white American ideal and distanced themselves, and at times, proactively reproduced anti-Black racism.[139] Toni Morrison wrote that "the organizing principle of becoming an American" was to partake in the deceits of whiteness.[140]

STATES ON THE MARGINS OF WHITENESS

Outside of white settler states, Ireland was another country whose premodern British-colonized history made its official country whitening in the early twentieth century even more instructive in showing how European racialized liminal whiteness was nonetheless still hierarchically above embodied nonwhite spaces and groups. During the debates for Irish Home Rule in 1866 and 1893–94 there was an "unambiguous" acceptance of Ireland as "white" from both British advocates and Irish nationalists, even if Irish nationalists asserted a "Celtic race" and English anti-Irish prejudice existed.[141] Irish whiteness, moreover, had already been revealed through the white racial necessity of the Irish diaspora in bolstering the European imperial rule addressed above.

Countries more racialized outside of whiteness, like Japan, attempted to structurally whiten by beating Europe at its own imperial game, and some non-Japanese elites globally promoted "Japan as Asia's 'white' country,"[142] and therefore worthy of equal international standing as fellow "white countries," even as Japan was largely excluded from global whiteness. Other countries like Iran, although transnationally racialized as "Aryan," were supposedly hurt by racial degeneration due to Arab and Mongol invasions. Iran was never colonized by Europeans but had lost much of its ancient empire. Iran's nationalist elite during the Pahlavi State era (1925–79), according to Reza Zia-Ebrahimi, were inspired by European racial thought and believed that the only way to circumvent "Iran's weakness" was to "eliminate the heritage of Arabs and Islam and reestablish racial and cultural purity" in Iran.[143] Therefore, the country embarked on a global image campaign that centered a Persian white identity away from Arabness.

Transnationally racialized Arab and Ottoman inferiority, and the use of inferred whiteness to solicit for autonomy, and, ultimately, statehood, took a particular form in the creation of Lebanon and its separation from Syria. Although "Syria" under the Ottoman empire was viewed as "Arab," under French scholarly influence Christian Maronites began to advocate for the creation of a Greater Lebanon encompassing Beirut under French protection.[144] Greater Lebanon was then administered separately from Syria during the French Mandate period (1923–46) following World War 1 and the ideology of "New Phoenicianism," encouraged by the French, "flourished."[145] The proclaimed "myth of Phoenicia" made Christian Lebanese the Phoenicians' ancestors and therefore the descendants of peoples who had helped build western European civilization, distinct from Arab Syrian Muslims.[146] "The term 'Phoenician' itself is a Greek invention" broadly encompassing maritime trading groups around 1200 BCE from Levantine ports who went on to establish settlements across the Mediterranean all the way to the Atlantic coast of Spain.[147] According to Josephine Quinn, "The Phoenicians provided an attractive prototype and parallel for the new state as well as a convenient alternative to Arab origins."[148] These narratives of glorious ancient pasts and advanced civilizational qualities, a preracial era callback strategy commonly evoked by other countries (and groups) navigating racialization, were further "crystalized" in the Syrian/Lebanese diaspora, who, as noted, struggled for whiteness in some new host geographies, and then further circulated back to "homeland communities."[149]

Bulgaria, inferiorly racialized as "Slavic" and/or hopelessly "'semi civilized' with racial mixtures"[150] from 500 years of Ottoman rule, similarly sought whiteness after it received independence from the Ottoman empire in 1878. Bulgarian nationalists, supported by western-trained intellectuals, Miglena Todorova argues, pursued a modernizing project to communicate to a white global audience that Bulgarians were biologically "white" (if mixed with multiple European "races"), "European," and had an advanced cultural civilization in contrast to the globally circulating and nationally adopted anti-Black and anti-Asian beliefs, and from the Roma and Jewish populations in its border.[151] "In the postsocialist period, Bulgarian claims to genetic and cultural Europeanness [were] equally important in the face of external . . . power" as western Europe looked to mark the E.U.'s boundaries of whiteness (see European Union expansion).[152]

Lastly, partial narrative justifications prior to and after Israel acquired statehood in 1948 included entreaties of global European racial ideas by some European and American leaders[153] and were adopted by some political thinkers.[154] Palestine, once under Ottoman rule before the British Mandate of Palestine (1920–48), was a majority multicultural population embedded in a wider region weary of new European imperial possibilities after not receiving independence following the fall of the Ottoman empire. For some Jewish thinkers, embracing the racial science and *volk* constructions of a "Jewish race" (although debated, with most Jewish intellectuals representing an "ambivalence" with the idea that then turned to distancing from after Nazi atrocities),[155] and supporting Jewish European colonialism in Palestine, was a way to negotiate antisemitism but also symbolically linked it to European cultural advancement.[156] Therefore, finding colonial solutions as one avenue to mitigate anti-Jewish acts and "violent repression" came out of the prevailing "national colonial habitus" of Europe at the time, contends Areej Sabbagh-Khoury.[157] Under the British-mandate Jewish organizations, land acquisition and spatial segregation strengthened, supported by a controlled, advanced immigration policy, making Jewish populations better able to develop "a semi-government apparatus" with eventual statehood.[158]

"Jewishness" was always a complicated racial marker, taking on different forms in or out of whiteness in specific colonial territories and/or being racialized outside of whiteness throughout much of Europe, culminating in the horrors of Nazi-conducted racial genocide. The United Nations 1947 partition plan to create separate Arab and Jewish states rejected by Palestinian Arab leaders, to be followed by decades of conflict and increased Israeli Jewish settlement in occupied territories, thus needs to be placed in the wider global historical context of European anti-Jewish racism and violence, global anti-Arab racial perceptions, and the rise of modern nationalisms scarred by, responding to, and acquiescing to colonial and postcolonial racial formations.[159]

STATES YEARNING FOR *BLANQUEAMIENTO*

As I highlighted with the case of Costa Rica at the beginning of the chapter, a group of mostly formerly Spanish colonized countries pursued a series of whitening immigration policies, modern "liberal" nation-building strategies, and white image cultivation discourses in the nineteenth and early twentieth centuries to challenge inferior transnational racialization centered on critiques of their supposed degenerate, mixed-race populations. *Blanqueamiento*, already practiced individually and in some Spanish Crown territories via royal decree or Spanish emigration, became a regionwide state strategy to put an end to "post-independence political turmoil," which was attributed to "racial deficiencies," develop modern institutions and practices, and thwart the budding U.S. imperial threats.[160] The hope was that by *mejorando la raza* (improving the race)[161] new dynamic national cultures and bodies that reflect whiteness could be fostered. Inspired and challenged by European and American scientific racist propositions and racial civilization hierarchies, elites in geographies pursued a modified form of "positive eugenics" to change local-national racial conditions. Encouraging and subsidizing European immigration was considered key. Ten to eleven million Europeans arrived between 1880 and 1930 with Brazil, Cuba, Uruguay, and Argentina receiving 90 percent of immigrants.[162] To varying degrees, immigrants were financially subsidized with transportation costs, given land grants, allowed autonomy over some municipal affairs, and were ushered into skilled work.[163]

Not all countries could make national whitening a reality or had only partial "success." The complementary ideology of *mestizaje* (see chapter 6) was pursued in tandem especially in the geographies whose demographics and national racial fault lines required alternative strategies to inferior transnational racialization. Brazil, where elites were extremely unnerved about having the largest African-descendent population in the Americas, implemented its *branqueamento* policies by creating the "most extensive legislative network of racial restrictions to regulate race after the abolition of slavery"[164] of any country in the region and encouraged over four million European emigrants, mostly from Portugal, Italy, and Spain,[165] to emigrate between 1872 and 1972. The most whitening Brazil could accomplish, nonetheless, was the white racialization of the southern states and controlling and policing access in the public domain. Cuba, similarly, had received over one million Spanish immigrants after it was granted independence by Spain, but the Afro-descendent population was simultaneously large, politically active, and, therefore, according to Tanya Hernández, attempts at *blanqueamiento* also included violent Black repression in the decades leading up to the Cuban Revolution.[166]

The U.S. was also mostly not interested in elites' regional whitening goals, particularly in Central America, Cuba, Dominican Republic, and Venezuela, as it already saw the region as inferior and racially nonwhite and was, thus, more interested in the availability of a cheap racialized labor force to work in U.S.-foreign direct investment–led export agriculture, extractive economies, and to construct the Panama Canal. To that end, U.S. global capitalists imported Black workers from the Caribbean to work the agriculture fields and dig the canal to the consternation of local white mestizo workers and national governments. Puerto Rico's pushback against U.S. regional racial dominance was a specific form of numerical whitening. In the decades after the U.S. acquired Puerto Rico from Spain, Puerto Rican census enumerators "subverted" the racial rigidity of U.S. racial classifications by classifying more Puerto Ricans as "white."[167] Already before the U.S. takeover, according to Emigh, Ahmed, and Riley, "liberal Puerto Rican elites promoted a single racial category, such as *'raza de color' 'hombres de color,'* or *'clase de color'*" that accelerated the whitening of the population after Spanish independence by "silencing the categories of Black."[168]

Argentina, Chile, Uruguay, and Costa Rica were the most symbolically successful at eventually becoming regionally and globally known as the "whitest" Latin American countries. Argentina, particularly under the political and intellectual leadership of Domingo Faustino Sarmiento (1868–1874), would go on to support the emigration of one million Europeans between 1880 and 1900.[169] Sarmiento was a regional intellectual, and once ambassador to the U.S., who wrote *Facundo: Civilización y barbarie* (Civilization and barbarism, 1845) and *Conflicto y armonías de las razas en América* (Conflict and harmonies of races in America, 1883). His views were emblematic of the tension and historic arc of white *criollo* elite-led *blanqueamiento* policies. Even with following European models, and supposedly fostering new national white blood lines, although in keeping with the "Black Legend" there was debate about the racial quality of "Spanish" and "Portuguese" immigrants, the region would always fall short of global, particularly, American Anglo-Saxon white judgment, nonetheless. Still, as Juliet Hooker argues, Sarmiento thought, "The only way to counter U.S. dominance was for Latin America to emulate it where race was concerned."[170] This meant for Sarmiento that by the 1880s his recommendations centered on following the polygenist ideas of Agassiz and stopping racial mixture, enhancing white local political equality, and keeping Black and indigenous communities out of the body politic as necessary for independent country survival and growth.[171]

Another pivotal factor to *blanqueamiento* was the discursive cultural work done by countries in tandem with exclusionary immigration policies "to favourably position [their national identities] above their neighbors [who had an] 'Indian' or 'Black' problem."[172] Just as Europeans were encouraged settlers through legislation, African-descendent groups were legislatively banned from entry or their movement was tightly restrained, and nonwhite regions of the countries were cut out of national identity cultural formation or their cultural production was whitened, like with Argentinian tango.[173] Eventually, over time, Buenos Aires became the "Paris of the New World," Chile was the "British of the Pacific," and Uruguay the "Switzerland of South America."

European Union Expansion and Centralizing Whiteness

More recently, the ability of "peripherally white" European countries to whiten via acceptance into the European Union community highlights the contemporary racial politics at play within the hierarchies of whiteness across a continent transnationally already positioned as "white." Since its proto-postwar founding with its six original country members in the late, supposedly decolonizing 1950s,[174] with the Treaties of Rome and the birth of the European Parliament, to its first enlargement in 1973 with Denmark, Ireland, and the U.K., to the subsequent 1980s enlargement of Greece, Spain, and Portugal after their dictatorships ended, to the post–Cold War expansion era of the 1990s, culminating with the largest period of expansion in the 2000s, when thirteen Central European and Balkan states subsequently joined, the core project of the European Union has been about rearticulating and preserving the "subject position of whiteness."[175] But, as already highlighted, since Europe's inception as a co-constitutive global racial idea and racial imperial practitioner, Europe was also an epistemological and geopolitical conflict zone where the various battles to define the articulations and degrees of difference within the hierarchies of whiteness were staged. Spain, and somewhat Portugal, were imperially scarred by the "Black Legend," Greece by the "Turks," Southern Italians by their proximity to "Africa," while Central and Eastern Europe and the Balkan Peninsula historically represented what scholars of the region describe as being racialized outside "the lands of western European Whiteness."[176] The lands east to west were placed at ambiguous "in-between" stages where historical Ottoman, Russian, or so-called "Oriental" influences made them ostensibly beyond the "borderlands of civilization, modernity, and progress."[177]

Yet, engagement with and ultimate acceptance into the European Union offered an outlet, a way for racially suspect Europeans to "strive toward [full whiteness and] become modern deserving subjects within wider intra-European hierarchies."[178] National whitening via European Union expansion (see table 5.1) is, therefore, possible when candidates adhere to a "conditionality regime"[179] that includes: (1) implementing required institutional mechanisms that follow the standards and procedures of western European values and rules; (2) introducing shared border policing and immigration management systems to protect and maintain Europe's exclusive borders; and (3) acquiescing to and practicing what Ivan Kalmar describes as the regional racial politics surrounding the "scale of prestige."[180] The scale of prestige ensures that regardless of whether white conditional countries embraced what József Böröcz describes as either "eurowhiteness" or "dirty whiteness," they all demand to be recognized as "white," definitively with the E.U., and distinct from the next country lower on the scale.[181] Of course, whitening as a process produces disparate rewards across the cartographies of the European borderland. The E.U. member privileges awarded, or partial privileges for "candidate" countries, are distributed and controlled by the traditionally white imperial elite states who also enact the "scale of prestige" supranationally, and when peripherally white bodies, despite being E.U. members, cross into its borders.

The fortification, policing, and either acceptance or rejection of certain types of traveling racial bodies across Europe's frontiers stand as the vanguard mechanism in which whiteness is practiced and solidified. The term "Fortress Europe" has been used since the 1980s to describe the hardening of the E.U. external borders as internal borders soften and requires new security procedures with each new global racial event.[182] These procedures include the vast network of "waiting zones, camps, new fences, new biometric methods of control," rapid border intervention teams (RABITs), the deployment of "various boats, helicopters, and planes,"[183] and as addressed in chapter 3, the use of North African countries as E.U. border enforcers. The visual, visceral assemblage of "border work"[184] manifests in "1800km of walls and fences either built or under construction," with the connected tools of heavily armed border guards who deploy sound cannons, loudspeakers, tear gas, along with other techniques to collectively terrorize migrants.[185] Since 2014 over 27,000 deaths occurred enroute to Europe, according to a 2021 report from the International Organization

TABLE 5.1. European Union Membership Expansion

Original Members	1970s Expansion	1980s Expansion	1990s Expansion	2000s Expansion	Candidate Members
Belgium	Denmark	Greece	Austria	Bulgaria	Albania
France	Ireland	Portugal	Finland	Cyprus	Bosnia and Herzegovina
Germany	UK (Leave 2020)	Spain	Sweden	Czechia	Moldova
Italy				Estonia	Montenegro
Luxembourg				Hungary	North Macedonia
Netherlands				Latvia	Serbia
				Lithuania	Türkiye
				Malta	Ukraine
				Poland	Georgia
				Romania	**Potential Candidates**
				Slovenia	Kosovo
				Slovakia	
				Croatia (2013)	

for Migration, with over 3,000 deaths since the beginning of 2021.[186] The depth and weight of "racial violence" across E.U.'s white racially manufactured borders is immense.[187]

Required symbolic and literal border violence, by first candidate countries and then member countries, is executed to defend the inhabitants of the border-free Schengen Area.[188] The "so-called white Schengen list," which marks who has visa free access to visit or transit through Schengen countries, versus those who do not on the "black Schengen list," is stunningly racially clear, and strikingly anti-Black.[189] Almost all North and South America, along with Australia, New Zealand, Malaysia, Japan, South Korea, along with various designations of British identities, are on the "white" list.[190] All of Africa, the Middle East, South Asia, Southeast Asia, Central Asia, China, and Russia, and much of the Caribbean are on the "black list."[191] Thus, racial threat is tagged and marked on regions depending on geographic proximity and ascribed fear of political instability. Moreover, those racialized nonwhite countries who have visa-free access represent a form of material visa whitening,[192] just as large economic investments in some E.U. geographies can lead to second citizenships and/or residency whitening.[193] Similarly, British, and other former imperial citizenship designations in now independent former colonial territories, allow for those (mostly) white persons in nonwhite racialized geographies access to the E.U., and depending on their legally defined nationality, provide the potential for an E.U. passport.[194]

Of all the countries that became members in the 2000s expansion, Slovenia and then Croatia, the last country to enter in 2013, represent a fealty to the E.U. "Return to Europe" call, along with an identification with the *antemurale myth,* and its connection to whiteness, the most.[195] The antemurale myth echoes back to early modern European discourses where certain countries act as a "'bulwark' of European and Christian civilization" in relation to the threats posed by its closest neighbors.[196] Slovenia and Croatia contrast themselves from their fellow former Yugoslavian states (who remain in E.U. "Candidate" or "Potential Candidate" status) and define themselves as western Europe's stewards in a religious and racially suspicious zone. These countries' expansion acceptance is particularly different from Turkey's. The never-ending cultural, religious, and racial conjectures surrounding Turkey's debated admission have kept the country in a thirty-six-year purgatory stalemate. Various public opinion polls throughout the Continent over the years show how many Europeans were "against Turkey's advancement."[197] These fears were lumped into the repertoire of racist imagery used by the Leave campaign to also justify U.K.'s needed separation from the E.U. Throughout its accession debate, Turkey was constructed as both a needed "bridge(head)," "role model," and "security buffer" to and from the "Arab world" and culturally "not European," essentially not white.[198]

Turkey historically tried to challenge its separation from whiteness with overtures in racial science (see chapter 6) and by the mid-1990s–2000s "White Turk" discourses emanating mostly from Istanbul positioned Turkey as a "pro-Western" "more civilized" country "different from its Middle Eastern" neighbors. The Justice and Development Party's (AKP) rise and its perceived backpedaling on "democratic norms," despite passage of multiple reform packages, helped to erode accession negotiations. Still, the E.U. needs Turkey now more than ever. Not as an equal E.U. member, however, but as the ultimate outside "buffer state."[199] An E.U.-Turkey deal signed in summer 2015, followed by funding in the billions of euros, "prevents migrants from leaving Turkish shores," returns migrants who crossed from Turkey to the Greek islands back to Turkey, and calls on Turkey to "prevent irregular migration from its territory" into the E.U.[200] Turkey currently houses over 3.5 million Syrian refugees and over 300,000 asylum seekers from other countries. Effectively, Turkey's role shields and protects European whiteness while ensuring that Turkey never becomes a central member. Turkey may not be "Arab," but it is "Muslim" and forever tied to the racialization of the Ottoman empire and the racial designation of the "Turk."[201] Therefore, shaky whiteness continues to shape and define its country racial movement limitations.

Unstable Racial Hinges

The malleability of whiteness, and potential for group and country racial movement, must be placed in its historical formation; local, state, regional, and global hierarchies; and relationally, proximally understood. The global field of whiteness is not static, but it is also not so loose and open that anyone and anyplace can achieve "whiteness." Whiteness is policed and guarded to ensure that there is always someone and someplace below to serve as the racial reference point to distance from. These below points across the racial field represent the cultural and phenotypical traits outside of whiteness attached to groups and countries variously symbolically and structurally placed either in the middle, closer to, or at the bottom where the global articulation of anti-Blackness is secured.

"Whitening" for most was also never about becoming "white" in the absolute sense. For the somewhat definitive cases where "total whiteness" in some contexts was secured, like the Irish and Portuguese, it is best to understand them as examples, where according to Ivan Kalmar, the group never "really need[ed] to 'become white,' but did struggle, successfully, to become *'more white.'*" Thus, these groups, and the countries in the E.U. expansion cases, were already historically embedded within the European zone of the hierarchy of whiteness, and, therefore, were not racially marked and constructed the same way as other groups and countries who were racialized outside of Europe and outside of whiteness. Moreover, when the U.S. and Australia, and others, shored up national whiteness, it was a continuation of imperial white settler practices that already placed these countries above its regional neighbors as white Anglo European paragons. Their spatial whiteness needs to be understood from their higher hierarchical standpoint than the Latin American varieties who, because of perceived Spanish and colonial racial degeneracy, were racialized as inferior and lower even if they also represented white settler lineages.

For most groups and countries, thus, the racial hinge may have opened for one aspect of whiteness but closed for another. Whitening is best articulated, therefore, as gaining disparate white privileges in specific temporalities, geographies, and scales. Limited structural reprieve from racial domination did not automatically protect from other forms of racism or make someone and someplace necessarily "white" or even "honorary white." The historical arc of Syria/Lebanon and Syrians, in general, is constructive. The Syrian struggle for whiteness in the United States and Australia only to become "legally white" did not protect them from anti-Arab racism before and after 9/11. Lebanon's overtures to Christian whiteness to bolster separation from Syria did not fully protect it from the inferior racialization of the "Arab Middle East." And, after the start of the Syrian civil war, when millions of Syrians had to flee, regardless of how Syrians racially saw themselves, they became a new global racial threat, unwanted in Europe, Turkey, and the Gulf States. Still, in relation to Black refugees and global anti-Black practices, Syrians may receive some privileges not awarded others.[202]

Ultimately, malleable whiteness, whitening, and negotiating racism by conforming to some aspects of it, intentionally or unintentionally, was an invidious way the global racial system powered on. This and the fact that global colorblindness also found a way historically and contemporarily to make the global racial hierarchy appear neutral and natural despite its obvious racist foundation. The E.U., for example, views itself as being against racism, for human rights, and believes its policies do not racially target.[203] I, therefore, turn to the last component of the contemporary global racial system, the production and maintenance of global colorblindness, in the next chapter.

Six
Global Colorblindness

In 1906 W.E.B. Du Bois elaborated on his famous and widely quoted assessment that the "problem of the twentieth century is the problem of the color line." While the global dimension of the quote is widely overlooked—specifically, Du Bois's assailment against the "European imperial politics" of expansion and violence[1]—what is less realized is that he also denounced a technique of colorblindness. Just prior to his "color line" statement he wrote how in America the construction of Black subjectivity is considered a "problem" that America wants to be "rid" of: "They do not want to understand it. They want to *simply be done with it* and *hear the last of it*. Of all possible attitudes this is *the most dangerous* because it fails to realize the most significant fact of the opening century" (emphasis added).[2]

Thus, over one hundred years ago, Du Bois placed the production of global white supremacy in tandem with and upheld by the deployment of colorblind tools.[3] In Du Bois's view, white Americans' exasperation with race hid their aggressive and ubiquitous racist praxis and was connected to the profound assuredness and naturalness those racialized as white across the globe held regarding their placement atop the color line. For Du Bois, "the global veil" always led to "blindness."[4] Powerfully, what this tells us, as exposed with racist modernity and empires, colorblindness always stood in concert with overt racist forms and is a global circulating ideological force that naturalizes the commonsense reality and perceived necessity of white global power and rule.

Global colorblindness in the twenty-first century is therefore both a reflection of past and current colorblind "technologies and strategies" that are repurposed and retooled to be most devastatingly effective in a supposedly post-empire, post-Apartheid, post–Civil Rights era.[5] The racial ideology of twenty-first-century global colorblindness functions in three ways. First, it is predicated on global racist erasure. Racist erasure is the varied globally dynamic assumption that racism is no longer a problem, no longer shapes life chances, and "race" itself is an arcane, inappropriate identity that divides societies. Racist erasure collectively distances the racist past from the racist present by dictating the terms of global and national racial collective memory and mythmaking.[6]

Second, the West-produced circulating global norms, practices, and policies about race, those in production and in process over the last four hundred–plus years, interact and intersect with regional and national fault lines creating distinct and unequal "politicultures," as Vilna Bashi Treitler labels them.[7] These colorblind politicultures, an amalgamation of the rules, policies, logics, and beliefs about race, tell us something about how global-local racial arrangements are interpreted and understood and hierarchies are justified through colorblindness. Collectively, colorblind politicultures embody an expansive global colorblind "racial paradigm."[8]

Lastly, all forms of global colorblindness are anchored by the authority of white racial knowledge and a performance of racial ignorance.[9] Necessarily, global colorblindness is propelled and hidden by whiteness. Those racialized as white, and in white racialized geographies, continue to set the rules of engagement, structure policy and language, and embody the authoritative standard on racial matters specific politicultures represent, or other politicultures must grapple with.

The racial ideology of global colorblindness is so significantly, dangerously effective, evoking Du Bois's warning, because it is omnipresent, multifaceted, and tellingly handles contradictions. The ubiquity of colorblindness is seen through its breadth and reach across scales, from material policies to discursive interpretive practice, and how it is baked into the banal, everyday workings of global and national social orders while appearing nonracial. Colorblindness's multifaceted character is acutely found in the varieties and overlapping examples of colorblind politicultures. Different politicultures adapt and pull into its local interpretive framework transnational workings of race in a manner that accentuates and prioritizes national-local folk tales of difference or sameness that erase the global project of race, racism, and white supremacy.

Finally, overt racial sentiment and diffuse, subtle, and coded language and representations are both handily incorporated into colorblindness's global reach. On the surface, the perceivably contradictory fact that overt and covert racist practices both occupy forms of colorblindness, as they always have, expertly exposes its insidious global ideological grip. Profound direct oppression and mundane, ubiquitous forms of subtle, coded white authority go smoothly together.

In this chapter, I highlight six colorblind politicultures that embody a global racial ideology of colorblindness (see table 6.1). These politicultures—post/antiracialism, multiculturalism, *mestizaje* and racial democracy, ethnic dominance, "the predicament of Blackness," and the conservative right—epitomize unequal power relations between and within politicultures across the global racial system. White transnational-dictating politicultures, such as specific geographies that represent post/antiracialism, multiculturalism, and the conservative right, and some ethnic dominant geographies influence and shape less dominant politicultures, notably the geographies that exhibit *mestizaje* and racial democracy, ethnic dominance, and most poignantly, "the predicament of Blackness." These latter politicultures must adapt and respond to global colorblind power dynamics and white dominant social structures.

TABLE 6.1. Panorama of Global Colorblindness

Colorblind Politiculture	Regions/Countries	Colorblind Mechanism
Post/Antiracialism	France, Germany, Italy, Spain, Nordic region	Obliterate race
Multiculturalism	U.S., U.K., Canada, Australia, New Zealand, Singapore, South Africa	Accentuate culture
Mestizaje and *Racial Democracy*	Central and South America, Spanish Caribbean, Hawaii	Accentuate mixture
Ethnic Dominance	East Asia, Eastern Europe, India, Iran, Turkey	Accentuate ethnic sameness
"The Predicament of Blackness"	East, West, South, Africa, Haiti, British Caribbean, Melanesia	Navigate anti-Blackness
Conservative Right	U.S., U.K., France, the Netherlands, Hungary, Russia	Claim white racial victimhood

Importantly, politicultures are not exact, static, and mutually exclusive. Some geographies have multiple, simultaneous politicultures but one politiculture typically ascends above others. These colorblind politicultures also react and stand in opposition to or accommodate and incorporate parts of historical and contemporary antiracist consciousness and praxis. Powerfully, opposing racial ideologies, notably Black consciousness, always sought to be a counterweight to racist ideological constructions, but the relentlessness and perpetual presence of colorblindness create an endless loop of the repackaged deployment of colorblind mechanisms.

Post/Antiracialism

Post/antiracialism as a colorblind politiculture is a complete expungement of the reality of race and racism in white western European racialized geographies. Post/antiracialism is especially seen in France, Germany, Italy, Spain, and Switzerland and conceptually began after WWII and decolonization, but always existed with explicit racist thought. In these geographies race is completely taken out of the national discourse as an identity and structural force that shapes life chances. More than a "transcendence" of race, as Sumi Cho describes postracialism in an American context,[10] it is an obliteration of race, an "anti-racialism"[11] against the "racialism" that stoked the historical flames of decolonization.[12] David Theo Goldberg describes this as "racial Europeanization," where race evaporates in a sea of unacknowledged European whiteness.[13] The weight of European whiteness is cloaked in the denial of Europe as the home to global racist thought and its pursuit of racist imperial practice, transatlantic racist enslavement, and racist colonial management and control. There is an "absent presence"[14] quality to post/antiracialism in Europe where the making of racism as something supposedly nonexistent underscores its subtle-yet-not-so-subtle ubiquity. If race is acknowledged, it is often through what Alana Lentin describes as an example of a "frozen racism," an event calcified in the past, such as the Holocaust, or outside of Europe, such as South African Apartheid and American Jim Crow.[15] As with other politicultures, American racism often becomes the reference point to inoculate the region against its connected and own racist production.

In this politiculture, the problem with race is the actual word "race." Therefore, the language, and even the possibility of the study of race, must be "deadened, taken away," expunged as a regional, national reality and as a social fact.[16] France, Germany, and Italy have proposed and/or officially eliminated race as a sociopolitical discursive legal category.[17] Even ethnic identity demarcations are considered too much. Within most national censuses across western Europe "ethnic categories are rejected in order to promote national unity."[18] Hence, with western European post/antiracialism we find an imagined world of delusion, disavowal, and self-aggrandizement. When race is taken out of society, Europe's global power is considered earned, emblematic of advanced civilization and development, and just in its democratic, capitalistic, and human rights examples it supposedly sets for the world. Specific countries across the region are connected in their shared representations of postracial representations and discourses, but these shared linkages also intersect with national and historic characteristics, circulating mythologies, and hierarchies of European whiteness.

WE'RE ALL EQUAL!—FRANCE

France is arguably the quintessential example of post/antiracialism. In France, post/antiracialism manifests in the specific ideology of *French Republicanism* as documented in the work of Mame-Fatou Niang, Jean Beaman, Crystal Fleming, and Trica Keaton.[19] French Republicanism harkens back to the French Revolution and the universalizing principles of equality and the French Enlightenment. Yet, while equality triumphed as emblematic of French citizenship, Black enslavement and colonial expansion would later proliferate. Thus, French colorblindness, what Keaton calls "raceblind Republicanism,"[20] historically always organized French racial subjectivity, a subjectivity accentuated by a cultivated sense of French cultural distinctiveness that was unique, but also represented a fetishization and denigration of Blackness. Achille Mbembe describes French racial assignation through the long arc of "occultation and denial," "restoration and disguise," and "frivolity and exoticism."[21] Through these practices slavery and Blackness were relegated to something out there or something to consume for pleasure, what Mbembe describes as a "willfully carefree, libertine, and frivolous racism."[22]

With French Republicanism, difference is ignored, French culture is homogenized and rendered static but also glorified as a current standard bearer of democracy, rights, taste, art, food, and fashion. The "category blindness" that ignores racial and ethnic demarcations of former colonized groups from the Maghreb and from the current French overseas *départements*—also forecloses acknowledgment of whiteness.[23] When whiteness embodies a default French citizen, then actions by nonwhite French groups are accused of being the pejorative, *communitariste*, the fomenting of separate ethnic identities, that is discriminatory toward "white" French.[24] The far-right National Front, the socialist mayor of Paris, and the French "antiracist" group, the International League Against Racism and Anti-Semitism—all decried the 2017 Nyansapo Festival organized by the French Afro-Feminist Mwasi Collective as being antiwhite and antithetical to French identity. Hence, French Republican colorblindness unites nationalists, socialists, and progressive activists, fomenting "the centrality of 'anti-white racism' to a right-left consensus," according to Alana Lentin.[25] A connected raceblind maneuver documented by Keaton was seen when filmmaker and scholar Mame-Fatou Niang and writer Julien Suaudeau spearheaded a petition in 2019 to remove a Hervé Di Rosa painting that deployed anti-Black visuals to chronicle the abolition of slavery from the French National Assembly only to be accused by Di Rosa "of prospering from racism" and that Niang and Suaudeau were *"inculte"* (uneducated/uncultured).[26]

The moderate government of Emmanuel Macron (2017–present) decried academics who study race, spoke against "Islamic separatism," and connected antiracist organizations to violence.[27] French mainstream academics also attacked decolonial scholars as "intellectual terror[ists]."[28] The notion of *laïcité*—secularism and a separation of church and state policed through public-private spatial activities—is particularly used with Republican ideology in a manner that facilitates anti-Muslim racial state policy under the guise of French universalism.[29] Moreover, Republicanism provides space for a limited acknowledgment of the history of enslavement if racism and the French perpetrators of enslavement are expunged. Fleming describes this as "asymmetrical racialization," where white French racist actors and policies remain invisible while marking visible nonwhite bodies.[30]

WE'RE GOOD AND FAIR!—THE NETHERLANDS, SWITZERLAND, AND NORDIC REGION

Some post/antiracial European and European-adjacent geographies minimize their history in empire, specifically, the profiting from empire despite some not having "colonies," deny contemporary racism, and center national identities around democratic justness and fairness. These geographies include the Netherlands, Switzerland, and the Nordic region: Norway, Sweden, Iceland, Finland, and Denmark, and to some extent Austria, which also highlights a "neutrality" position. The presence of the Netherlands in this cohort of post/antiracial European nations is extraordinary considering its prolific racist imperial past. Its collective national imagination is contemporarily informed by a sense of goodness and beneficence that comes from its constructed historical "underdog" status. According to Gloria Wekker, the Dutch are the "good guys" in history's battles. The Dutch fought against the water, against the Hapsburg empire, against the forces of religious intolerance, against Nazi occupation—only to doggedly become a prosperous global trade leader, an emblem of culture, and contemporarily a "just, ethical" nation that tries human rights abusers.[31] This national mythos fosters "white innocence," according to Wekker, where white Dutch citizenry protect themselves from the reality of the "formidable" and deadly Dutch empire, ongoing colonial arrangements in the Caribbean, and acknowledgment of contemporary racism.[32]

Switzerland, like the Netherlands, touts its role as an arbiter of fairness on the global stage but within its distinctly constructed position as a neutral, stable, and democratic European landscape.[33] The Swiss cultivate what Noémi Michel describes as *Swiss Sonderfall*, where the Swiss believe they are "more prosperous, more harmonious, more democratic, more self-reliant, more able to solve its problems and more moral" because of the cultural practices of neutrality, federalism, and direct democracy.[34] Switzerland champions its lack of formal colonies, not practicing enslavement, and its "noninvolvement" ethos as emblematic of its neutral and objective spirt. Because the country absolves itself from any racist past it ignores how it embodies "colonialism without colonies," and how race structures Swiss identity today.[35] Regardless of formal colonial and enslavement statutes, Switzerland was involved and profited from colonial trade, banking, and commerce. Swiss actors also participated in racial science, the slave trade, and the South African Apartheid regime.[36] When racist political caricature campaign posters were used by the Swiss People's Party in 2017, degrading nonwhite immigrants and veiled Muslim women, the antiracist response summoned the postracial ideology of *Swiss Sonderfall* and "renewed a regime of raceless racism."[37]

Kristín Loftsdóttir and Lars Jensen label the Nordic region as "*Nordic exceptionalism.*"[38] Nordic exceptionalism centers the geographies' peripheral status to colonialism, to contemporary globalization, and to a self-perception of "'good citizen'[ship], peace-loving, conflict-resolution orientated," and as social welfare providers.[39] These countries engage in practices of post/antiracial mythmaking in relation to each other's colonial past and present (Denmark in Greenland) and for some countries its peripheral white status (Iceland and Finland). Therefore, post/antiracialism in Nordic spaces stands in unison with essentialized white European geographic cultural valorization but within the context of hierarchical European whiteness and perceived homogeneity within the region. Accentuating ethnic homogeneity exposes how these countries also straddle an ethnic dominance politiculture as part of the negation of racism.

FASCIST HAUNTINGS—GERMANY, ITALY, SPAIN, AND PORTUGAL

Germany, Italy, Spain, and Portugal employ a post/antiracialism that diminishes its colonial footprints and consolidates white European identity but from disparate historical dioramas of the politics of whiteness and Nazi fascist wounds. The long shadow of the Holocaust engulfs all of Europe but is acutely felt and navigated in Germany. The German response to the horrors of the Holocaust was to remember the atrocities but purge the Nazi-believed biological reality of race and therefore racism. Thus, eliminating the term *rasse* (or *race* by the French and *razza* by the Italians) is necessary and the only way to break the chain to a horrendous, fascist genocidal past.[40] Cengiz Barskanmaz calls the Nazi imaginative grip on German post/antiracialism, which also overpowers the racial history of German colonialism and genocide in southwest Africa, "German exceptionalism," a colorblind ideal, like Nordic exceptionalism, that preserves a "white narration" of German identity.[41] Whiteness continues to symbolize an unmarked "real German" despite multicultural, multiracial cityscapes[42] and attempts at Nazi atonement. The antiforeign, anti-Muslim racial discourses following the acceptance of Syrian refugees underscore that who counts as German is continuously racially sealed.[43]

Italy also seeks to exorcise its fascist, Nazi allyship and hide its colonial projects. Yet Italian post/antiracialism is less simmering under the surface as seen in reserved German practicality, or in assured universal French republican glorification, and in circumspect Nordic fairness. Italian postracialism is loudly proclaimed through contemporary colorblind interpretations of *italianità* that praises whiteness. A white racial interpretation of *italianità* was a central component to *Risorgimento*, the unification of Italy in 1861.[44] Italian whiteness unified the new nation-state, challenged the "superstition of Catholicism," and rebuffed the inferior transnational racialization of Italian emigrants and the international image of Italy as "backwards and under-developed."[45] Hence, the cultivation of Italian whiteness was well under way before fascism but was strategically forgotten in the post-WWII project of de-fascistization. De-fascistization cocooned the Italian racial project to a singular temporal war past, one that laid the blame on Hitler for Italian racist laws, and in the process, racist colonial violence and continued colonial pursuits post-WWII were expunged from history.[46] Postwar Italy presented itself as a "clean, sanitized, homogenously white" nation embarking on a fresh, new era of Italian modernity.[47]

The contemporary full embrace of Italian post/antiracialism decries *razza* as an "ugly word," according to Ann Morning and Marcello Maneri,[48] but also exhumes, deploys, and reinterprets racist thought as somehow not racist but natural and cultural. Even though "widespread racism permeates the political discourse, societal behavior, and popular culture"[49] racism is nowhere to be found, "implicitly deemed meaningless."[50] Mackda Ghebremariam Tesfau' and Giovanni Picker outline how the "genealogy" of Italian post/antiracial articulation over the last two decades unfolded through discourses surrounding security, immigration, and citizenship laws only to become "consolidated" by 2015 with the rise of the Five Star Movement (M5S), left political appeasement, and discursive colorblind defenses of anti-Black violence.[51] Extreme Italian post/antiracialism reached a zenith with the 2022 election of the neo-fascist Brothers of Italy under the leadership of Georgia Meloni.[52] Meloni supporters even evoked *rossobrunismo* (red-brownism), appropriating anti-imperialist and Marxist-leaning language to convey racist nationalist positions wrapped in colorblindness.[53] Black Italians challenge *italianità* enveloped in whiteness but must contend with a profound national post/antiracial mindset excluding their existence.[54]

Similar to Italy's navigation of historical challenges to its whiteness *bona fides,* Spain's post/antiracialism is informed by an even longer "crisis of whiteness."[55] Spain had to negotiate the European regional and U.S. transnational racialization that constructed Spain as never quite white or racially pure. Impurity reflected 800 years of "Moor" rule, and, therefore, Spaniards purportedly brought racial degeneracy to their American empire projects, which precipitated its late nineteenth-century decline.[56] The external historical perception of Spanish mixedness, while Christianity was perceived to be under threat, initiated the state-sponsored obsession with controlling ancestry that, as addressed in chapters 1 and 2, evolved from religious lineage claims among Christian, Spanish, Jewish, and Muslim identities to racial demarcations that linked Christianity with whiteness, and after the American conquest, Europeanness.[57] Thus, Spanish whiteness in relation to the rest of western Europe, even compared to Italy that claimed Aryan and Mediterranean racial roots at different moments, was an anxious whiteness, one that could be flexible and buyable, but also challenged by "Spanish Orientalism."[58]

Ironically, regardless of this history and the importance of premodern Spain toward facilitating racial categorization and control, along with Spain's vast empire project, in contemporary Spain, most Spaniards are "unwilling to acknowledge the role that racial identity, or ethnic differences, has played in forging Spanish notions to national identity."[59] "So-called colorblind Spain" forecloses any possibility of an acknowledgment of current structural racism and the history of Spanish racial enslavement, and as the last European enslavers, and as practitioners of colonial brutality.[60] Essentially, there is a forced historical amnesia that precludes any acknowledgment of being a racist empire trendsetter.[61] The violent havoc and isolation wrecked by the fascist Franco dictatorship (1939–75), where Franco cultivated the idea of a traditional "Spanish race,"[62] is conjured to argue that Spaniards are racially homogenous but also anchors the contemporary desire to move beyond this painful past even as the neo-Francoist Vox political party ascends. Moreover, if racism exists it is a "new import" through recent immigration.[63] A connected, and seemingly contradictory, postracial Spanish move celebrates Spanish "openness and tolerance" vis-à-vis the rest of Europe because of its multicultural history.[64] These multiple colorblind Spanish techniques reinforce Spanish whiteness and the reality that racism organizes nonwhite Spaniards lives.

Portuguese post/antiracialism, in contrast to Spain, Italy, and Germany, is less about the denial, minimization, or a desire to forget its fascist past, and for Portugal until very recently, its colonial holdings, but a disavowal that colonialism was produced through racist practice at all.[65] Therefore, with this logic Portugal today cannot be racist. To some extent, this belief mirrors other former European imperial powers, notably, France. *Luso-tropicalism*, the ideology created by Brazilian Gilberto Freyre (see "Brazilian Racial Democracy"), was strategically used by Portuguese dictator António de Oliveira Salazar to deflect criticism of its continued colonial activities and to encourage "imperial nationalism" in the post–World War II era.[66] Within Portugal the ideology was less about racial mixture,[67] as it was understood with Brazil, and more about the "originality of the Portuguese territorial expansion" project that centered a shared linguistic commonality and history.[68] *Luso-tropicalism* today deflects any attempts to acknowledge ongoing racism in Portugal, continued racial inequities in its former colonies, and Portugal's larger fundamental role in the transatlantic slave trade.[69]

Multiculturalism

In contrast to post/antiracialism, multiculturalism acknowledges difference but prioritizes ethnic and cultural group virtues and qualities. As a colorblind politiculture, multiculturalism embodies a strategy of incorporation, diversity, and pluralism that is detached from the deep history and continued forms of racial domination.[70] Multiculturalism slowly rose over the last forty years, most predominantly in white settler geographies (U.S., Canada, Australia, New Zealand) and sparingly, but with great tension, in Europe, such as in the U.K. and somewhat in Sweden and the Netherlands, where, nonetheless, anti-Black and anti-Muslim racism cloaked its promotion. In the global South, multiculturalism is less extensive as colorblind praxis (despite the prevalence of vast diverse groups across geographies), except in Singapore, which is possibly the most institutionalized form, and in Indonesia. A new emerging multiculturalism in Central and South America is present but has yet to break the hold of *mestizaje*. Across much of Africa, expansive group identities are mostly subsumed and must maneuver under the weight of the transnational racialization of Blackness throughout the continent.

Broadly, multiculturalism allows states to present an image to the world that celebrates diversity and is used to manage global and national demands for antiracist transformation.[71] As a colorblind politiculture, multiculturalism is a global "diversity ideology."[72] Multiculturalism deftly handles the problem of race by eliminating racism.[73] If racism is acknowledged it is typically expressed as something between individuals not structured in society or globally resonate. Racial categorization, consequently, becomes just another category of group difference, equal to ethnicity, and through the mirage of multiculturalism all groups can equally contribute to a shared national kaleidoscope of cultural difference.[74] Subsequently, when structural racism is flattened through multicultural celebration, whiteness sustains its hold as the norm in white and nonwhite geographies alike.[75] In white geographies, "white" is simply another group; in nonwhite geographies the group positioned closest to global whiteness remains atop the hierarchy.

There are differences, nonetheless, between multicultural landscapes in the manner and form of direct policies and interventions pursued or if states merely perform public image maintenance. In Canada, multiculturalism is an essential part of Canadian national identity, codified in the Multiculturalism Policy of Canada (1985), but is handled through pluralism, constructed divisions between "good" vs. "bad" multicultural subjects,[76] an erasure of Black Canadians,[77] and by reproducing indigeneity as static and/or consumed for aesthetics or white remorse.[78] Swedish multiculturalism never fully formed despite its post-1968 attempts at "white solidarity" against colonialism and racism and its relatively large foreign-born population.[79] More recently since the 2000s, Sweden drifted to post/antiracialism in what Tobias Hübinette and Catrin Lundström label as a form of Swedish "white melancholy" where Swedes (an expansive malleable white category) yearn for a return to conservative, Christian, white welfare rights protections supposedly under threat from Communities of Color.[80] As in other post/antiracial states, the Swedish government also abolished the word "*ras*" from existing legislation and as a legitimate basis of discrimination.[81]

Bhinneka Tunngal Ika (Unity in Diversity) as a motto in Indonesia since 1999 highlights the country's expansive diversity and supposed regional autonomy, but the Javanese state operates as the "metaphorical and geographical center."[82] Possibly, the most unique form of multiculturalism is found in Antarctica. As a "continent of science and peace" it symbolizes *scientific multiculturalism*.[83] A global array of scientific researchers and support staff with grit and solemnity monitor the health of our planet while the imperial fights for Antarctica, racial inequities embodied in the Antarctic Treaty of 1959, Nazi mythological lore, and a landscape framed by "cultural connotations of [white] purity, fragility, and even superiority," recede into the figurative and literal white background.[84]

Post–Civil Rights, and after the 2020 murder of George Floyd, many institutions in the U.S. embrace Diversity, Equity & Inclusion (DEI) initiatives, and for some, even a language of addressing "racism"; but many do not, and much are shallow and tokenistic in effect.[85] The U.S.'s global representation as both emblematic of a history of ultimate white supremacy *and* racial consciousness and confrontation underscores its fraught, overlapping colorblind politicultures. The U.S.'s binary dialectic, between ongoing racial oppression and direct resistance, limits the ability of post/antiracialism as seen in Europe to fully dominate,[86] but U.S. multiculturalism has yet to produce meaningful, comprehensive racial material redistribution.[87] Regardless of its limited effects it still entreats pronounced conservative and liberal pushback, most pronouncedly since 2023 with "DEI" becoming a pejorative term weaponized to delegitimize any nonwhite inclusion. The tension of U.S. multiculturalism, and its ultimate roots in colorblindness, is acutely symbolized through the lauded, and globally performed, musical *Hamilton*. A multiracial cast performs a retelling of Revolutionary America with a hip-hop beat but renders invisible actual nonwhite subjectivity and resuscitates and revels in a national narrative of "great white men" who just happened to be enriched by racial enslavement.[88]

WHITE ATTACKS ON MULTICULTURALISM: U.K.–BRITAIN

On the surface, even though still practicing definitive racist citizenship and immigration policies, the United Kingdom in the 1990s and 2000s also presented to some a "new kind of cosmopolitanism," one of "diaspora, transnationalism, and hybridity."[89] Cosmopolitan multicultural ideals, however, quickly gave way to a narrative of multiculturalism "in crisis" and as a "failed experiment" across western Europe.[90] After the fierce backlash to the recommendations in the 2000 Runnymede Trust Commission's *The Future of Multi-Ethnic Britain* report,[91] the U.K.'s multiracial reality crashed against the growing sentiment that multiculturalism stokes division, segregation, and gratuitous political correctness.[92] The counter to multiculturalism was the cultivation and call for a preservation of what Damian Breen and Nasar Meer identify as "Fundamental British Values" (FBV)—"democracy, the rule of law, individual liberty, mutual respect."[93] FBV as multicultural backlash challenged multiculturalism's perceived danger in schools, most notoriously exhibited in the 2013 "Trojan Horse letter" sent to the Birmingham City Council alleging an "Islamic takeover" in local schools.[94]

The final death knell, however, to British multiculturalism was Brexit in 2016. The Leave Campaign to withdraw the U.K. from the European Union successfully lumped most nonwhite Britons together in an amalgam category of the racial "immigrant" threat[95] and cultivated a white "politics of Englishness" identity.[96] The politics of Englishness harnessed resentment against the decline of empire, class mobility, and the aura of prestige.[97] Only sovereignty from the European Union, it was argued, could resuscitate true British strength—a strength only white British descendants of empire could affirm. Regardless of the pummeling against multiculturalism the "lived multiculture" remains, according to Paul Gilroy, and haunts the critics of multiculturalism as "a zombie phenomenon" refusing to die, and, ultimately, impeding pure post/antiracial colorblindness from taking complete hold.[98] Within the United Kingdom's political states, Scotland emerged strongest against Brexit politics, and Scots construct themselves separate from the English with an "emphasis on collectivism over individualism . . . [and] welcoming [of] increased migration."[99] Yet, distancing from the English, and hailing Scotland as embodying the popular expression *"We 're a' Jock Tamson's bairns"* (all God's children), also obscures and silences contemporary acknowledgment of racism in Scotland and Scotland's deep historical participation within the British empire.[100]

WHITE PARANOID MULTICULTURALISM— AUSTRALIA, SOUTH AFRICA

Australia and South Africa represent a contemporary production of multiculturalism that is tied to an acute sense and history of what Ghassan Hage labels "white paranoia."[101] Both geographies' white settlers had to navigate isolation and distance from Britain and the Netherlands and a large local population of constructed "threatening" nonwhite inhabitants. Australia's white paranoia emanated from its perceived white geographic fragility within the Asia Pacific and its white class-based anxieties as partial descendants of British convicts. In South Africa, dueling constructions of whiteness between Dutch and British settlers created competing racial strategies of territorial dominance in relation to "native" populations. Therefore, "living up to [and commanding] whiteness" was always in process and strategically deployed within the hierarchies of whiteness of racially divided empires.[102] Ultimately, white colonial anxiety culminated as addressed in chapter 5 with the White Australia policy and South African Apartheid (1948–94) and now rearticulates and informs modern projects of multiculturalism.

A modern Australian multicultural ideal sits side by side with the ideological pursuit of "Australian Values" secured during the White Australia era. Australian Values are codified in immigration and naturalization procedures, citizenship tests, and signing Australian Values statements while signaling a multicultural spirit of a "'fair go' for all."[103] A distinct form of white Australianness is consolidated, by critics and supporters alike of Australian Values, through investments in symbolic multicultural posturing that never fully breaks from White Australia reverberations.[104] In South Africa, multiculturalism is less of a mindset and more of a presence that lightly ideologically represents a racial order of white economic and social dominance with Black political rule. With the fall of Apartheid, Black political representation navigates a global political economic landscape that demands a colorblind approach to participation in the global economy that ensures the maintenance of white racial power within South Africa.[105] Profound racial inequality in South Africa, however, is excused by "neoliberal racial articulation" of "deracialized choice," which centers individual freedoms and removes race as an organizing force.[106]

Despite the firm grip of whiteness in South Africa, white paranoia and anxiety is deep, and structures the evolution of South African "nonracialism."[107] Originally heralded as a "practical anti-racist strategy" by the African National Congress (ANC) to promote unity and directly meet the needs of Black South Africans, it was co-opted and weaponized to demand a form of South African post/antiracialism.[108] Now nonracialism commands "White Talk":[109] discourses that insist on a "new South Africa" with a hodgepodge narrative of democracy, social development, individual achievement, and ethnic pluralism; where class-accounts explain inequality, and an end to racial categories, university affirmative action, and Black Economic Empowerment policies are advocated.[110] In this milieu, a heightened sense of white South Africans, particularly Afrikaners, being under siege and victim to Black politics globally circulates as supposed proof of antiwhite racism.[111]

STATE MULTICULTURALISM—SINGAPORE, MALAYSIA

Singapore pursued a postcolonial nation-building strategy of "racial harmony"[112] and institutionalized an official policy of "state multiracialism"[113] by discarding any reference to racism. State multiracialism, nonetheless, reinscribes British colonially crafted racial identities and ignores the unequal racial foundation and assumptions that continue to structure postcolonial racial hierarchies between Chinese, Indian, and Malay Singaporeans. With Singapore state multiracialism, racial categories are turned into ethnic cultural groups and all groups are institutionally given "fair and equal opportunity" to achieve meritocratically without privileging one group over the other.[114] The perception of racial harmony overrides any claims by Indians and Malays of unequal racial practice and "racism remains an unspoken word."[115] Globally, Singapore symbolizes the city-state presented in the Hollywood film *Crazy Rich Asians*, one of prosperity, upward mobility, and multicultural colorblindness, and is emblematic of a "multicultural redemptive narrative."[116] With multicultural redemption, however, global anti-Asian racism is only overcome by "assimilat[ing] to the [colorblind] values of whiteness" that discursively and symbolically devalues "darker skinned Asians" under a veneer of celebrated multicultural politics.[117]

Malaysia, governed together with Singapore under colonialism, had a different transnational racialization process to navigate in its nation-building project. The Bumiputera—ethnic Malays—were inferiorly racialized by the British as "lazy" and "ill-suited for commercial work" and subsequently excluded from trade economies during colonialism.[118] The postcolonial state pursued "a united Malaysian nation made up of one *Bangsa Malaysia* (Malaysian Race)" that acknowledges minority ethnicities but structurally privileges ethnic Malays.[119] This strategy operates in negotiation with the postindependence regional dynamic to Singapore and others and within a larger global anti-Muslim context.

Mestizaje and Racial Democracy

Different from multiculturalism, which looks at ethnic groups through the prism of discrete cultural difference, *mestizaje* and racial democracy extol racial group mixture, hybridity, and fluidity across much of Mexico, Central and South America, and formerly Spanish-colonized Caribbean states.[120] *Mestizaje* is connected to perceptions of miscegenation accentuated by historical racial-gender mythologies that Spanish and Portuguese colonialism was less brutal and racist compared to British because intimate relationships formed between European men and indigenous and African-enslaved women.[121] Miscegenation purportedly "proves" that the region is "less racist, that racial distinctions cannot be made because of great fluidity among categories and that nearly everyone has Black or Indian blood."[122] The colorblind racial ideological underpinning of everyone being "mixed together" gives way to the most dominant "amorphous" racial category that personifies this ideology: the *"mestizo."*[123] The "mestizo" simultaneously represents all races yet only strategically incorporates, when productive, surface indigenous symbolism, excludes Blackness, and renders invisible Asian identities.[124] *Mestizaje*, in its historical and sometimes contemporary manifestations, declares mixture while longing for whiteness.

Mestizaje as a colorblind politiculture is profoundly shaped by the historical transnational circulations of nineteenth-century scientific racism, and the global implementation of eugenics policies, with the ongoing racial domineering influence of the U.S.[125] Following independence from Spain in the mid–late nineteenth century, Spanish-descendent *creole* elites throughout the region had to negotiate the global reality of scientific racism that proclaimed the region racially inferior due to degeneration from mixture and the U.S.'s threat to annex or significantly control the region "because of the greatness of the [white] race."[126] The U.S.'s successes in the 1848 Mexican-American War and the 1898 Spanish-American War loomed large, as did the denigration of Spanish Americans as "mongrels."[127] *Pliable mestizaje* emerged as the ideological answer to both symbolically challenge and adhere to global whiteness. *Mestizaje* strategies ranged from what Virginia Tilley describes as *"indo-mestizaje,"* a form of *mestizaje* that channeled a romanticized, indigenous heritage, to *"latino-mestizaje"* where a "Latin" identity was summoned and proclaimed.[128]

Both forms of pliable *mestizaje* responded to the global politics of whiteness. *Indo-mestizaje*, or *indigenismo*, mythologized "Indians" as symbolic heroes of past resistance and as cultural folklore, but superior Spanish-descendent traits were a given; and *latino-mestizaje* saw value only in *"La Raza"* as found in its European, "Latin" roots. Indeed, the invention of the term "Latin America" was a means for elites to both identify with whiteness and maintain a symbolic connection with Europe, and thwart the power plays of the "Anglo-Saxon" whiteness of the U.S.[129] Simultaneously, Mexican Americans were also beginning to deploy the term to mitigate anti-Mexican racism.[130] When Mexican writer José Vasconcelos extolled the hybrid "cosmic race" in *La Raza Cósmica* (1997 [1925]), he was fundamentally outlining a battle between forms of whiteness, northern *"sajones"* (Saxons) and southern *"latinos,"* a Spanish-French amalgamation. The future of the region was to be protected by strengthening its "Latin" roots through broad whitening policies in support of European immigration, economic development, cultural aesthetic production, and education achievement as noted in chapter 5.[131] The *mestizo*, therefore, was a new way to claim whiteness. The best traits of Latin European whiteness were infused with Latin-dominated southern geographies to create a "superior, and universal race."[132] *El Día de La Raza* (Day of the Race) continues to be celebrated across much of the region as a tribute to Columbus's arrival and the birth of the Spanish Latin American race.

Therefore, *mestizaje* as a colorblind politiculture embodies the historic reality of transnational racialization, elite fragile whiteness,[133] and its contemporary national manifestations. Yet mixture dominated by whiteness with strategic indigenous touches only further denigrates Blackness and renders invisible Asian subjectivities. The national symbols of the *"mestizo,"* or the *"indio"* in Dominican Republic, or the *"ladino"* in Guatemala, serve to mark racism as an impossibility while contemporary European-descendent elites, and those closest to global whiteness, sustain power and continue to "control[] access to whiteness"[134] across vast color pigmentocracies. The circuitous racial maneuvering to whiteness and away from Blackness across the region is also informed by distinct national dynamics connected to racialized borders and transnational forces.

Andean communities and countries exhibit indigenous politics of deep exclusion and violent repression that produces discordant *mestizo* inflection points. In Guatemala *ladinos* are more directly connected to whiteness than to Maya indigenous, *mestizo* categories[135] while in Ecuador *mestizo* is really "white mestizos" who are "no longer indigenous" and control sociopolitical possibilities and ethnic classification.[136] The rise of the indigenous presidency of Aymara Evo Morales (2006–19) in Bolivia was seen as a threat to racial and class interests[137] that spurred anti-indigenous backlash, a retrenchment on indigenous rights,[138] and the capturing of power in 2019 by white *mestizo* Jeanine Áñez.[139]

Across parts of the Caribbean there are different types of what Shirley

Tate and Ian Law describe as *Caribbean mestizaje* informed by colonial plantation racial divisions, forced labor diasporas, and transnational racial power dynamics.[140] In Puerto Rico, the expression *tres razas una cultural la puertorriqueña* (three races, one culture, the Puerto Rican) symbolically connects the indigenous Taíno, the colonial Spaniard, and the enslaved African descendent through mixture as the heart of the nation.[141] *Cubanidad* in Cuba, and *dominicanidad* in the Dominican Republic, eradicates Blackness in the latter and depoliticizes it in the former.[142] Anti-Blackness travels through these countries marked by *antihationismo* in the Dominican Republic[143] and by denying its power, influence, and existence in post-revolutionary Cuba,[144] and through the use of pejorative racialized terms of constructed Black endearment that "invokes the paternalism of slavery's past."[145]

Of course, what most of these colorblind *mestizaje* landscapes have in common is the hegemony and transnational racial power of the United States. As addressed in chapters 2, 4, and 5 the mostly Spanish-Portuguese historical colonial processes of racialization deeply structured the emergence of contemporary racial categories and divisions, the early language of fluidity, and movement through whitening. Yet, once the U.S. became the dominant regional white racial geography it dictated how the region and specific countries were transnationally racialized with direct practices of U.S.-led global capitalism, support of militarism and dictatorships, and in direct colonial forms, as seen in Puerto Rico.[146] The U.S. represents a symbolic imaginary and a broad wheel of influence that national ideologies navigate.[147] Altogether in the various national contexts, the U.S. is the foil shaping historic *mestizaje* strategies, the key to global economic success and development funds, the direct and indirect colonizing presence, and the racist global exemplar that shields national acknowledgments of racism, what Tanya Hernández calls national entreaties of "racial innocence."[148]

The U.S. is also influencing the multicultural turn in *mestizaje* politics. Indigenous and Afro-descendent activism over the last decades challenged national failures to address racism. In response, and with support by U.S. global multilateral institutions like the World Bank, various governments began a "multicultural alignment"[149] such as collecting national statistics on ethnoracial categories, acknowledging cultural claims, and pursuing policy attempts to modify discrimination.[150] Rather than challenge *mestizaje*, however, these practices are best understood as new neoliberal colorblind articulations that turn racialized groups into de-racialized ethnic actors for neoliberal market incorporation and participation.[151] Like *mestizaje*, they also continue Black marginalization by accentuating a form of cultural group minority rights framework in tension with the realities of anti-Blackness in the region.[152] Essentially, as Juliet Hooker analyzed in Central America, "cultural accommodation does not get to the problem of racial hierarchy and inequality."[153] Even traditionally constructed white Latin American geographies (Argentina, Chile, and Costa Rica) that eschewed *mestizaje* to hail "white exceptionalism"[154] in relation to the "non-white" region, now embody a form of "white multiculturalism."[155] White multiculturalism, argue Prisca Gayles and Marianela Muñoz-Muñoz, invests in a "normative logic of homogeneous whiteness . . . within a late multicultural scaffolding."[156] Multicultural overture, therefore, accommodates and absorbs *mestizaje* and whiteness rather than dislodging them.[157]

BRAZILIAN RACIAL DEMOCRACY

Racial democracy and *mestiçagem* is the Portuguese colonially formed version of *mestizaje* in Brazil. Made prominent in anthropologist Gilberto Freyre's *Casa-Grande e Senzala* (The Masters and the Slaves), Brazilian racial democracy constructed a mythologized Portuguese colonial system that was more benign and racially tolerant in juxtaposition to the British.[158] Racial democracy, the Brazilian variant of Portuguese *Luso-tropicalism*, professed racial mixture, harmonious social relations, and its version of a *mestiço* nation that embraced Afro-Brazilian culture as Brazilian.[159] Under Freyre's urging, the United Nation's Educational Scientific and Cultural Organization (UNESCO) studied Brazil in a post-WWII context as an exemplar racial model.[160] Although the UNESCO study documented racial inequality, class, not race, was considered the main driver. Across the decades and into the twenty-first century, "racism in a racial democracy" was an impossibility.[161]

The colorblind ideological practices in Brazilian racial democracy broadly encompass a "hegemonic architecture" that hides the reality of Black Brazilian marginalization and violence, indigenous dispossession, and a broad racist history.[162] This history encompasses racial labor exploitation, Brazilian whitening immigration policies, and the use of Freyre's ideas by the Salazar dictatorship to justify late Portuguese colonialism in Africa. There is also a pronounced gendered-sexualized component to racial democracy as the *"mulata"* emerged as Brazil's "national erotic icon" in a continuum where Black Brazilian women were "marked as outside the bounds of sexual respectability."[163]

Fundamentally, the "hyperconsciousness/negation of race dialectic" of race in Brazil accentuates its profound visibility.[164] The commonsense naturalism of the ideology notably bleeds into all aspects of life, underscoring how whiteness is preserved and valued. We find the ideology shaping how racialized "affective capital" is captured within families in ways that reproduce racial inequality.[165] The ideology also limits the racial justice possibilities available and exposes the challenges Black Brazilian activists face.[166] To be sure, Black Brazilian women-led movements over the last two decades were able to demand the social policies of redress begun under the Brazilian Workers' Party leadership (2003–16, 2023–present), but the power and lure of racial democracy remains. Jair Bolsonaro's (2016–22) rise harnessed white Brazilian backlash and his supporters viewed addressing and even acknowledging racism as destroying Brazil's racial democracy.[167]

ALOHA SPIRIT IN HAWAII

Outside of Brazil, and Latin America more widely, Hawaii is a geography also hailed as a "racial paradise." In 2019 the *New York Times* published an extensive opinion article, "Want to Be Less Racist? Move to Hawaii," with accompanied black-and-white photographs of content multiracial Hawaiians.[168] Like Brazil, the myth of racial harmony is connected to a scholar in the early twentieth century, in this case sociologist Romanzo Adams, and centers a history of multiple racial groups living integrated lives immune to the Jim Crow segregation that marked mainland U.S. According to Adams, Hawaiians cultivated a set of values surrounding equality and egalitarianism that supported interracial marriages, and he argued one day "there will be no Portuguese, no Chinese, no Japanese—only American."[169]

The romanticized "Aloha spirit" that permeates constructions of Hawaii as a colorblind paradise by the media, tourism development, and scholars of an earlier era dwarfs the history of white American imperial expansion, racially divided plantation economies, land displacement, and the perpetual racialized-gendered tourist marketing of the "hula maiden."[170] Moreover, the historical racialization of native Hawaiians as Polynesian distanced from "Black" Melanesians within Oceania;[171] current inequities surrounding homelessness, unemployment, and healthcare access experienced by legal migrant Micronesians in Hawaii;[172] and the variously historically hierarchically positioned, mostly, East Asian labor by white Americans,[173] calls our attention to complex racial formations and material inequalities within Hawaii along with an erasure of Blackness[174] that gets lost in simplistic tropes of racial harmony.

Ethnic Dominance

The colorblind politiculture of ethnic dominance proclaims an ethnic homogeneous identity divorced from any construction of race. Rather than multicultural celebration, group mixture, or assertions of being beyond race, ethnic identity is typically constructed as being primordial to a geography or distinctly cultivated over time through state cultural identity formation practices. We see ethnic dominant colorblindness in East Asia and parts of Southeast Asia (China, Japan, South/North Korea, Cambodia), in Eastern Europe (Russia and the countries once incorporated in the Soviet Union), the former Yugoslav region, Turkey, India, Iran, and broadly the Middle East. Sometimes ethnic identity fuses with other markers, like religion and ancestral lineage affirmations, that coalesce around an accepted and demanded homogeneity. Proclamations of ethnic sameness, however, do not preclude the reality of racial diversity. To the contrary, many geographies have vast racial group demarcations within their borders but use ethnic-dominant claims to deny group rights and benefits, which is often connected to larger projects of political ethnic nationalism.[175]

As a colorblind politiculture, ethnic dominance underscores the work geographies do to eliminate the role of race in shaping their identities and the identities of those in their borders. What Anikó Imre describes as state "discourses that have taken advantage of the flexibility of 'ethnicity' in order to disavow the realities of racism."[176] Like *mestizaje* and racial democracy, ethnic-dominant geographies must balance the forces of transnational racialization that place countries along a global field between whiteness and anti-Blackness. Accordingly, ethnic-dominant geographies through entangled racial state relations compete, compare, and attempt to control in regional negotiations how they are positioned in the transnational field in ways that are informed by their historic transnational racialization and how global racial cultural codes were applied, adapted, and contested in their specific local geographies.

The end results are manufactured essentialized ethnic national identities that allegedly have nothing to do with race and everything with ethnicity and nationality. Race is also often neglected by scholars studying these regions as a legitimate area of study and form of analysis.[177] For most of these geographies, the precarity of their global structural position in relation to global whiteness motivates or shapes and constrains their national identity constructions in relation to neighboring countries. Across many ethnic-dominant geographies, anti-Blackness sits at the opposite end of national racialization, with geographies consuming and enacting different forms of global anti-Blackness, while also exposing fissures and potential rupture points. Pointedly, in many countries we find a "new racial science"[178] emerging where ethnic biological essentialism is accepted but constructed separate from the language of "race."[179]

EAST ASIA NATIONAL ESSENCES

In Japan, China, and North and South Korea we see forms of ethnic dominance informed by these countries' relation to each other and the wider transnational racialization that historically and contemporarily distances them from European whiteness. As addressed in chapter 2, Japan personified Yellow Peril globally and in consequence responded by placing itself at the top of the pan-Asian hierarchy and enacted colonial racial practices in China and Korea. In Japan there was an evolution in how the terms *Jinshu, Minzoku,* and *Nihonjin* were positioned, typically connected to geopolitical and national racial concerns.[180] *Jinshu* was often used to connect Japan with the rest of Asia in defiance of Western inferior transnational racialization, but would be replaced by *Minzoku* to separate Japan from other Asian peoples in connection to Japanese colonial projects.[181] Following the end of the Allied Powers' General Headquarters occupation (1945–52),[182] *Nihonjin* (Japanese people) was used to accentuate the Japanese as a cultural group, and *Nihonjinron* (theories on Japanese people) sought to accentuate homogeneity and pinpoint the uniqueness and national character of being Japanese.[183] What Kazuko Suzuki equates as the Japanese formulation of "race = ethnicity = culture."[184] Altogether, according to Yuko Kawai this process "depoliticize[s] and dehistoricize[s] the Japanese as a *non-jinshu* and *minzoku* group on the surface but still let[s] the Japanese people keep employing the underlying [racial] meanings" of the terms.[185] In consequence, Japan's imperial past, its effects across Asia and with other Asian groups, and the idea that racism is not a problem in Japanese society goes unchallenged.[186]

Like Japan, Korea and China had to navigate the western transnational forces that racially inferiorized its populations while contending with Japanese aggression and occupation, and British colonialism in Hong Kong, Portuguese colonialism in Macau, and German colonialism in Kiaochow along the southern coast of Shandong Province. That multilevel negotiation produced specific claims regarding their own distinct ethnic national identities. In South Korea, the *minjok* ideology promotes a shared and common ethnic Korean identity connected to pure patrilineal Korean bloodlines.[187] Consolidating ethnic Korean sameness was a way to perpetually negotiate what Nadia Kim describes as a "shared sense of collective inferiority" vis-à-vis external oppressive forces but also sits neatly within a global racial order that validates whiteness.[188] *Minjok* also undergirds calls for South and North Korean unification; yet the discriminatory experiences of North Koreans in South Korea also suggest a new form of contemporary co-ethnic and regional racialization.[189] Similarly, in China, the racial discourse creating and sustaining Han-superiority presumptions was cultivated in the crucible of global racial colonial geopolitics, scientific racism, Confucian traditions, Chinese nationalism, and communist propaganda.[190] Across each stage only Han people could "forestall racial destruction," according to nationalist leader Sun Yat-sen, or under later communist regimes save China from western capitalism because they were "endowed with superior political and cultural attributes."[191]

INDIA, TURKEY, IRAN—ARYAN MYTHOLOGIES

In India, Turkey, and Iran there are different political ethnic-dominant claims connected to the larger history of how the Aryan myth was historically applied, appropriated, and evolved and how countries and groups were regionally positioned against each other. India, particularly, exposes the complexities of the "intricate braiding"[192] of multiple social stratification systems with overlapping forms of racialization to create one homogenized "Indian" South Asian category, out of a country, and broad South Asian region, with vast ethnic, religious, indigenous divisions. Rohini Rai outlines the racialized construct of the "Indian category" as "being upper-caste, Hindi-speaking, Hindu, particularly of the North Indian region"[193]—an identity that harkens back to the British racialization of caste and colonially crafted racial divisions.[194] Contemporary *Hindutva* (Hindu nationalism), with the political dominance of the Bharatiya Janata Party (BJP), harnesses a twenty-first-century evolution of western Orientalist scholarship on the Indo-Aryan race, and the Golden Age of Hinduism, with early twentieth-century Hindu nationalist thinkers.[195] These thinkers adopted transnational constructions of the "Hindu race" and adapted and integrated them into a national project of "cultural, racial, and linguistic homogenization."[196]

Modern *Hindutva* state-building erases this global racial foundation while excluding the sociopolitical claims of Muslims, Dalits, and Northeastern groups.[197] The logic of formal equality, as well as cultural distinction, is also manipulated in *Hindutva* to attack "special treatment accorded to religious minorities" and other groups under the constitution as a "violation of the principle of equality, while simultaneously using the right to enrich Hindu majoritarianism."[198] Similarly, caste-blind arguments minimize the racialization of caste, and caste-induced inequities, to rail against legislative practices that mitigate caste discrimination and a formal reservation system. Caste-blind narratives also travel outside the region through the Indian diaspora movement. Google canceled a talk on caste discrimination in 2020 because of complaints that any acknowledgment of caste equates to creating an "anti-Hindu" environment.[199] With this example we see how different sociopolitical diasporic Indian identities in America can become racially homogenized as "Indian," and equally subject to anti-Asian racism, but also denies the possibility of nuanced discussions on the interaction between global racism and its interaction with caste divisions.

Contemporary essentialized Turkish identity is associated with discourses and notions of perceived Turkish "immutability" and a "chromatic fascination with whiteness."[200] Of course, the cultivation of an unchangeable Turkish essence connected to an aesthetics of whiteness was in response to the historic transnational racialization of the "sub-human Turk," and the racial-identity strategies pursued by the Turkish Republic in a world saturated by scientific racism after the fall of the Ottoman empire.[201] Early claims that the Turkish race founded the ancient civilization of Anatolia made Turkey a facilitator of European whiteness—the real ancestors of modern Aryan race(s).[202]

Turkey still finds itself negotiating the transnational forces of racialization as addressed in the last chapter vis-à-vis its struggles for E.U. membership. "White Turk" responses sustained earlier Republic projects and rendered whiteness a given fact connected to a performance of modern development and culture.[203] Even when the cynical use of a "Black Turk" counterdiscourse arose with the AKP to argue that conservative Muslims were "Turkey's 'Blacks,'"[204] the discourse was never about solidarity with pro-Blackness but more reflected the globally circulating politics of resentment (see "Conservative Right"). Moreover, there is space for the "consumption of the Ottoman past" that both embraces symbolic diversity while maintaining a distinct Turkish identity.[205] New significations of a Turkish essence support the minimization of racial inequalities experienced by Kurdish communities,[206] and Syrian and Afghan refugees,[207] and further separates Turkey from Arabness and the constructed "backward" Middle East even as its media products cater to Arab audiences.

Iran, like Turkey, negotiates a precarious transnational racialization that distances the country from whiteness while at the same time most of the country adopts the belief of embodying the quintessential "Aryan" geography. The "resiliency" of modern Aryan discourse is rooted in a history where Iranian nationalists, negotiating European dominance and a sense of inferiority from a loss of Persian imperial territory, embraced Europe, and sought "dislocation" or distance from western racialization of the Middle East.[208] According to Neda Maghbouleh, "The idea that Iranians are racial Aryans remains pervasive in Iran and its diaspora, despite a century of successive revolutions, governments, and uprises opposed to the very regimes that concretized the myth."[209] Thus, Aryan discourses are baked in a discursive contemporary common sense that is beyond race because Aryans have supposedly existed since "time immemorial."[210] Yet, despite a constructed ancestral linkage to Europe, Iran, like Turkey, and India and its diaspora find that they fall outside the hierarchical boundaries of global whiteness and must negotiate their global and diasporic national racial placements.

RUSSIAN AND EASTERN EUROPEAN ETHNIC WHITES

Russia and Eastern Europe highlight the "contingencies of whiteness,"[211] even for "European" bodies, and the long arc of first tsarist Russian, then Soviet imperialist race-making, in response to western Europe—but all couched within a discourse of race denial.[212] Now, as in the post-Soviet era, the Russian Federation affirms a "patriotic white Slavic Russian identity"[213] while minimizing race, which sustains the privileged position of Slavic whiteness. Evocations of "Russian faces," in contrast to Tajiks, Kyrgyz, Uzbeks, and Caucasians, are constructed as ethnic biological facts to justify inequality in the name of ethnic Russian belonging, the "real" *Rossiya*.[214] Countries like Ukraine, Estonia, Belarus, and Lithuania are companions to Slavic Russian whiteness, but those identities may find themselves excluded within Russian structures, or choose to distance themselves from Russia, depending on how whiteness is shored up in their borders or being captured when bodies migrate across Europe.[215] Nevertheless, the claim is always about ethnicity, a postsocialist colorblind regional stance of "we don't have races, we have ethnicities."[216] Race is always somewhere else and not within the former Yugoslav, eastern European and Eurasian regions, or studied as such.[217]

The Predicament of Blackness

"The predicament of Blackness" colorblind politiculture applies the title of Jemima Pierre's revelatory book on postcolonial African racial formations informed and produced through historical and contemporary forces of global white supremacy.[218] The title exposes the tensions and complexities of conceptualizing colorblindness in geographies that carry the weight of global anti-Black racism. Geographies of this politiculture, notably throughout continental Africa, Haiti, parts of the Caribbean, and Oceania, experience the full force and devastating consequences of global colorblindness material praxis—security, militarization, and capitalist development policies—that enact global white supremacy and anti-Blackness under a veneer of colorblindness. The circulation of colorblind global discourses emanating from post/antiracial, multicultural, and some ethnic dominant politicultures marks these geographies as "underdeveloped," "undemocratic," "prone to violence," "corrupt," "lacking in capabilities," and/or ripe for fetishized white consumption of safaris, beaches, and bodies. These narratives resurrect calcified racial colonial tropes of racial backwardness and exotic allure with entreaties to culture and essentialized group formations prior to European colonialism. When conflicts emerge, they are also described as proof of naturalized ancient antagonisms rather than products of colonial-devised racial divisions.[219]

Moreover, there is also a lack of robust scholarship and framing of race, racism, and anti-Blackness, and its multiple forms, across many geographies. In African geographies outside of South Africa, Pierre exposes this "race-blindness" within academic and media analyses, and the ongoing "silence around race and racial structures" in the African postcolonial moment.[220] Or what Bruce Hall describes as the denial of race in Africa when race is clearly at play.[221] The irony is deep as "Africa stands in for 'race' [in the global imaginary] but, paradoxically race doesn't seem to exist for Africanists,"[222] and there is a prominent "disavowal" to racial analyses in North Africa and North African studies, according to Leslie Gross-Wyrtzen.[223] The production of a colorblind perspective for any issue shaping the continent, therefore, creates the view that global processes, racialized group divisions, and contemporary inequities are natural or explained by class reductionist or ethnic essentialist and lineage arguments. Race-blindness also creates a platform for white African subjectivities to make claims of racism centered on notions of "victimhood or besiegement."[224] Through these procedures the "centrality of race" in contemporary global-national racial formations across Africa subsequently gets lost.[225]

Lastly, local Black geographies respond to and negotiate with global colorblindness in what Achille Mbembe calls the "duality" of Blackness, the simultaneous process of understanding the construction of global anti-Blackness with forms of resistance and reclamation.[226] A long tradition of Black resistance, agency, and epistemologies is often evoked and centered by states and groups seeking emancipatory decolonial futures adopting Black nationalist liberation histories, Pan-Africanism, and interconnections across a transnational Black diaspora community (see the concluding chapter 7). Resisting colorblindness, nonetheless, contends with the pressures and limitations that can occur when choosing specific narratives and representations as collective national counterpoints to global white supremacy. For example, Angola still adheres to a form of colonial *lusotropicalism,* positioning "a nation of creole" that is not about mixture but praising assimilation to Portuguese culture.[227] Therefore, the terrain is fraught for geographies within "the predicament of Blackness" colorblind politiculture, which are left with the colonial vestiges of transatlantic Black enslavement, late colonialism, construed "native" hierarchies, and the modern replications of global racial capitalism and racial politics.

THE CARIBBEAN, HAITI, BLACKNESS IN OCEANIA

In the postindependence era, formerly British colonized Caribbean geographies created national strategies of cultural diversity and "mixing," *"All ah we is one"* within the *callaloo nation,* but the forces of anti-Blackness were hard to rupture. In Trinidad and Tobago, regardless of the "national ideal" of "mixing and multiculturalism," popular representations and political and economic practices also expose that "African and Indian don't mix especially in the Indian community."[228] This reality was drastically seen in the anti-Black political visuals and messaging created by the United National Congress Party in the 2020 general elections.

Thus, "mixing," in Black transnationally racialized geographies, what Tate and Law and others describe as "browning," is always connected and in negotiation with globally circulating anti-Black expressions and how they unfold across historical and national demarcations in ways that "obscure[] continuing persistent anti-darker skinned African descent racism."[229] Nonetheless, Deborah Thomas identifies how a subaltern aesthetics of "modern Blackness" in Jamaica challenges and attempts to move beyond these earlier "national representations" by positing a "blackness in the here and now,"[230] just as Jovan Scott Lewis underscores a "reparative" Black ethics that demands, defines, and takes its freedom.[231]

The long, devasting, continuous arc of global white supremacy and anti-Blackness in Haiti still generated what Angela Davis described as "a collective resilience, a ubiquitous beauty."[232] The profound anti-Black racist practices Haiti endured—brutal enslavement for the global consumption of sugar, Spanish and French colonization, 200-plus years of punishment for being the first multiracial democracy,[233] U.S. direct and indirect intervention, anti-Haitian exclusion and exploitative treatment in neighboring Caribbean countries—now hide within a cornucopia of global colorblind discourses and policies around development, security, and humanitarianism that never mention race but are explicitly about race. The 2022 production of "manufactured consent" to keep the U.N. in Haiti, and support U.S. and global capital interests, evoked recycled coded language of stopping "gang violence" and providing "humanitarian relief" that has circulated within the last 100 years of racist global intervention justifications.[234]

The Oceanic islands, those racialized as "Melanesian," similarly, navigate global anti-Blackness but within the context of Oceania and the colonial racialization that racially divided the islands between Polynesian and Melanesian. Literally "islands of Black people," Melanesia is the largest subregion in Oceania but widely marginalized and unrecognized within the principle and romanticized construction of Oceania as Polynesian.[235] Akin to discourse surrounding Africa and parts of the Caribbean, Melanesia is "portrayed predominantly as a place of conflicts, political instabilities, and poor social and economic development."[236] The permeation of anti-Blackness across Oceania hinders the facilitation of a collective Oceanic identity.[237]

Conservative Right

The conservative right colorblind politiculture overlaps and runs alongside other politicultures. Within the politiculture we find an abundance of conservative right racist discourse and praxis that denies racism at every turn and harnesses a politics of "repressive victimhood."[238] Repressive victimhood renders whiteness not only neutral, and white supremacy nonexistent, but if racism does exist, antiwhite racism is the most prominent form. The racial common sense of the politiculture includes overt declarations to whiteness, degrading and disparaging language to talk about nonwhite groups, and coded racial cues couched within an assemblage of liberal, seemingly reasonable positions that call for the celebration of western civilization, democracy, individual freedoms, and meritocracy. Essentially, when the contours and potential for racial claim-making is centered on whiteness as an oppressed group, a new discursive colorblind landscape and arena of possibilities is created: "fascists are [now] populists," white supremacists are now antiracist activists, and white racial preservation policies are merely a response to "demographic challenges" and a means to enact "reciprocal decolonization."[239] Indeed, the usurpation of antiracist, antidiscrimination, and decolonization language and praxis "agile[ly]" works to immobilize its original intent, making whites, naturally, like all groups, merely "ethnically self-interested."[240] Thus, in the conservative right politiculture we find global colorblindness at its most insidious, invidious, and exceedingly violent—a combined and contradictory logic where nothing is racist, but where those racialized as white are "victims" and or "entitled" to be racist,[241] and where overt racism is "legitimized" as acceptable, reasonable, and appropriate.[242]

The topsy-turvy orbit of the conservative right politiculture further exposes the intimate braiding of white supremacy with colorblindness. As an evolution of racist modernity, the two concepts have always worked together, underscoring how those who have racial power define what counts as a racial matter: what is racist and what is not.[243] Most succinctly, when "the very possibility of naming facts, organizational logics, official discourses and circumstances as racist is foreclosed," upon, as noted by Ghebremariam Tesfau' and Picker, the groundwork is ripe for racist expressions and policies to flourish.[244] Aurelien Mondon and Aaron Winter characterize this politiculture as the global "mainstreaming of the far right" where "movements and parties espouse a racist ideology, but do so in an indirect, coded or even covert manner," occupying a fluid relational space that oscillates between overt and colorblind racial tools.[245]

The mainstreaming of far-right discourse is only possible, however, by its adoption and acceptance broadly within institutions, particularly the media. Traditional, conservative, and social media alike have all played a role. We find mainstreaming when traditional media outlets report on race with an approach of "bothsidesism" objectivity. We find mainstreaming when conservative media outlets, most strikingly editorial cable news shows, regurgitate white racist talking points as nonracist fact. And we find mainstreaming in global social media companies who refuse to fully moderate their platforms of racist hate speech, or simply disinformation, under a guise of free speech protections, personal liberties, and a cultivated benign neglect due to English-language dominance within the companies. Even when social media firms have attempted to curtail content, a false equivalency between racial groups, the perception of "race-blind" algorithms and designers, and the financial allure of techno racial capitalism impede limiting actual racist content and forums.[246]

Most dramatically we find that the racial ideas, strategies, and discursive significations of the conservative right politiculture transnationally travels and is nationally adopted to suit local conditions. The appeal to a cultivated aggrieved global white precarity interacts with local regional geographic varieties of whiteness. Notably, the global collective toolkit of this politiculture predominantly centers on the construction of internal and external racial threats, a form of "racial nativism," and adroitly conjures deep emotions, self-righteousness, and entitlement.[247] We find the global movement of conservative right racial thought and practice mainly through (1) the transmission of conservative intellectual ideals, (2) global-national cultivation of conservative celebrity culture, and (3) in the flow and appropriation of white symbolic iconography. The U.S. and specific states within Europe commonly serve as cultural ideological reference points, producing and shaping discursive narratives and representative imagery.

Signatories to the Netherlands-based Edmund Burke Foundation's "National Conservatism: A Statement of Principles" include American conservative groups such as the *National Review*, Heritage Foundation, Claremont Institute, *Washington Times*, and Turning Point USA with organizations from the U.K, Israel, Poland, Portugal, France, and Hungary. The statement invokes colorblind ideals on race while displaying the mainstreaming of far right talking points by advocating for "Western civilization" standards, "restrictive immigration policies," Christian dominance, "traditional families," and against racial consciousness where "state and private institutions discriminate and divide us against one another on the basis of race."[248] Other right and far-right think tanks and international organizations in Europe make similar pronouncements, like the European and Latin American–focused Madrid Forum. Fundamentally, European and American–dominant conservative thinkers under a veneer of intellectualism and populism yell into a global bullhorn that the world is on a crash course of destruction caused by globalists, feminists, socialists, LGBTQ+ communities, and critical race theory.[249]

Astonishingly popular American conservative former Fox cable news personality Tucker Carlson sensationally and loudly echoed similar principles on his show every night between 2016–23. He vehemently stated "we," as in him and his viewers, were not racist, and then proceeded to declare, according to the *New York Times* expose, that we "inhabit a civilization under siege—by Black Lives Matter . . . by diseased migrants from south of the border, by refugees importing alien cultures, and by tech companies and cultural elites who . . . silence [us], or label [us] racist if [we] complain."[250] Carlson's conservative celebrity appeal was enthusiastically globally consumed.[251] The show broadcast from Hungary in 2021 and effusively praised the policies of Prime Minister Viktor Orbán. A visit to interview then president of Brazil Jair Bolsonaro in 2019 included a call from Bolsonaro to broadcast a local form of Fox Cable News; and Carlson championed the plight of white South African farmers who went on a global campaign to demand "white rights" and claim they were targets of antiwhite racial violence. Undoubtedly, Carlson, and this wider brand of celebrity firebrand conservatism that includes the rise of specific comedy and culture podcasters and content creators, bask in the "pleasure" of spewing slurs, racist epithets, and aggressive speech[252] that is interconnected to the ways racist humor[253] and racist entertainment enacts what Stuart Hall called "ritualized degradation" that "is so natural that it requires no explanation or justification."[254] Essentially, Carlson and his contemporaries found in academia, politics, entertainment, and media punditry as seen in France, the U.K, the Netherlands, and other geographies embody the entertaining value and profit of political racist spectacle for the twenty-first century.

In addition to global conservative celebrity, the "transcultural dimensions to confederate" iconography,[255] and other far right–appropriated insignia, like the Gadsden flag, and Trump's "Make America Great Again" branding, also cross borders in an interactive global-local process of white racial meaning-making. Sweden's Social Democrats adopted the saying "Make Sweden Great Again" and won national elections in 2022. Australia's United Australia Party hopes to make "Australia Great Again." From Russia to Poland, to Germany to Sweden, and to Brazil we see the Confederate flag being celebrated and used to signify local political meanings that range from overt declarations of white superiority to more coded references to "rebel" sensibilities.[256] The annual *Festa Confederada* in rural São Paulo celebrates the Brazilian descendants of American confederates who fled the U.S. for Latin America in the thousands after the Civil War rather than accept Reconstruction.[257] Regardless that the U.S. is contemporarily wrestling with the racist imagery of the flag, along with the racist legacy of memorializing Confederate leaders in public spaces, the global adoption of Confederate iconography highlights its adaptable global attraction. Similarly, the co-option of Norse symbolism exposes the allure of a globally cultivated and constructed form of white cultural production. Different white identity groups in Sweden, Germany, Canada, and the U.S. appropriate Thor's hammer, and/or the ancient Týr rune symbol, and the Valknut as their logo to signify the purity of whiteness.[258] The continuous reappropriation of Greek Hellenic, neo-pagan white ideal representations follows a comparable logic.[259]

Altogether then, across geographies, we find a broad synergy of mainstreaming far right global conservative discourse and imagery unfolding, but also commonly couched within a media frame of twenty-first-century authoritarianism and populist politics rather than race. These practices, parties, and elections are undoubtedly about race, nonetheless, and the preservation of whiteness for traditionally or suspect white groups. Ishan Ashutosh argues that global conservative right political leaders all compromise and participate in a "transnational dialogue" where the "global mapping of racial identity and difference" demands managing and creating nationally constructed racial crises and threats.[260] Viktor Orbán speaks repeatedly about how Hungary needs to preserve its ethnic homogeneity, infamously stating, "We [Hungarians] are not a mixed race and we don't want to become a mixed race either."[261] And Vladimir Putin's politics "made it possible for white [Russian] militarism to flourish" as he virtually created "a [modern] model for white nationalist rule [across Europe] and around the world."[262] According to Ivan Kalmar, Orbán, Putin, and other Central/Eastern European conservative right leaders construct themselves as "the last stand of the white man," global defenders of "patriarchal, heteronormative conservatism."[263] Interestingly, connected are the "reactionary discourses" emanating from some far right nationalists in global South geographies, such as the anti-*baizu* ("anti-woke") narratives in China, that chastise "the West" for its fall into a "progressive liberalism" of multiracialism, immigration, and leftist politics that undermines its more admirable traits of white racial homogeneity and technological and military prowess, all while reproducing global-national entangled racial logics and hierarchies in its borders.[264]

Most devastatingly we are living in the "present wreckage" of the global advancement of the conservative right politiculture and its most violent consequences.[265] As a global society we have become inured by overlapping and overwhelming acts of racist violence: Mob violence in the thousands against non-Slavic-looking people in Russia (2010); the neo-Nazi massacre of seventy-one people including teenagers in Norway (2011); the killing of nine Black congregants at Mother Emanuel church in Charleston, South Carolina (2015); the Unite the Right rally in Charlottesville, Virginia (2017); the shooting and deaths of eleven worshippers at a Pittsburgh, Pennsylvania synagogue (2018); the assassinations of Marielle Franco (2018) and Maria Bernadete Pacífico (2023) in Brazil; the beatings of thirty Nicaraguans in Costa Rica (2018); the massacre of fifty people in two Christchurch, New Zealand mosques (2019); the targeting and killing of twenty-two Latinx shoppers in El Paso, Texas (2019), ten Black shoppers in Buffalo, New York (2022), and three Black Floridians in Jacksonville (2023). And lastly, the attempted coups against multiracial democracy in the U.S. (2022) and Brazil (2023). The brutality from these racist events falls along with the global quotidian deadly assaults on Black life, anti-Asian attacks in the wake of Covid-19, anti-Muslim and anti-Jewish violence, and the rampages of indigenous land and environment destruction. The alarming conceptual seepage from the overt white supremacist pronunciations of these acts to more palpable coded references of the Great Replacement Theory in mainstream discourse shows just how frighteningly easy contemporary colorblindness cojoins with violent avowed white supremacy. These dynamics reached their pinnacle when Donald Trump was again elected president of the United States on November 5, 2024, with a racist, misogynistic, homophobic, and transphobic campaign of grievance.

Racial Exceptionalism

In these six global colorblind politicultures we see how disastrously effective colorblindness is at sustaining the global racial system. Global colorblindness shows itself as expansive, flexible, abundant, and in many ways, an all-inclusive ideology of overt and coded racist thought and practice. The evaporation of race as a global force, with the continued global circulation and national and local incorporations of racial meanings, exposes the profound adaptability of race and the ease at which the racial hierarchy between whiteness and anti-Blackness remains in the twenty-first century. The diverse colorblind tools found in post/antiracialism, multiculturalism, *mestizaje* and racial democracy, ethnic dominance, "the predicament of Blackness," and the conservative right politicultures collectively expose how global racial inequality effortlessly reproduces just as race is obliterated, celebrated as culture, mixed out of existence, discarded for ethnicity, rendered invisible through hypervisibility, and created victims out of perpetrators.

Global colorblindness is principally about the abundant forms of racial exceptionalism. In a world where racism is everywhere but believed to be nowhere, racial exceptionalism operates through elusion, artifice, arrogance, and performativity in the pronouncement and elevation of whiteness.[266] Claiming racial exceptionalism is essentially the ultimate form of what Jean Beaman describes as "racial gaslighting," the white narratives that vigorously shut down antiracist demands.[267] Clearly, the ideology of global colorblindness tells us something about contemporary racial knowledge: who has the power to create it, who has the power to claim it, and who has the power to wield it.[268] Across the politicultures, the colorblind strategy of eliminating the possibility of acknowledging racism in social systems alongside the ability to study it in scholarship is notably striking. Equally, the U.S. functioning as a global racist strawman by many geographies to discount and trivialize racism within its borders obscures the relational, interactional effects between the forces of global white supremacy and national negotiations. Collectively then, though in disparate forms, the ideological wheels of the global racial system keep assuredly turning, but vital counterknowledges, disruption points, and refusal also never abate. That is where we turn in the final chapter, to the resistance moves and defiant proclamations and counteractions against global racism.

Seven
Fighting Global White Supremacy

In 1956 Black American writer, sociologist, and voluntary exile living in Paris, Richard Wright, described the Bandung Conference of 1955 as a gathering of "the despised, the insulted, the hurt, the disposed—in short the underdogs of the human race"[1] to unite around a "shared background of colonial experience, of subjection, of color consciousness."[2] The twenty-nine newly independent Asian and African nations who gathered in Bandung, Indonesia, sought new pathways, new insights, and new strengthened connected solidarities to decry the historical forces and continued practices of imperialism and colonialism.[3] Imperialism, what was then described through "racialism," was a lived reality, one which delegates and observers had an intimate understanding of, even if their personal colonial racialized experiences were divergently felt and understood. All told, the certitude of shared colonial racialization and exploitations of their homelands bound these new nations, and all of the soon-to-be-free territories of the "Dark World,"[4] together to demand decolonization and negotiate new modes of global engagement all with a declared commitment to "equal races" and "equal nations."[5] Bandung marked a step in the long, always present, but arduous process since its inception of fighting global white supremacy from those who labored, struggled, and dreamed of a new world.

The global kernels of transnational racial solidarity, however, did not begin with Bandung. As mentioned in chapter 1, maronnage, Haiti's revolution, and abolitionism connected racialized subject positionalities across geographies in global, national, and local collective calls for liberation and freedom. Black internationalism, and the global Black Left, particularly, cultivated a form of Black transnationalism that linked geographically disparate Black subjectivities to a common experience of anti-Black enslavement, oppression, movement, and resistance.[6] The 1911 First Universal Races Congress held in London, at the peak of racist imperial expansion and scientific racist rationale, forged a space where "the voices of the oppressed alone can tell the real meaning of oppression," according to Du Bois, and decried the problems of race and colonialism.[7] Connected, between 1900 and 1945, six Pan African Conferences took place after Trinidadian Henry Sylvester Williams established the African Association in 1897 to become the Pan African Association in 1900.[8] A shared racialized Black experience and the colonial subjugation of Africa allied diasporic communities to produce what Michelle Commander considers a "speculative philosophy" of "freedom and elevation of African-descended peoples."[9] Cultural movements like *Afrocriollo*, the Harlem Renaissance, and *Negritude* also expanded Black expression and curated a "transnational Black resistant subjectivity."[10]

Du Bois, who organized four Pan African Congresses, used the prism of the color line, addressed throughout this book, as a frame to couple the world's subjected races together, all suffering under the weight of global white supremacy. Other colonized thinkers did as well. India's independence and anticolonial intellectuals, and those in its vast diaspora, produced global analyses between racism and colonialism in journals such as *Anti-Caste* (1888–93). And the Black-run, British-based *African Times and Orient Review* (1912–18) devoted itself to "the interests of Colored Races of the World," laying the foundation for "anti-racist, anti-imperialist coalition[s]."[11] *Présence Africaine* started publication in Paris in 1947 and went on to create a publishing house and bookstore devoted to Pan-Africanism, anticolonialism, and *Negritude*. Altogether, the material and epistemic anticolonial battles of Asian, African, and Caribbean liberation movements ushered in the project of Third World Internationalism, the right to self-determination, and a call to redistribute the world's resources.[12] The 1958 All African People's Conference in newly liberated Ghana, under the leadership of Kwame Nkrumah and the organizing prowess and intellect of George Padmore, extolled the slogan "Hands off Africa!" and made the continent the center and heart of the world decolonization movement.[13]

This era of "worldwide revolution" was heralded by Malcolm X, who always saw the struggle against "white world supremacy" as one fought on the global stage.[14] The revolutionary fervor that extended throughout the globe was believed to finally make possible the "decrease in power of the white world over the dark world."[15] A year after the devastation of Malcolm X's assassination, the 1966 Tricontinental Conference in Cuba brought together eighty-two liberation movements in a defiant act of unification of the world's oppressed peoples.[16]

Thus, just as race emerged through the transnational, fighting white supremacy was also always a global project. Antiracist thinkers, revolutionaries, and anticolonialists were in dialogue with each other and sought solace in solidarity through a shared lived experience of colonial racism and racial domination. Despite common charges on the supposed parochialism of U.S. race theory, when "institutional racism" analyses first emerged in the 1960s with Black American scholars theorizing structural forces within the context of Black urban spaces, they were in conversation with anticolonial, global perspectives,[17] just as Du Bois's work had been for the fifty years prior. Amílcar Cabral's late anticolonial fight against the Portuguese empire in Africa emphasized "a commitment to every just cause in the world."[18] Solidarity through liberatory antiracist practice, nonetheless, was also difficult, marked by the open scars of racist imperial and colonial divisions and the evolving new nation-state fault lines of the global racial system, what Du Bois in *Dark Princess* called "the color line within the color line."[19] Building global unity around shared transnational racialization and colonialism collided with the realities of the ongoing production of racial hierarchies in national racial orders, and in some geographies, the continuation of local logics of anti-Blackness.[20] For example, there were different perspectives on the degree to which race should shape analysis at Bandung, and the Turkish delegates, who saw themselves as "white," complained about the framing of Bandung as "a meeting of colored races" by North Americans.[21] After decolonization, the new states that emerged from colonially demarcated borders had to operate within an international order defined by liberal "sovereignty," and lacked the leverage of being "powerful state[s]" that could enforce their material distributive social compact and the pursuit of broad-based interpretations of socialism.[22] Hence, "colonial debris"[23] followed new nation-building dynamics, and as I argue throughout the book, the global racial system reformed and intensified in core countries but under the prism of global colorblindness.

Therefore, global resistant connections and solidarities were constantly present and practiced across the global racial system but also had to negotiate tensions, the contours of global and national racial hierarchies, and the ability of global white supremacy to reorganize and respond to new threats to its power. This global connected history of the ever-present, perpetual battles against global white supremacy, and its global and national articulations, helps us situate the current moment of post–Global Black Lives Matter eruptions and solidarities, and the vicious attacks, racist policies, and discursive crackdowns across many geographies against its liberatory potential. In the midst of the Covid-19 global pandemic in 2020, an estimated twenty-six million people took to the streets in the United States and throughout the world, including Denmark, Belgium, Japan, South Korea, the Philippines, South Africa, Jamaica, France, England, Brazil, Liberia, and many more, in protest rage against the police murder of George Floyd.[24] Intrinsically, "the Black Spring rebellion of 2020" did not only speak against the ongoing production of state violence and anti-Blackness in the U.S. Rebellion also simultaneously became a vehicle for those racially marginalized in disparate national racialized social systems to lay claim to their connected experiences of racial domination.[25] In a stunning turn of colorblind reversal, if not completely genuine, the language of "systemic racism," "structural racism," and in some cases even "white supremacy" and "anti-Black racism" were now spoken by some global elite institutions, in national halls of power, in school districts, within the biggest corporate brands throughout the world, and between neighbors on the block.[26]

The global reckoning on racism, however, was short-lived, and white supremacy reconstituted itself to deal with this latest challenge. In an unexpected twist, the weapon of choice to double-down on maintaining the status quo of whiteness was to go after critical race theory (CRT), with the 1619 project, that was supposedly tearing America apart, and that its practitioners were the actual perpetrators of "racism."[27] "Trufism," according to David Theo Goldberg, an amalgamation of the racial politics in the global age of Trumpism with the advocated racist tactics of conservative celebrity chaos fomenter Christopher Rufo, dances in the complete "make-believe" to reassure those racialized white that not only does systemic racism not exist but they must fight against any practice that smells of "wokeism," "wokery," "wokeness," and "anti-racism."[28] Diversity Equity & Inclusion, along with a sustained assault on LGBTQ+ rights, especially transgender rights, was added to the target list.[29] Not surprising, global anti-CRT propaganda, and the English language term "woke," traveled throughout former imperial and settler colonial geographies and adapted to national-local political landscapes.[30] Collective elite appeals to a white aggrieved set railed against "decolonization," "CRT," "migrants," and any "woke ideology," *el wokismo*, while also deploying nonwhite representatives as spokespeople to further inoculate from charges of racism.[31] Basically, by perniciously attacking Black knowledge through the global war on CRT and "woke," the conservative right politiculture found its latest rallying cry. Unsurprising, many global leftist politicians and thinkers have also jumped on, to various degrees, the "anti-woke" bandwagon.

Of course, this phenomenon of "reform-retrenchment" was deftly articulated by Derrick Bell, Kimberlé Crenshaw, and other critical race scholars, along with Du Bois at the turn of the twentieth century, to challenge assessments that presupposed racial progress, and to highlight how racism maintains itself through formal legal equality and both "modest" and "major" reform," while the inevitable "tremendous backlash" follows and retrenchment ensues.[32] Emancipation brought Black Codes and white racial terrorism, Civil Rights brought resegregated schools and mass incarceration, Black Lives Matter brought anti-CRT/"divisive concepts" laws and labeling protestors "terrorists." National liberation movements and formal decolonization brought what Nkrumah coined as "neocolonialism," debt, structural adjustment, the denial of racism, the sealing of borders in the metropoles, and later the War on Terror. Nasar Meer reminds us there is a "cruel optimism" in presupposing progress and "racial justice" when "racial injustice" is the "convention . . . not exception."[33] What is often misunderstood, nevertheless, about this racial realist approach is claiming that it is "pessimistic" and a "prescription for paralysis," when in reality Derrick Bell saw it as an understanding that brought forward new tactics, new actions, and new visions that would never cease to challenge white domination.[34] Bell poignantly noted the struggle was always what brought meaning. The struggle was what breathed life.[35]

With that I turn to the meaning and struggle of continuing the global fight against white supremacy into the twenty-first century even as its tentacles remain and evolve. I do not have all the answers, nor do I think my voice should be privileged. Rather I look to and follow the lead of how Black transnational thinkers, Black activists, Scholars of Color, and other critical race intellectuals have addressed themes on what the pursuit of collective liberation might entail. As a former student simply reminded me in our discussion about this chapter, "Freedom doesn't have to be hard, we can practice it every day." Quotidian freedom praxis thus coincides with what Michelle Alexander, evoking Dr. Martin Luther King, extols as the small solidarity acts of "revolutionary love" in pursuit of justice.[36] Accordingly, to practice and cultivate freedom outside yet still within the contours of a world drenched with racism, I highlight the importance of building racial consciousness, literacy, and solidarity alongside imagining and practicing new worlds while working to meet urgent material needs.

Building Racial Consciousness, Literacy, Solidarity

Like Bandung, and the myriad of global antiracist gatherings and solidarity calls throughout the twentieth century, we need to proactively build a global racial consciousness about white supremacy; outline a language and develop a literacy about how it functions and operates transnationally, nationally, and locally; and cultivate racial solidarity that works to disinvest from the reproduction of global whiteness and global anti-Blackness. Doing the epistemological work to unpeel the multiscaled practices of racialization that shape and situate divergent and hierarchically rendered racial positionalities brings race and racism out of the shadows of the many geographies where it is often forced into colorblind oblivion while racism goes unabated. Acknowledging the dynamic and power-laden forces of race-making does not essentialize or reify race. On the contrary, it forces a reckoning with the racist practices that produced race alongside the reclamation practices that defied race's ascribed limitations. Therefore, the layers to racial consciousness will reveal the global workings of racism and its formation and intersectional markers in diverse geographies. Thus, racial consciousness and racial positionalities will not look the same across the globe, but we will have a shared cultivated racial literacy to interpret positionalities as interconnected, relational, and historically rendered. The long, ever-present production of counterframes, storytelling, allegory, and "soul" cultural production that emanated from Black, indigenous, non-white groups and spaces marks pathways for distinct revelations and recognitions alongside shared communion.[37]

Knowing our connected histories that produced the global racial system and our own distinct but linked racial subject positionalities is the "deep understanding of reality"[38] necessary to do the work of addressing, and then dismantling, how white supremacy created alienating relationships between racialized groups,[39] incentivized and coerced others toward whiteness, and fostered and bred anti-Blackness. These dynamics play out in diverse ways in imperial and postcolonial geographies depending on which groups are racialized closer to whiteness and which groups are placed at "the bottom";[40] but all demand that a spotlight is placed on the construction of global, national, and locally embedded racial hierarchies and power differentials so we can neutralize them and work toward multiscale coalition organizing across disparate "places, conditions, and multiple [racial] relations."[41] Through this racial literacy work a form of solidarity politics is practiced that "maps racial resistance" to the layered forms of global-national racial "triangulations," that reproduces strained relations between groups and the ongoing forces of global anti-Blackness, according to Diane Wong.[42] In the past, anti-Apartheid activist Steve Biko's Black Consciousness sought to unite racially oppressed groups around a collective construction of "Blackness."[43] In this regard, centering pro-Blackness, or what Achille Mbembe calls "Becoming Black of the World,"[44] can operate today as a global solidarity base to build what Patricia Hill Collins identifies as "coalitions of conscience"[45] while still acknowledging different racialized group experiences, histories, and intersectional embodiments to meet both shared and differential group needs.

Collectively, learning, processing, engaging, and constantly reflecting on the ways in which white supremacy inflicts epistemic, material, and symbolic violence and creates different lived experiences and pathways based on one's racialized positionality sets the groundwork for the possibilities for an "inclusionary resistant subjectivity."[46] This subjectivity is united through a shared value to struggle against white supremacy but must also acknowledge racial difference, inequities, and the way "race operates in our lives, relentless, pervasively."[47] Essentially, a "solidarity produced through race talk" that advances antiracist action[48] and modeled through various varieties of "crafted democratic communities" of coalition building.[49] With this we can work toward the freedom dreams outlined by Robin Kelley. Kelley writes, "Every freedom dream shares a common desire to find better ways of being together without hierarchy and exclusion, without violence and domination but with love, compassion, care and friendship."[50]

Black Lives Matter's global crossings, and the wider platform proscriptions of the Movement for Black Lives (M4BL), offer a window into the potential for a contemporary global radical resistance politics of global and local social transformation against global white supremacy, national structural racism, and anti-Blackness.[51] From the beginning of Black Lives Matter, with the hashtag first used by sociologist Marcus Hunter in 2012, then further deployed from the absolute anguish after the acquittal of the murderer of Trayvon Martin in 2013, Ayọ Tometi, Patrisse Cullors, and Alicia Garza saw the power and importance of a global movement and made connections to the experiences of Palestinians, Haitians in the Dominican Republic, LGBTQ+ Ugandan refugees, and Nigerians fighting police violence within the mantra of uplifting all Black lives.[52] From France to Yemen to Egypt to Australia to Indonesia to India the national-local groups connected to constructions of Blackness and the bottom of national hierarchies used the mantra of Black Lives Matter to call out silence around anti-Black racism in their geographies and their collective experiences with racial domination.[53] The global-local formations of Blackness in the global racial system expose the overlapping and distinct ways a pro-Black global consciousness is embodied, signified, and harnessed across space in ways that open the door to typically nonexistent regional and national introspections on racism. In North Africa this has brought attention to long-practiced anti-Black discourse and treatment of Black migrants, foreign residents, and citizens alike.[54]

Of course, the resonance of Black Lives Matter across global landscapes today is rooted in the long history of on-the-ground local movements and the even longer histories of Black transnationalism and anticolonial struggles and solidarities addressed. Black Lives Matter "invigorated" already established antiracist, Afro-feminist, Queer of Color critique collectives and movements in Brazil, across Africa, Latin America, in Europe, and other locales.[55] For example, Brazilian Black women have long organized for better material livelihoods and political representation in a challenge to the myth of racial democracy.[56] While the 2015–16 Rhodes Must Fall and Fees Must Fall Movements in South Africa found inspiration in South Africa's decades-long anti-Apartheid struggle and ongoing attempts at decolonization practices across the Continent in conjunction with global Black Lives Matter.[57] And across the U.K. and Europe antiracist and feminist collectives centered empire's ongoing entanglements in modern metropoles.[58]

Jean Beaman credits decades-old Black European movements' long-fought battles against race erasure, colorblindness, and police violence, while advocating for public social goods, as keeping the flame of Black

Lives Matter percolating prior to the actual beginning of the movement.[59] And Fatima El-Tayeb showed how over the last twenty years Europeans of Color pursued a "transgressive approach to identity" through culture work and activist collectives to challenge their erasure as what she calls "queer impossible subjects."[60] In Europe's not fully white Balkan "borderlands," Miglena Todorova also documented how "postsocialist cultural 'third space'" activists mobilized "anti-racist vernaculars and imaginations" of transnational feminist and antiracist crossings.[61] These histories, and the ongoing exposure of a globally resonant commitment to Black lives, came to a head when mass protests engulfed France during the summer of 2023 after the French police killed French Algerian Moroccan seventeen-year-old Nahel Merzouk. The young activists who took to the streets, thus, represented the long tradition of fighting against colonial and metropole violence and the denial of European, specifically French, racism while being forced to endure its material depravity.

Moreover, Black Lives Matter's global embrace, and its Vision for Black Lives policy proscriptions, particularly, demonstrates important similarities to the historically recent internationalization of the Black Power Movement, the Black Panthers, and their Ten-Point program.[62] The Panthers interwove, complemented, and sought inspiration in global anticolonial liberation movements just as local racial liberation movements "interpreted and reinterpreted" Black Power ideas and its use of a visual politics. Black Power helped to create "new forms of unity and collaboration" and inspired "racial border crossing" while cultivating cohesive yet specific forms of "global Black Powers."[63] The Caribbean, Australian, Polynesian, Dalit, and Israeli Panther groups, alongside wider Black Power, Civil Rights, and Third World Left organizations in the U.S., participated in a diverse transnational politics of Blackness and solidarity building between the "submerged peoples of the world"[64] that was also rooted in an understanding of distinct forms of racial repression and racialized lived experiences that often revealed layered and complex racialization.[65] Therefore, global Black Lives Matter actions and ontology move this recent historical foundation forward but in an even more intentional intersectional, Black feminist grounding, that always historically had a global footing at its core.[66]

Solidarity movement work through race consciousness and literacy demands constant care and attention to the interracial wounds and divisions global white supremacy excelled at producing. Delicate and honest discussions about the creation of racial hierarchies and how groups are racialized in relation to each other and across different scales in the global racial system expose both the tensions to and necessity for radical solidarity. Because, as Laura Pulido notes, different racializations can lead to distinct forms of radical politics and demands based on groups' specific subjugation, strategies and priorities can diverge and indirectly or directly impact other groups and strain coalition building.[67] This is particularly seen, for example, in the avenues made available for indigenous and Black communities to make appeals for decolonization, sovereignty, Treaty rights, and reparations redress,[68] and how certain Asian and Latino/a/x groups in the U.S. were turned into wedge groups to decry policies like affirmative action, immigration reform, etc.[69] Within broad racialized categories there also exist ethnic-class divisions, and their different incorporations into racial states, that can inhibit pan-racial solidarities, along with state ideological forces that force activists to negotiate the semiotics of global colorblindness and its national form. The Black Freedom Movement fighter Ella Baker–inspired practice of "political quilting" that Barbara Ransby outlines may serve as an antidote to fraught relations by bringing movement communities together,[70] just as the adoption of an expansive form of Hawaiian Kanaka epistemologies may, according to Nitasha Sharma.[71] Defiantly, Mari Matsuda, an early CRT scholar and self-identified "descendent of Okinawan radicals and *Miyagi ken* plantation workers," declared "We will not be used" and called for nonwhite, non-Black groups to reject the white supremacist scripts that coerce them into color line maintenance.[72] Addressing the many ways anti-Blackness can strain movement relations alongside the different appropriations of Black Lives Matter politics without a dedicated commitment to all forms of Black Lives[73] is also necessary to build "principled multiethnic [and intersectional] coalitions."[74]

Lastly, it is those racialized traditionally white in the global racial system who need to do the heavy lifting of personal racial consciousness and literacy work outside of burdening Black-led movements and Communities of Color. Beyond antiracist knowledge work, a commitment to radical racial redistribution of the cumulated unjust rewards gleaned from 400 years of white supremacy is also crucial. U.S. organizations like Standing Up for Racial Justice (SURJ),[75] and the longer history of white "race traitors" in abolitionism, decolonization, worker rights, feminism, and Black Power, offer lessons and models. Yet, any politics that works toward what Noel Ignatiev calls a "treason to whiteness" by "violating the rules of whiteness"[76] needs to be situated in a racial realist approach. Through racial realism the endeavor toward abolishing whiteness is a never-ending process for those racialized as white.[77] Because the history of whiteness has shown its slippery, expansive adaptability, with the ability to maintain itself with new terms and significations, alongside the societally structured ease that allows white folks to simply fall back into whiteness because they remain "embedded within white structures of power," abolishing whiteness is always processual and potentially never complete.[78] "Seeing whitely" forces those racialized as white to recognize directly how the white epistemology of ignorance, white socialization, and white beneficial material formations collectively function to advantageously blind them to the operation of global and national racisms and nonwhite suffering even as they may choose to identify as "antiracist" or not "white."[79]

Therefore, the struggle of racial sight demands continuous obligation and white disinvestment from the global racial contract.[80] Working against the way white (self) interests are baked into global, national, local systems also entails more than just finding common cause through class-based or other shared marginalized identities, and the disavowal of a white identity. Essentially, white folks (in all its different global varieties) must organize against white supremacy within white spaces, white communities, white families, and white geographies in service to and in solidarity with Black- and nonwhite-led movements to construct cross-racial coalition spaces.[81] Like George Lipsitz writes, "Sitting on the sidelines is inexcusable,"[82] as it is our responsibility to confront how whiteness always vigorously "defends itself."[83] Since whiteness representation varies across the global racial system, organizing and confrontation will look different as there are differential white statuses and varying degrees of power between groups malleably racialized as white. Thus, a complex scale of who receives the most rewards of whiteness will shape the layered politics of white disinvestment and global and national movement building.

Building and Practicing New Worlds

Collective racial solidarity and ending the war on Black lives includes pursuing practices that dismantle the racialized social systems that keep it afloat to build new models of collective social relations. These systems—racial capitalism, racial states, racial militarism and policing, racist cultural production, unjust education arrangements, and others—have maintained racism for over 400 years. Finding collective abundance particularly outside and beyond the procedures of global racial capitalism is particularly vital. We can therefore imagine and practice in our everyday politics a new world beyond white supremacy that actively attempts to build systems of care, repair, reciprocity, mutuality,[84] and a *global-commons for all* while acknowledging white supremacy's ongoing grip. Much of this revolves around centering knowledges and epistemologies beyond western racial liberalism in order to disrupt nature-human antagonisms, priorities granted toward the individual above all else, and the constant forces of coloniality, accumulation, competition, and the politics of scarcity.[85] In her beautiful treatise *Viral Justice*, Ruha Benjamin reminds us that we are all "patternmakers" and "each twist, coil and code offers a chance for us to weave new patterns, practices and politics . . . new blueprints" at all levels, at all scales, from small to big, individual to collective.[86] Each of us can plant the seeds for "new worlds in [our] own backyards."[87]

These seeds can nourish both our material urgent needs in our specific villages, communities, cities, geographies, and dream beyond the immediate now. Anticolonial leader Amílcar Cabral wrote, "People struggle in order to gain material advantages, to be able to live a better life in peace . . . to see their lives progress and ensure their children's future . . . [for] a real improvement in standard of living."[88] My time working and researching over the last ten years alongside friend, collaborator, and Ugandan labor organizer Assumpta Namaganda has shown me the importance of urgent material reprieve for those most marginalized through global racial capitalism and racial coloniality, and how workers themselves are demanding and creating change in the systems they are placed in. Working from the systems one is in does not alleviate the challenge of using the "master's tool" Audre Lorde warned us about, but acknowledges how the adoption of what Olúfẹ́mi Táíwò calls "constructivist politics" "starts [from] where we are but imagines where we want to be."[89] A constructivist approach works to redistribute resources and goods, some as a part of current institutions, others newly created, "all to make people's lives better" at multiple scales.

At global and national levels, a global wealth tax, shoring up workers' rights, basic universal income, freedom schools, universal healthcare, land redistribution and a return to indigenous communities, debt relief, race-conscious institutional policies at all levels, and a global reparations apparatus are just a few practices that can meet immediate needs. Above all, the urgency for safety and the protection of life through immediate ceasefires—globally, nationally, and locally—is paramount. We must "reject[] militarism and state violence as the answer to our most profound, seemingly intractable conflicts and struggles,"[90] marked by the alienations fostered by global white supremacist logics and practice and its reproduction in manufactured postcolonial spaces, borders, and regional fractures.

Of all these, dialogue and action toward reparations has received more recent traction thanks to the Movement for Black Lives, even though calls for reparations from racial enslavement have been around since the days of slavery. Currently, there are several models proposed but most are kept within the parameters of the nation-state or regionally such as the Caribbean CARICOM project;[91] a "constructivist view of reparations" for Táíwò is "a world making project" of "thinking about justice and injustice in distributive terms" with an end target of remaking the world while embodying just one practice in how we get there.[92] Important discussions on how to link reparations to broader models of decolonization, climate justice, and away from the tenets of racial capitalism, alongside praxis geared toward meeting collective needs, should be at the forefront.[93] For example, CARICOM's Ten-Point Plan includes addressing the forces of enslavement and indigenous dispossession and genocide, building new institutions, the importance of healing from the trauma of racism, technology transfer, and debt eradication.[94] Correspondingly, Red Nation's "The Red Deal: Indigenous Action to Save the World" draws inspiration from Black abolitionism and its areas of struggle crossed with shared liberatory pursuits including divestment from the military and police, healing bodies and the planet, and universal rights and social goods for all peoples and communities.[95]

Meeting the needs of the here and now corresponds to the greater pursuit of curating "epistemic freedoms," "abolition democracy," and a "global commons" beyond colonial borders and the multiplied harms inflicted by damaged racist societies. The Ten-D's of the decolonial turn advocated by Sabelo Ndlovu-Gatsheni seek a world where epistemic freedom, informed by and rooted in the "struggles against patriarchy, racism, sexism, capitalism," and all repressive modern logics, nourishes new knowledges that embody a "mosaic epistemology."[96] The mosaic is a reservoir of vast knowledges on ways of being, knowing, and doing in relation to each other and the environment that was never lost despite the ravages of the global racial system, and is contemporarily tended to every day by challenges and refusals to our unjust racist world by those who dare to dream, build, and thrive. Spreading wisdom and connecting through epistemic freedom found in a mosaic epistemology is also seen through practices of what Michelle Commander describes as "neoteric Pan-Africanism," where finding ways to "live more freely in the present and [learning and discovering] how to fly resolutely into the future" grounds new futures.[97]

We can also meet the material conditions of life and quilt patterns of connectivity, art, sound, beauty, knowledge, taste, and love by pursuing what Du Bois originally coined as abolition democracy and was expanded upon by Ruth Wilson Gilmore.[98] Abolition democracy rebuilds from the smolders of our racist world with new models, institutions, and cultural practices outside of carceral regimes, racial capitalism, militarism, and racist knowledge.[99] A form of abolition democracy also erupts how we currently mark and define our world. "No Borders" is a political project that dismantles modern nation-state borders as ideological vestiges of racist empires to imagine modes of social organization centered on "the gaining of a global commons."[100] The global commons are "more than a resource: it is a practice—a practice of communing . . . [and the] nurturing of relationships of mutuality with fellow commoners." Ugandan Afro-feminist legal scholar Sylvia Tamale reminds us that when we embrace decolonization through the *ubuntu* philosophy we see "the interconnectedness of all things" through communal, interpersonal relations and harmony with others and nature.[101] If we root ourselves in local ecologies, local knowledges, and collective rights, we all have the right to move, grow, become, and be.

To Know, to Feel, to Move

The global racial system of white supremacy marks us all but does not have to solely define us. We all can seek meaning in the struggle. For those racialized as white, by dealing with our own experiences with racialization, how we received the rewards of a racist system we did not build but benefit from and participate in, even as we embody other diverse identities, we can begin to do the fundamental work of understanding what whiteness and white supremacy are while doing all that we can to pursue redistribution, redress, atonement, and knowledges and practices outside of whiteness. We can lean into the reality of being defined as racially "white" while living a life against whiteness and the reproduction of white supremacy. The wisdoms and tools created by global Black intersectional knowledges to envision and practice a shared collective global future, as has always been the case, is where our collective freedom lies. This is a long road, a jagged road, a road that must have waystations for "radical" and "transformative" healing for all global Communities of Color against the intergenerational and interracial traumas of global white supremacy,[102] waystations for care and sustenance, and waystations for mourning, tears, and defiant, loud, unabashed joy. Today, tomorrow, forever; we keep on moving.

Afterword

I hope you found *The Global Journey of Racism* a useful guide for understanding how our world came to be. There are three important takeaways I imagine will spur discussion, debate, and rage at the insidiousness of racism's damages alongside the perpetuation of its global erasure.

First, racism began in the global sphere, spread through roaming material domination and discursive praxis, and connected all spaces and peoples together unequally. Resistance to racism was therefore necessarily also always fought against as a global articulation even if nationally and locally conceived. Second, racism, and the racial categories, ideas, and representations that emerged from it, transformed across time and geography but was always connected to a single global system and history. The connective, entangled histories of racism thus dictated the parameters of how we relationally defined and knew racial categorical meanings across local, national, regional, and global levels. Lastly, racism has always been and continues to be about white supremacy, even as global colorblindness demands its expungement and deep and malleable whiteness hides its procedures.

The global journey of racism continues. Each step, propulsion, sound, exclamation, and imprecise impression marking its pathway overwhelms but it does not reduce. The beauty of the everyday, the movement of audacity, and the politics of relentless refusal guard and protect so one can continue the next day, and the next, and the next. My biggest wish is that readers find inspiration in some of the conceptual tools developed throughout the book and go on their own journeys of discovery and resistance. *The Global Journey of Racism* is an imperfect work. There are ideas not addressed, geographies not exhumed, stories I cannot tell. Thus, I eagerly anticipate learning from all those who come next in chronicling racism's disorientation, its concealed permanence yet always present defiant ruptures.

Notes

Prologue

1. Du Bois put the conceptual pieces to the global mechanisms of racism, imperialism, and white supremacy together a hundred years ago, and the late Charles Mills and Manning Marable, alongside David Theo Goldberg, Howard Winant, Jemima Pierre, José Itzigsohn and Karida Brown, Julian Go, Kehinde Andrews, Gurminder Bhambra, Zine Magubane, Melissa Weiner, Ali Meghji, and Marzia Milazzo, all center the global, colonial roots of racism today. See Du Bois, *Darkwater*; Mills, *The Racial Contract*; Marable, "Race and Globalization"; Goldberg, *Threat of Race*; Winant, *The World*; Pierre, *Predicament of Blackness*; Itzigsohn and Brown, *Sociology of W.E.B*; Go, "Postcolonial Possibilities"; Andrews, *The New Age*; Bhambra, "Possibilities of"; Magubane, "American Sociology's Racial"; Weiner, "Towards Critical Global"; Meghji, "Toward Theoretical Synergy"; Milazzo, *Colorblind Tools*.

2. Bacchetta, Maira, and Winant, *Global Raciality*; Thompson, "Through, Against, Beyond," 139, 133.

3. Marable, "Introduction"; Mullings, "Interrogating Racism"; Thomas and Clark, "Globalization and Race"; Weiner, "Towards Critical Global."

4. Beliso-De Jesús and Pierre, "Anthropology of White Supremacy"; Mills, *From Class to Race*, 186; Mills, *The Racial Contract*.

5. Morrison, *Playing in the Dark*, 4.

6. Mills, *Black Rights*, 33.

7. I am particularly indebted to the work of Charles Mills, David Theo Goldberg, Philomena Essed, Alana Lentin, Ali Meghji, and Melissa Weiner, all of whom frame "critical" in their understandings of global racial analyses. There is some semantic dif-

ference in the framing of "race critical" or "critical race," but both speak to the forces of racial power. See Goldberg and Essed, "Introduction: From Demarcations"; Mills, *From Class to Race*.

8. Terreblanche, *Western Empires*.

9. My perspective differs from a segment of global race scholarship that advocates for a "polyracism" or "multiple modernities" perspective where racism is said to have "multiple origins in different regions" within modernity, or for some even prior to modernity. I agree that there is much to learn from different regions' historical stratification and domination forms, but I believe that those regions' hierarchical inequities informed and interacted with European-created racialization praxis operating through a global racial system. As Ivan Hannaford writes, "Race does not lie dormant in every society on all occasions and at all times, simply waiting to be discovered." The charge of "arrogance" or "oppositional Eurocentrism" against scholars who implicate Europe for creating a global racial system of white supremacy is reminiscent of the judgmental and dismissive tone of French theorists Pierre Bourdieu and Loïc Wacquant in 1999 against what they described as the "racial (or racist) sociodicy" of scholars, notably Black American scholars, who dared to address race and racism as a global phenomenon and outside the borders of the U.S. More recently, in 2024, Wacquant challenged the analytic rigor of critical sociology of race scholars and more or less dismissed their scholarship as an "epistemological obstacle" to producing robust and precise theories of race. These intellectual attacks reveal much about what is constructed as legitimate theory and who are knowledge producers. They also politically work to limit European countries, settler-colonial offshoots, and those traditionally racialized as "white" from accountability for present-day accumulated and ongoing material and symbolic racial domination. I nonetheless commend and cite much of the contemporary scholarship from many authors who fall in various divisions within this camp, for example those in the Mapping Global Racisms book series. See Mapping Global Racisms, https://link.springer.com/series/14813/books?page=1. For a critique of West originating racism, see Law, *Mediterranean Racisms*, 3; Bonnet, *Multiracism*; Bourdieu and Wacquant, "On the Cunning"; Wacquant, *Racial Domination*. Hannaford, *Race*, 9; French, "The Missteps"; and Terreblanche, *Western Empires*, challenge some of their arguments.

10. Gathii, "Beyond Color-Blind," 63; Roithmayr, *Reproducing Racism*.

11. Howard Winant describes this moment as a "break" from overt global white supremacy. See Winant, *The World*.

12. Acharya, "Race and Racism."

13. How to incorporate race and racism into the world system is an ongoing theoretical discussion. Du Bois and Frantz Fanon were among the first anticolonial intellectuals to pinpoint the role of race and racism in the functioning of the world system through exploitative capital imperial relations. Oliver Cox outlined in the late 1940s the utility of racism and racial prejudice in maintaining an economically stratified world system where racial antagonisms emerged from economic structural arrangements. The Tanzanian school of radical scholars, including Walter Rodney, Samir Amin, and Immanuel Wallerstein, pinpointed the challenges of postcolonial rebuilding due to an unequal world

system. Cedric Robinson, inspired by the Black Radical Tradition and South African anti-Apartheid intellectuals who coined the concept "racial capitalism," "popularized" and theoretically developed the term. Around the same time cultural theorist Stuart Hall challenged the bifurcation between race and class analyses by applying Antonio Gramsci and Louis Althusser's insights to document how race articulates in different historical capital formations, producing one complex overdetermined system with commonsense understandings. Immanuel Wallerstein would go on to write how racism was the totality of the global division of labor that produces an "ethnicization of work," whereas his coauthor, Étienne Balibar, defined racism as "a true social phenomenon" that gave expression to state nationalist racist communities that hid behind ethnic fictions. More recently, Roderick Bush, Ramón Grosfoguel, James Fenelon, Vilna Bashi Treitler, and Manuela Boatcă have applied a racial analysis to world systems. See Du Bois, *World and Africa*; Fanon, *Wretched of Earth*; Cox, *Caste, Class and Race*; Jenkins and Leroy, "Introduction"; Robinson, *Black Marxism*; Hall, "Race, Articulation," "Gramsci's Relevance"; Wallerstein, "Ideological Tensions," 33–34; Balibar, "Racism and Nationalism," 41, 49; Bush, *End of White World*; Grosfoguel, "What Is Racism?"; Fenelon, "Critique"; Bashi Treitler and Boatcă, "Dynamics of Inequalities."

14. Bonilla-Silva, "Rethinking Racism." Ali Meghji similarly argues for the utility of stretching Bonilla-Silva's racialized social systems lens to global formations that complement decolonial thought, and Moon-Kie Jung "retools" racialized social systems to include global formations. See Meghji "Toward Theoretical Synergy"; Jung, *Beneath the Surface*, 26.

15. Many scholars invoke the framing of a racial world system but do not always operationalize it. Howard Winant has provided many conceptual terms to temporally contextualize the racial world system and compare national racial formations over the last two decades. Junaid Rana describes a racial world system through modern labor chains and racist subject-making. Jemima Pierre contextualizes the limitations of autonomy and development in African postcolonial countries experience because of the continuation of a racial world system. See Winant, *The World*; Rana, *Terrifying Muslims*; Pierre, *Predicament of Blackness*.

16. Wolfe, "Race and Racialisation," 5. For more detailed descriptions of racialization, also see Omi and Winant, *Racial Formation*; Garner and Selod, "Racialization of Muslims." Inferiorized racialized groups also enact "self" racialization practices but must negotiate the power dynamics of racialization processes.

17. Small, "Theorizing Visibility," 1189.
18. Kim, *Imperial Citizens*, 6, 13.
19. Patil and Purkayastha, "Transnational Assemblage," 16.
20. Goldberg, *Are We All*, 123.
21. Feagin, *White Racial Frame*, 3.
22. Thompson, *Schematic State*, 10.
23. Zakharov, *Race and Racism*, 4.
24. Farnia, "Law's Inhumanities."
25. Suzuki, "Empire and Racialization," 25.

26. Farnia, "Law's Inhumanities."

27. The oft-quoted "scavenger" qualities of racism were as much about the "continuity" of racist constructions over time as they were about excavating, repurposing, and applying local belief systems and divisions into a mélange of perceived racial credibility and naturalness. See Mosse, *Toward a Final*, 234–36; Solomos and Back, *Racism and Society*, 210–13; Fields and Fields, *Racecraft*; Gross-Wyrtzen, "'There Is No Race,'" 7, for a discussion of "race as an ensemble," full of cross-pollinating historical and contemporary logics.

28. Goldberg, "Racial Comparisons," 1274.

29. Maldonado-Torres, "On the Coloniality"; Quijano, "Coloniality of Power"; Tamale, *Decolonization and Afro-Feminism*.

30. Goldberg, "Racial Comparisons," 1273.

31. Racial state literature explains how states govern race through structuring what David Theo Goldberg describes as "racist exclusions" and "racist expressions" of racial definition, management, and control and what Vilna Bashi Treitler outlines as "politicultures" and "paradigms." States, however, are not actors, according to Glenn Bracey, but are a "tool" used by the racial dominant group in that geography "to advance their collective racial interests." States are also internally heterogeneous and "fragmented," which produces racial practices sometimes disparately across a myriad of racial state institutions. See Goldberg, *Racist Culture*, 9, *Racial State*; Bashi Treitler, *Ethnic Project*, 35; Bracey, "Toward a Critical"; Brown, "Who Is," 776.

32. Dikötter, "Racialization of Globe," 1482.

33. Joseph, *Race on the Move*, and Roth, *Race Migrations*, also explore how this movement shapes individual perceptions of race.

34. Bashi Treitler, *Ethnic Project*. Imani Perry argues we should view race as an "architecture" that centers historical contexts and the distribution of power within the racial structure, and incorporates different markers and meta-narratives of racial signification. See Perry, "Of Desi," 141–52, *South to America*.

35. Molina, HoSang, and Gutiérrez, *Relational Formations*.

36. Molina, HoSang, and Gutiérrez, *Relational Formations*, 2; Patil, *Webbed Connectivities*.

37. Perry, "Of Desi."

38. Costa Vargas and Jung, "Antiblackness of Social," 5.

39. McMillan Cottom, *Thick*, 112. Also see Costa Vargas and Jung, "Antiblackness of Social," 3; Sharpe, *In the Wake*, 4; Hartman, *Scenes of Subjection*; Matsuda, "Planet Asian America."

40. Carbado, "Race to Bottom," 1283; Bell, *Faces at the Bottom*.

41. Mills, "Illumination of Blackness," 32.

42. What Devon Carbado calls "interracial distancing," Vilna Bashi Treitler terms "ethnic project," and Lani Guinier and Gerald Torres describe as partaking in a "racial bribe" that entails making claims away from Blackness. See Carbado, "Race to Bottom," 130; Bashi Treitler, *Ethnic Project*, 112; Guinier and Torres, *Miner's Canary*, 224–29.

43. Gokh Amin Alshaif describes a "gradation of Blackness and anti-Blackness" and Kaiya Aboagye "hierarchies of blackness" in specific geographies embedded in global forces. See Alshaif, "Black and Yemeni," 131; Aboagye, "Australian Blackness," 79.

44. For some a relational racial analysis eschews the importance of hierarchy to avoid any presumption of a "hierarchy of suffering" among racial groups. It is important to not adjudicate between groups' lived experiences of racial oppression, but if we ignore how racial hierarchies function then we minimize how they operate as a system of power that reproduces across geographies in service of global white supremacy.

45. The complex relationship between Blackness and indigeneity is an example of the importance of a relational and hierarchical analysis. Because "Indigeneity" and "Nativeness" was colonially racialized across the global white-Black scale, we find that "Native" embodied different racial subject positionalities in divergent spatial geographic landscapes, creating the disparate contexts in which anti-Blackness, anti-Indigeneity, anti-Asianness, and anti-Arabness were practiced together, through, or away from each other. See King, Navarro, and Smith, "Introduction," for a deeper analysis of indigeneity and Blackness.

46. Levine-Rasky, *Working through Whiteness*, 2.
47. Boucher, Carey, and Ellinghaus, *Re-Orienting Whiteness*, 5, 6.
48. Arat-Koç, "New Whiteness(es)," 148.
49. Beaman and Petts, "Towards a Global," 7.
50. Doane, "Beyond Colorblindness," 981.
51. Goldberg, *Threat of Race*, 23, 25.
52. Lentin, *Why Race Still*, 61.
53. Titley, "On Are We," 2270.
54. Solomos and Back, *Racism and Society*, 27.
55. Beaman and Petts, "Towards a Global," 2.
56. Milazzo, "The Rhetorics," 8.
57. Milazzo, "On the Transportability," 106, 112.
58. Andrews, *New Age*, 130.
59. Hartman, *Scenes of Subjection*, xxx–xxxi.
60. Omi and Winant, *Racial Formations*; Hanchard, *Spectre of Race*.
61. McKittrick, *Dear Science*, 28.
62. McKittrick, *Dear Science*, 26.
63. Morrison, *Playing in the Dark*, 8.
64. Morrison, *Playing in the Dark*, 4.
65. Toward the end of Brand's poem, "No Language is Neutral," she writes, "Each sentence realized or dreamed jumps like a pulse with history and takes a side." See *No Language*, 22–34, 34.
66. Ndlovu-Gatsheni, *Empire, Global Coloniality*, 112.
67. Wynter, "1492," 9, 20.
68. Brand, *No Language*; *Mapping the Door*.
69. Goméz, *Manifest Destinies*, 58.
70. Keaton, *#YouKnowYour*.
71. Perry, *South to America*.
72. Crenshaw, "Race, Reform, and Retrenchment."
73. Thompson, *The Schematic State*, 7; Morning, "Ethnic Classification"; Moore, *Reproducing Racism*.

74. Bashi Treitler, *Ethnic Project*, 35–40.
75. Desautels-Stein, *Right to Exclude*.
76. Crenshaw et al., "Introduction," 5.
77. Mills, *Racial Contract*, 19.

Chapter 1

1. Hall, *Things of Darkness*; Strings, *Fearing the Black Body*.
2. Heng, "Invention of Race."
3. Hall, *Things of Darkness*, 6.
4. Christofides, "Hamlet Verses Othello," 6.
5. Hall, *Things of Darkness*.
6. Rana, *Terrifying Muslims*. See Gilman, *On Blackness Without*, xii, for a breakdown of the different designations: "The Old High German term '*Môr*' with roots in Latin '*Mauri*' referred to the inhabitants of North Africa" to become "*Moor*" in England and "*Mohr*" in Germany. France had "*Maure*," Italy "*More*," and Spain "*Moro*." Gilman writes that the term was ultimately a "portmanteau concept of dark skinned, non-Christian." In the Netherlands, "Moor" was associated more with Africa and dark skin and less associated with "Muslim"; see Hondius, "Blacks in Modern," 32.
7. Shohat, "Spectre of Blackamoor," 158.
8. Hall, *Things of Darkness*, 7.
9. Ponce, "Genealogy of Islamophobia," 9, adopting terms originally used by Nadhiri.
10. Hannaford, *Race*, 107.
11. Fredrickson, *Racism*; Hannaford, *Race*.
12. French, *Born in Blackness*; Kendi, *Stamped*.
13. French, *Born in Blackness*, 62.
14. French, *Born in Blackness*, 82.
15. French, *Born in Blackness*, 112–18.
16. Groebner, "The Carnal Knowing."
17. French, *Born in Blackness*.
18. Wynter, "1492," 9.
19. Hannaford, *Race*.
20. Goldberg, *Racist Culture*, 22, 23.
21. Heng, "Invention of Race."
22. David Theo Goldberg argues that the debate between Bartolomé de las Casas and Juan Ginés Sepulveda on the nature of indigeneity "marks a watershed" in the periodization of modernity because both "premised their positions upon the unquestioned racial difference, between European, American Indian, and Negro" groupings. The racialization of African descent for enslavement would have unimaginable consequences regardless of Las Casas later changing his position on African enslavement. See Goldberg, *Racist Culture*, 26; Kendi, *Stamped*.
23. There are many other contexts that can be added. The English colonization of Ireland in the twelfth century and the subsequent discourse that culturally separated the "wild Irish" from the English, together with oppressive practices against the Catholic Irish during Elizabethan and Cromwell eras, influenced later emerging racial discourses

in the "New World," along with the use of Irish bonded labor in English colonies. See Garner, *Racism in the Irish*, and Smedley and Smedley, *Race in North America*, for a more thorough analysis. Moreover, Cedric Robinson rightly pinpoints how incipient capitalism in medieval Europe was organized through ethnic and cultural differentiation, but I find describing this phenomenon as proto-racial, ultimately strengthening the racialization of the world system to be more analytically helpful. See Robinson, *Black Marxism*.

24. Smedley and Smedley, *Race in North America*.

25. There is a debate within Arab/Islamic slavery (AIS) scholars about whether race existed and played a role in enslavement. I find the argument that race exists as a primordial universal fact and therefore was present in AIS because some Muslim scholars of that era wrote about phenotypes and geographic groupings falls short because their analysis is detached from a broader theoretical understanding of race as not just an idea but rooted in a global material system. I agree with Dahlia Gubara, who writes that scholars who impose a racial lens to AIS falsely position race as an "essential object, that is eternal and universal." Similarly, Haroon Bashir argues that we cannot apply the "racial logics of Europe" to the "Islamicate prior to the advent of the colonial world order." This is not to say that there was not nascent anti-Blackness in some geographies of AIS or by specific thinkers and rulers shaping enslavement, particularly in Morocco in the seventeenth century, and later in modern notions of anti-Blackness. But we cannot equate this to the European system of global white supremacy that would later inform, influence, and interact with local ideas of difference in Arab-identified regions. See Gubara, "Revisiting Race," 223; Bashir, "Black Excellence," 94. El Hamel, *Black Morocco*, 155–84, makes a stronger claim for how racial slavery was facilitated.

26. Beyond acknowledging ancient group bias formations and antagonisms, some scholars even argue that "the ancient evidence for self-identification as what we would call an ethnic group is very weak." Quinn, *In Search of the Phoenicians*, xxii.

27. Isaac, Ziegler, and Eliav-Feldon, "Introduction," 10.

28. Mills, *Illumination of Blackness*, 23

29. Goldberg, *Racist Culture*, 27. Also see Wolfe, "Race and Racialisation," 52.

30. Winant, *The World*, 2.

31. Wynter, "1492," 13.

32. Bauman, "Modernity," 552.

33. Hesse, "Racialized Modernity," 643.

34. Itzigsohn and Brown, *Sociology of W.E.B*, 19.

35. Wynter, "1492," 12.

36. Wynter, "1492," 13.

37. Hesse, "Racialized Modernity," 657.

38. Hesse, "Racialized Modernity"; Itzigsohn and Brown, *Sociology of W.E.B*; Mbembe, *Critique of Black Reason*; Winant, *The World*, 30.

39. Hesse, "Racialized Modernity," 657.

40. Bauman, "Modernity," 553, 554.

41. Goldberg, *Racist Culture*; Mbembe, *Critique of Black Reason*, 12; Quijano, "Questioning, 'Race.'"

42. Baker, *From Savage to Negro*, 2.

43. Mbembe, *Critique of Black Reason*, 40.
44. Robinson, *Black Marxism*.
45. Ndlovu-Gatsheni, "Ali A. Mazrui," 213.
46. Du Bois, *Darkwater*; Fanon, *Black Skin*; Bhattacharyya, Gabriel and Small, *Race and Power*, 12; Horne, *Apocalypse*; Mbembe, *Critique of Black Reason*.
47. Ndlovu-Gatsheni and Mhlanga, *Bondage of Boundaries*.
48. Matereke, "Space Matters."
49. Wynter, "1492," 9. Strings, *Fearing the Black*.
50. Brand, "A Map," 18.
51. Barder, "Scientific Racism," 207.
52. Goldberg, *Racist Culture*; Fredrickson, *Racism*.
53. Mills, *Black Rights*, xv.
54. Mills, *Racial Contract*, 56.
55. Elkins, *Legacy of Violence*; Goldberg, *Racist Culture*; Mills, *Black Rights*.
56. Lowe, *Intimacies*, 57.
57. Hartman, *Scenes of Subjection*, 213.
58. Garrett and Sebastiani, "David Hume."
59. Goldberg, *Racist Culture*, 31.
60. Goldberg, *Racist Culture*; Lowe, *Intimacies*.
61. Moreton-Robinson, *White Possessive*.
62. Harris, "Whiteness as Property"; Lowe, *Intimacies*.
63. Harris, "Whiteness as Property," 279–80.
64. Lowe, *Intimacies*.
65. Goldberg, *Racist Culture*, 3.
66. Mills, *Black Rights*; Taylor, "Forward," xxvi.
67. Elkins, *Legacy of Violence*, 16.
68. Bernasconi and Lott, *Idea of Race*; Du Bois, *World and Africa*.
69. Painter, *History of White People*, 79.
70. Smedley and Smedley, *Race in North America*.
71. Muslim intellectuals, such as Ibn Khaldūn (1332–1406), are often evoked as counterexamples to the singular importance of the emergence of racial discourse in Europe because of his descriptions of derogatory physical features and intellect between peoples. His writings are early examples of theorizing the role of climate and culture on peoples; yet he similarly places what gets translated as "white Slavic peoples" and "Black" together rather than separately when addressing intellect. Haroon Bashir cautions against applying modern understandings of race to Arabic translations because they often flatten the diversity of meanings for specific terms. Moreover, as addressed by Ramzi Rouighi, ideologically driven European translations of Ibn Khaldūn's work were used by colonial powers, notably in Algeria, to view the region through a hierarchical racial lens that he argues did not exist in Ibn Khaldūn's original text. See Gubara, "Revisiting Race"; Bashir, "Black Excellence"; Rouighi, "Race on the Mind."
72. Hudson, "'Hottentot,'" 20.
73. Strings, *Fearing the Black Body*; Wekker, *White Innocence*.

74. Hudson, "From Nation," 248.
75. See Hannaford, *Race*, "Origins of the Word 'Race'" table. He highlights the western etymology of the word in Arabic, Czech, Dutch, English, French, German, Icelandic, Italian, Latin, Portuguese, Slavonic, and Spanish examples.
76. Douglas, "Notes on 'Race,'" 334.
77. Douglas, "Notes on 'Race,'" 334.
78. Painter, *History of White People*, 44.
79. Fredrickson, *Racism*, 56.
80. Kendi, *Stamped*, 83.
81. Hudson, "From 'Nation.'"
82. Hudson, "From, 'Nation,'" 253.
83. Smedley and Smedley, *Race in North America*, 219.
84. Hudson, "From 'Nation,'" 254.
85. Strings, *Fearing the Black Body*, 77.
86. Douglas, "Notes on 'Race,'" 336.
87. Black Central Europe, "Kant, Über die Verschiedenen Rassen Der Menschen (1777)."
88. Bernasconi and Lott, *Idea of Race*, ix.
89. Hudson, "'Hottentot"; Mills, *Black Rights*.
90. Hudson, "'Hottentot.'"
91. Gould, *Mismeasure of Man*.
92. There is a large literature on colonial racial science that analyzes the numerous texts produced by first explorers, then anthropologists and colonial administrators, outlining the physical and cultural characteristics of the peoples Europeans encountered. For examples, see Roque, "Transnational Isolates" (about Portugal); Sysling, *Racial Science* (about Netherlands); Douglas and Ballard, "Race, Place" (about colonial powers in Oceania). Also see Du Bois, *World and Africa*.
93. Roberts, *Fatal Invention*, 82, 83.
94. Johnson, "Introduction," v.
95. Stanton quoted in Smedley and Smedley, *Race in North America*, 233.
96. Zuberi, *Thicker than Blood*, 23. Although it is commonly argued that Spencer's application was a distorted view of Darwin, Darwin was not an egalitarian; he encouraged the research of Galton, and his writing on human racial variation tends to essentialize racial differences and the larger racial worldview. See Charles Darwin, "On the Races of Man," in Bernasconi and Lott, *Idea of Race*.
97. Zuberi, *Thicker than Blood*, 23.
98. Smedley and Smedley, *Race in North America*, 237.
99. Bunche, *World View*.
100. Zuberi, *Thicker than Blood*, 34.
101. Barder, "Scientific Racism," 214.
102. Hudson, "From 'Nation,'" 258.
103. Mosse, *Toward Final Solution*, 34.
104. Garner, *Racism in the Irish*.

105. Garner, *Racism in the Irish*; Painter, *History of White People*.
106. Motadel, "Iran," 120.
107. Rai, "From Colonial."
108. Zia-Ebrahimi, "Self-Orientalization," 450.
109. Motadel, "Iran," 124.
110. Fredrickson, *Racism*, 90.
111. Motadel, "Iran."
112. Law, *Mediterranean Racisms*; Törngren, "Does Race Matter"; Baker, *Race and the Yugoslav*.
113. Zakharov, *Race and Racism*.
114. Law, *Red Racisms* 7.
115. Avrutin, *Racism in Modern Russia*, 11.
116. Law, *Red Racisms*, 7.
117. Avrutin, *Racism in Modern Russia*, 14.
118. Avrutin, *Racism in Modern Russia*, 14.
119. Mogilner, "When Race Is Language," 208.
120. Kawai, "Japanese as Both"; Suzuki, "Empire and Racialization."
121. Kawai, "Japanese as Both," 372; Suzuki, "Empire and Racialization," 38.
122. Dikötter, *Discourse of Race*.
123. Dikötter, *Discourse of Race*, 53.
124. Cheng, *Discourses of Race*, 16.
125. Kim and Jung, "Not to Be Slaves," 150–52, 155.
126. Kim and Jung, "Not to Be Slaves," 145.
127. Dikötter, *Discourse of Race*.
128. Kowner and Demel, *Race and Racism*, 4.
129. Adams, "Eugenics in History."
130. Duster, *Backdoor to Eugenics*.
131. Sebring, "Reproductive Citizenship."
132. Mosse, *Toward the Final*.
133. Bunche, *World View*, 4.
134. Hartman, *Scenes of Subjection*, 96.
135. Baker, *From Savage*.
136. Baker, *From Savage*.
137. Webby, "Images of Europe."
138. Matthewson, "Satirising Imperial Anxiety."
139. Berkhofer, *White Man's Indian*.
140. Lorimer, *Science, Race*, 112, 135.
141. Merrill, "Exhibiting Race," 323.
142. The 1900 exhibition famously included the American Negro Exhibit, where a young Du Bois showed stunning visuals of sociological analyses regarding America's and Georgia's Black communities. The exhibition was "contested ground" between different representations of African American culture but as an "archive," according to Marcus Bruce, the exhibit resisted the white gaze that sought to homogenize Blackness. See Bruce, "New Negro," 209, 214–15.

143. Hale, *Races on Display*, 18.
144. Baker, *From Savage*.
145. Baker, *From Savage*; Michel, "Sheepology."
146. Francis Galton in his *Narrative of an Explorer in Tropical South Africa* (1853) describes Khoikhoi as "yellow" and not part of the race of "Black Africans." He also admires the beauty of Khoikhoi women and labels them the "favoured race." His admiration, nonetheless, was cloaked in European white superiority. The "Hottentots" were also "savages."
147. Strings, *Fearing the Black Body*, 91.
148. Collins, *Black Sexual Politics*, 26–27.
149. Strings, *Fearing the Black Body*.
150. A 2023 *Washington Post* report determined that the U.S. National Smithsonian still held 254 human brains and over 30,700 human bones collected by former curator Ales Hrdlicka in pursuit of racial science. See Dungca and Healy, "Revealing the Smithsonian's."
151. Baker, *From Savage*; Wells-Barnett, *On Lynchings*; Equal Justice Initiative, *Lynching in America*.
152. Baker, *From Savage*; Elsaket, "Jungle Films"; Thelwell, *Exporting Jim Crow*.
153. Thelwell, *Exporting Jim Crow*, 5.
154. Hartman, *Scenes of Subjection*, 37.
155. Hoxworth, "Jim Crow," 444.
156. Hoxworth, "Jim Crow."
157. Thelwell, *Exporting Jim Crow*, 30.
158. Baghoolizadeh, "Myths of Haji."
159. Troutt Powell, *Different Shade*.
160. Thelwell, *Exporting Jim Crow*, 3.
161. Roediger, *Wages of Whiteness*; Thelwell, *Exporting Jim Crow*; Troutt Powell, *Different Shade*.
162. Berkhorfer, *White Man's Indian*; Nagel, *Race, Ethnicity, Sexuality*; Thelwell, *Exporting Jim Crow*.
163. Thelwell, *Exporting Jim Crow*.
164. Smalls, "'Race' as Spectacle."
165. McClintock, *Imperial Leather*, 209.
166. Elkins, *Legacy of Violence*, 28.
167. Thelwell, *Exporting Jim Crow*, 195.
168. Purtschert, Falk, and Lüthi, "Switzerland and Colonialism," 297.
169. Hale, *Races on Display*; Keaton, *#You Know You're*; Purtschert, Falk, and Lüthi, "Switzerland and Colonialism," 297.
170. Kim, *Imperial Citizens*.
171. Thelwell, *Exporting Jim Crow*.
172. Kim, *Imperial Citizens*; Thelwell, *Exporting Jim Crow*.
173. Rouleau, "In the Wake."
174. Lowe, *Intimacies*.
175. Strings, *Fearing the Black Body*, 57.

176. Surinamese Anton de Kom's 1934 book on the extreme Dutch practices of enslavement addresses the enslaved women who carried the famed Brazilian wood, under torture of the whip, that was exported to the Netherlands to build the famous Mauritshius museum in the Hague. See De Kom, *We Slaves*.

177. Strings, *Fearing the Black Body*, 53; Smalls, "'Race' as Spectacle"; Weiner, "Ideologically Colonized."

178. Smalls, "'Race' as Spectacle," 378.

179. Hooker, *Theorizing Race*; Itzigsohn and Brown, *Sociology of W.E.B.*

180. Zuberi, "Sociology," 248.

181. McKittrick, *Dear Science*, 3, 186–87.

Chapter 2

1. Bacchetta, Maira, and Winant, *Global Raciality*; Mbembe, *Critique of Black Reason*.
2. Lowe, *Intimacies*.
3. Wolfe, *Traces of History*, 18.
4. Go, "'Racism' and Colonialism"; Steinmetz, *Devil's Handwriting*.
5. Sartre, "Introduction," xxiii.
6. Winant, *The World*.
7. Cooper, "Afterword"; Small, "Theorizing Visibility."
8. Chatterjee, *The Nation*, 14–34.
9. Steinmetz, *Devil's Handwriting*, 37.
10. Goldberg, *Racial State*.
11. Go, *Patterns of Empire*; Wolfe, *Traces of History*.
12. Stoler, *Haunted by Empire*, 9.
13. Elkins, *Legacy of Violence*, 9.
14. Some of the first usages of white supremacy as a term are found in the calls to uphold racial enslavement in the South of the United States and applied to a view of world history and the fear of white civilizational decline in the late nineteenth and early twentieth centuries. See Smedley and Smedley, *Race in North America*, 243–47; Garner, *Racism in the Irish*, 6.
15. Goldberg, *Racial State*, 108.
16. Terreblanche, *Western Empires*, 57.
17. Steinmetz, *Devil's Handwriting*; Wilcox, *Italian Empire*.
18. Maríscal, "Role of Spain."
19. Wilcox, *Italian Empire*, 24.
20. Krishan Kumar argues that "Ottoman" was a political category, not an ethnic one. There were inequalities against non-Muslims, but groups mostly had autonomy and control over their affairs. Enslavement was not legally racialized. See Kumar, *Visions of Empire*.
21. Delatolla, *Civilization and the Making*; Ponce, "Genealogy of Islamophobia."
22. Gevers, "Unwhitening the World."
23. According to Kazuko Suzuki, Japan implemented different racial projects across its Pan-Asian empire that varied between the groups within its empire. "*Dobun doshu* (common culture, common race)" logics were used to justify its colonization of Taiwan

and Korea and grant them "imperial subject" status with intense assimilation requirements. But when Japan received the South Seas Mandate following WWI, Micronesians were not considered assimilable. See Suzuki "Empire and Racialization," 36.

24. Delatolla, *Civilization and the Making*; Lake and Reynolds, *Drawing the Global Colour*.

25. Wilcox, *Italian Empire*.

26. Delatolla, "Global Phenomenology," 5.

27. Baker, *Race and the Yugoslav*; Du Bois, *World and Africa*; Horne, *Apocalypse*.

28. Harrison, "Introduction," 4.

29. Maori oral tradition describes encountering Antarctica first. James Cook attempted three voyages in the late 1700s. American sealer Captain John Davis was the first to step on the continent in 1821. By the end of the 1830s the seal population had been decimated, followed by British- and Norwegian-dominated whaling exhibitions in the late nineteenth and early twentieth centuries. See Day, *Antarctica*, 15.

30. Van der Watt and Swart, "Whiteness of Antarctica," 137.

31. Fanon, *Wretched of the Earth*; Du Bois, *World and Africa*.

32. Wolfe, *Traces of History*.

33. Anderson, *Ethnic Cleansing*.

34. Ethridge, "Global Capital," 50.

35. Churchill, *A Little Matter*; Woolford, Benvenuto, and Laban Hinton, *Colonial Genocide*.

36. French, *Born in Blackness*.

37. Churchill, *A Little Matter*, 129.

38. Wynter, "1492."

39. Horne, *Apocalypse*.

40. Gómez, *Manifest Destinies*, 53.

41. Woolford, "Discipline, Territory," 35.

42. Woolford and Benvenuto, "Canada and Colonial Genocide."

43. Go, *Patterns of Empire*; Steinmetz, *Devil's Handwriting*.

44. Shaw, *Colonial Inscriptions*, 27.

45. Steinmetz, *Devil's Handwriting*.

46. Hesse, "Of Race," 26.

47. The region, according to eighteenth-century Cook voyage naturalist Johann Reinhold Foster, had "'two great varieties of people,'" an "'aboriginal black race of people' who had been subdued by the 'more civilized Malay tribes.'" See Douglas and Ballard, "Race, Place, Civilization," 253. French explorer Jules Dumont d'Urville's 1832 division categorized Oceania between Polynesia and Melanesia.

48. Douglas and Ballard, "Race, Place, Civilization."

49. Aboagye, "Australian Blackness."

50. French, *Born in Blackness*, 239–40.

51. Historian Robin Blackburn documented the total enslaved populations in the Americas from 1550–1888. See Table 1, Slave Populations of the Americas; Blackburn, *Making New World Slavery*, 6.

52. Andrews, *New Age*; Du Bois, *World and Africa*; Williams, *Capitalism and Slavery*.
53. Eltis, "Volume and Structure."
54. Terreblanche, *Western Empires*.
55. Andrews, *New Age*, 71.
56. French, *Born in Blackness*, 165.
57. French, *Born in Blackness*, 170.
58. De Kom, *We Slaves*.
59. Horne, *Apocalypse*.
60. French, *Born in Blackness*, 8.
61. French, *Born in Blackness*; Williams, *Capitalism and Slavery*.
62. French, *Born in Blackness*, 397.
63. Wynter, "1492."
64. Du Bois, *World and Africa*, 13.
65. Hudson, "From Nation," 252; Robinson, *Black Marxism*.
66. Mbembe, *Critique of Black Reason*, 15.
67. Hunter, "Blackness Everywhere," 112.
68. Hartman, *Scenes of Subjection*, 207.
69. French, *Born in Blackness*.
70. Harris, "Whiteness as Property."
71. Smedley and Smedley, *Race in North America*, 116. Also see Hartman's figure, "Cycles of Accumulation and Dispossession," which outlines the domains of chattel subjection and the practices of refusal. See *Scenes of Subjection*, 218–19.
72. Chandler quoted in Hesse, "Of Race," 15.
73. Hartman, *Scenes of Subjection*, 207, 208.
74. Lowe, *Intimacies*.
75. Cheng, *Discourses of Race*, 183.
76. Lowe, *Intimacies*, 25.
77. Kim, *Asian Americans*, 67.
78. Sharma, *Empire's Garden*, 67, 70–75.
79. Swan, *Pasifika Black*.
80. King, "Black Arabs."
81. Du Bois, *Black Reconstruction*.
82. Carby, "On the Threshold"; Elkins, *Legacy of Violence*.
83. Vinson, *Before Mestizaje*; Horne, *Apocalypse*; Navarro, *Virgin Capital*.
84. Robinson, *Black Marxism*.
85. James, *Black Jacobins*.
86. Dahl, "Black American Jacobins."
87. Wu and Edmonds, "Trump."
88. Andrews, *New Age*, 55–59.
89. French, *Born in Blackness*.
90. Rodney, *How Europe Underdeveloped Africa*.
91. Carby, "On the Threshold"; El-Tayeb, "Blood"; Stoler, *Carnal Knowledge*; Wells-Barnett, *On Lynchings*; Vink, *Creole Jews*.

92. James, *Black Jacobins*, 9.
93. Keevak, *Becoming Yellow*.
94. Keevak, *Becoming Yellow*.
95. Lee, *Orientals*.
96. Kowner, "Race and Racism," 96.
97. Kowner, "Race and Racism," 96; Keevak, *Becoming Yellow*, 135.
98. Stoddard, *Rising Tide*, 3, 4.
99. Stoddard, *Rising Tide*, 20, 21.
100. Lake and Reynolds, *Drawing the Global Colour*, 3.
101. Lee, "The 'Yellow Peril,'" 52.
102. Lee, "The 'Yellow Peril,'" 52.
103. Lee, "The 'Yellow Peril.'"
104. Avrutim, *Racism in Modern Russia*.
105. Lee, "The 'Yellow Peril.'"
106. Horne, *Race War!*; Füredi, *Silent War*.
107. Japan sought to position itself as a "champion to colored races," but Horne describes this claim as "fraudulent." Du Bois had initial hopes for what a Japanese empire might do to global white supremacy, but in 1945 wrote: "So far as she [Japan] tried to substitute for European, an Asiatic caste system under a 'superior' Japanese race; and for the domination and exploitation of the peasants of Asia by Japanese trusts and industrialists, she was offering Asia no acceptable exchange for Western exploitation." See Horne, *Race War!*; Du Bois, "Japan, Color," 86.
108. Füredi, *Silent War*, 91–93.
109. Winant, *World*; Said, *Orientalism*.
110. Douglas and Ballard, "Race, Place, and Civilization"; Steinmetz, *Devil's Handwriting*.
111. Omi and Winant, *Racial Formations*.
112. Stoler, *Race and Education*.
113. Small, "Theorizing Visibility," 1188.
114. de Napoli, "Between Governmentality"; Luttikhuis, "Beyond Race."
115. Memmi, *The Colonizer*, 74.
116. Memmi, *The Colonizer*, 74. Although a leading anticolonial intellectual, Albert Memmi would emphasize fifty years later a more essentialist interpretations of culture and religion as an explanation for the wounds that marked postcolonial state formations, particularly in Arab states. There is much to be learned nevertheless from his classic text, *The Colonizer and the Colonized*, and how we can understand his own intellectual change as part of the larger fallout to disparate forms of colonial and postcolonial racializations and response.
117. Césaire, *Discourse on Colonialism*, 42.
118. Kennedy, *Islands of White*.
119. Vinson, *Before Mestizaje*; Law, *Mediterranean Racisms*.
120. Vinson, *Before Mestizaje*.
121. Edwards, *Hiding in Plain Sight*, xv.

122. Rodríguez-García, "Persistence of Racial"; Vinson, *Before Mestizaje*, 47.

123. Fisher and O'Hara, *Imperial Subjects*, 11. Artist Miguel Cabrera famously depicted the wide *casta* categories in a sixteen-panel series in the eighteenth century. *Casta* paintings were popular in the eighteenth century, and according to Magali Carrera produced a form of visual surveillance of nonnormative whiteness. See Carrera, *Imagining Identity*.

124. Vinson, *Before Mestizaje*, 49.

125. Telles and Flores, "Not Just Color."

126. Mattos, "'Pretos' and 'Pardos.'"

127. Mattos, "'Pretos' and 'Pardos,'" 50.

128. Patrick Wolfe, in "Land, Labor, Difference," identifies a color classification in the late colonial, early independence era of Brazil as divisions among *branco, mulato, mulato claro, moreno claro, negro, escuro, claro roxo, sarará escuro, preto claro, cor de cinza, caboclo escuro, branco sarará branco caoclado, mulato sarará, cor de cinza clara, louro, mambebe roxo de cabelo bom, preto moreno multao escuro, aboclo, cabo verde, araçuaba, amarelo, cor de canela, roxo claro, vermelho, pardo, mambebe, moreno escuro, creole vermelho, pelé, preto escuro.*

129. Horne, *Apocalypse*, 54.

130. Koekkoek, Richard, and Weststeijn, "Visions of Dutch Empire."

131. Thelwell, *Exporting Jim Crow*, 31.

132. Fredrickson, *White Supremacy*.

133. Jones and de Hart, "(Not) Measuring Mixedness," 371.

134. Vink, *Creole Jews*, 167.

135. Marchand, *Being Dogla*, 83. According to Guno Jones and Betty de Hart, twentieth-century colonial Surinamese censuses included these categories: in 1938—Europeans, "native born," "Dutch-East Indians," "British-East Indians," "Chinese," "Bushnegroes," and "Indians"; in 1950—"Bushnegroes," "Chinese," "Creoles," "Europeans," "half-bloods," "Hindostanis," "Indians," "Indonesians," "Coloreds," and "Negroes"; in 1964—"Creole," "Hindustani," "Indonesian," "Indian," "Chinese," "European," "Bushnegroe," and "Indian." See, "(Not) Measuring."

136. Luttikhuis, "Beyond Race."

137. Wesseling and Dane, "Are 'the Natives,'" 29.

138. Houben, "Boundaries of Race."

139. Darwin, *Empire Project*, 3.

140. Newman, *Dark Inheritance*, 15.

141. Newman, *Dark Inheritance*, 15.

142. Christopher, "Race and Ethnicity."

143. Kumar, *Visions of Empire*.

144. Rana, *Terrifying Muslims*; Rai, "From Colonial."

145. Streets, *Martial Races*, 1.

146. Rana, *Terrifying Muslims*.

147. Kumar, *Visions of Empire*.

148. Christopher, "Race and Ethnicity," 39.

149. Dirks, *Castes of Mind*.

150. Rai, "From Colonial."
151. Mamdani, "Race and Ethnicity."
152. Thomas and Clark, "Globalization and Race," 308.
153. Milner-Thornton, "Measuring Mixedness."
154. Steinmetz, *Devi's Handwriting*.
155. Mamdani offers a limited racial analysis to colonialism, using race solely to describe its legal use in colonialism. I agree with Goldberg in *The Racial State* that limiting race in that regard distorts the full range of global, national, and local racialization forms during and after the colonial order.
156. Kumar, *Visions of Empire*, 429.
157. Law, *Mediterranean Racisms*.
158. Fleming, *Resurrecting Slavery*, 15.
159. A French planter elite from Martinque, Louis-Élie Moreau de Sant-Méry, wrote *Description Topographique, Physique, de la Partie Française de l'Isle Saint-Domingue* in 1797, which outlined a racial taxonomy for the island. See Garraway, "Race, Reproduction, and Family."
160. Garraway, "Race, Reproduction, and Family."
161. Kumar, *Visions of Empire*, 441.
162. Collins and Nam, "Between the Law," 234.
163. Muckle, "Presumption of Indigeneity," 314.
164. Collins and Nam, "Between the Law," 234.
165. Kumar, *Visions of Empire*, 446; Law, *Mediterranean Racisms*, 27; Rouighi, "Race on the Mind."
166. Muckle, "Presumption of Indigeneity," 315.
167. El-Tayeb, "Blood," 151.
168. Steinmetz, *Devil's Handwriting*, 321.
169. Steinmetz, *Devil's Handwriting*.
170. Steinmetz, *Devil's Handwriting*, 54.
171. Steinmetz, *Devil's Handwriting*, 54.
172. Madley, "From Africa."
173. Steinmetz, *Devil's Handwriting*.
174. El-Tayeb, "We Are Germans," 192; Madley, "From Africa," 439.
175. Wilcox, *Italian Empire*, 23.
176. Wilcox, *Italian Empire*, 29.
177. Wilcox, *Italian Empire*.
178. Barrera, "Mussolini's Colonial"; Wilcox, *Italian Empire*.
179. Pesarini and Tontori, "Mixed Identities."
180. Wilcox, *Italian Empire*.
181. Wilcox, *Italian Empire*.
182. De Napoli, "Between Governmentality," 21, 3.
183. Di Stefano, "System of Differences."
184. Pergher, "Allure of Citizenship."
185. Pergher, "Allure of Citizenship."

186. Fusari, "Orphanages and Citizenship."
187. Barrera, "Mussolini's Colonial."
188. Pesarini and Tintori, "Mixed Identities," 356.
189. Barrera, "Mussolini's Colonial," 425.
190. Law, *Mediterranean Racisms*, 30.
191. Mbembe, *Critique of Black Reason*, 48.
192. Bledsoe, "Marronage as a Past," 30.
193. Moulton, "Towards the Arboreal."
194. Zuberi, "Sociology and the African," 248. See Robert Alexander Young's "The Ethiopian Manifesto, Issued in Defense of the Black Man's Rights in the Scale of Universal Freedom" (1829) and David Walker's "Appeal to the Coloured Citizens of the World, but in Particular, and Very Expressly, to Those of the United States" (1829).
195. Hartman, *Wayward Lives*, xv.
196. Hunter and Robinson, *Chocolate Cities*, 10.
197. Carby, "On the Threshold," 265.
198. Vitalis, *White World Order*, 5.
199. Elkins, *Legacies of Violence*, 294.
200. Davies, *Left of Karl Marx*.
201. Tate, "The War Aims," 532.

Chapter 3

1. Chancel, Piketty, Saez, and Zucman, *World Inequality Report*, 3, 11.
2. International Labour Organization, *World Employment*.
3. Chancel, Piketty, Saez, and Zucman, *World Inequality Report*, 11.
4. Bledsoe and Wright, "Anti-Blackness."
5. *World Social Report*, xiii.
6. *World Social Report*, 22.
7. Achiume, "Report of the Special," 3.
8. Terreblanche, "Wealth Tax," 16, 17.
9. Terreblanche, "Wealth Tax," 18.
10. Oliver and Shapiro, *Black Wealth*; Feagin, *Racist America*; Táíwò, *Reconsidering Reparations*. There are also U.S. and European legal definitions of "unjust" and "unjustified" "enrichment."
11. Daria Roithmayr uses the framing of "locked in" to describe the transmission of white racial advantage and nonwhite disadvantage. See Roithmayr, *Reproducing Racism*.
12. Lipsitz, *Possessive Investment*.
13. Ahmed, "Phenomenology of Whiteness," 160.
14. Yancy, "When Heaven," 14.
15. Lipsitz, *Possessive Investment*.
16. powell, "Race: Power."
17. Dicken, *Global Shift*.
18. Gereffi, Humphrey, and Sturgeon, "The Governance."
19. Thomas, "Race as a Technology," 1860.

20. McMichael, *Development Social Change*.
21. Hall, "Race, Articulation."
22. Bair and Werner, "Commodity Chains," 989.
23. I apply Bhattacharyya's application of Nancy Fraser's framing of racial capitalism based on the "three exes—exchange, exploitation, and expropriation," but I do not singly analyze "expulsion," which Bhattacharyya adds. I embed expulsion procedures in expropriation mechanisms. I also add an analysis of "replication" and "protection." These inclusions uncover how nonwhite racial groups and geographies contribute to global racial capitalism and how global legal institutions and frameworks "protect" white global interests. Although I do not discretely examine "exchange," I place aspects of exchange dynamics in the other components. Most clearly, I view exchange value as a form of racialized value. The price points of final products (tangible and intangible), and the price points of the myriads of products and services that make up the components to a final product, are all racialized. See Bhattacharyya, *Rethinking Racial Capitalism*, 37; Fraser, "Race, Empire, Capitalism"; Harris, "Whiteness as Property."
24. Fraser, "Race, Empire, Capitalism," 27.
25. Dicken, *Global Shift*.
26. Raj-Reichert, "Role of Transnational."
27. Pierre, "Racial Vernaculars"; Wilson, *Race, Racism, and Development*.
28. Christian and Namaganda, "Transnational Intersectionality"; Collins and Bilge, *Intersectionality*.
29. Barrientos, "Gender Dynamics," 326.
30. Romero, *Introducing Intersectionality*.
31. Barrientos, "Gender Dynamics"; Boeri, "Challenging the Gendered"; Cabezas, *Economies of Desire*.
32. Williams, *Sex Tourism*.
33. The exploitation of Black women carework goes back to racial enslavement and colonial arrangements. Nonwhite and immigrant women typically provide carework in global North geographies now. See Glenn, *Forced to Care*; Romero, *Maid in USA*.
34. Christian and Namaganda, "Ugandan Domestic Worker"; Parreñas, *Unfree*.
35. Bledsoe and Wright, "Anti-Blackness," 12.
36. Barndt, *Tangled Routes*.
37. Holmes, *Fresh Fruit*.
38. Lincoln, "Labour Migration."
39. Rifai-Hasan, "Development, Power."
40. Frasier, "Race, Empire, Capitalism," 18, 20. Fraser also conceptualizes expropriation as what occurred during colonial racial slavery, making those enslaved not just exploited like with free labor but also a "dependent racialized expropriable subject," 26.
41. Harvey, *New Imperialism*, 63.
42. Dicken, *Global Shift*, 405, 414.
43. Jenkins and Leroy, *Histories of Racial Capitalism*.
44. Corporate Accountability Lab, "Fifty Years of Exploration."
45. Environmental Justice Atlas, "Amungme against Freeport."

46. International Coalition for Papua, *Special Report: PT*, 20.
47. Wakenge, "Referees Become."
48. Nathan and Sarkar, "Blood on Mobile Phone."
49. Nathan and Sarkar, "Blood on Mobile Phone."
50. Nathan and Sarkar, "Blood on Mobile Phone."
51. Wakenge, "Referees Become Players," 69.
52. Wakenge, "Referees Become Players," 72.
53. Mollett, "Power to Plunder," 414; Christian, "Kenya's Tourist Industry."
54. Christian, "Racial Neoliberalism"; Mollet, "Power to Plunder," 424.
55. Christian, "Kenya's Tourist Industry."
56. Christian, "Kenya's Tourist Industry"; Christian, "Tourism Global Production."
57. Mbaria and Ogada, *Big Conservation Lie*.
58. Sheller, *Consuming the Caribbean*.
59. Dunaway and Clelland emphasize BRICS, particularly Asia's rise as a displacement of white supremacy, and delink current BRICS economic practices from ongoing global white economic forces. Mignolo positively sees the rise of BRICS as a legacy of the Bandung Conference and "dewesternization," and as a hope that the "rules of the game" will change. See Dunaway and Clelland, "Challenging Global Apartheid"; Mignolo, "Role of BRICS."
60. See chapter 6, "The Non-White West" in Andrews, *New Age*, for an analysis of how the racial logic of empire continues through the economic practices of these countries.
61. Boatcă, "Centrality of Race," 446.
62. Kimari and Ernston, "Imperial Remains," 827.
63. Boatcă, "Centrality of Race," 466.
64. Nonini and Ong, "Chinese Transnationals," 4.
65. Kang'ara, "China and Africa," 377.
66. Kimari and Ernston, "Imperial Remains," 825.
67. Kang'ara, "China and Africa"; Kimari and Ernston, "Imperial Remains."
68. Castillo, "'Race,' and 'Racism'" 324.
69. Cheng, *Discourses of Race*.
70. Boatcă, "Centrality of Race," 471.
71. UNCTAD, *World Investment Report*.
72. Cheng, *Discourses of Race*, 207.
73. Castillo, "'Race,' and 'Racism,'" 311.
74. Valdes and Cho, "Critical Race Materialism," 1516.
75. Valdes and Cho, "Critical Race Materialism," 1526; Gathii, "Beyond Color-Blind."
76. Rahman, "White Adjacent Muslim," 264.
77. McMichael, *Development and Social Change*, 100–107.
78. McMichael, *Development and Social Change*, 103.
79. McMichael, *Development and Social Change*; Quince, "Racism by Design."
80. McMichael, *Development and Social Change*, 139.
81. Dicken, *Global Shift*, 200.

82. Mgbeoji, *Global Biopiracy*.
83. Wilson, *Race, Racism, Development*
84. Rahman, "White-Adjacent Muslim," 261.
85. King, "A Time to Break Silence," 240.
86. Kramer, "Shades of Sovereignty," 261.
87. Williams, *White Malice*, 30.
88. Williams, *White Malice*; Trenta, "Remote Killing."
89. See W. J. Hennigan's op-ed from the *New York Times* that explores the multigenerational harmful impacts on communities across the globe from nuclear testing. Hennigan, "What Over 2,000."
90. Branche, "Torture of Terrorists?"; Elkins, *Legacy of Violence*.
91. Elkins, *Legacy of Violence*; Kramer, "Shades of Sovereignty," 261.
92. Branche, "Torture of Terrorists?"; Elkins, *Legacy of Violence*.
93. Goldberg, *Are We Postracial*, 118–22.
94. Husain, "Deracialization, Dissent," 211.
95. Achiume, "Report of the Special," 7.
96. Daulatzai and Rana, "Writing Muslim Left," xvii.
97. Selod, Islam, and Garner, *Global Racial Enemy*, 22.
98. Husain, "Deracialization, Dissent," 208.
99. Meier, "Idea of Terror," 20.
100. Selod, *Forever Suspect*.
101. Razac, "Catastrophically Damaged."
102. Lipsitz, *Possessive Investment*.
103. Selod, Islam, and Garner also use the framing of "a global domino effect" to describe antiterror policies. See *Global Racial Enemy*, 4.
104. Silverstein and Sprengel, "An (Un)marked Foreigner."
105. *Al Jazeera*, "Timeline."
106. Human Rights Watch, "Break Their Lineage."
107. Moreton-Robinson, Casey, and Nicoll, *Transnational Whiteness*, ix.
108. Oxfam, "Fueling Conflict."
109. Oxfam, "Fueling Conflict," 12; Alshaif, "Black and Yemeni."
110. Clarno, *Neoliberal Apartheid*, 162.
111. Lentin, *Traces of Racial Exception*, 8.
112. Clarno, *Neoliberal Apartheid*, 165.
113. Savell, "How Death Outlives War."
114. Savell, "How Death Outlives War."
115. Vine, *Base Nation*, 216.
116. Thomson, *Outsourced Empire*, 8.
117. Chisholm, "Silenced and Indispensible," 36.
118. Chisholm, "Silenced and Indispensible," 40.
119. Chisholm, "Silenced and Indispensible," 27; Streets, *Martial Races*.
120. Chisholm, "Silenced and Indispensible."
121. Jones et al., *Russia's Corporate Soldiers*, 1.

122. Zakaria, "White Russian Empire."
123. Jones et al., *Russia's Corporate Soldiers*, 37.
124. Jones et al., *Russia's Corporate Soldiers*, 57.
125. Jones et al., *Russia's Corporate Soldiers*, 2.
126. The August 2023 suspicious death via plane crash of Wagner leader Yevgeny Prigozhin may come to represent the consequence of dissent.
127. Vine, *Base Nation*, 3, 5.
128. Vine, *Base Nation*, 6.
129. Vine, *Base Nation*, 83–84.
130. Vine, *Base Nation*, 74.
131. Vine, *Base Nation*, 71.
132. Vine, *Base Nation*, 75–76.
133. Vine, *Base Nation*, 63, 67.
134. Sand, "Diego Garcia," 113.
135. Sand, "Diego Garcia," 114.
136. Yusuf and Chowdhury, "Persistence of Colonial."
137. Sand, "Diego Garcia," 115.
138. Rana, *Terrifying Muslims*.
139. Vine, *Base Nation*; Enloe, *Bananas, Beaches, and Bases*.
140. Gross-Wyrtzen and Gazzotti, "Telling Histories."
141. Baker, "Contingencies of Whiteness," 124.
142. Doherty, "Short History Nauru"; Lentin, *Why Race Still Matters*, 54.
143. Yaron, Hashimshony-Yaffe, and Campbell, "'Infiltrators' or Refugees."
144. Gidron, "How Israel's Secret."
145. Garner, "European Union," 71.
146. Garner, "European Union," 71.
147. Bahri, "Race and Color."
148. Smith, "What's Behind the Deaths."
149. Tondo and Bellingreri, "Tunisian Cemeteries."
150. Faiola et al., "With Europe's Support, North African Nations Push Migrants to the Desert," *Washington Post*, May 20, 2024. Their report is a detailed accounting of the policing and abuses against migrants with funding from European countries in specific North African countries. See https://www.washingtonpost.com/world/interactive/2024/eu-migrant-north-africa-mediterranean/.
151. Gross-Wyrtzen, "There Is No Race."
152. Tondo and Bellingreri, "Tunisian Cemeteries."
153. Gross-Wyrtzen and Gazzotti, "Telling Histories," 827.
154. Hall, *Representation*, 234.
155. Hall, *Representation*, 258.
156. Valluvan, "What Is 'Post Race,'" 2247.
157. Russell, "Race and Reflexivity"; Kim, *Asian Americans*, 305.
158. Mullings, "Interrogating Racism."
159. Wekker, *White Innocence*.
160. Rodríguez-García, "The Persistence,"

161. Roper, "Blackface at the Andean Fiesta."
162. Morris, "Music."
163. Castillo, "The Han Saviour"; Kimari and Ernston, "Imperial Remains," 835.
164. White, "Use of Blackface."
165. Hartman, *Scenes of Subjection*, 39.
166. Morris, "Music," 361.
167. Jackson, *White Negroes*, 6.
168. Smith, *Shine Bright*, 51; Ramsey, *Race Music*.
169. Morrison, "Sound(s) of Subjection," 13.
170. Morrison, "Sound(s) of Subjection," 16, 19–20.

171. "Race music" is the umbrella term that segregated all genres of Black musical expression, was marketed as such, and whose songs were often appropriated by white artists. White singer Pat Boone was one of the artists who became (in)famous in the 1950s by covering the songs of Black artists. For more on rock music see the *Little Richard: I Am Everything* documentary, which re-centers Black Queer pioneers as the architects of rock and roll who were rooted in what Fredara Hadley calls the "well spring of Black creativity; Black community." Hadley, "The World We Make," 206. Also see Guthrie Ramsey's *Race Music* for a broader history of what he calls the "community theatres" of everyday Black life that produced a celebratory, jubilant, intergenerational aesthetic rooted in multiple spaces of community gathering.

172. Perry, "Global Black Self-Fashioning," 636.
173. Ho, "Consuming Women."
174. Anderson, *Soul in Seoul*.
175. Examples according to Claire Jean Kim include Girls' Generation, BEAST/B2ST, Bubble Sisters, and Mamamoo. See Kim, *Asian Americans*, 315.
176. Garza, "Where All My," 3, 8.
177. Garza, "Where All My," 24. Black K-Pop fans have pushed K-Pop idols to address themes of appropriation and anti-Black racism, particularly in the wake of George Floyd's murder, but have also received pushback. The band BTS is described as one that more authentically centers Black cultural influences and demonstrates support for Black Lives Matter. See Cho, "BTS for BLM."
178. Oh, "Performing Post-Racial Asianness," 124.
179. Cho, "BTS for BLM," 275.
180. Kim, "Racialization of the Cultural Toolkit."
181. Rivera-Rideau, *Remixing Reggaetón*.
182. The *LA Times* published "Latinx Files: Reggaeton Has a Colorblindness Problem" by Shaadi Devereaux, April 2023, after global reggaeton superstar Bad Bunny minimized racism in Puerto Rico. Also see Rivera-Rideau and Torres-Leschnik, "The Colors," 92, for an analysis of the white racial practices of the Luis Fonsi global smash, *Despacito*.
183. Rivera-Rideau and Torres-Leschnik, "The Colors," 91–92, 94.
184. Rivera-Rideau, *Remixing Reggaetón*, 86.
185. Jackson, *White Negroes*; Tate, "I Do Not See."
186. Tate, "I Do Not See," 208.
187. Tate, "I Do Not See," 208.

188. Jackson, *White Negroes*, 31–36.
189. Pérez, "Ontology of Twerk."
190. Roth-Gordon, Harris, and Zamora, "Producing White Comfort."
191. Parker et al., "From 'Fight the Power.'" See Carson, "Owning My Masters."
192. El Zein, "Hip Hop Revolutionaries."
193. Glenn, "Yearning for Lightness."
194. Jackson, *White Negroes*, 98.
195. Lu, "The Many Faces," 171–72.
196. Brzeski, "How Japanese Anime."
197. Kowner and Demel, *Race and Racism*, 19.
198. Fleming and Indelicato, "Introduction: On Transnational."
199. Lee and Kolluri, *Hong Kong and Bollywood*, 14.
200. Gehlawat, "The Gori."
201. Beeman and Narayan, "If You're White."
202. Raghuram, "New Racism."
203. Chakraborty, "Bollywood and Hindu," 94.
204. Tsika, *Nollywood Stars*, 7.
205. Tsika, *Nollywood Stars*, 8.
206. Uzuegbunam, "Oppositional Gaze," 122.
207. Ekwenchi, "Seeing Colours," 1.
208. Rêgo and Pastina, "Brazil and Globalization."
209. Rêgo and Pastina, "Brazil and Globalization," 90.
210. Erlick, *Telenovelas*, 95; Rivadeneyra, "Gender and Race," 216.
211. Dos Santos Soares, "Look, Blackness," 7.
212. Gillam, *Visualizing Black Lives*, 2.
213. In 2023, Black American actor Taraji P. Henson painfully spoke publicly about the narratives she heard over her career to justify her lower pay relative to white actors. See Sharf, "Taraji P. Henson."
214. Kraidy and Al-Ghazzi, "Neo-Ottoman Cool," 18.
215. Ergin, "Is the Turk," 836.

Chapter 4

1. Feldman, "Do the Right Thing," 248.
2. Kelley, *Race Rebels*.
3. Horne, *Race War!*
4. Bush, "Black Internationalism," 311.
5. Bell, "*Brown v. Board*," 22.
6. Melamed, *Represent and Destroy*, 2.
7. Sidaway and Power, "'The Tears of Portugal,'" 538.
8. The CIA financially supported over 225 different organizations across the globe, many billed as anticolonial and antiracist, to spread U.S. influence during the Cold War. NATO military equipment was provided to Portugal to fight against decolonization. See Batalha, *Cape Verdean*; Williams, *White Malice*, 56.

9. According to Luca Trenta the U.S. was involved in three regime changes in the 1960s—the Dominican Republic, South Vietnam, and Chile—that "included the assassination of a foreign official." See Trenta, "Remote Killing?" 476.
10. Füredi, *Silent War*, 226.
11. Melamed, *Represent and Destroy*, 6.
12. Freeman, Kim and Lake, "Race in International Relations," 180.
13. Commander, *Afro-Atlantic Flight*, 12.
14. Gathii, "Retelling Good," 988; Chatterjee, *The Nation*, 6.
15. Quijano, "Coloniality of Power"; Tamale, *Decolonization*.
16. Elkins, *Legacy of Violence*, 20.
17. Táíwò, *Reconsidering Reparations*, 24.
18. The UK has 5 Overseas Territories in the Caribbean—1 in Gibraltar, 1 Oceania, 1 in Africa, and 2 in the Polar Region—and 1 "Total Dependence" in Asia. France has 2 Overseas Departments and 2 Overseas Collectivities in the Caribbean, 1 Special Collectivity and 2 Overseas Collectivities in Oceania, 2 Overseas Departments and 1 Overseas Territory in Africa, and 1 Overseas Territory in the Polar Region. The Netherlands has 3 Constituent Countries of the Kingdom of Netherlands and 1 Special Municipality of Netherlands in the Caribbean. Spain has 2 "Places of Sovereignty" in Morocco. Denmark has 1 Overseas Territory and 1 Self Governing Dependency. Norway has 3 Overseas Territories in the Polar Regions. The U.S. has 3 Unincorporated Unorganized Territories in the Caribbean, and 2 Unincorporated Organized Territories, 1 Commonwealth in Political Union, 1 Free Association, and 1 Unincorporated Organized Territory in Oceania. Australia has 4 Non Self Governing Overseas Territories, and 2 Non Self Governing Overseas Territories in Oceania. New Zealand has 2 Free Associations and 1 Territory in Oceania. Source: CIA World Factbook, https://www.cia.gov/the-world-factbook/
19. Yusuf and Chowdhury, "The Persistence," 160, 157.
20. Táíwò, *Reconsidering Reparations*, 21.
21. Dikötter, "Racialization of the Globe," 1482.
22. Thompson, "Through, Against," 145.
23. Delatolla, *Civilization*, 19.
24. Pierre, *Predicament of Blackness*.
25. Bonilla-Silva, "Rethinking Racism"; *White Supremacy*.
26. Doane, "Beyond Colorblindness," 978.
27. Pierre, *Predicament of Blackness*, 39.
28. See Grosfoguel, "What Is Racism"; Fanon, *Wretched of the Earth*.
29. There is a long and vast literature on race, racism, and inequality in the U.S. from W.E.B. Du Bois, to Kwame Ture and Charles Hamilton, to the emergence of Black Studies, Ethnic Studies, and Critical Race Theory. Important modern critical race studies books in sociology include Omi and Winant, *Racial Formation*; Ladner, *Death of White Sociology*; Feagin, *Racist America*; Glenn, *Unequal Freedom*; Collins, *Black Feminist Thought*; Romero, *Maid in USA*; Jung, *Beneath the Surface of White Supremacy*; and all the works of Eduardo Bonilla-Silva.
30. Lopez, *White by Law*.

31. Strmic-Pawl, Jackson, and Garner, "Race Counts."
32. Bashi Treitler, *Ethnic Project*.
33. Massey and Denton, *American Apartheid*; Kozol, *Shame of the Nation*.
34. Alexander, *New Jim Crow*; Muhammad, *Condemnation of Blackness*
35. Oliver and Shapiro, *Black Wealth*; Taylor, *Race for Profit*; Darity and Mullen, *From Here*.
36. Gómez, *Inventing Latinos*.
37. Gómez, *Inventing Latinos*, 9.
38. Gómez, *Inventing Latinos*; Hernández, *Racial Innocence*.
39. Wade, *Race and Ethnicity*.
40. Hernández, *Racial Subordination*, 14
41. Pérez, "Cuba," 391.
42. Derham, "Construction," 379.
43. Hernández, *Racial Innocence*, 13, 24.
44. Tate and Law, *Caribbean Racisms*.
45. Navarro, *Virgin Capital*, 48.
46. Navarro, *Virgin Capital*.
47. García-Peña, *Borders of Dominicanidad*, 2.
48. Hernández, *Racial Innocence*, 16.
49. Emigh, Ahmed, and Riley, *How Everyday Forms*, 51.
50. Childers, *In Someone Else's Country*.
51. García-Peña, *Borders of Dominicanidad*.
52. Farmer, *Haiti after the Earthquake*; Wu and Edmonds, "Trump and the Continent"; Forgie, "US Imperialism."
53. Sandoval García, *Otros Amenazantes*.
54. Bonhomme, "We're a Bit Browner."
55. Olivieri et al., "Labour Market."
56. Weinstein, *Color of Modernity*.
57. Perry, *Black Women*, 35; Williams, *Sex Tourism*.
58. Warren, *Racial Revolutions*.
59. Villén Pérez et al., "Brazilian Amazon."
60. See Twine, *Racism Racial Democracy*; Hanchard, *Orpheus and Power*; Caldwell, *Negras in Brazil*. As Keisha-Khan Perry notes, much of the scholarship that globally spread this important analytic shift was conducted by Black American scholars who were subject to charges of American "ethnocentrism," and from early critical Brazilian and international scholars who began debunking the myth of racial democracy in the late 1970s. For more on the history of the research trajectory and critique see French, "Missteps of Anti-Imperialist"; Perry, *Black Women*.
61. Hernández, *Racial Subordination*.
62. Hernández, *Racial Subordination*, 99.
63. Hordge-Freeman, *Second-Class Daughters*.
64. Perry, "Resurgent Far-Right," 158.
65. Perry, "Resurgent Far-Right," 159.

66. Hernández, *Racial Subordination*.
67. Alves and Ravindran, "Racial Capitalism," 188.
68. Alves and Ravindran, "Racial Capitalism," 190
69. Ravindran, "What Undecidability," 976.
70. Hernández, *Racial Subordination*, 81.
71. Ravindran, "What Undecidability"; "Power of Phenotype."
72. Quoted in Backhouse, *Colour-Coded*, 14. See Dionne Brand, *A Map to the Door of No Return*, for her writing on the Black Diasporic, Canadian experience and the operation of anti-Blackness.
73. Backhouse, *Colour-Coded*, 9.
74. McKittrick, "Their Blood."
75. Woolford and Benvenuto, "Canada and Colonial Genocide," 375.
76. Francis, *Creative Subversions*, 12–13.
77. Stelkia, "Police Brutality."
78. Marrison, "Canada's 'Freedom Convoy.'"
79. Zakharov, *Race and Racism*, 13.
80. Small, "Theorizing Visibility," 1187.
81. The Center for Contemporary Cultural Studies published *The Empire Strikes Back* in 1982. Strongly influenced by Stuart Hall's work, it was one of the first books to apply a structural perspective of race and racism to Europe, in this case Britain. The insights from the text about political economic fault lines and state changes in the 1970s, white nationalist politics, racial ideological constructions, and structural inequalities still mirror the realities in England today, according to Claire Alexander, "Empire Strikes Back."
82. Harrison, "White Minority," 116.
83. Portugal held on to Macau until 1999, having originally tried to return the island to China during its decolonization push, but China did not want to accept it at that time.
84. Lubkemann, "Unsettling the Metropole."
85. Lisbon already had a historical Black population of enslaved and free individuals in the fifteenth and sixteenth centuries. See Curington, *Laboring in the Shadow*, 14, 39.
86. Rocha, "Race and Society."
87. Goode, "Race, Crime," 175.
88. Repinecz, "Unearthing Spanish Racism."
89. Goode, "Race, Crime," 174.
90. Rodríguez-García, "Persistence of Racial."
91. Goode, "Race, Crime."
92. Lombardi-Diop and Romeo, *Postcolonial Italy*.
93. Houben, "Boundaries of Race."
94. Weiner, "Ideologically Colonized."
95. Keaton, *Muslim Girls*, 9.
96. In 2005 two young men were electrocuted while hiding from the police and triggered a twenty-one-day uprising throughout the *banlieues* in hundreds of French towns.
97. Keaton, *Muslim Girls*, 90.
98. Essed and Trienekens, "Who Wants," 53; Wekker, *White Innocence*.

99. Essed and Trienekens, "Who Wants," 57.
100. Essed and Trienekens, "Who Wants," 57–58.
101. El-Tayeb, "Blood Is," 149.
102. Novati, "Battle for the *Jus Soli*."
103. Hawthorne, *Contesting Race*.
104. Lefkaditou, "Blood Affairs," 329; Lefkaditou, "Observations on Race." Lefkaditou addresses the history of racial blood group studies in Greece and the resurfacing of biological racial essentialism.
105. Law, *Mediterranean Racisms*, 39.
106. Hawthorne, *Contesting Race*, 3.
107. Giannis Antetokounmpo, a current NBA player in the U.S., only received Greek citizenship after he was drafted. His life story is often evoked to call attention to the stateless Greek-born residents of undocumented parents who experience racism and material hardship and the hypocrisy of the Greek state for cheering his successes while denying citizenship and rights to other nonwhite Greek populations. See Kokkindis, "the 'Lost Antetokounmpos.'"
108. Samaras, "End of Golden Dawn."
109. Baker, *Race and the Yugoslav*.
110. Said, *Orientalism*.
111. Böröcz, "Goodness Is Elsewhere," 129.
112. Kalmar, *White but Not Quite*.
113. Kalmar, *White but Not Quite*, 148.
114. Poland is instructive here. Polish citizens were racialized when they traveled within the E.U. for work, and now Poland has become one of the region's main destinations of migrant workers. According to Daria Krivonos, Poland prefers Ukrainian workers due to a perceived shared affinity with cultural whiteness. See Krivonos, "Racial Capitalism."
115. Phelps, "Scientific Racism," 413, 416–19.
116. Baker, *Race and the Yugoslav*, 66, 66–69.
117. Baker, *Race and the Yugoslav*, 106–9. Baker is quick to note the tensions of race under state socialism. Even when raceblindness was espoused and similar experiences with western inferior racialization supposedly linked Yugoslavs with nonwhite colonized groups, South Slavs had participated in colonial pursuits in Africa.
118. Baker, *Race and the Yugoslav*, 128.
119. It is important to contextualize and unpack the Soviet position on race. Simple characterizations that racism did not exist because of the communist emphasis on class are inaccurate, as is merely equating race in the Soviet era to that of the West. Promoting Soviet antiracism was a political tool used to differentiate from the West, but in practice Soviet classification, although under the language of nation and ethnicity, hierarchically ranked "civilized" geographies, with classically nonwhite spaces labeled as "backward." Stalin's famous 1913 essay, which led to the state policy on ethnic groups, may not have positioned "an exclusive form of racial nationalism" but neither did it "challenge the reality of race," according to Ian Law. Moreover, the political way "Blackness" was used as international propaganda both shows how Blackness is positioned differently outside

the West, and sometimes benefitted those racialized as Black, as in the reception in the Soviet Union of Black intellectuals, but also how anti-Blackness festered under the surface. Moreover, one can argue that the Soviet Union was somewhat racialized outside of whiteness by the West. Therefore, our analysis must always be relational, contextual, and understood within this global hierarchy of the global racial system and the national maneuvers pursued. See Zakharov, *Race and Racism*; Law, *Red Racisms*, 15.

120. Djagalov, "Racism," 291–292.
121. Kakışım, "Racism in Russia," 105.
122. Avrutin, *Racism in Modern Russia*; Law, *Red Racisms*.
123. Avrutin, *Racism in Modern Russia*, 7.
124. Laruelle, "Central Asian Labor Migrants."
125. Edgar, "Fragmented Nation," 256.
126. Haugen, *Establishment of National Republics*.
127. Haugen, *Establishment of National Republics*, 43, 48.
128. Krivonos, "Racial Capitalism."
129. Henriksen and Rahbek-Clemmensen, "The Greenland Card."
130. Jensen, "Greenland, Arctic Orientalism."
131. Kakışım, "Racism in Russia," 113.
132. Patel, "How Imperial Hopes."
133. See Costley White, "Oceanic Negroes"; Aboagye, "Australian Blackness."
134. MacPherson, *Reinventing the Nation*.
135. Keane, *The World's People*.
136. MacPherson, *Reinventing the Nation*, 220.
137. MacPherson, *Reinventing the Nation*.
138. Vowles and Gibbons, "Representation, Identity."
139. Houkamau, Stronge, and Sibley, "Prevalence and Impact."
140. Nicoll, "Consuming Pathologies."
141. Ang and Colic-Peisker, "Sinophobia in the Asian Century."
142. Ang, Ho, and Yeoh, "Migration and New Racism," 589.
143. Ang and Colic-Peisker, "Sinophobia in the Asian Century."
144. Matsuoka, "Unveiling Race," 12.
145. Yonezawa, "Memories of Japanese"; Baber, "'Class and "Race"'; Owens, "Traveling Yellow Peril."
146. Kim, *Imperial Citizens*.
147. Owens, "Traveling Yellow Peril," 30.
148. Dikötter, *Discourse of Race*; Harrell, "Introduction: Civilizing Projects."
149. Zang, *Ethnicity in China*.
150. Cheng, *Discourses of Race*, 203.
151. Black writes, "When war correspondent Wallace Terry arrived in Saigon reporting for Time Magazine, African American combat casualties, at 22%, were higher than whites and double actual African American representation. 'The front line soldiers were all brothers,' says Terry, 'So much so that between 1965–1967 it was called Soulville." See Black, "Soul Soldiers," 27.
152. Frey, "Agent Orange."

153. Kiernan, *Pol Pot Regime*, 4.
154. Su, "Becoming Cambodian," 278.
155. Železný, "More than Just Hedging," 236.
156. Mukherjee, "Race Relations."
157. MacLean, "Rohingya Crisis," 88.
158. Mukherjee, "Race Relations."
159. MacLean, "Rohingya Crisis," 89.
160. The three categories of citizenship—full, associate, and naturalized—adjudicated rights based off discrete ideals of Burman lineage. See MacLean, "Rohingya Crisis," 88
161. MacLean, "Rohingya Crisis," 93.
162. Hoon, "Assimilation, Multiculturalism," 151
163. Hoon, "Assimilation, Multiculturalism," 151.
164. Hoon, "Assimilation, Multiculturalism," 151, 152.
165. Roque, "Colonial Ethnological Line," 389, 390.
166. Simpson, "'Illegally and Beautifully,'" 281; Kusumaryati, "#Papuanlivesmatter," 457.
167. Tan, "We Are Not."
168. Philpott, "Fear of the Dark," 381, 386.
169. Kabutaulaka, "Re-Presenting Melanesia."
170. Ballard, "Oceanic Negroes."
171. Pryke, "Risks of China's Ambitions."
172. Grossman, "China's Pacific Push."
173. Abu-Laban and Bakan, "Anti-Palestinian Racism," 145.
174. Goldberg, *Threat of Race*; Spangler, *Understanding Israel/Palestine*.
175. Abu-Laban and Bakan, "The Racial Contract," 643.
176. Abu-Laban and Bakan, "The Racial Contract," 643.
177. Erakat, "Whiteness as Property," 85.
178. Lentin, *Traces of Racial Exception*; Erakat, "Whiteness as Property."
179. UNHCR, *Statistics of Foreigners*; Mehrotra, "Israel Turns to Indian Workers."
180. Christie, *Race and Nation*, 195.
181. Rocha and Aspinall, "Introduction: Africa," 417.
182. Cooke, *Tribal Modern*, 34.
183. Cooke, *Tribal Modern*, 36.
184. Le Renard, *Western Privilege*, 28
185. Vitalis, *America's Kingdom*.
186. Vitalis, *America's Kingdom*; Le Renard and Vora, "Interrogating Race," 97.
187. Lori and Kuzmova, "Who Counts," 107.
188. Le Renard and Vora, "Interrogating Race," 98.
189. Zia-Ebrahimi, "'Arab Invasion,'" 1043, 1044.
190. Cooke, *Tribal Modern*; Le Renard, *Western Privilege*; Le Renard and Vora, "Interrogating Race."
191. International Labour Organization, "Labour Migration."
192. Kassamali, "The Kafala System."

193. Le Renard and Vora, "Interrogating Race," 100.
194. Cooke, *Tribal Modern*, 14; Le Renard, *Western Privilege*.
195. Labib, *Imagining the Arab Other*, ix.
196. Nevola, "Black People."
197. Nevola, "Black People."
198. Alshaif, "Black and Yemeni," 130.
199. Alshaif, "Black and Yemeni," 130.
200. Alshaif, "Black and Yemeni," 131.
201. Nevola, "Black People," 95.
202. Hahonou, "Blackness, Slavery," 41, 42.
203. Mauritania did not outlaw slavery until 1980. Stephen King estimates 450,000–900,000 "Black Arabs" in the country are enslaved. See King, "Black Arabs."
204. Ltifi, "Disarticulating Blackness," 56.
205. Ltifi, "Disarticulating Blackness," 56.
206. Tayeb, "What Is Whiteness."
207. Silverstein, "Racial Politics," 50, 53; Rouighi, "Race on the Mind."
208. Troutt Powell, *Different Shade*, 17; Elsaket, "Jungle Films."
209. See Troutt Powell, *Different Shade*; Abubakr, "Contradictions of Afro-Arab"; Moll, "Narrating Nubia"; Elsaket, "Jungle Films."
210. Troutt Powell, *Different Shade*.
211. Moll, "Narrating Nubia."
212. Tahrir Institute, "Egypt's Racial Nationalism."
213. Gross-Wyrtzen, "'There Is No Race.'"
214. Khoury, "Western Sahara."
215. Parikh, "Limits of Confronting."
216. El Hamel, *Black Morocco*, 5.
217. Bahri, "Race and Color," 148.
218. Gross-Wyrtzen, "'There Is No Race.'"
219. Parikh, "Limits of Confronting"; Gross-Wyrtzen, "'There Is No Race.'"
220. Parikh, "Limits of Confronting"; King, "Black Arabs."
221. Ndlovu-Gatsheni, *Empire, Global Coloniality*, 126.
222. Pierre, *Predicament of Blackness*.
223. Ndlovu-Gatsheni, *Empire, Global Coloniality*, 86, 90.
224. Commander, *Afro-Atlantic Flight*, 1, 3.
225. Commander, *Afro-Atlantic Flight*, 110.
226. Augusto and King, "'Skilled White Bodies'"; Christian and Namaganda, "Good Mzungu?".
227. Pallister-Wilkins, "Saving the Souls"; Remers, "Voluntourism."
228. Sharkey, "Arab Identity," 30.
229. Sharkey, "Arab Identity," 39.
230. Sharkey, "Arab Identity," 32.
231. Mondesire, "Race after Revolution," 87.

Chapter 5

1. Villafranca, *Costa Rica*, 28.
2. The 1862 *Ley de Bases y Colonización* (Law of Settlement and Colonization) was based on fears that the U.S. following the Civil War would send Black Americans to Central America. See Harpelle, *West Indians*, 12.
3. Longley, *Sparrow and the Hawk*, 12.
4. Ahmed, "Phenomenology of Whiteness," 153.
5. Shahjahan and Edwards, "Whiteness as Futurity," 3.
6. Shahjahan and Edwards, "Whiteness as Futurity," 3; Tayeb, "What Is Whiteness."
7. Shome, "Whiteness and Politics," 111.
8. McMillan Cottom, *Thick*, 112.
9. Ahmed, "Phenomenology of Whiteness," 154.
10. I published an earlier version of Figure 5.1. See Christian, "Global Critical Race," 180.
11. Kim's figure shows how Asian Americans are racialized and triangulated in relation to white and Black Americans across the different racialization dimensions of civic ostracism and relative valorization. I do not engage with these dimensions specifically; rather, I address how capital is captured and harnessed by groups and countries across the globe. See Kim, "Racial Triangulation," 108.
12. Kim, "Racial Triangulation," 106.
13. Frankenberg, "The Mirage," 76.
14. Tayeb, "What Is Whiteness."
15. Tayeb, "What Is Whiteness."
16. Eduardo Bonilla-Silva argues that some middle groups achieve "honorary white" status in the U.S. His grouping only includes the U.S. but draws from racialized labels that are globally resonate and include "light skinned Latinos, Japanese Americans, Korean Americans, Asian Americans, Chinese Americans, Middle Eastern Americans, most multiracial, Filipino Americans." Nadia Kim critiques this designation as flattening the racial experiences of Asian Americans. Through a global racial field perspective, I argue that some nonwhite groups for mixed reasons can get access to some white capital but that does not mean they do in all forms, and most never fully become "white." See Bonilla-Silva, "From Bi-Racial," 933; Kim, "Critical Thoughts."
17. Harris, "Whiteness as Property," 282.
18. Sociological racial applications to Pierre Bourdieu's field theory of power are seen in Ghassan Hage's "field of whiteness" analysis to understand white Australian power through an axis of belonging and not belonging and George Steinmetz's examination of empires in what he labels "imperial global relations." Steinmetz also addresses how there are different kinds of fields, some embedded in others, and "social spaces" where unequal groups compete for resources through capital. While acknowledging these field scales and social space differences, I believe it is important to outline a broad globally expansive field of racial positions because country and group racial rankings were always globally, relationally understood. See Hage, *White Nation*, 55–57. See Steinmetz, "Sociology of Empires," "Social Fields," and endnote 23 in this chapter for more analysis on Bourdieu and race.

19. Kaiwar and Mazumdar, "Introduction," 3.
20. Arat-Koç, "New Whiteness(es)," 156; Joseph, "Taking Race Seriously," 346.
21. Shahjahan and Edwards, "Whiteness as Futurity."
22. Babcock, "(De)Coupling Positional Whiteness," 32.
23. Hage, *White Nation*, 55. Bourdieu's analysis of cultural and symbolic capital and habitus is adopted in several sociological studies of race (see Twine, *Racism in Racial Democracy*; Bonilla-Silva, Goar, and Embrick, "When Whites Flock"); but his primary analytic emphasis was on class. When he addressed race, the scale remained in the colonial geography of Algeria and not its production in metropole France. Wacquant, in *Racial Domination*, more recently argues that Bourdieu did use a broader framing of racism. My work both uses Bourdieu's analytic tools and critiques the more common default color-blind interpretations of capital. See Richards et al., "What's Race Got."
24. Breen and Meer, "Securing Whiteness," 599.
25. Todorova, "Race Travels," 144.
26. Pierre, *Predicament of Blackness*, 26.
27. Bandelj and Wherry, "Introduction," 8, 7.
28. Andrucki, "Visa Whiteness Machine."
29. Gómez, *Manifest Destines*; Kim, "Critical Thoughts."
30. Stoler, *Haunted by Empire*, 2.
31. Painter, *History of White People*, 58.
32. See Jacobson, *Whiteness of a Different Color*, and Painter, *History of White People*, for examples of the "untidy" taxonomy and struggles over whiteness and white categories.
33. Blumenbach, "On the Variety," 27.
34. Morton, *Crania Americana*, 5.
35. Keane, *The World's Peoples*, 24–28.
36. Frankenberg, "The Mirage," 74.
37. Critical race theory is at the forefront of analyzing how the law constructs race through both "coercion and ideology" and in the distribution of rights, privileges, and through created racialized institutional and spatial boundaries of belonging. See Lopez, *White by Law*, 10; Harris, "Whiteness of Property"; Gómez, *Manifest Destines*.
38. Jacobson, *Whiteness of Different Color*, 25; Newman, *Dark Inheritance*, 271.
39. Luttikhuis, "Beyond Race," 542.
40. Twinam, "Purchasing Whiteness," 146–47.
41. *Cédulas de gracias al sacar* have a long history and include petitioning for legitimacy and noble title, among others, that go back to the fifteenth century.
42. Hernández, *Racial Subordination*, 20; Twinam, "Purchasing Whiteness," 142; Twinam, *Purchasing Whiteness*.
43. Twinam, *Purchasing Whiteness*, 27–29.
44. Twinam, *Purchasing Whiteness*, 28.
45. Twinam, *Purchasing Whiteness*, 29.
46. Twinam, *Purchasing Whiteness*, 29.
47. Twinam, *Purchasing Whiteness*, 104.
48. Twinam, "Purchasing Whiteness," 141–44.

49. Forbes, "Black Pioneers," 243.
50. Edwards, *Hiding in Plain Sight*, 8.
51. Edwards, *Hiding in Plain Sight*, 6.
52. Edwards, *Hiding in Plain Sight*, 7.
53. Navarro, *Virgin Capital*, 52–53.
54. Crawford, "Individuals of Part-African"; Newman, *Dark Inheritance*, 10.
55. Crawford, "Individuals of Part-African."
56. Newman, *Dark Inheritance*, 10.
57. Newman, *Dark Inheritance*, 114.
58. Hurwitz and Hurwitz, "Token of Freedom," 424
59. Newman, *Dark Inheritance*, 20, 22.
60. Garrigus, *Before Haiti*, 37.
61. Garrigus, *Before Haiti*, 167, 142.
62. Twinam, "Purchasing Whiteness," 143.
63. Lopez, *White by Law*, 1.
64. Lopez, *White by Law*, 1. See chapters 3 and 4 in *White by Law* for details on the white prerequisite cases and specifics on the *Ozawa* and *Thind* cases that went to the Supreme Court.
65. Lopez, *White by Law*.
66. Farnia, "Law's Inhumanities," 466.
67. Mansour, "Undesirable Alien," 144–45.
68. Kawasaki, "Policy of Apartheid," 57.
69. Kawasaki, "Policy of Apartheid," 57–60.
70. Farnia, "Law's Inhumanities."
71. Tehranian, "Compulsory Whiteness."
72. Garner, *Racism in the Irish*.
73. Tate and Law, *Caribbean Racisms*.
74. Bastos, "Luso-Tropicalism Debunked," 3.
75. Jung, *Reworking Race*.
76. Bastos, "Luso-Tropicalism Debunked"; Jung, *Reworking Race*.
77. Yerushalmi, "Between Amsterdam," 169.
78. Yerushalmi, "Between Amsterdam," 173.
79. Perry, *South to America*, 189–190.
80. Yerushalmi, "Between Amsterdam," 182.
81. Yerushalmi, "Between Amsterdam," 186.
82. Roitman, "Mediating Multiculturalism," 94.
83. Vink, *Creole Jews*.
84. Vink, *Creole Jews*, 147.
85. Leibman and May, "Making Jews."
86. Davis, "'Incommensurate Ontologies.'" Regarding Jewish peoples in Tunisia, Memmi writes, "For better or worse, the Jew found himself one small notch above the Moslem on the pyramid which is the basis of all colonial societies." See *The Colonizer*, xiv.
87. I use Syrian/Lebanon because although Lebanon did not exist as a state at the

time, and immigrants were mostly referred to as Syrian (or sometimes Turk as in Brazil) when they arrived in disparate geographies, they mostly came from the region that is modern Lebanon. See Gualtieri, *Between Arab*; Lesser, *Immigration, Ethnicity*.

88. Gualtieri, *Between Arab*, 37–40.
89. Najar, "Privileges of Positivist Whiteness."
90. Najar, "Privileges of Positivist Whiteness," 2.
91. Gualtieri, *Between Arab*.
92. Najar, "Privileges of Positivist Whiteness," 266.
93. Lesser, *Immigration, Ethnicity*, 155–57.
94. Kawasaki, "Policy of Apartheid."
95. Collins and Nam, "Between the Law."
96. Lesser, *Immigration, Ethnicity*, 161–64.
97. Barnes, "Aryanizing Projects," 64–65, 69–70, 73.
98. Habecker, "Not Black"; Jalata, "Being In"; Woldemikael, "Eritrea's Identity."
99. Batalha, *Cape Verdean*, 50–51; Ture and Hamilton, *Black Power*, 30.
100. Curington, *Laboring in the Shadow*, 46.
101. Batalha, *Cape Verdean*, 27, 51.
102. Bastos, "Race, Medicine," 30.
103. Frenz, "Global Goans."
104. Frenz, "Global Goans."
105. Monaville, "Politics of Elegance."
106. Van Hooste, "Metis in the Belgian Congo," 17.
107. Kumar, *Visions of Empire*; Monaville, "Politics of Elegance"; van Hooste, "Metis in the Belgian Congo"; Williams, *White Malice*, 70.
108. Stoler, *Race and the Education*.
109. Edwards, *Hiding in Plain Sight*, 72.
110. Charlton-Stevens, "Anglo-Indians."
111. Wekker, *White Innocence*, 23.
112. Edwards, *Hiding in Plain Sight*, 71.
113. Laforteza, *The Somatechnics*, 43.
114. Laforteza, *The Somatechnics*, 44.
115. Firpo, "Métis of Vietnam," 54.
116. Firpo, "Métis of Vietnam," 55–56.
117. Fusari, "Orphanages and Citizenship," 188.
118. "Belgium Apology."
119. Hartman, *Lose Your Mother*, 6.
120. Firpo, "Métis of Vietnam," 56.
121. Firpo, "Métis of Vietnam," 56.
122. Wildenthal, "Race, Gender, and Citizenship," 268.
123. Lindner, "Contested Concepts," 69.
124. Wildenthal, "Race, Gender, and Citizenship," 270
125. El-Tayeb, "Blood Is," 161.
126. Pesarini and Tintori, "Mixed Identities," 356.

127. Garner, *Racism in the Irish*, 136.
128. Edwards, *Hiding in Plain Sight*, 5.
129. Lopez, *White by Law*.
130. Gómez, *Manifest Destinies*.
131. Gómez, *Manifest Destinies*, 88–89.
132. Gómez, *Manifest Destinies*, 8–9.
133. Lake and Reynolds, *Drawing the Global Colour Line*, 315.
134. Marczuk, "Origins of Immigration"; Snoek, "Empire, Race."
135. Marczuk, "Origins of Immigration."
136. Hage, *White Nation*, 18.
137. Monsour, "Undesirable Alien," 132.
138. The 1870 U.S. Naturalization Law gave "aliens of African nativity and persons of African descent" the ability to be naturalized. Citizenship rights were granted with the Reconstruction bills, but those rights were gutted in late nineteenth and early twentieth centuries with southern Jim Crow statutes. Native Americans were given citizenship in 1924, but many could not vote. In Australia and New Zealand, indigenous groups were "British subjects" but denied rights in other ways.
139. There is a long literature on whitening in the U.S. The classic studies include Theodore Allen, *The Invention of the White Race*; David Roediger, *The Wages of Whiteness*; Noel Ignatiev, *How the Irish Became White*; Karen Brodkin, *How Jews Became White Folks*; Matthew Freye Jacobson, *Whiteness of a Different Color*.
140. Morrison, "On the Backs," 148.
141. Garner, *Racism in the Irish*, 136.
142. Lesser, *Immigration, Ethnicity*, 152.
143. Zia-Ebrahimi, "Arab Invasion," 1044.
144. Delatolla, *Civilization and Making*, 120–21.
145. Quinn, *In Search of*, 9.
146. Delatolla, *Civilization and Making*, 121.
147. Quinn, *In Search of*, xv–xviii.
148. Quinn, *In Search of*, 5.
149. Gualtieri, *Between Arab*, 16.
150. Todorova, "Race Travels," 8.
151. Todorova, "Race Travels," 133–34.
152. Todorova, *Unequal under Socialism*, 154.
153. Attiah, "The Colonial History"; Goldberg, *Threat of Race*.
154. Christie, *Race and Nation*; Lentin, *Traces of Racial*, 90–95; Spangler, *Understanding Israel/Palestine*; Sabbagh-Khoury, *Colonizing Palestine*, 3. Sabbagh-Khoury describes Zionism as being a "polyvalent term" with "various ideological movements."
155. Mosse, *Toward Final Solution*, 122–25.
156. Lentin, *Traces of Racial Exception*, 28; Christie, *Race and Nation*.
157. Sabbagh-Khoury, *Colonizing Palestine*, 18.
158. Bunche, "Review and Appraisal," 177; Sabbagh-Khoury, *Colonizing Palestine*. Darwin argues that the British wanted to maintain their interests in Palestine partic-

ularly in gaining Jewish support of the World War I effort and to "help guard the approaches to Europe," even as they tried to find solutions that would appease both Arab and Jewish groups. See Darwin, *Empire Project*, 537–38.

159. Lentin, *Traces of Racial Exception*.
160. Hooker, *Theorizing Race*, 73.
161. Hernández, *Racial Subordination*, 20.
162. Hernández, *Racial Subordination*, 26.
163. Hernández, *Racial Subordination*, 26–29.
164. Hernández, *Racial Subordination*, 48.
165. Lesser, *Immigration, Ethnicity*, 15.
166. Hernández, *Racial Subordination*, 29–30.
167. Emigh, Ahmed, and Riley, *How Everyday Forms*, 49.
168. Emigh, Ahmed, and Riley, *How Everyday Forms*, 44.
169. Hernández, *Racial Subordination*, 23.
170. Hooker, *Theorizing Race*, 105.
171. Hooker, *Theorizing Race*, 105.
172. Christian, ". . . Latin America Without," 3.
173. Castro, *Afro-Argentine*, 85

174. Among the six first members at the time of the 1958 founding, France still had colonies in equatorial Africa, was fighting a war with Algeria, and continued to govern its Caribbean Departments. Netherlands still controlled Dutch New Guinea, the contemporary Papua region of Indonesia, and some Caribbean colonies. Belgium governed Ruanda-Urundi and the Belgium Congo. Italy, although lost its colonies after WWII, administered Somaliland, then a U.N. Trust Territory.

175. Böröcz, "Eurowhite," 1126.
176. Böröcz, "Eurowhite," 1128.
177. Narkowicz, "White Enough," 4; Boatcă, "Eastern Margins"; Kalmar, "Race, Racialisation"; Todorova, *Unequal under Socialism*.
178. Narkowicz, "White Enough," 2.
179. Baker, *Race and the Yugoslav*, 143.
180. Kalmar, *White but Not Quite*, 54.
181. Böröcz, "Eurowhite," 1129.
182. Baker, *Race and the Yugoslav*, 142.
183. Van Houtum, "Human Blacklisting," 163, 175, 176.
184. Van Houtum, "Human Blacklisting."
185. Rigby and Crisp, "Fortress Europe."
186. International Organization for Migration, "Missing Migrants Project."
187. Hawthorne, *Contesting Race*, 138.

188. There are twenty-nine member countries of the Schengen Area. Iceland, Norway, Switzerland, and Lichtenstein are associate members but not part of the E.U. See https://www.schengenvisainfo.com/schengen-visa-countries-list/.

189. Van Houtum, "Human Blacklisting," 169.
190. All British nationals (Overseas), British overseas territories citizens (BOTC),

British overseas citizens (BOC), British protected persons (BPP), and British Subjects have visa-free access.

191. See the European Commission's website on Migration and Home Affairs for a map of the countries who do and do not need visas; https://home-affairs.ec.europa.eu/policies/schengen-borders-and-visa/visa-policy_en.

192. Andrucki, "Visa Whiteness Machine"; Le Renard, *Western Privilege*.

193. Boatcă, "Centrality of Race," 469.

194. Andrucki, "Visa Whiteness Machine."

195. Baker, *Race and the Yugoslav*, 21–22, 116–17.

196. Suljagić, "Role of Croatia," 124.

197. Engert, *EU Enlargement*, 49.

198. Engert, *EU Enlargement*, 42.

199. Zaragoza-Cristiani, "Containing the Refugee Crisis," 63.

200. Zaragoza-Cristiani, "Containing the Refugee Crisis," 68.

201. See Delatolla's racial analysis on why Turkey was unable to accede to the E.U. "Global Phenomenology," 8–12,

202. Silverstein and Sprengel, "An (Un)Marked Foreigner."

203. Garner, "European Union."

Chapter 6

1. Quisumbing King, "Recentering US Empire."

2. See "The Color Line Belts the World," published in *Collier's Weekly*, October 20, 1906, republished in Lewis, *W.E.B. Du Bois*, 30. Du Bois used the phrasing of the "color line," which is originally credited to Frederick Douglass, earlier in his 1900 address to the Pan-African Conference in London. Du Bois commonly conceptualized race and subjectivity with the framing of "a problem," but this example also exposes the colorblind aspects of its rendering.

3. Milazzo, *Colorblind Tools*.

4. Itzigsohn and Brown, *Sociology of W.E.B.*, 79.

5. Milazzo, *Colorblind Tools*.

6. Goldberg, *Threat of Race*.

7. Bashi Treitler, "Racialization and its Paradigms."

8. Bashi Treitler, "Racialization and its Paradigms."

9. Melamed, *Represent and Destroy*; Mills, *Black Rights*; Mueller, "Racial Ideology."

10. Cho, "Post-Racialism," 1601.

11. Curington, *Laboring in the Shadow*, 21.

12. Wright, *The Color Curtain*.

13. Goldberg, *Threat of Race*, 152.

14. Taras adopted by Duyvendak, Kesic, and Stacey, *Return of the Native*, 86.

15. Lentin, "Europe and the Silence," 8.

16. Goldberg, *Threat of Race*, 157.

17. France voted to remove *race* from legal texts in 2005. In 2010 the German Institute of Human Rights initiated a campaign to remove *rasse* from the Constitution. In 2016

the Italian Anthropological Association and the Italian Institute of Anthropology wrote a joint letter asking for the removal of *razza* from the Constitution. See Fleming, *Resurrecting Slavery*; Barskanmaz, "Traveling Theory"; Ghebremariam Tesfau' and Picker, "Italian Postracial Archive."

18. Morning, "Ethnic Classification," 239.
19. See Niang, "Innocence, Ignorance"; Beaman, *Citizen Outsider*; Fleming, *Resurrecting Slavery*; Keaton, *Muslim Girls, #You Know You're*.
20. Keaton, *#You Know You're*, 6.
21. Mbembe, *Critique of Black Reason*, 67, 68.
22. Mbembe, *Critique of Black Reason*, 68.
23. Beaman and Petts, "Towards a Global," 3.
24. Beaman, "Are French People White?"
25. Lentin, *Why Race Still*, 61.
26. Keaton, *#You Know You're*, 138–45.
27. Davis, "Macron's Speech."
28. Lentin, *Why Race Still*, 73.
29. Almeida, "Space and Secularism"; Beaman and Petts, "Toward a Global," 5.
30. Fleming, *Resurrecting Slavery*, 19.
31. Wekker, *White Innocence*, 2, 22.
32. Wekker, *White Innocence*, 3.
33. Boulila, "Race and Racial," 1402.
34. Michel, "Sheepology," 413.
35. Purtschert, Falk, and Lüthi, "Switzerland and 'Colonialism,'" 287.
36. Boulia, "Race and Racial."
37. Michel, "Sheepology," 411.
38. Loftsdóttir and Jensen, "Nordic Exceptionalism," 2.
39. DeLong quoted in Loftsdóttir and Jensen, "Nordic Exceptionalism," 2.
40. Barskanmaz, "Traveling Theory"; Müller, "Far Away."
41. Barskanmaz, "Traveling Theory."
42. Müller, "Far Away."
43. Sadeghi, "Racial Boundaries."
44. Wilcox, *Italian Empire*.
45. Wilcox, *Italian Empire*, 154.
46. Mellino, "De-Provincializing Italy," 92.
47. Lombardi-Diop, "Postracial/Postcolonial," 176.
48. Morning and Maneri, *An Ugly Word*.
49. Lombardi-Diop, "Postracial/Postcolonial," 175.
50. Ghebremariam Tesfau' and Picker, "Italian Postracial Archive," 2.
51. Ghebremariam Tesfau' and Picker, "Italian Postracial Archive."
52. Ben-Ghiat, "Return of Fascism."
53. Lanzano "Italian Fascists."
54. Hawthorne, *Contesting Race*.
55. Fra-Molinero, "Suspect Whiteness," 148.

56. Mariscal, "Role of Spain."
57. Fra-Molinero, "Suspect Whiteness."
58. Tofiño-Quesada, "Spanish Orientalism," quoted in Goode, "Race, Crime," 149.
59. Goode, "Race, Crime," 162.
60. Rodríguez-García, "Persistence of Racial," 4.
61. When empire is acknowledged, positive attributes are proclaimed. In 2022 King Felipe VI praised early Spanish colonialism while in Puerto Rico, stating: "All Hispanic communities in the Americas should feel 'proud of [a] shared past, of those values Spain provided." See "Spanish King Praises."
62. Rodríguez-García, "Persistence of Racial," 6.
63. Goode, "Race, Crime," 163.
64. Goode, "Race, Crime," 174.
65. Bastos, "Luso-Tropicalism Debunked."
66. Power, "Anti-Racism, Deconstruction"; Sidaway and Power, "'Tears of Portugal,'" 532.
67. Salazar and elites supposedly thought that Freyre's emphasis on "the African contribution of the new civilization was repellent," but the idea of "new Brazils" was a useful way to challenge anticolonial sentiment. See Rocha, "Race and Society," 339.
68. Rocha, "Race and Society," 339.
69. According to Bastos *Luso-tropicalism discourses* have been used to minimize the transatlantic slave trade, counter journalist reports of incidents of racism in Portugal, and oppose any initiative to gather racial and ethnic statistics. See Bastos, "Luso-Tropicalism Debunked"; Curington, *Laboring in the Shadow*.
70. Lentin and Titley, *Crises of Multiculturalism*.
71. Gilroy, *There Ain't No*.
72. Sarah Mayorga-Gallo distinguishes diversity ideology from colorblind ideology. I find, however, that incorporating diversity ideology, as exhibited in multiculturalism, continues the project of global colorblindness. See Mayorga-Gallo, "White-Centering Logic," 1789.
73. Lentin, "Europe and the Silence"; Lentin, "Post-Race, Post Politics"; McKittrick, "Wait Canada."
74. Lentin, "Replacing 'Race.'"
75. Lentin, "Replacing 'Race.'"
76. Winter, "Rethinking Multiculturalism."
77. McKittrick, "Their Blood Is There."
78. Daigle, "Spectacle of Reconciliation."
79. Hübinette and Lundström, "Three Phases," 429.
80. Hübinette and Lundström, "Three Phases," 432.
81. Törngren, "Does Race Matter," 127.
82. Tan, "We are Not," 276.
83. Roberts, "White (Supremacist) Continent," 105.
84. Van der Watt and Swart, "Whiteness of Antarctica," 126.
85. Corley, Pamphile, and Sawyer, "What Has (and Hasn't)."

86. There is a robust literature that identifies the U.S. as postracial, particularly after the election of Barack Obama in 2008. See Bonilla-Silva, "Structure of Racism"; Cho, "Post-Racialism"; powell, "Post-Racialism or Targeted." Different to Europe, postracial techniques in the U.S. center notions of progress and the idea that we have "solved the race problem." If the U.S. is viewed in a global colorblind context, however, I find that multiculturalism is a more apt description because solving includes celebration of difference and even acknowledgment of continued problems. Clearly, in the U.S. we see overlapping colorblind politicultures depending on region, who is in power, and how racial politics are deployed.

87. Darity and Mullen, *From Here to Equality*.

88. Monteiro, "Race-Conscious Casting," 90.

89. Favell, "Crossing the Race," 4.

90. Lentin and Titley, *Crises of Multiculturalism*, 3.

91. The report argued for a "multi-racial future" and "embraced super diversity" as "multi-ethnicity," and several recommendations advocated for institutionalizing multiculturalism and including intersectional identities for protection in the Equality Act. The report was accused "of branding Britain as racist" by several newspapers for its discussion of empire and national collective memory and members of the commission were attacked; see Favell, "Crossing the Race," 4.

92. Gilroy, "My Britain Is"; Lentin and Titley, *Crises of Multiculturalism*, 2l; Lentin, "Post-Race."

93. Breen and Meer, "Securing Whiteness," 599.

94. Breen and Meer, "Securing Whiteness."

95. Favell, "Crossing the Race," 1.

96. Virdee and McGeever, "Racism, Crisis, Brexit," 1804.

97. Virdee and McGeever, "Racism, Crisis, Brexit."

98. Gilroy, "My Britain Is," 384.

99. Davidson and Virdee, "Introduction: Understanding Racism," 9.

100. Davidson and Virdee, "Introduction: Understanding Racism," 9, 11.

101. Hage, "Multiculturalism and White Paranoia," 417.

102. Hage, "Multiculturalism and White Paranoia," 420.

103. Meeting Australian Values is underscored in the Home Affairs website; see Australian Government, "Australian Values," https://www.homeaffairs.gov.au/about-us/our-portfolios/social-cohesion/australian-values.

104. Cheng, "Talking about 'Australian' Values."

105. Terreblanche, "A Wealth Tax."

106. Goldberg, *Threat of Race*, 314, 312.

107. Steyn and Foster, "Repertoires for Talking White."

108. Milazzo, "Rhetorics of Racial Power," 8.

109. Steyn and Foster, "Repertoires of Talking White."

110. Milazzo, "Rhetorics of Racial Power," "On the Transportability."

111. Van Zyl-Hermann and Boersema, "Introduction."

112. Velayutham, "Everyday Racism," 258.

113. Velayutham, "Races without Racism?" 458.
114. Velayutham, "Everyday Racism."
115. Velayutham, "Everyday Racism," 15.
116. Sugino, "Multicultural Redemption," 3.
117. Sugino, "Multicultural Redemption," 3.
118. Velayutham, "Races without Racism?" 457.
119. Allison-Reumann and He, "Federalism, Race."
120. Sue, *Land of the Cosmic*; Tilley, "Mestizaje"; Telles, "Race and Ethnicity"; Tate and Law, *Caribbean Racisms*.
121. Tate and Law, *Caribbean Racisms*.
122. Telles, "Race and Ethnicity," 188.
123. Telles and Flores, "Not Just Color," 1565.
124. Ng'weno and Siu, "Comparative Raciality."
125. Tilley, "Mestizaje"; Gobat, "Invention of Latin America."
126. Jung, *Menace to Empire*, 32.
127. Gobat, "Invention of Latin America."
128. Tilley, "Mestizaje," 58, 63.
129. Gobat, "Invention of Latin America."
130. Gómez, *Inventing Latinos*.
131. Manrique, "Dreaming of a Cosmic Race"; Tilley, "Mestizaje"; Sue, *Land of the Cosmic*.
132. Manrique, "Dreaming of a Cosmic Race," 1.
133. Gobat, "Invention of Latin America," 1355,
134. Goméz, *Inventing Latinos*, 71.
135. Telles and Flores, "Not Just Color."
136. Roitman, *Race, Ethnicity*.
137. Telles and Flores, "Not Just Color."
138. Hale, Calla and Mullings, "Race Matters."
139. Wood, "Could Bolivia's Current Politics."
140. Tate and Law, *Caribbean Racisms*.
141. Tate and Law, *Caribbean Racisms*.
142. Candelario, *Black behind the Ears*; García Peña, *Borders of Dominicanidad*; Tate and Law, *Caribbean Racisms*.
143. Tate and Law, *Caribbean Racisms*.
144. Clealand, *Power of Race*; Garth, "There Is No Race."
145. Hernández, *Racial Innocence*, 14.
146. Gill, *Future of U.S. Empire*.
147. Gómez, *Inventing Latinos*.
148. Hernández, *Racial Subordination*, 3.
149. Loveman, *National Colors*; Sue, "Is Mexico Beyond."
150. Sue, "Is Mexico Beyond."
151. Christian, "Racial Neoliberalism."
152. Hooker, "Indigenous Inclusion."

153. Hooker, *Race and the Politics*, 134.
154. Christian, ". . . Latin America Without."
155. Gayles and Muñoz-Muñoz, "Unveiling Latin American."
156. Gayles and Muñoz-Muñoz, "Unveiling Latin American," 2.
157. Sue, "Is Mexico Beyond"; Telles and Flores, "Not Just Color."
158. Milazzo, "On the Transportability."
159. Williams, *Sex Tourism*.
160. Anderson, Roque, and Santos, *Luso-Tropicalism*.
161. Twine, *Racism in a Racial Democracy*.
162. Costa Vargas, "Hyperconsciousness of Race," 446.
163. Williams, *Sex Tourism*, 51.
164. Costa Vargas, "Hyperconsciousness of Race," 449.
165. Hordge-Freeman, *Color of Love*, 5.
166. Dos Santos Soares, "Look, Blackness"; Perry, *Black Women*.
167. De Castro, "Why Did Bolsonaro's."
168. The author complicates the racial paradise narrative somewhat, but the overall tone affirms it. See Velasquez-Manoff, "Want to Be Less Racist?".
169. Adams (*The Peoples of Hawaii*, 1925) quoted in Pierce, "Creating a Racial Paradise," 78. Adams came out of the University of Chicago and was inspired by the Chicago School race-relations cycle that mostly ignored structural racism and instead focused on natural antagonisms between groups that would eventually wither with assimilation.
170. Jung, *Reworking Race*; Glenn, *Unequal Freedom*; Pierce, "Creating a Racial Paradise"; Sharma, *Hawai'i Is My Haven*. Hawaii does have an important history of multiracial labor organizing that Moon-Kie Jung in *Reworking Race* addresses as a form of "interracialism." There also existed precolonial interconnected structures and group relations within the islands. There are lessons to be learned from these experiences, but they get drowned out by ideologically simplifying Hawaii as a racial paradise.
171. Kabutaulaka, "Re-presenting Melanesia."
172. Citizens of the Freely Associated States of the Federated States of Micronesia, the Republic of the Marshall Islands, and the Republic of Palau "are legal nonimmigrants allowed . . . to live, work, and study in U.S. without a visa" but due to legal reforms have lost access to most federal public benefits. See United States Commission on Civil Rights, *Micronesians in Hawaii*.
173. Jung, *Reworking Race*.
174. Sharma, *Hawai'i Is My Haven*.
175. There is a long literature on ethnic nationalism, particularly studied in political science, and it is the main framing used in the media to describe these nations. Through a colorblind lens, however, we can see how an overt focus on ethnic nationalist frames hides the racial practices across the global racial system shaping ethnic-dominant claims.
176. Imre, "Whiteness in Post-Socialist."
177. Thompson, "Democratic Hauntings."
178. Roberts, *Fatal Invention*.
179. Kim, *Imperial Citizens*; Kowner, "Race and Racism."

180. Kawai, "Japanese as Both."
181. Kawai, "Japanese as Both."
182. The GHQ censored any mention of race and racism and any reference to the Japanese being a "colored race" in the media to counter any claims of American racism at home and in Japan. U.S.'s colorblindness helped to distance Japan from engaging with the history of its colonial projects. See Kawai, "Japanese as Both," 377.
183. Kowner, "Race and Racism," 100.
184. Suzuki, "Empire and Racialization," 30.
185. Kawai, "Japanese as Both," 388.
186. Kawai, "Japanese as Both," 388.
187. Hough, "Racialization of North Koreans"; Kim, *Imperial Citizens*.
188. Kim, *Imperial Citizens*, 25.
189. Hough, "Racialization of North Koreans."
190. Dikötter, *Discourse of Race*.
191. Dikötter, *Discourse of Race*, 79, 124.
192. Baber, "Race Might Be a Unicorn," 161.
193. Rai, "From Colonial 'Mongoloid,'" 453.
194. Dirks, *Castes of Mind*.
195. Baber, "Race Might Be a Unicorn."
196. Kapur "Colonial Debris," 316.
197. Kapur, "Colonial Debris"; Rai, "From Colonial 'Mongoloid.'"
198. Kapur, "Colonial Debris," 319.
199. The California Department of Fair Employment and Housing filed a lawsuit against Cisco for caste discrimination in 2020. See Chotiner, "Google's Caste-Bias Problem."
200. Ergin, "Is the Turk," 840.
201. Ergin, "Is the Turk," 836.
202. Eissenstat, "Metaphors of Race"; Gökay and Aybak, "Identity, Race, and Nationalism," 109.
203. Gökay and Aybak, "Identity, Race, Nationalism."
204. Arat-Koç "Culturalizing Politics," 392, 401.
205. Ergin and Karakaya, "Between Neo-Ottomanism," 34.
206. Ergin, "Racialization of Kurdish Identity."
207. Karaman, "Coding Whiteness."
208. Zia-Ebrahimi, "Self-Orientalization" 446, 447.
209. Maghbouleh, *Limits of Whiteness*, 55.
210. See Zia-Ebrahimi, "Self-Orientalization."
211. Baker, "Contingencies of Whiteness," 124.
212. Avrutin, *Racism in Modern Russia*; Law, *Red Racisms*; Yusupova, "Invisibility of Race."
213. Zakharov, *Race and Racism*, 13.
214. Zakaria, "White Russian Empire."
215. Avrutin, *Racism Modern Russia*.

216. Todorova, "Race Travels," 168, quoted in Baker, *Race and the Yugoslav*, 12.
217. Baker, *Race and the Yugoslav*; Rucker-Chang and Ohueri, "Moment of Reckoning."
218. Pierre, *Predicament of Blackness*.
219. Mama, "Challenging Subjects."
220. Pierre, "Race in Africa," 549.
221. Hall critiques Mahmood Mamdani's (*Saviors and Survivors*, 2009) interpretation of race in addressing the Darfur conflict and how it was globally politicized. Mamdani seems to claim that because the British labeled communities using racial terms, somehow race is not meaningful (because they are not real), rather than to acknowledge that racism creates race and is exactly about this ascriptive process. See Hall, "Reading Race."
222. Pierre, "Race in Africa," 550.
223. Gross-Wyrtzen, "'There Is No Race," 4–6.
224. Van Zyl-Hermann and Boersema, "Introduction."
225. Pierre, "Race in Africa."
226. Mbembe, *Critique of Black Reason*, 6, 27–31.
227. Augusto and King, "Skilled White Bodies," 120.
228. Law, *Mediterranean Racisms*, 126.
229. Law, *Mediterranean Racisms*, 51.
230. Thomas, *Modern Blackness*, 13.
231. Lewis, *Scammer's Yard*, 162.
232. Davis, "Reflections on Haiti," 9.
233. Davis, "Reflections on Haiti," 8.
234. Wu and Edmonds, "Trump and Continent."
235. Swan, *Pasifika Black*.
236. Kabutaulaka, "Re-presenting Melanesia," 118.
237. Kabutaulaka, "Re-presenting Melanesia," 124.
238. Kelly, "Whiteness, Repressive Victimhood," 59.
239. Meer, "Wreckage of White Supremacy," 501; Harrison, "The White Minority," 111.
240. Harrison, "The White Minority." Eric Kaufmann, academic "poster boy for the far and radical right," supports white self-interests in the name of ethnic self-interests. Former Trump adviser Stephen Miller and his America First Legal, alongside other conservative law firms, are using antidiscrimination civil rights law to sue "woke" companies, universities, and the federal government for initiating antiracist initiatives of redress and diversity enhancement. See Duyvendak, Kesic, and Stacey, *Return of the Native*; Draper, "America First Legal."
241. Essed and Muhr, "Entitlement Racism."
242. McKay, "Masking Legitimized Racism."
243. Lentin, *Why Race Still*.
244. Ghebremariam Tesfau' and Picker, "Italian Postracial Archive," 3.
245. Mondon and Winter, "Racist Movements," 151.
246. Benjamin, *Race after Technology*.

247. Duyvendak, Kesic, and Stacey, *Return of the Native*, 85; Bonilla-Silva, "Feeling Race."

248. See the full statement and signatories at https://nationalconservatism.org/national-conservatism-a-statement-of-principles/.

249. The Heritage Foundation, Claremont Institute, and Manhattan Institute are at the forefront of the anti-CRT, anti-woke, anti-DEI propaganda campaigns. Their talking points are recycled through conservative and even "liberal" editorials in such prestigious outlets as the *New York Times* without any acknowledgment of the connections to conservative think tanks and their mainstreaming of once far right positions.

250. The *New York Times* details all the incidents and ways the program profits from white racial grievance politics, writing, "Mr. Carlson has constructed what may be the most racist show in the history of cable news." See Confessore, "How Tucker Carlson."

251. Lawton, "Tucker Carlson's Embrace."

252. Hill, *Everyday Language*, 50.

253. Peréz, *Souls of White Jokes*.

254. Hall quoted in Wekker, *White Innocence*, 140.

255. Brasher, "Crisis of Confederate," 1317.

256. Mathias, "This Is Why."

257. Brasher, "Crisis of Confederate."

258. Kim, "White Supremacists."

259. Law, *Mediterranean Racisms*.

260. Ashutosh, "Transnational Routes."

261. Walker and Garamvolgyi, "Viktor Orbán."

262. Avrutin, *Racism in Modern Russia*, 92.

263. Kalmar, *White but Not Quite*, 149.

264. Zhang, "Race, Gender, and Occidentalism," 9–12.

265. Meer, "Wreckage of White Supremacy," 501.

266. See Baker, *Race in the Yugoslav*; Christian, ". . . Latin America Without"; Anderson, Roque and Santos, *Luso-Tropicalism*.

267. Beaman, "Racial Gaslighting," 407.

268. Lentin, *Why Race Still*.

Chapter 7

1. Wright, *Color Curtain*, 12.
2. Wright, *Color Curtain*, 176.
3. Mignolo, "The Role of BRICS."
4. Bush, "Black Internationalism," 312.
5. Acharya, "Race and Racism," 40.
6. Bush, *The End of White*; Hanchard, "Black Transnationalism."
7. Mays, *Afro-Indigenous History*, 93, 95; Agathocleous and Neary, "Before Bandung." The conference, however, still had to contend with a common assumption of "pure" races among some contributors. Mosse, *Toward Final Solution*, 121–22.
8. The interpretations and politics of Pan-Africanism evolved, connected to global

currents of the moment, e.g., the Scramble for Africa, World War I, the founding of the League of Nations, the interwar period, World War II, and decolonization. Sabelo J. Ndlovu-Gatsheni identifies six eras of Pan Africanism—Trans Atlantic, Black Atlantic, Continental, Sub-Saharan, Pan-Arab, and Global—that speak to historical debates and complex histories regarding race and African unity. Marcus Garvey's Universal Negro Improvement Association (UNIA) also sought an African homeland for the Black diaspora. See Ndlovu-Gatsheni, *Empire, Global Coloniality*.

9. Commander, *Afro-Atlantic Flight*, 82.
10. Bush, "Black Internationalism"; Mahler, "Beyond the Color."
11. Agathocleous and Neary, "Before Bandung."
12. Prashad, *The Darker Nations*; Táíwò, *Reconsidering Reparations*.
13. Williams, *White Malice*; Worrell, "George Padmore."
14. Bush, *The End of White*.
15. Bush, *The End of White*, 324–35.
16. Mahler, *From the Tricontinental*.
17. See Ture and Hamilton, *Black Power*; Clark, *Dark Ghetto*.
18. Cabral, *Unity and Struggle*, 255.
19. Agathocleous and Neary, "Before Bandung," 617; Eslava, Fakhri, and Nesiah, "Spirit of Bandung."
20. Abubakr, "Contradictions of Afro-Arab"; Labelle, "Tensions of Decolonization."
21. Vitalis, "The Midnight Ride," 268.
22. Bush, *The End of White*; Eslava, Fakhri, and Nesiah, "Spirit of Bandung."
23. Kapur, "Colonial Debris," 312.
24. Beaman, "Towards a Reading"; Kelley, *Freedom Dreams*, xvi; Kirby, "'Black Lives Matter"; Shahin, Nakahara, and Sánchez, "Black Lives Matter."
25. Kelley, *Freedom Dreams*. Shahin, Nakahara and Sánchez, "Black Lives Matter."
26. Táíwò, *Elite Capture*.
27. Crenshaw, "This Is Not a Drill."
28. Goldberg, *War on Critical Race Theory*, 17.
29. In the United States, attacks on CRT are most pronounced in the passage of so-called "divisive concepts" education laws. The CRT-Forward project from the UCLA Law School mapped 807 local, state, and federal efforts as of summer 2024. See CRT Forward Tracking Map, https://crtforward.law.ucla.edu/map/, and their report by Alexander et al., "CRT Forward Tracking."
30. Meghji, *Racialized Social System*.
31. Andrews, "Identity Politics."
32. Hamilton, "Reform, Retrench"; Crenshaw, "This Is Not," 1707.
33. Meer, *Cruel Optimism*, 127.
34. Feldman, "Do the Right Thing," 251–52.
35. Bell, "Racial Realism."
36. Alexander, "Only Revolutionary Love."
37. Bell, *Faces at the Bottom*; Feagin, *White Racial Frame*; Hunter and Robinson, *Chocolate Cities*.

38. Kelley, *Freedom Dreams*, xix.
39. Feagin, *Systemic Racism*.
40. Carbado, "Race to the Bottom."
41. Goldstein, "Introduction," 361–62; Collins, *On Intellectual Activism*, 339–40.
42. Wong, "Future Is Ours," 499.
43. See Biko, *I Write*, and his "Definition of Black Consciousness," 48–53; "Black Consciousness," 97.
44. Mbembe, *Critique of Black Reason*, 6.
45. Collins, *On Intellectual Activism*, 242.
46. Mahler, *From the Tricontinental*, 119.
47. Wu, *Yellow*, 325.
48. Prashad, *Karma of Brown Folk*, 196–97.
49. Collins, *On Intellectual Activism*, 236.
50. Kelley, *Freedom Dreams*, xxxix.
51. Taylor, *From #BlackLivesMatter*.
52. Célestine, Martin-Breteau, and Recoquillon, "Introduction"; Ransby, *Making All Black*.
53. Aboagye, "Australian Blackness"; Alshaif, "Black and Yemeni"; Shahin, Nakahara, and Sánchez, "Black Lives Matter"; Kusumaryati, "#Papuanlivesmatter."
54. Gross-Wyrtzen, "There Is No Race."
55. Célestine, Martin-Breteau, and Recoquillon, "Introduction"; Busey and Coleman-King, "All Around World"; Paschel, "From Colombia."
56. Perry, *Black Women Against*.
57. Ndlovu-Gatsheni, "Cognitive Empire," 895.
58. Fisher, *What's Left*; Mama, *Beyond the Masks*.
59. Beaman, "Black Feminism."
60. El-Tayeb, *European Others*, xxxv.
61. Todorova, *Unequal under Socialism*, 161.
62. The Ten-Point Plans and the BLM Policy Platform both focus on Black self-determination and freedom, an end to racial capitalism, freedom from police violence and militarism, seeking unity with other racial groups and the most marginalized in the Black communities. See M4BL, Vision for Black Lives; Pulido, *Black, Brown, Yellow*, 168.
63. Slate, "Introduction," 1–5.
64. One of the resolutions in 1959 from the first Southwide Institute on Violent Resistance to Segregation stated: "We make common cause with the oppressed and submerged peoples of the world." See Slate, "Dalit Panthers," 135.
65. Pulido, *Black, Brown, Yellow*; Slate, "Introduction."
66. Gumbs, *Survival Is a Promise*.
67. Pulido, *Black, Brown, Yellow*, 33, 153.
68. Within some corners of decolonization scholarship there is a charged discussion that implies working toward antiracism ignores, or worse, actively undermines indigenous sovereignties. Some have even labeled Black subjectivities as "settlers." As Nandita Sharma and Cynthia Wright and others point out, this often exposes exclusionary ideas

of who constitutes as "native" and "non-native" (both colonial identities) and ignores Black native subjectivities and how Blackness was globally rendered through racial enslavement and domination and, therefore, should not be equated with white settlers. Tiffany Lethabo King and colleagues' delicate account of Black-Native relations addresses the tensions and complexities that speak to the importance of a relational analysis. The important U.S. history of how "indigenous" groups are legally rendered as "political" identities over racial, while simultaneously embodying racialized processes and meanings, underscores much of the complex parameters of how indigenous communities seek decolonization. See Brown, "Who Is an Indian"; King, Navarro, and Smith, "Introduction"; Sharma and Wright, "Decolonizing Resistance"; Mays, *Afro-Indigenous History*.

69. Gómez, *Inventing Latinos*; Kim, *Asian Americans*.
70. Ransby, *Making All Black*, 148.
71. Sharma, *Hawai'i Is My Haven*, 21, 218.
72. Matsuda, "We Will Not Be Used"; "Planet Asian America."
73. El Zein, "Introduction."
74. Ransby, *Making All Black*, 99.
75. See Standing Up for Racial Justice's web site for details on values and campaigns, https://surj.org/.
76. Ignatiev, *Treason to Whiteness*, 232.
77. George Yancy explains how even whites who attempt to "undo" and "dis-identify" "with whiteness are still implicated within the systemic structures of racial injustice." See Yancy, "When Heaven and Earth," 198.
78. Yancy, "When Heaven and Earth," 201.
79. Hooker, *Race and the Politics*, 6.
80. Lipsitz, "Rejecting the Racial Contract."
81. Biko, *I Write*, specifically "Black Souls," 25.
82. Lipsitz, "Rejecting Racial Contract," 6.
83. McMillan Cottom, *Thick*, 118.
84. Mbembe, *Critique of Black Reason*, 179–83.
85. Tamale, *Decolonization and Afro-Feminism*.
86. Benjamin, *Viral Justice*, 283.
87. Benjamin, *Viral Justice*, 270.
88. Cabral, *Unity and Struggle*, 241.
89. Táíwò, *Reconsidering Reparations*, 12.
90. Alexander, "Only Revolutionary Love."
91. See Darity and Mullen, *From Here to Equality*, for U.S. models and history; CARICOM, "Ten Point Plan for Reparatory Justice."
92. Táíwò, *Reconsidering Reparations*, 72–74.
93. Kelley, *Freedom Dreams*, xxxv, 115.
94. CARICOM, "Ten Point Plan."
95. Red Nation, "The Red Deal,"17; Kelley, *Freedom Dreams*.
96. Ndlovu-Gatsheni, "The Cognitive Empire," 884, 896.
97. Commander, *Afro-Atlantic Flight*, 18.

98. Gilmore, *Abolition Geography*.
99. Kelley, "Making History."
100. Anderson, Sharma, and Wright, "Why No Borders?"; Sharma and Wright, "Decolonizing Resistance," 131.
101. Tamale, *Decolonization and Afro-Feminism*, 21.
102. French et al., "Toward a Psychological Framework"; Destine, "#Reclaiming My Time."

Bibliography

Aboagye, Kaiya. "Australian Blackness, the African Diaspora and Afro/Indigenous Connections in the Global South." *Transition* 126 (2018): 72–85.

Abu-Laban, Yasmeen, and Abigail B. Bakan. "The Racial Contract: Israel/Palestine and Canada." *Social Identities* 14, no. 5 (2008): 637–60.

———. "Anti-Palestinian Racism: Analyzing the Unnamed and Suppressed Reality." In *Racial Formations in Africa and the Middle East: A Transregional Approach*, 135–42. Middle East Political Science and Program on African Social Research, 2021.

Abubakr, Bayan. "The Contradictions of Afro-Arab Solidarity(ies): The Aswan High Dam and the Erasure of the Global Black Experience." In *Racial Formations in Africa and the Middle East: A Transregional Approach*, 73–80. Middle East Political Science and Program on African Social Research, 2021.

Acharya, Amitav. "Race and Racism in the Founding of the Modern World Order." *International Affairs* 98, no. 1 (2022): 23–41.

Achiume, E. Tendayi. "Report of the Special Rapporteur on Contemporary Forms of Racism, Racial Discrimination, Xenophobia and Related Intolerance." Note by the Secretary-General Seventy-Seventh Session Agenda Item 66, no. 1 (October 25, 2022).

Adams, Mark B. "Eugenics in the History of Science." In *The Wellborn Science: Eugenics in Germany, France, Brazil, and Russia*, edited by Mark Adams, 3–7. New York: Oxford University Press, 1990.

Agathocleous, Tanya, and Janet Neary. "Before Bandung: Afro-Asian Cross-referencing and Comparative Racialization." *Journal of Social History* 54, no. 2 (2020): 599–622.

Ahmed, Sara. "A Phenomenology of Whiteness." *Feminist Theory* 8, no. 2 (2007): 149–68.

Aidi, Hisham, Marc Lynch, and Zachariah Mampilly. "Introduction." In *Racial Forma-*

tions in Africa and the Middle East: A Transregional Approach, 3–9. Middle East Political Science and Program on African Social Research, 2021.

Al Jazeera. "Timeline: Nine Years of French Troops in Mali." February 17, 2022. https://www.aljazeera.com/news/2022/2/17/timeline-what-led-france-to-withdraw-its-troops-from-mali.

Alexander, Claire. "The Empire Strikes Back: 30 Years On." *Ethnic and Racial Studies* 37, no. 10 (2014): 1784–92.

Alexander, Michelle. *The New Jim Crow: Mass Incarceration in the Age of Colorblindness*. New York: New Press, 2010.

———. "Only Revolutionary Love Can Save Us Now." *The Nation*, March 8, 2024. https://www.thenation.com/article/activism/mlk-vietnam-war-speech-gaza-democracy/.

Alexander, Taifha, LaToya Baldwin Clark, Kyle Reinhard, and Noah Zatz. "CRT Forward: Tracking the Attack on Critical Race Theory." CRT Forward's Tracking Project, UCLA School of Law Critical Race Studies, 2023. https://crtforward.law.ucla.edu/wp-content/uploads/2023/04/UCLA-Law_CRT-Report_Final.pdf.

Allen, Theodore W. *The Invention of the White Race*. New York: Verso, 1994.

Allison-Reumann, Laura, and Baogang He. "Federalism, Race, and Ethnicity in Southeast Asia." In *Routledge Handbook of Race and Ethnicity in Asia*, edited by Michael Weiner, 93–107. New York: Routledge, 2022.

Almeida, Dimitri. "Space and Secularism: *Laïcité*, Spatial Governmentality, and Exclusion in French Hijab Stories." *Social Compass* 70, no. 1 (2023): 3–19.

Almeida, Pedro. "Football, Race, and National Identity in Portugal." *Soccer & Society* 23, no. 1 (2022): 75–88.

Alshaif, Gokh Amin. "Black and Yemeni: Myths, Genealogies, and Race." In *Racial Formations in Africa and the Middle East: A Transregional Approach*, 129–34. Middle East Political Science and Program on African Social Research, 2021.

Alves, Jaime Amparo, and Tathagatan Ravindran. "Racial Capitalism, the Free Trade Zone of Pacific Alliance, and Colombian Utopic Spatialities of Antiblackness." *ACME* 19, no. 1 (2020): 187–209.

Anderson, Bridget, Nandita Sharma, and Cynthia Wright. "Why No Borders?" *Refuge* 26 (2009): 5–18.

Anderson, Crystal S. *Soul in Seoul: African American Popular Music and K-Pop*. Jackson: University Press of Mississippi, 2020.

Anderson, Gary Clayton. *Ethnic Cleansing and the Indian: The Crime that Should Haunt America*. Norman: University of Oklahoma Press, 2014.

Anderson, Warwick, Ricardo Roque, and Ricardo Ventura Santos, eds. *Luso-Tropicalism and Its Discontents: The Making and Unmaking of Racial Exceptionalism*. New York: Berghahn Books, 2019.

Andrews, Kehinde. "Black Is a Country: Building Solidarity across Borders." *World Policy Journal* 33, no. 1 (2016): 15–19.

———. *The New Age of Empire: How Racism and Colonialism Still Rule the World*. New York: Bold Type Books, 2021.

———. "Identity Politics from Cruella Braverman to Uncle (Clarence) Thomas." *Make It*

Plain, March 17, 2023. https://make-it-plain.org/2023/03/17/identity-politics-from-cru ella-braverman-to-uncle-clarence-thomas/.

Andrucki, Max J. "The Visa Whiteness Machine: Transnational Motility in Post-Apartheid South Africa." In *Geographies of Privilege*, edited by France Winddance Twine and Bradley Gardener, 121–34. New York: Routledge, 2013.

Ang, Sylvia, and Val Colic-Peisker. "Sinophobia in the Asian Century: Race, Nation and Othering in Australia and Singapore." *Ethnic and Racial Studies* 45, no. 4 (2022): 718–37.

Ang, Sylvia, Elaine Lynn-Ee Ho, and Brenda S. A. Yeoh. "Migration and New Racism beyond Colour and the 'West': Co-Ethnicity, Intersectionality and Postcoloniality." *Ethnic and Racial Studies* 45, no. 4 (2022): 585–94.

Aoki, Keith. "Space Invaders: Critical Geography, the Third World in International Law and Critical Race Theory." *Villanova Law Review* 45 (2000): 913.

Arat-Koç, Sedef. "New Whiteness(es), Beyond the Colour Line? Assessing the Contradictions and Complexities of 'Whiteness' in the (Geo)political Economy of Capitalist Globalism." In *States of Race: Critical Race Feminism for the 21st Century*, edited by S. Razack, M. Smith, and S. Thobani, 147–68. Toronto: Between the Lines, 2010.

———. "Culturalizing Politics, Hyper-Politicizing 'Culture': 'White' vs. 'Black Turks' and the Making of Authoritarian Populism in Turkey." *Dialectical Anthropology* 42, no. 4 (2018): 391–408.

Ashutosh, Ishan. "The Transnational Routes of White and Hindu Nationalisms." *Ethnic and Racial Studies* 45, no. 2 (2022): 319–39.

Attiah, Karen. "The Colonial History of Israel-Palestine: Bringing the Receipts." *Washington Post,* November 3, 2023. https://www.washingtonpost.com/opinions/2023/11/03/colonial-history-britain-israel/.

Augusto, Asaf, and Russell King. "'Skilled White Bodies': Portuguese Workers in Angola as a Case of North–South Migration." *Geographical Journal* 186, no. 1 (2020): 116–27.

Avrutin, Eugene. *Racism in Modern Russia: From the Romanovs to Putin*. London: Bloomsbury, 2022.

Azuma, Eiichiro. "Japanese Immigrant Settler Colonialism in the U.S.-Mexican Borderlands and the U.S. Racial-Imperialist Politics of the Hemispheric 'Yellow Peril.'" *Pacific Historical Review* 83, no. 2 (2014): 255–76.

Babcock, Joshua. "(De)coupling Positional Whiteness and White Identities through "Good English" in Singapore." *Signs and Society* 11, no. 1 (2023): 23–44.

Baber, Zaheer. "'Race Might Be a Unicorn, But Its Horn Could Draw Blood': Racialization, Class and Racism in a Non-Western Context." *Critical Sociology* 48, no. 1 (2022): 151–69.

———. "'Class and 'Race' . . . the Two Antinomic Poles of a Permanent Dialectic': Racialization, Racism and Resistance in Japan." *Current Sociology* (2023): 1–19.

Bacchetta, Paola, Sunaina Maira, and Howard Winant, eds. *Global Raciality: Empire, Postcoloniality, Decoloniality*. New York: Routledge, 2019.

Backhouse, Constance. *Colour-Coded: A Legal History of Racism in Canada, 1900–1950*. Toronto: University of Toronto Press, 1999.

Baghoolizadeh, Beeta. "Seeing Race and Erasing Slavery: Media and the Construction of Blackness in Iran." PhD diss., University of Pennsylvania, 2018.

———. "The Myths of Haji Firuz: The Racist Contour of the Iranian Minstrel." *Lateral* 10, no. 1 (2021).

Bahri, Hamid. "Race and Color in North Africa and the Arab Spring." *Multiculturalism and Democracy in North Africa: Aftermath of the Arab Spring*, edited by Moha Ennaji, 135–56. New York: Routledge, 2014.

Bair, Jennifer, and Marion Werner. "Commodity Chains and the Uneven Geographies of Global Capitalism: A Disarticulations Perspective." *Environment and Planning A* 43 (2011): 988–97.

Baker, Catherine. *Race and the Yugoslav Region*. Manchester: Manchester University Press, 2018.

———. "Contingencies of Whiteness: Gendered/Racialized Global Dynamics of Security Narratives." *Security Dialogue* 52 (2021): 124–32.

Baker, Lee D. *From Savage to Negro: Anthropology and the Construction of Race, 1896–1954*. Berkeley: University of California Press, 1998.

Balibar, Étienne. "Racism and Nationalism." In *Race, Nation, Class: Ambiguous Identities*, by Immanuel Wallerstein and Étienne Balibar, 37–68. New York: Verso, 1991.

Ballard, Chris. "'Oceanic Negroes': British Anthropology of Papuans, 1820–1869." In *Foreign Bodies: Oceania and the Science of Race, 1750–1940*, edited by Bronwen Douglas and Chris Ballard, 157–201. Canberra: Australian National University Press, 2008

Bandelj, Nina, and Frederick F. Wherry. "Introduction: An Inquiry into the Cultural Wealth of Nations." In *The Cultural Wealth of Nations*, edited by Nina Bandelj and Frederick F. Wherry, 1–20. Palo Alto, CA: Stanford University Press, 2011.

Banerjee-Dube, Ishita. "Caste, Race, and Difference: The Limits of Knowledge and Resistance." *Current Sociology* 62, no. 4 (2014): 512–30.

Barder, Alexander D. "Scientific Racism, Race War and the Global Racial Imaginary." *Third World Quarterly* 40, no. 2 (2019): 207–23.

Barndt, Deborah. *Tangled Routes: Women, Work, and Globalization on the Tomato Trail*. Lanham, MD: Rowman & Littlefield, 2008.

Barnes, Andrew E. "Aryanizing Projects, African 'Collaborators' and Colonial Transcripts." In *Antinomies of Modernity Essays on Race, Orient, and Nation*, edited by Vasant Kaiwar and Sucheta Mazumdar, 62–97. Durham, NC: Duke University Press, 2003.

Barr, Jeremy. "Fox News Host Tucker Carlson Takes Show—and His Message—to Hungary." *Washington Post*, August 3, 2021. https://www.washingtonpost.com/media/2021/08/03/tucker-carlson-hungary/.

Barrera, Giulia. "Mussolini's Colonial Race Laws and State-Settler Relations in Africa Orientale Italiana (1935–41)." *Journal of Modern Italian Studies* 8, no. 3 (2003): 425–43.

Barrientos, Stephanie. "Gender Dynamics in Global Value Chains." In *Handbook on Global Value Chains*, edited by Stefano Ponte, Gary Gereffi, and Gale Raj-Reichert, 324–38. Northampton: Elgar, 2019.

Barskanmaz, Cengiz. "Traveling Theory: Anti-Racism without Racism." Presentation Teaching Truth to Power: Critical Race Theory Summer School, African American Policy Forum, July 18, 2022.

Bashi Treitler, Vilna. *The Ethnic Project: Transforming Racial Fiction into Ethnic Factions*. Palo Alto, CA: Stanford University Press, 2013.

———. "Racialization and Its Paradigms: From Ireland to North America." *Current Sociology* 64, no. 2 (2016): 213–27.

Bashi Treitler, Vilna, and Manuela Boatcă. "Dynamics of Inequalities in a Global Perspective: An Introduction." *Current Sociology* 64, no. 2 (2016): 159–71.

Bashir, Haroon. "Black Excellence and the Curse of Ham: Debating Race and Slavery in the Islamic Tradition." *ReOrient* 5, no. 1 (2019): 92–116.

Bastos, Christiana. "Race, Medicine and the Late Portuguese Empire: The Role of Goan Colonial Physicians." *Journal of Romance Studies* 5, no. 1 (2005): 23–35.

———. "Luso-Tropicalism Debunked, Again: Race, Racism, and Racialism in Three Portuguese-Speaking Societies." In *Luso-Tropicalism and Its Discontents: The Making and Unmaking of Racial Exceptionalism*, edited by Warwick Anderson, Ricardo Roque, and Ricardo Ventura Santos, 243–64. New York: Berghahn Books, 2019.

Batalha, Luís. *The Cape Verdean Diaspora in Portugal: Colonial Subjects in a Postcolonial World*. Lanham, MD: Lexington Books, 2004.

Bauman, Zygmunt. "Modernity." In *The Oxford Companion to Politics of the World*, 2nd ed., edited by Joel Krieger, 551–73. Oxford: Oxford University Press, 2001.

Beaman, Jean. "As French as Anyone Else: Islam and the North African Second Generation in France." *International Migration Review* 50, no. 1 (2015): 41–69.

———. *Citizen Outsider: Children of North African Immigrants in France*. Berkeley: University of California Press, 2017.

———. "Are French People White? Towards an Understanding of Whiteness in Republican France." *Identities* 26, no. 5 (2019): 546–62.

———. "Black Feminism and Transnational Solidarity: Mobilization against Police Violence in France." *Esclavages & Post-Esclavages* 6 (2022).

———. "Towards a Reading of Black Lives Matter in Europe." *JCMS: Journal of Common Market Studies* 59 (2021): 103–14.

———. "Racial Gaslighting in a Non-racial France." *Contemporary French and Francophone Studies* 26, no. 4 (2022): 406–17.

Beaman, Jean, and Amy Petts. "Towards a Global Theory of Colorblindness: Comparing Colorblind Racial Ideology in France and the United States." *Sociology Compass* 14, no. 4 (2019): 1–11.

Beeman, Angie, and Anjana Narayan. "If You're White You're Alright: The Reproduction of Racial Hierarchies in Bollywood Films." In *Covert Racism: Theories, Institutions, and Experiences*, edited by Rodney D. Coates, 155–73. Boston: Brill, 2011.

Begum, Neema. "Revolt on the Right: Explaining Support for the Radical Right in Britain." *Commonwealth & Comparative Politics* 55, no. 1 (2017): 108–10.

"Belgium Apology for Mixed-Race Kidnappings in Colonial Era." *BBC News*, April 4, 2019. https://www.bbc.com/news/world-europe-47817530.

Beliso-De Jesús, Aisha M., and Jemima Pierre. "Anthropology of White Supremacy." *American Anthropologist* 122, no. 1 (2020): 65–75.

Bell, Derrick A. "*Brown v. Board of Education* and the Interest Convergence Dilemma." In *Critical Race Theory: The Key Writings that Formed the Movement*, edited by Kimberlé Crenshaw, Neil Gotanda, Gary Peller, and Kendall Thomas, 20–29. New York: New Press, 1995.

———. "Racial Realism." In *Critical Race Theory: The Key Writings that Formed the Movement*, edited by Kimberlé Crenshaw, Neil Gotanda, Gary Peller, and Kendall Thomas, 302–29. New York: New Press, 1995.

———. *Faces at the Bottom of the Well: The Permanence of Racism*. New York: Basic Books, 2018.

Ben-Gihat, Ruth. "The Return of Fascism in Italy." *The Atlantic*, September 23, 2022. https://www.theatlantic.com/international/archive/2022/09/giorgia-meloni-italy-election-fascism-mussolini/671515/.

Benjamin, Ruha. *Race after Technology: Abolitionist Tools for the New Jim Code*. Medford, MA: Polity Press, 2019.

———. *Viral Justice: How We Grow the World We Want*. Princeton, NJ: Princeton University Press, 2022.

Berkhofer, Robert. 1979. *The White Man's Indian*. New York: Vintage Books, 1979.

Bernasconi, Robert, and Tommy L. Lott, eds. *The Idea of Race*. Indianapolis: Hackett, 2000.

Bhambra, Gurminder. "The Possibilities of, and for, Global Sociology: A Postcolonial Perspective." *Postcolonial Sociology* 24 (2013): 295–314.

Bhattacharyya, Gargi. *Rethinking Racial Capitalism: Questions of Reproduction and Survival*. London: Rowman & Littlefield, 2018.

Bhattacharyya, Gargi, John Gabriel, and Stephen Small. *Race and Power: Global Racism in the Twenty-First Century*. London: Routledge, 2002.

Biko, Steve. *I Write What I Like: Selected Writings*. Chicago: University of Chicago Press, 2015.

Black, Samuel W. "Soul Soldiers: African Americans and the Vietnam Era." *Western Pennsylvania History:1918–2018* (2006): 22–31.

Black Central Europe. "Kant, Über die Verschiedenen Rassen Der Menschen (1777)." July 17. https://blackcentraleurope.com/quellen/1750-1850-deutsch/kant-uber-die-verschiedenen-rassen-der-menschen-1777/.

Blackburn, Robin. *The Making of New World Slavery: From the Baroque to the Modern 1492–1800*. London: Verso, 1997.

Blanton, Robert, David Mason, and Brian Athow. "Colonial Style and Post-Colonial Ethnic Conflict in Africa." *Journal of Peace Research* 38, no. 4 (2001): 473–91.

Bledsoe, Adam. "Marronage as a Past and Present Geography in the Americas." *Southeastern Geographer* 57, no. 1 (2017): 30–50.

Bledsoe, Adam, and Willie Jamaal Wright. "The Anti-Blackness of Global Capital." *Environment and Planning D: Society and Space* 37, no. 1 (2019): 8–26.

Blumenbach, Johann Friedrich. "On the Variety of Mankind." In *The Idea of Race*, edited by Robert Bernasconi and Tommy L. Lott, 26–37. Indianapolis: Hackett, 2000.

Boatcă, Manuela. "The Eastern Margins of Empire: Coloniality in 19th Century Romania." *Cultural Studies* 21, no. 2/3 (2007): 368–84.

———. "The Centrality of Race to Inequality across the World-System." *Journal of World-Systems Research* 23, no. 2 (2017): 465–73.

Boeri, Natascia. "Challenging the Gendered Entrepreneurial Subject: Gender, Development, and the Informal Economy in India." *Gender & Society* 32, no. 2 (2018): 157–79.
Bonhomme, Macarena. "'We're a Bit Browner but We Still Belong to the White Race': Making Whiteness in the Context of South-South Migration in Chile." *Latin American and Caribbean Ethnic Studies* 18, no. 2 (2023): 227–43.
Bonilla-Silva, Eduardo. "Rethinking Racism: Toward a Structural Interpretation." *American Sociological Review* 62, no. 3 (1997): 465–80.
———. *White Supremacy and Racism in the Post–Civil Rights Era*. Boulder, CO: Lynne Reinner, 2001.
———. "From Bi-Racial to Tri-Racial: Towards a New System of Racial Stratification in the USA." *Ethnic and Racial Studies* 27, no. 6 (2004): 931–50.
———. "The Structure of Racism in Color-Blind, 'Post-Racial' America." *American Behavioral Scientist* 59, no. 11 (2015): 1358–76.
———. "Feeling Race: Theorizing the Racial Economy of Emotions." *American Sociological Review* 84, no. 1 (2019): 1–25.
Bonilla-Silva, Eduardo, Carla Goar, and David G. Embrick. "When Whites Flock Together: The Social Psychology of White Habitus." *Critical Sociology* 32, no. 2/3 (2006): 229–53.
Bonnet, Alastair. *Multiracism: Rethinking Racism in Global Context*. New York: John Wiley & Sons, 2021.
Böröcz, József. "Goodness Is Elsewhere: The Rule of European Difference." *Comparative Studies in Society and History* 48, no. 1 (2006): 110–38.
———. "'Eurowhite' Conceit, 'Dirty White' Ressentment: 'Race' in Europe." *Sociological Forum* 36, no. 4 (2021): 1116–34.
Boucher, Leigh, Jane Carey, and Katherine Ellinghaus, eds. *Re-Orienting Whiteness*. New York: Palgrave Macmillan, 2009.
Boulila, Stefanie Claudine. "Race and Racial Denial in Switzerland." *Ethnic and Racial Studies* 42, no. 9 (2019): 1401–18.
Bourdieu, Pierre. *Distinction a Social Critique of the Judgement of Taste*. Cambridge, MA: Harvard University Press, 1984.
Bourdieu, Pierre, and Loïc Wacquant. "On the Cunning of Imperialist Reason." *Theory, Culture & Society* 16, no. 1 (1999): 41–58.
Bracey, Glenn. "Toward a Critical Race Theory of State." *Critical Sociology* 41, no. 3 (2015): 553–72.
Branche, Raphaëlle. "Torture of Terrorists? Use of Torture in a 'War against Terrorism': Justifications, Methods and Effects: The Case of France in Algeria, 1954–1962." *International Review of the Red Cross* 89, no. 867 (2007): 543–60.
Brand, Dionne. *No Language Is Neutral*. Toronto: Coach House Press, 1990.
———. *A Map to the Door of No Return: Notes on Belonging*. Toronto: Vintage Canada, 2002.
Brasher, Jordan P. "The Crisis of Confederate Memory in the Interior of São Paulo, Brazil." *Memory Studies* 14, no. 6 (2021): 1314–32.
Breen, Damian, and Nasar Meer. "Securing Whiteness: Critical Race Theory and the Securitization of Muslims in Education." *Identities* 26, no. 5 (2019): 595–613.

Brodkin, Karen. *How Jews Became White Folks and What that Says about Race in America.* New Brunswick, NJ: Rutgers University Press, 1998.

Brown, Hana E. "Who Is an Indian Child? Institutional Context, Tribal Sovereignty, and Race-Making in Fragmented States." *American Sociological Review* 85, no. 5 (2020): 776–805.

Bruce, Marcus. "The New Negro in Paris." In *Black France/France Noire,* edited by Trica Danielle Keaton, T. Denean Sharpley-Whiting, and Tyler Stovall, 207–20. Durham, NC: Duke University Press, 2012.

Brzeski, Patrick. "How Japanese Anime Became the World's Most Bankable Genre." *Hollywood Reporter,* May 16, 2022. https://www.hollywoodreporter.com/business/business-news/japanese-anime-worlds-most-bankable-genre-1235146810/.

Bunche, Ralph J. *A World View of Race.* Port Washington: Kennikat Press, 1936.

———. "Review and Appraisal of Israeli-Arab Relations." In *Ralph J. Bunche: Selected Speeches and Writings,* edited by Charles P. Henry, 165–74. Ann Arbor: University of Michigan Press.

Bush, Roderick. *The End of White World Supremacy: Black Internationalism and the Problem of the Color Line.* Philadelphia: Temple University Press, 2009.

———. "Black Internationalism and Transnational Africa." In *Rod Bush: Lessons from a Radical Black Scholar on Liberation, Love, and Justice,* edited by Melanie E. L. Bush, Rose Brewer, Robert Newby, and Daniel Douglas, 301–39. Belmont, MA: Ahead, 2019.

Busey, Christopher L., and Chonika Coleman-King, "All around the World Same Song: Transnational Anti-Black Racism and New (and Old) Directions for Critical Race Theory in Educational Research." *Urban Education* 58, no. 6 (2020): 1–28.

Cabezas, Amalia L. *Economies of Desire: Sex and Tourism in Cuba and the Dominican Republic.* Philadelphia: Temple University Press, 2009.

Cabral, Amílcar. *Unity and Struggle, Speeches and Writings.* New York: Monthly Review Press, 2016.

Caldwell, Kia. *Negras in Brazil: Re-Envisioning Black Women, Citizenship, and the Politics of Identity.* New Brunswick, NJ: Rutgers University Press, 2007.

Candelario, Ginetta E.B. *Black behind the Ears: Dominican Racial Identity from Museums to Beauty Shops.* Durham, NC: Duke University Press, 2007.

Carbado, Devon W. "Race to the Bottom." *UCLA Law Review* 49 (2001): 1283.

Carby, Hazel V. "'On the Threshold of Woman's Era': Lynching, Empire, and Sexuality in Black Feminist Theory." *Critical Inquiry* 12, no. 1 (1985): 262–77.

CARICOM Reparations Commission. "CARICOM Ten Point Plan for Reparatory Justice." https://crtforward.law.ucla.edu/map/.

Carrera, Magali M. *Imagining Identity in New Spain: Race, Lineage, and the Colonial Body in Portraiture and Casta Paintings.* Austin: University of Texas Press, 2003.

Carson, A.D. "Owning My Masters: The Rhetorics of Rhymes & Revolutions." PhD diss., Clemson University, 2017. https://tigerprints.clemson.edu/all_dissertations/1885.

Castillo, Roberto. "'Race' and 'Racism' in Contemporary Africa-China Relations Research: Approaches, Controversies and Reflections." *Inter-Asia Cultural Studies* 21, no. 3 (2020): 310–36.

---. "The Han Saviour behind the Blackface: Racialised and Gendered Media Representations in Africa-China Popular Geopolitics." *Inter-Asia Cultural Studies* 22, no. 3 (2021): 421–39.

Castro, Donald. *The Afro-Argentine in Argentine Culture: El Negro del Acordeón*. New York: Edwin Mellon Press, 2001.

Célestine, Audrey, Nicolas Martin-Breteau, and Charlotte Recoquillon. "Introduction—Black Lives Matter: A Transnational Movement?" *Esclavages & Post-esclavages (Slaveries & Post-Slaveries)* 6 (2022).

Center for Contemporary Cultural Studies. *The Empire Strikes Back: Race and Racism in '70s Britain*. London: Routledge, [1982] 2005.

Césaire, Aimé. *Discourse on Colonialism*. New York: Monthly Review Press, [1955] 2000.

Chakraborty, Chandrima. "Bollywood and Hindu Nationalism." *Global Media Journal* 13, no. 1 (2021): 94–107.

Chancel, Lucas, Thomas Piketty, Emmanuel Saez, and Gabriel Zucman. *World Inequality Report*. World Inequality Lab, 2022.

Chandler, Nashum Dimitri. *X—The Problem of the Negro As a Problem for Thought*. New York: Fordham University Press, 2013.

Charlton-Stevens, Uther. "Anglo-Indians in Colonial India: Historical Demography, Categorization and Identity." In *The Palgrave International Handbook of Mixed Racial and Ethnic Classification,* edited by Z. L. Rocha and P. J. Aspinall, 669–92. New York: Springer, 2020.

Chatterjee, Partha. *The Nation and Its Fragments: Colonial and Postcolonial Histories*. Princeton, NJ: Princeton University Press, 1993.

Cheng, Jennifer. E. "Talking about 'Australian Values' in the Australian Parliament: How Politicians Contest Culturalist Racism." *Critical Race and Whiteness Studies*, 9, no. 2 (2013).

Cheng, Yinghong. *Discourses of Race and Rising China*. Switzerland: Palgrave Macmillan, 2019.

Childers, Trenita Brookshire. *In Someone Else's Country: Anti-Haitian Racism and Citizenship in the Dominican Republic*. Lanham, MD: Rowman & Littlefield, 2020.

Chisholm, Amanda. "The Silenced and Indispensible." *International Feminist Journal of Politics* 16, no. 1 (2014): 26–47.

Cho, Michelle. "BTS for BLM: K-Pop, Race, and Transcultural Fandom." *Celebrity Studies* 13, no. 2 (2022): 270–79.

Cho, Sumi. "Post-Racialism." *Iowa Law Review* 94 (2008): 1589–644.

Chotiner, Isaac. "Google's Caste-Bias Problem." *New Yorker*, August 11, 2022. https://www.newyorker.com/news/q-and-a/googles-caste-bias-problem.

Christian, Michelle. "'. . . Latin American without the Downside': Racial Exceptionalism and Global Tourism in Costa Rica." *Ethnic and Racial Studies* 36, no. 10 (2013): 1599–618.

---. "Racial Neoliberalism in Costa Rican Tourism: *Blanqueamiento* in the Twenty-First Century." *Current Perspectives in Social Theory* (2015): 157–189.

———. "Kenya's Tourist Industry and Global Production Networks: Gender, Race and Inequality." *Global Networks* 16, no. 1 (2016): 25–44.
———. "Tourism Global Production Networks and Uneven Social Upgrading in Kenya and Uganda." *Tourism Geographies* 18, no. 1 (2016): 38–58.
———. "A Global Critical Race and Racism Framework: Racial Entanglements and Deep and Malleable Whiteness." *Sociology of Race and Ethnicity* 5, no. 2 (2019): 169–85.
Christian, Michelle, and Assumpta Namaganda. "Transnational Intersectionality and Domestic Work: The Production of Ugandan Intersectional Racialized and Gendered Domestic Worker Regimes." *International Sociology* 33, no. 3 (2018): 315–36.
———. "The Ugandan Domestic Worker Global Labor Chain to Gulf States: Transnational Intersectionality, Violence, and Resistance." In *IV ISA Forum of Sociology*, February 23–28, 2021. International Sociological Association.
———. "Good Mzungu? Whiteness and White Supremacy in Postcolonial Uganda." *Identities* (2022): 1–20.
Christie, Clive J. *Race and Nation*. London: I.B. Tauris, 1998.
Christofides, R.M. "Hamlet Versus Othello: Or, Why the White Boy Keeps Winning." *Shakespeare* 17, no. 1 (2021): 6–14.
Christopher, Anthony. "Race and Ethnicity Classification in British Colonial and Early Commonwealth Censuses." In *The Palgrave International Handbook of Mixed Racial and Ethnic Classification*, edited by Zarine L. Rocha and Peter J. Aspinall, 27–48. New York: Springer, 2020.
Churchill, Ward. *A Little Matter of Genocide: Holocaust and Denial in the Americas 1492 to the Present*. San Francisco: City Lights Books, 1997.
Clark, Kenneth B. *Dark Ghetto: Dilemmas of Social Power*. New York: Harper & Roe, 1965.
Clarno, Andy. *Neoliberal Apartheid: Palestine/Israel and South Africa after Apartheid*. Chicago: University of Chicago Press, 2017.
Clealand, Danielle. *The Power of Race in Cuba: Racial Ideology and Black Consciousness during the Revolution*. Oxford: Oxford University Press, 2017.
Collins, Erin, and Sylvia Nam. "Between the Law and the Actual Situation: Failure as Property Formation in French Colonial Indochina." *Society and Space D* 40, no. 2 (2022): 227–44.
Collins, Patricia Hill. *Black Feminist Thought: Knowledge, Consciousness, and the Politics of Empowerment, Second Edition*. New York, Routledge, 2000.
———. *Black Sexual Politics: African Americans, Gender, and the New Racism*. New York: Routledge, 2004.
———. *On Intellectual Activism*. Philadelphia: Temple University Press, 2013.
Collins, Patricia Hill, and Sirma Bilge. *Intersectionality*. Hoboken, NJ: John Wiley & Sons, 2020.
Commander, Michelle. *Afro-Atlantic Flight: Speculative Returns and the Black Fantastic*. Durham, NC: Duke University Press, 2017.
Confessore, Nicholas. "How Tucker Carlson Stoked White Fear to Conquer Cable." *New York Times*, May 4, 2022. https://www.nytimes.com/2022/04/30/us/tucker-carlson-gop-republican-party.html?action=click&module=RelatedLinks&pgtype=Article.

Cooke, Miriam. *Tribal Modern: Branding New Nations in the Arab Gulf.* Berkeley: University of California Press, 2014.

Cooper, Frederick. "Afterward: Citizenship and Subjecthood, Empire, and Nation." In *Citizens and Subjects of the Italian Colonies: Legal Constructions and Social Practice*, edited by Simona Berhe and Olindo de Napoli, 245–56. New York: Routledge, 2021.

Corley, Todd, Vontrese (Voni) Pamphile, and Katina B.S. Sawyer. "What Has (and Hasn't) Changed about Being a Chief Diversity Officer." *Harvard Business Review*, September 23, 2022. https://hbr.org/2022/09/what-has-and-hasnt-changed-about-being-a-chief-diversity-officer.

Corporate Accountability Lab. "Fifty Years of Corporate Exploitation, Environmental, Labor and Human Rights Abuses by US Mining Giant Free Port (Part II)." July 28, 2022. https://corpaccountabilitylab.org/calblog/2022/7/28/fifty-years-of-corporate-exploitation-environmental-labor-amp-human-rights-abuses-by-us-mining-giant-freeport-part-ii.

Cortés, Lisa. *Little Richard: I Am Everything.* Magnolia Pictures, 2023.

Costa Vargas, João H. "Hyperconsciousness of Race and Its Negation: The Dialectic of White Supremacy in Brazil." *Identities* 11, no. 4 (2004): 443–70.

Costa Vargas, João H., and Moon-Kie Jung, "Antiblackness of the Social and the Human." In *Antiblackness,* edited by Joao H. Costa Vargas and Moon-Kie Jung, 1–14. Durham, NC: Duke University Press, 2021.

Costley White, Khadijah. "Oceanic Negroes: Communicating Pacific Blackness Down, Out, and Under." *International Journal of Communication* 15 (2021): 4184–207.

Cox, Oliver C. *Caste, Class, and Race.* Garden City, NY: Doubleday, 1948.

Crawford, Edward. "Individuals of Part-African or African Descent Named in the Acts of the Jamaican Assembly, 1760–1810." Jamaica Family Search. http://www.jamaicanfamilysearch.com/Samples/acts.htm.

Crenshaw, Kimberlé W. "Race, Reform, and Retrenchment: Transformation and Legitimation in Antidiscrimination Law." *Harvard Law Review* 101, no. 7 (1988): 1331–87.

———. "This Is Not a Drill: The War against Antiracist Teaching in America." *UCLA Law Review* 68, no. 6 (February 2022): 1702–30.

Crenshaw, Kimberlé Williams, Luke Charles Harris, Daniel Martinez HoSang, and George Lipsitz. "Introduction." In *Seeing Race Again: Countering Colorblindness across the Disciplines*, edited by Kimberlé Crenshaw, Luke Charles Harris, Daniel Martinez HoSang, and George Lipsitz Berkeley, 1–19. Berkeley: University of California Press, 2019.

Curington, Celeste. *Laboring in the Shadow of Empire: Race, Gender, and Care Work in Portugal.* New Brunswick, NJ: Rutgers University Press, 2024.

Dahl, Adam. "Black American Jacobins: Revolution, Radical Abolition, and the Transnational Turn." *American Political Science Association* 15, no. 3 (2017): 633–46.

Daigle, Michelle. "The Spectacle of Reconciliation: On (the) Unsettling Responsibilities to Indigenous Peoples in the Academy." *Society and Space D* 37, no. 4 (2019): 703–21.

Darity Jr, William A., and A. Kirsten Mullen. *From Here to Equality: Reparations for Black Americans in the Twenty-First Century.* Chapel Hill: University of North Carolina Press, 2022.

Darwin, Charles. "On the Races of Man." In *The Idea of Race*, edited by Robert Bernasconi and Tommy L. Lott, 54–78. Indianapolis: Hackett, 2000.

Darwin, John. *The Empire Project: The Rise and Fall of the British World-System, 1830–1970*. Cambridge: Cambridge University Press, 2009.

Daulatzai, Sohail, and Junaid Rana. "Writing the Muslim Left: An Introduction to Throwing Stones." In *With Stones in Our Hands: Writings on Muslims, Racism, and Empire*, edited by Sohail Daulatzai and Junaid Rana, ix–xxiii. Minneapolis: University of Minnesota Press, 2018.

Davidson, Basil. "The Revolution of People's Power: Notes on Mozambique 1979." *Race and Class* 21, no. 2 (1979): 127–43.

Davidson, Neil, and Satnam Virdee. "Introduction: Understanding Racism in Scotland." In *No Problem Here: Understanding Racism in Scotland*, edited by Neil Davidson, Minna Liinpää, Maureen McBride, and Satnam Virdee, 9–12. Edinburgh: Luath Press, 2018.

Davies, Carole Boyce. *Left of Karl Marx: The Political Life of Black Communist Claudia Jones*. Durham, NC: Duke University Press, 2008.

Davis, Angela Y. "Reflections on Haiti." *Black Scholar: Journal of Black Studies and Research* 51, no. 2 (2021): 8–10.

Davis, Muriam Haleh. "'Incommensurate Ontologies?' Anti-Black Racism and the Question of Islam in French Algeria." *Lateral* 10, no. 1 (2021).

———. "Macron Speech Purposefully Misdiagnosed the Real Issues Facing the French Republic." *Jadaliyya*, March 20, 2022. https://www.jadaliyya.com/Details/43965/Macron's-Speech-Purposefully-Misdiagnosed-the-Real-Issues-Facing-the-French-Republic.

Day, David. *Antarctica: What Everyone Needs to Know*. Oxford: Oxford University Press, 2019.

De Castro, Vanessa Maria. "Why Did Bolsonaro's Supporters Vote for Him?" In *In Spite of You: Bolsonaro and the New Brazilian Resistance*, edited by Conor Foley, 71–85. OR Books, 2019.

De Kom, Anton. *We Slaves of Suriname*. Medford, MA: Polity, [1934] 2022.

De Napoli, Olindo. "Between Governmentality and Interdeterminacy: The Birth of the Legal Category of Subjecthood, 1882–1909." In *Citizens and Subjects of the Italian Colonies: Legal Constructions and Social Practice*, edited by Simona Berhe and Olindo de Napoli, 3–24. New York: Routledge, 2021.

Delatolla, Andrew. *Civilization and the Making of the State in Lebanon and Syria*. Switzerland: Palgrave Macmillan, 2021.

———. "A Global Phenomenology of Whiteness: Turkey, Europe, and Institutional Global Racism." *Sociology Lens* (2024): 1–17.

DeLong, Robert D. "Danish Military Involvement in the Invasion of Iraq in Light of the Scandinavian International Relations." *Scandinavian Studies* 81, no. 3 (2009): 367–80.

Derham, Michael. "Construction of a Culture of Privileged Immigrants in Venezuela." *Journal of Iberian and Latin American Studies* 27, no. 3 (2021): 377–401.

Desautels-Stein, Justin. *The Right to Exclude: A Critical Race Approach to Sovereignty, Borders, and International Law*. Oxford: Oxford University Press, 2023.

Destine, Shaneda L. "#Reclaiming My Time: Structural Violence, Racial Trauma and the Case for a Transformative Healing Justice for Black Women Movement Actors." *Societies without Borders* 13, no. 1 (2021): 13.

Devereaux, Shaadi. "Latinx Files: Reggaetón Has a Color Blindness Problem." *LA Times*, April 6, 2023. https://www.latimes.com/world-nation/newsletter/2023-04-06/latinx-files-bad-bunny-colorism-tego-calderon-racism-time-interview-latinx-files.

Di Stefano, Alessia Maria. "The System of Differences: Justice and Citizenship in Libya (1911–1922)." In *Citizens and Subjects of the Italian Colonies: Legal Constructions and Social Practice,* edited by Simona Berhe and Olindo de Napoli, 68–87. New York: Routledge, 2021.

Dicken, Peter. *Global Shift. Mapping the Changing Contours of the World Economy, Seventh Edition.* New York: Guilford Press, 2015.

Dikötter, Frank. "The Racialization of the Globe: An Interactive Interpretation." *Ethnic and Racial Studies* 31, no. 8 (2008): 1478–96.

———. 2015. *The Discourse of Race in Modern China, Second Edition.* Oxford: Oxford University Press.

Dirks, Nicholas. *Castes of Mind: Colonialism and the Making of Modern India.* Princeton: Princeton University Press, 2002.

Djagalov, Rossen. "Racism, the Highest Stage of Anti-Communism." *Slavic Review* 80, no. 2 (2021): 290–98.

Doane, Ashley "Woody." "Beyond Colorblindness: (Re)Theorizing Racial Ideology." *Sociological Perspectives* 60, no. 5 (2017): 975–91.

Doherty, Ben. "A Short History of Nauru, Australia's Dumping Ground for Refugees." *The Guardian,* August 9, 2016. https://www.theguardian.com/world/2016/aug/10/a-short-history-of-nauru-australias-dumping-ground-for-refugees.

Dos Santos Soares, Maria Andrea. "Look, Blackness in Brazil! Disrupting the Grotesquerie of Racial Representation in Brazilian Visual Culture." *Cultural Dynamics* 24, no. 1 (2012): 75–101.

Douglas, Bronwen. "Notes on 'Race' and the Biologisation of Human Difference." *Journal of Pacific History* 40, no. 3 (2005): 331–38.

Douglas, Bronwen, and Chris Ballard. "Race, Place, and Civilization: Colonial Encounters and Governance in Greater Oceania." *Journal of Pacific History* 47, no. 3 (2012): 245–62.

Draper, Robert. "America First Legal, A Trump-Aligned Group, Is Spoiling for a Fight." *New York Times,* March 21, 2024. https://www.nytimes.com/2024/03/21/us/politics/stephen-miller-america-first-legal.html.

Du Bois, W.E.B. *Black Reconstruction in America: Toward a History of the Part Which Black Folk Played in the Attempt to Reconstruct Democracy in America, 1860–1880.* New York: Free Press, [1935] 1998.

———. *Darkwater: Voices from with the Veil.* New York: Harcourt, Brace and Howe, 1920.

———. *The World and Africa: An Inquiry into the Part Which Africa Has Played in World History.* International, 1965.

———. "The Color Line Belts the World." In *W.E.B. Du Bois: A Reader*. Edited by David L. Lewis. New York: Holt, 1995.

———. "Japan, Color, and Afro-Americans." In *W.E.B. Du Bois: A Reader*. Edited by David Lewis, 86–87. New York: John Macrae, 1995.

Dunaway, Wilma A., and Donald A. Clelland. "Challenging the Global Apartheid Model: A World-Systems Analysis." *Journal of World-Systems Research* 22, no. 1 (2016): 16–22.

Dungca, Nicole, and Claire Healy. "Revealing the Smithsonian's 'Racial Brain Collection.'" *Washington Post*, August 14, 2023. https://www.washingtonpost.com/history/interactive/2023/smithsonian-brains-collection-racial-history-repatriation?itid=hp-top-table-main_p001_f001.

Duster, Troy. *Backdoor to Eugenics*. New York: Routledge, 2003.

Duyvendak, Jan Willem, Josip Kesic, and Timothy Stacey. *The Return of the Native: Can Liberalism Safeguard Us Against Nativism?* Oxford: Oxford University Press, 2022.

Edgar, Adrienne. "The Fragmented Nation: Genealogy, Identity, and Social Hierarchy in Turkmenistan." In *Race and Nation: Ethnic Systems in the Modern World*, edited by Paul Spickard, 257–72. New York, Routledge, 2005.

Edwards, Erika Denise. *Hiding in Plain Sight: Black Women, the Law, and the Making of a White Argentine Republic*. Tuscaloosa: University of Alabama Press, 2020.

Eissenstat, Howard. "Metaphors of Race and Discourse of Nation: Racial Theory and State Nationalism in the First Decades of the Turkish Republic." In *Race and Nation: Ethnic Systems in the Modern World*, edited by Paul Spickard, 239–55. New York, Routledge, 2004.

Ekwenchi, Ogochukwu C. "Seeing Colours: Race in Nollywood." *International Journal of Social Sciences and Humanities Reviews* 5, no. 1 (February 2015): 1–12.

El-Tayeb, Fatima. "'Blood Is a Very Special Juice': Racialized Bodies and Citizenship in Twentieth-Century Germany." *International Review of Social History* 44, no. 7 (1999): 149–69.

———. "'We Are Germans, We Are Whites, and We Want to Stay White!': African Germans and Citizenship in the Early 20th Century." *Amsterdamer Beitrague zur neueren Germanistik* 56, no. 1 (2004): 185–205.

———. *European Others: Queering Ethnicity in Postnational Europe*. Minneapolis: University of Minnesota Press, 2011.

El Hamel, Chouki. *Black Morocco: A History of Slavery, Race, and Islam*. Cambridge: Cambridge University Press, 2013.

El Zein, Rayya. "Introduction: Cultural Constructions of Race and Racism in the Middle East and North Africa/South West Asia and North Africa." *Lateral* 10, no. 1 (2021).

———. "From 'Hip Hop Revolutionaries' to 'Terrorist-Thugs': 'Blackwashing' between the Arab Spring and the War on Terror." *Lateral* 5, no. 1 (2016).

Elgenius, Gabriella, and Jens Rydgren. "Frames of Nostalgia and Belonging: The Resurgence of Ethno-Nationalism in Sweden." *European Societies* 21, no. 4 (2019): 583–602.

Elkins, Catherine. *Legacy of Violence: A History of the British Empire*. New York: Alfred A. Knopf, 2022.

Elsaket, Ifdal. "Jungle Films in Egypt." *Arab Studies Journal* 25, no. 2 (2017): 8–33.
Eltis, David. "The Volume and Structure of the Transatlantic Slave Trade: A Reassessment." *William and Mary Quarterly* 58, no. 1 (2001): 17–46.
Emigh, Rebecca Jean, Patricia Ahmed, and Dylan Riley. *How Everyday Forms of Racial Categorization Survived Imperialist Censuses in Puerto Rico.* New York: Palgrave Macmillan, 2021.
Engert, Stefan. *EU Enlargement and Socialization: Turkey and Cyprus.* New York: Routledge, 2010.
Enloe, Cynthia. *Bananas, Beaches and Bases: Making Feminist Sense of International Politics.* Berkeley: University of California Press, 2014.
Environmental Justice Atlas. "Amungme against Freeport." https://ejatlas.org/conflict/amungme-against-freeport-mcmoran-indonesia.
Equal Justice Initiative. *Lynching in America: Confronting the Legacy of Racial Terror, Third Edition.* Montgomery, Alabama, 2017.
Erakat, Noura. "Whiteness as Property in Israel: Revival, Rehabilitation, and Removal." *Harvard Journal of Racial and Ethnic Justice* 69 (2015): 69–104.
Ergin, Murat. "'Is the Turk a White Man?' Towards a Theoretical Framework for Race in the Making of Turkishness." *Middle Eastern Studies* 44, no. 6 (2008b): 827–50.
———. "The Racialization of Kurdish Identity in Turkey." *Ethnic and Racial Studies* 37, no. 2 (2014): 322–41.
Ergin, Murat, and Yağmur Karakaya. "Between Neo-Ottomanism and Ottomania: Navigating State-Led and Popular Cultural Representations of the Past." *New Perspectives on Turkey* 56 (2017): 33–59.
Erlick, June Carolyn. *Telenovelas in Pan-Latino Context.* New York: Routledge, 2017.
Eslava, Luis, Michael Fakhri, and Vasuki Nesiah. "The Spirit of Bandung." In *Bandung, Global History and International Law*, edited by Luis Eslava, Michael Fakhri, and Vasuki Nesiah, 3–31. Cambridge: Cambridge University Press, 2017.
Essed, Philomena, and Sandra Trienekens. "'Who Wants to Feel White?': Race, Dutch Culture and Contested Identities." *Ethnic and Racial Studies* 31, no. 1 (2008): 52–72.
Essed, Philomena, and Sara Louise Muhr. "Entitlement Racism and Its Intersections: An Interview with Philomena Essed, Social Justice Scholar." *Ephemera: Theory & Politics in Organization* 18, no. 1 (2018): 183–201.
Ethridge, Robbie. "Global Capital, Violence, and the Making of a Colonial Shatter Zone." In *Colonial Genocide in Indigenous North America*, edited by Andrew Woolford, Jeff Benvenuto, and Alexander Laban Hinton, 49–69. Durham, NC: Duke University Press, 2014.
Faiola, Anthony, Imogen Piper, Joyce Sohyun Lee, Klaas van Dijken, Maud Jullien, and May Bulman. "With Europe's Support: North African Nations Push Migrants to the Desert." *Washington Post*, May 20, 2024. https://www.washingtonpost.com/world/interactive/2024/eu-migrant-north-africa-mediterranean/.
Fanon, Frantz. *Wretched of the Earth.* New York: Grove Press, 1963.
———. *Black Skin, White Masks.* New York: Grove Press, 2008.
Farmer, Paul. *Haiti after the Earthquake.* New York: PublicAffairs, 2012.

Farnia, Nina. "Law's Inhumanities: Peripheral Racialization and the Early Development of the Iranian Race." *Comparative Studies of South Asia, Africa and the Middle East* 31, no. 2 (2011): 455–73.

Favell, Adrian. "Crossing the Race Line: 'No Polish, No Blacks, No Dogs' in Brexit Britain? Or, The Great British Brexit Swindle." In *Europe's Malaise: The Long View*, edited by Francesco Duina and Frédéric Mérand, 103–30. London: Emerald, 2020.

Feagin, Joe R. *Racist America: Roots, Current Realities, & Future Reparations*. New York: Routledge, 2000.

———. *Systemic Racism: A Theory of Oppression*. New York: Routledge, 2006.

———. *The White Racial Frame: Centuries of Racial Framing and Counter-Framing*. New York: Routledge, 2020.

Feldman, Stephen M. "Do the Right Thing: Understanding the Interest-Convergence Thesis." *Northwestern University Law Review Colloquy* 106 (2011–12): 248–60.

Fenelon, James V. "Critique of Glenn on Settler Colonialism and Bonilla-Silva on Critical Race Analysis from Indigenous Perspectives." *Sociology of Race and Ethnicity* 2, no. 2 (2016): 237–42.

Fields, Barbara J., and Karen E. Fields. *Racecraft: The Soul of Inequality in American Life*. New York: Verso, 2012.

Firpo, Christina. "Metis of Vietnam: An Historical Perspective on Mixed-Race Children from the French Colonial Period." In *Mixed Race in Asia*, 52–64. New York: Routledge, 2017.

Fisher, Andrew B., and Matthew D. O'Hara, eds. *Imperial Subjects: Race and Identity in Colonial Latin America*. Durham, NC: Duke University Press, 2009.

Fisher, Tracy. *What's Left of Blackness: Feminisms, Transracial Solidarities, and the Politics of Belonging in Britain*. New York: Springer, 2012.

Fleming, Crystal. *Resurrecting Slavery: Racial Legacies and White Supremacy in France*. Philadelphia: Temple University Press, 2017.

Fleming, David H., and Maria Elena Indelicato. "Introduction: On Transnational Chinese Cinema(s), Hegemony and Huallywood(s)." *Transnational Screens* 10, no. 3 (2019): 137–47.

Fofiu, Adela. "Stories of a White Apocalypse of the Romanian Internet." In *Unveiling Whiteness in the Twenty-First Century: Global Manifestations, Transdisciplinary Interventions*, edited by Veronica Watson et al., 29–47. Lanham, MD: Lexington Books, 2014.

Forbes, Jack D. "Black Pioneers: The Spanish-Speaking Afroamericans of the Southwest." *Phylon (1960–)* 27, no. 3 (1966): 233–46.

Forgie, Keir. "US Imperialism and Disaster Capitalism in Haiti." In *Good Intentions: Norms and Practices of Imperial Humanitarianism*, 57–75. Montreal: Alert Press, 2014.

Fra-Molinero, Baltasar. "The Suspect Whiteness of Spain." In *At Home and Abroad: Historicizing Twenty-First Century Whiteness in Literature and Performance*, 147–69. Knoxville: University of Tennessee Press, 2009.

Francis, Margot. *Creative Subversions: Whiteness, Indigeneity, and the National Imaginary*. Vancouver: UBC Press, 2011.

Frankenberg, Ruth. "The Mirage of an Unmarked Whiteness." In *The Making and Unmaking of Whiteness*, edited by Birgit Brander Rasmussen, Eric Klinenberg, Irene J. Nexica, and Matt Wray, 72–96. Durham, NC: Duke University Press, 2001.

Fraser, Nancy. "Race, Empire, Capitalism: Theorizing the Nexus." Contributions to Contemporary Knowledge Lecture Series, Faculty of Social Sciences, South Asian University, 2018.

Fredrickson, George M. *White Supremacy: A Comparative Study of American and South African History*. Oxford: Oxford University Press, 1981.

———. *Racism: A Short History*. Princeton, NJ: Princeton University Press, 2002.

Freeman, Bianca, D.G. Kim, and David A. Lake. "Race in International Relations: Beyond the 'Norm against Noticing.'" *Annual Review of Political Science* 25 (2022): 175–96.

French, Bryana H., Jioni A. Lewis, Della V. Mosley, Hector Y. Adames, Nayeli Y. Chavez-Dueñas, Grace A. Chen, and Helen A. Neville. "Toward a Psychological Framework of Radical Healing in Communities of Color." *Counseling Psychologist* 48, no. 1 (2020): 14–46.

French, Howard W. *Born in Blackness: Africa, Africans, and the Making of the Modern World, 1471 to the Second World War*. New York: Liveright, 2021.

French, John D. "The Missteps of Anti-Imperialist Reason: Bourdieu, Wacquant and Hanchard's Orpheus and Power." *Theory, Culture & Society* 17, no. 1 (2000): 107–28.

Frenz, Margret. "Global Goans: Migration Movements and Identity in a Historical Perspective." *Lusotopie* 15, no. 1 (2008): 183–202.

Frey, R. Scott. "Agent Orange and America at War in Vietnam and Southeast Asia." *Human Ecology Review* 20, no. 1 (2013): 1–10.

Frye Jacobson, Matthew. *Whiteness of a Different Color: European Immigration and the Alchemy of Race*. Cambridge, MA: Harvard University Press, 1998.

Füredi, Frank. *The Silent War: Imperialism and the Changing Perception of Race*. London: Pluto Press, 1998.

Fusari, Valentina. "Orphanages and Citizenship: Abandoned Italo-Eritreans Accessing Italian Citizenship." In *Citizens and Subjects of the Italian Colonies: Legal Constructions and Social Practice*, edited by Simona Berhe and Olindo de Napoli, 180–201. New York, Routledge, 2021.

Galton, Francis. *The Narrative of an Explorer in Tropical South Africa*. London: Ward, Lock, 1854.

García, Carlos Sandoval. *Otros Amenazantes: Los Nicaragüenses y la Formación de Identidades Nacionales en Costa Rica*. San Jose: University of Costa Rica, 2002.

García Peña, Lorgia. *The Borders of Dominicanidad: Race, Nation, and Archives of Contradiction*. Durham, NC: Duke University Press, 2016.

Garth, Hanna. "'There Is No Race in Cuba': Level of Culture and the Logics of Transnational Anti-Blackness." *Anthropological Quarterly* 94, no. 3 (2021): 385–410.

Garner, Steve. *Racism in the Irish Experience*. London: Pluto Press, 2004.

———. "The European Union and the Racialization of Immigration, 1985–2006." *Race/Ethnicity: Multidisciplinary Global Contexts* 1, no. 1 (2007): 61–87.

Garner, Steve, and Saher Selod. "The Racialization of Muslims: Empirical Studies of Islamophobia." *Critical Sociology* 41, no. 1 (2015): 9–19.
Garraway, Doris. "Race, Reproduction and Family Romance in Moreau de Sant-Méry's Description . . . de la partie française de l'isle Saint-Domingue." *Eighteenth Century Studies* 38, no. 2 (2005): 227–46.
Garrett, Aaron, and Silvia Sebastiani. "David Hume on Race." In *The Oxford Handbook of Philosophy and Race*, 31–43. Oxford: Oxford University Press, 2017.
Garrigus, John D. *Before Haiti: Race and Citizenship in French Saint-Domingue*. New York: Palgrave Macmillan, 2006.
Garza, Joyhanna Yoo. "Where All My Bad Girls At? Cosmopolitan Femininity through Racialised Appropriations in K-Pop." *Gender and Language* 15, no. 1 (2021): 1–31.
Gathii, James Thuo. "Retelling Good Governance Narratives on Africa's Economic and Political Predicaments: Continuities and Discontinuities in Legal Outcomes between Markets and States." *Villanova Law Review* 45 (2000): 971.
———. "Beyond Color-Blind International Law." *Symposium on Race, Racism and International Law* (2023).
Gayles, Prisca, and Marianela Muñoz-Muñoz. "Unveiling Latin American White Multiculturalism: Black Women's Politics in Argentina and Costa Rica." *Latin American and Caribbean Ethnic Studies* (2022): 1–17.
Gehlawat, Ajay. "The Gori in the Story: The Shifting Dynamics of Whiteness in Bollywood Film." *TOPIA: Canadian Journal of Cultural Studies* 26 (2011): 105–26.
Gereffi, Gary, John Humphrey, and Timothy Sturgeon. "The Governance of Global Value Chains." *Review of International Political Economy* 12, no. 1 (2005): 78–104.
Gevers, Christopher. "'Unwhitening the World': Rethinking Race and International Law." *UCLA Law Review* 67 (2020): 1652.
Ghebremariam Tesfau', Mackda, and Giovanni Picker. "The Italian Postracial Archive." *Ethnic and Racial Studies* 44, no. 2 (2021): 195–214.
Gidron, Yotam. "How Israel's Secret Refugee Deals Collapsed in the Light of Day." *New Humanitarian*, May 3, 2018. https://deeply.thenewhumanitarian.org/refugees/community/2018/05/03/how-israels-secret-refugee-deals-collapsed-in-the-light-of-day.
Gill, Tim, Ed. *The Future of U.S. Empire in the Americas*. New York: Routledge, 2020.
Gillam, Reighan. *Visualizing Black Lives: Ownership and Control in Afro-Brazilian Media*. Champaign: University of Illinois Press, 2022.
Gilman, Sander. *On Blackness without Blacks: Essays on the Image of the Black in Germany*. Boston: G.K. Hall, 1982.
Gilmore, Ruth Wilson. *Abolition Geography: Essays towards Liberation*. New York: Verso Books, 2022.
Gilroy, Paul. *There Ain't No Black in the Union Jack*. New York: Routledge, 1987.
———. "'My Britain Is Fuck All': Zombie Multiculturalism and Race Politics of Citizenship." *Identities* 19, no. 4 (2012): 380–98.
Glenn, Evelyn Nakano. *Unequal Freedom: How Race and Gender Shaped American Citizenship and Labor*. Cambridge, MA: Harvard University Press, 2004.
———. "Yearning for Lightness: Transnational Circuits in the Marketing and Consumption of Skin Lighteners." *Gender & Society* 22, no. 3 (2008): 281–302.

———. *Forced to Care: Coercion and Caregiving in America*. Cambridge, MA: Harvard University Press, 2010.

Go, Julian. "'Racism' and Colonialism: Meanings of Difference and Ruling Practices in America's Pacific Empire." *Qualitative Sociology* 27, no. 1 (2004): 35–58.

———. *Patterns of Empire: The British and American Empires, 1688 to the Present*. Cambridge: Cambridge University Press, 2011.

———. "Postcolonial Possibilities for the Sociology of Race." *Sociology of Race and Ethnicity* 4, no. 4 (2018): 439–51.

Gobat, Michel. "The Invention of Latin America: A Transnational History of Anti-Imperialism Democracy and Race." *American Historical Review* 118, no. 5 (2013): 1345–75.

Gökay, Bülent, and Tunç Aybak. "Identity, Race, and Nationalism in Turkey." *Journal of Balkan and Near Eastern Studies* 18, no. 2 (2016): 107–10.

Goldberg, David Theo. *Racist Culture: Philosophy and Politics of Meaning*. Malden, MA: Blackwell, 1993.

———. *The Racial State*. Malden, MA: Wiley, 2001.

———. *The Threat of Race: Reflections on Racial Neoliberalism*. Malden, MA: Wiley Blackwell, 2009.

———. "Racial Comparisons, Relational Racisms: Some Thoughts on Method." *Ethnic and Racial Studies* 32, no. 7 (2009): 1271–82.

———. *Are We All Postracial Yet?* Cambridge: Polity, 2017.

———. *War on Critical Race Theory: Or, the Remaking of Racism*. Hoboken, NJ: John Wiley & Sons, 2023.

Goldberg, David Theo, and Philomena Essed, "Introduction: From Demarcations to Multiple Identifications." In *Race Critical Theories*, edited by Philomena Essed and David Theo Goldberg, 1–11. Malden, MA: Blackwell, 2002.

Goldstein, Alyosha. "Introduction, Abolitionist Worldmaking: A Forum on Ruth Wilson Gilmore Abolition Geography." *American Quarterly* 75, no. 2 (2023): 359–64.

Gómez, Laura E. *Inventing Latinos: A New Story of American Racism*. New York: New Press, 2020.

———. *Manifest Destinies, Second Edition*. New York: New York University Press, 2018.

Goode, Joshua. "Race, Crime and Criminal Justice in Spain." In *Race, Crime and Criminal Justice: International Perspectives*, edited by Anita Kalunta-Crumpton, 162–84. Basingstoke: Palgrave MacMillan, 2010.

Gould, Stephen J. *The Mismeasure of Man*. New York: W.W. Norton, 1996.

Groebner, Valentin. "The Carnal Knowing of a Coloured Body: Sleeping with Arabs and Blacks in the European Imagination, 1300–1550." In *The Origins of Racism in the West*, edited by Miriam Eliav-Feldon, Benjamin Isaac, and Joseph Ziegler, 217–31. Cambridge: Cambridge University Press, 2009.

Grosfoguel, Ramón. "What Is Racism?" *Journal of World-Systems Research* 22, no. 1 (2016): 9–15.

Grossman, Derek. "China's Pacific Push Is Backfiring; Rand Corporation." *Rand Blog*, July 26, 2022. https://www.rand.org/blog/2022/07/chinas-pacific-push-is-backfiring.html.

Gross-Wyrtzen, Leslie. "'There Is No Race Here': On Blackness, Slavery, and Disavowal in North Africa and North African Studies." *Journal of North African Studies* 28, no. 3 (2023): 635–65.

Gross-Wyrtzen, Leslie, and Lorena Gazzotti. "Telling Histories of the Present: Postcolonial Perspectives on Morocco's 'Radically New' Migration Policy." *Journal of North African Studies* 26, no. 5 (2021): 827–43.

Gualtieri, Sarah. *Between Arab and White: Race and Ethnicity in the Early Syrian American Diaspora*. Berkeley: University of California Press, 2009.

Gubara, Dahlia E.M. "Revisiting Race and Slavery through 'Abd al-Rahman al-Jabarti's 'Aja'ib al-athar." *Comparative Studies of South Asia, Africa and the Middle East* 38, no. 2 (2018): 230–45.

Guinier, Lani, and Gerald Torres. *The Miner's Canary*. Cambridge, MA: Harvard University Press, 2002.

Gumbs, Alexis Pauline. *Survival Is a Promise: The Eternal Life of Audre Lorde*. New York: Farrar, Straus and Giroux, 2024.

Habecker, Shelly "Not Black, but Habasha: Ethiopian and Eritrean Immigrants in American Society." *Ethnic and Racial Studies* 35, no. 7 (2012): 1200–219.

Hadley, Fredara Mareva. "The World We Make: Black Colleges and Black Music Studies." *American Music* 41, no. 2 (2023): 205–10.

Hage, Ghassan. *White Nation: Fantasies of White Supremacy in a Multicultural Society*. New York: Routledge, 2000.

———. "Multiculturalism and White Paranoia in Australia." *JIMI/RIMI* 3, no. 4 (2002): 417–37.

Hahonou, Eric. "Blackness, Slavery and Anti-Racism Activism in Contemporary North Africa." In *Racial Formations in Africa and the Middle East: A Transregional Approach*, 41–48. Project on African Social Research, 2021.

Hale, Charles R., Pamela Calla, and Leith Mullings. "Race Matters in Dangerous Times: A Network of Scholar-Activists Assesses Changing Racial Formations across the Americas—and Mobilizes against Renewed Racist Backlash." *NACLA Report on the Americas* 49, no. 1 (2017): 81–89.

Hale, Dana S. *Races on Display: French Representations of Colonized Peoples, 1886–1940*. Bloomington: Indiana University Press, 2008.

Hall, Bruce S. "Reading Race in Africa and Middle East." *Anthropologia* 7, no. 1 (2020): 33–44.

Hall, Kim. *Things of Darkness: Economies of Race and Gender in Early Modern England*. Ithaca, NY: Cornell University Press, 1995.

Hall, Stuart. "Race, Articulation, and Societies Structured in Dominance [1980]." In *Selected Writings on Race and Difference*, edited by Paul Gilroy and Ruth Wilson Gilmore, 195–245. Durham, NC: Duke University Press, 2020.

———. "Gramsci's Relevance for the Study of Race and Ethnicity [1986]". In *Selected Writings on Race and Difference*, edited by Paul Gilroy and Ruth Wilson Gilmore, 295–28. Durham, NC: Duke University Press, 2020.

———. *Representation: Cultural Representations and Signifying Practice*. Thousand Oaks, CA: Sage, 1997.

Hamilton, Vivian E. "Reform, Retrench, Repeat: The Campaign against Critical Race

Theory, through the Lens of Critical Race Theory." *William & Mary Journal of Race, Gender, and Social Justice* 28, no. 1 (Fall 2021): 61–102.

Hanchard, Michael G. *Orpheus and Power: The Movimento Negro of Rio de Janeiro and São Paulo, Brazil, 1945–1988*. Princeton, NJ: Princeton University Press, 1998.

———. "Black Transnationalism, Africana Studies, and the 21st Century." *Journal of Black Studies* 35, no. 2 (2004): 139–53.

———. *The Spectre of Race: How Discrimination Haunts Western Democracy*. Princeton, NJ: Princeton University Press, 2018.

Hannaford, Ivan. *Race: The History of an Idea in the West*. Baltimore: Johns Hopkins University Press, 1996.

Harpelle, Ronald N. *West Indians of Costa Rica: Race, Class, and the Integration of an Ethnic Minority*. Montreal: McGill-Queens University Press, 2001.

Harrell, Stevan. "Introduction: Civilizing Projects and the Reaction to Them." In *Cultural Encounters in China's Ethnic Frontiers*, edited by Stevan Harrell, 3–36. Seattle: University of Washington Press, 1995.

Harris, Cheryl I. "Whiteness as Property." In *Critical Race Theory: The Key Writings that Formed the Movement*, edited by Kimberlé Crenshaw, Neil Gotanda, Gary Peller, and Kendall Thomas, 276–91. New York: New Press, 1995.

Harrison, Olivia C. "The White Minority: Natives and Nativism in Contemporary France." *Boundary 2* 50, no. 1 (2023): 105–35.

Harrison, Rachel. "Introduction: The Allure of Ambiguity: The 'West' and the Making of the Thai identities." In *The Ambiguous Allure of the West: Traces of the Colonial in Thailand*, edited by Rachel V. Harrison, Peter A. Jackson, and Dipesh Chakrabarty, 1–36. Ithaca, NY: Cornell University Press.

Hartman, Saidiya. *Lose Your Mother: A Journey along the Atlantic Slave Route*. New York: Farrar, Straus and Giroux, 2007.

———. *Scenes of Subjection: Terror, Slavery, and Self-Making in Nineteenth-Century America*. New York: W.W. Norton, [1997] 2022.

———. *Wayward Lives, Beautiful Experiments: Intimate Histories of Social Upheaval*. New York: W.W. Norton, 2019.

Harvey, David. *The New Imperialism*. Oxford: Oxford University Press, 2005.

Haugen, Arne. *The Establishment of National Republics in Soviet Central Asia*. New York: Palgrave Macmillan, 2003.

Hawthorne, Camilla. *Contesting Race and Citizenship: Youth Politics in the Black Mediterranean*. Ithaca, NY: Cornell University Press, 2022.

Heng, Geraldine. "The Invention of Race in the Middle Ages, 1: Race Studies, Modernity, and the Middle Ages." *Literature Compass* 8, no. 5 (2011): 258–74.

Hennigan, W.J. "What over 2,000 Nuclear Tests Have Revealed." *New York Times*, June 20, 2024. https://www.nytimes.com/interactive/2024/06/20/opinion/nuclear-weapons-testing.html.

Henriksen, Anders, and Jon Rahbek-Clemmensen. "The Greenland Card: Prospects for and Barriers to Danish Arctic Diplomacy in Washington." *Danish Foreign Policy Yearbook* 1 (2017): 75–98.

Hernández, Tanya K. *Racial Subordination in Latin America: The Role of the State, Cus-*

tomary Law, and the New Civil Rights Response. Cambridge: Cambridge University Press, 2012.

———. Racial Innocence: Unmasking Latino Anti-Black Bias. Boston: Beacon Press, 2022.

Hesse, Barnor. "Racialized Modernity: An Analytics of White Mythologies." *Ethnic and Racial Studies* 30, no. 4 (2007): 643–63.

———. "Of Race: The Exorbitant Du Bois." *Small Axe* 20, no. 2 (2016): 14–27.

Hill, Jane H. 2009. *The Everyday Language of White Racism*. Malden, MA: Wiley-Blackwell.

Ho, Michelle H. S. "Consuming Women in Blackface: Racialized Affect and Transnational Femininity in Japanese Advertising," *Japanese Studies* 37, no. 1 (2017): 49–69.

Holmes, Seth. *Fresh Fruit, Broken Bodies: Migrant Farmworkers in the United States*. Berkeley: University of California Press, 2013.

Hondius, Dienke. "Blacks in Modern Europe: New Research from the Netherlands." In *Black Europe and the African Diaspora*, edited by Darlene Clark Hine, Tricia Danielle Keaton, and Stephen Small, 29–47. Urbana: University of Illinois Press.

Hooker, Juliet. "Indigenous Inclusion / Black Exclusion: Race, Ethnicity and Multicultural Citizenship in Latin America." *Journal of Latin American Studies* 37, no. 2 (2005): 285–310.

———. *Race and the Politics of Solidarity*. Oxford: Oxford University Press, 2009.

———. *Theorizing Race in the Americas: Douglass, Sarmiento, Du Bois, and Vasconcelos*. Oxford: Oxford University Press, 2017.

Hoon, Chang-Yau. "Assimilation, Multiculturalism, Hybridity: The Dilemmas of the Ethnic Chinese in Post-Suharto Indonesia." *Asian Ethnicity* 7, no. 2 (2006): 149–66.

Hordge-Freeman, Elizabeth. *The Color of Love: Racial Features, Stigma, and Socialization in Black Brazilian Families*. Austin: University of Texas Press, 2015.

———. *Second-Class Daughters: Black Brazilian Women and Informal Adoption as Modern Day Slavery*. Cambridge: Cambridge University Press, 2022.

Horne, Gerald. *Race War! White Supremacy and the Japanese Attack on the British Empire*. New York: New York University Press, 2004.

———. *The Apocalypse of Settler Colonialism: The Roots of Slavery, White Supremacy, and Capitalism in the Seventeenth–Century North America and the Caribbean*. New York: Monthly Review Press, 2016.

Houben, Vincent J.H. "Boundaries of Race: Representations of Indisch in Colonial Indonesia Revisited." In *Empires and Boundaries: Race, Class, and Gender in Colonial Settings*, edited by Harold Fisher-Tiné and Susanne Gehrmann, 66–85. New York: Routledge, 2008.

Hough, Jennifer. "The Racialization of North Koreans in South Korea: Diasporic Co-Ethnics in the South Korean Ethnolinguistic Nation." *Ethnic and Racial Studies* 45, no. 4 (2022): 616–35.

Houkamau, Carla A., Samantha Stronge, and Chris G. Sibley. "The Prevalence and Impact of Racism toward Indigenous Māori in New Zealand." *International Perspectives in Psychology: Research, Practice, Consultation* 6, no. 2 (2017): 61–81.

Hoxworth, Kellen. "The Jim Crow Global South." *Theatre Journal* 72, no. 4 (2020): 443–67.

Hübinette, Tobias, and Catrin Lundström. "Three Phases of Hegemonic Whiteness: Understanding Racial Temporalities in Sweden." *Social Identities* 20, no. 6 (2014): 423–37.
Hudson, Nicholas. "From 'Nation' to 'Race': The Origin of Racial Classification in 18th Century Thought." *Eighteenth-Century Studies* 29, no. 3 (1996): 247–64.
———. "The 'Hottentot Venus,' Sexuality, and the Changing Aesthetics of Race, 1650–1850." *Mosaic: An Interdisciplinary Critical Journal* 41, no. 1 (2008): 19–41.
Human Rights Watch and Mills Legal Clinic. "Break Their Lineage, Break Their Roots: Chinese Government Crimes against Humanity Targeting Uyghurs and Other Turkic Muslims." April 19, 2021. https://www.hrw.org/report/2021/04/19/break-their-lineage-break-their-roots/chinas-crimes-against-humanity-targeting.
Hunter, Marcus Anthony. "Blackness Everywhere: How the State Maintains and Manifests Racialized Power." In *Routledge International Handbook of Contemporary Racisms*, edited by John Solomos, 110–20. New York: Routledge, 2020.
Hunter, Marcus Anthony, and Zandria F. Robinson. *Chocolate Cities: The Black Map of American Life*. Berkeley: University of California Press, 2018.
Hurwitz, Samuel, and Edith F. Hurwitz. "A Token of Freedom: Private Bill Legislation for Free Negroes in Eighteenth-Century Jamaica." *William and Mary Quarterly* 24, no. 3 (1967): 423–31.
Husain, Atiya. "Deracialization, Dissent, and Terrorism in the FBI's Most Wanted Program." *Sociology of Race and Ethnicity* 7, no. 2 (2021): 208–25.
Ignatiev, Noel. *How the Irish Became White*. Cambridge, MA: Harvard University Press, 1994.
———. *Treason to Whiteness Is Loyalty to Humanity*. New York: Verso Books, 2022.
Imre, Anikó. "Whiteness in Post-Socialist Eastern European: The Time of Gypsies, the End of Race." In *Postcolonial Whiteness A Critical Reader on Race and Empire*, edited by Alfred J. Lopez, 79–102. New York: State University of New York Press, 2005.
International Coalition for Papua. *Special Report: PT Freeport Indonesia and Its Trail of Violations in Papua: Human, Labour and Environmental Rights*. International Coalition for Papua, December 2020. https://www.tapol.org/sites/default/files/sites/default/files/pdfs/PT_Freeport_Indo_tail_of_violations_in_Papua_Dec20.pdf.
International Labour Organization. "Labour Migration." N.d. https://www.ilo.org/regions-and- countries/ilo-arab-states/areas-work/labour-migration.
International Labour Organization. *World Employment and Social Outlook Trends 2022*. ILO Flagship Report. https://industrialrelationsnews.ioe-emp.org/news/article/world-employment-and-social-outlook-trends-2022-ilo-report-1#:~:text=ILO%20expects%20total%20hours%20worked,level%20by%20about%2021%20million.
International Organization for Migration. "Missing Migrants Project." 2023. https://missingmigrants.iom.int/.
Isaac, Benjamin, Joseph Ziegler, and Miriam Eliav-Feldon. "Introduction." In *The Origins of Racism in the West*, edited by Miriam Eliav-Feldon, Benjamin Isaac, and Joseph Ziegler, 1–31. Cambridge: Cambridge University Press, 2009.
Itzigsohn, José, and Karida L. Brown. *The Sociology of W.E.B. Du Bois: Racialized Modernity and the Global Color Line*. New York: New York University Press, 2020.

Jackson, Lauren Michele. *White Negroes: When Cornrows Were in Vogue . . . and Other Thoughts on Cultural Appropriation*. Boston: Beacon Press, 2019.

Jacobson, Matthew Frye. *Whiteness of a Different Color: European Immigration and the Alchemy of Race*. Cambridge, MA: Harvard University Press, 1998.

Jalata, Asafa. "Being In and Out of Africa: The Impact of Duality of Ethiopianism." *Journal of Black Studies* 40, no. 2 (2009): 189–214.

James, C.L.R. *The Black Jacobins: Toussaint L'Ouverture and the San Domingo Revolution*. New York: Vintage Books, [1963] 1989.

Jefferson, Thomas. *Notes on the State of Virginia: Edited with an Introduction & Notes by William Peden, Second Edition*. Chapel Hill: University of North Carolina Press, 1996.

Jenkins, Destin, and Justin Leroy. "Introduction: The Old History of Capitalism." In *Histories of Racial Capitalism*, edited by Destin Jenkins and Justin Leroy, 1–26. New York: Columbia University Press, 2021.

Jensen, Lars. "Greenland, Arctic Orientalism and the Search for Definitions of a Contemporary Postcolonial Geography." *KULT-Postkolonial Temaserie* 12 (2015): 139–53.

Johnson, Howard. "Introduction." In *History of Jamaica, Volume 1: Reflections on Its Situation, Settlements, Inhabitants, Climate, Products, Commerce, Laws and Government*, i–xxv. Montreal: McGill-Queens University Press, [1774] 2002.

Jones, Guno, and Betty de Hart. "(Not) Measuring Mixedness in the Netherlands." In *The Palgrave International Handbook of Mixed Racial and Ethnic Classification*, 367–87. New York: Palgrave, 2020.

Jones, Seth, Catrina Doxsee, Brian Katz, Eric McQueen, and Joe Moye. *Russia's Corporate Soldiers: The Global Expansion of Russia's Private Military Companies*. Report of the Center for Strategic and International Studies. Lanham, MD: Rowman and Littlefield, 2021.

Joseph, Galen. "Taking Race Seriously: Whiteness in Argentina's National and Transnational Imaginary." *Identities* 7, no. 3 (2000): 333–71.

Joseph, Tiffany D. *Race on the Move: Brazilian Migrants and the Global Reconstruction of Race*. Palo Alto, CA: Stanford University Press, 2015.

Jung, Moon-Ho. *Menace to Empire: Solidarities and the Transpacific Origins of the US Security State*. Oakland: University of California Press, 2022.

Jung, Moon-Kie. *Reworking Race: The Making of Hawaii's Interracial Labor Movement*. New York: Columbia University Press, 2006.

———. *Beneath the Surface of White Supremacy: Denaturalizing U.S. Racisms Past and Present*. Palo Alto, CA: Stanford University Press, 2015.

Kabutaulaka, Tarcisius. "Re-presenting Melanesia: Ignoble Savages and Melanesian Alter-Natives." *Contemporary Pacific* 27, no. 1 (2015): 110–45.

Kaiwar, Vasant, and Sucheta Mazumdar. "Introduction." In *Antinomies of Modernity: Essays on Race, Orient, and Nation*, edited by Vasant Kaiwar and Sucheta Mazumdar, 1–12. Durham, NC: Duke University Press, 2003.

Kakışım, Can. "Racism in Russia and Its Effects on the Caucasian Region and Peoples." *Tesam Akademi Dergisi* 6, no. 1 (2019): 97–121.

Kalmar, Ivan Davidson. *White but Not Quite: Central Europe's Illiberal Revolt*. Bristol: Bristol University Press, 2022.

———. "Race, Racialisation, and the East of the European Union:. An Introduction." *Journal of Ethnic and Migration Studies* 49, no. 6 (2023): 1465–80.

Kang'ara, Sylvia Wairimu. "China and Africa: Development, Land, and the Colonial Legacy." In *Bandung, Global History and International Law*, edited by Luis Eslava, Michael Fakhri, and Vasuki Nesiah, 367–80. Cambridge: Cambridge University Press, 2017.

Kaplan, Yosef. "The Curaçao and Amsterdam Jewish Communities in the 17th and 18th Centuries." *American Jewish History* 72, no. 2 (1982): 193–211.

Kapur, Ratna. "The Colonial Debris of Bandung: Equality and Facilitating the Rise of the Hindu Right in India." In *Bandung, Global History and International Law*, edited by Luis Eslava, Michael Fakhri, and Vasuki Nesiah, 311–21. Cambridge: Cambridge University Press, 2017.

Karaman, Nuray. "Coding Whiteness: Living in the Space as an Insider-Outsider." *Journal of International Studies* 12, no. 2 (2022): 124–40.

Kassamali, Sumayya. "The Kafala System as Racialized Servitude." In *Racial Formations in Africa and the Middle East: A Transregional Approach*, 102–6. Project on African Social Research, 2021.

Kawai, Yuko. "'Japanese as Both a "Race" and a 'Non-Race': The Politics of Jinshu and Minzoku and the Depoliticization of Japaneseness." In *Race and Racism in Modern East Asia: Interactions, Nationalism, Gender and Lineage*, edited by Rotem Kowner and Walter Demel. 368–88. Boston: Brill, 2015.

Kawasaki, Seiro. "The Policy of Apartheid and the Japanese in the Republic of South Africa (1)." *Tokyo Kasei Gakuin Tsukiba Jyoshi Daigaku Kiyō* (2001): 53–79.

Keane, A.H. *The World's Peoples: A Popular Account of Their Bodily & Mental Characters, Beliefs, Traditions, Political and Social Institutions*. England: Hutchinson, 1908.

Keaton, Trica. *Muslim Girls and the Other France*. Indianapolis: Indiana University Press, 2006.

———. *# You Know You're Black in France When: The Fact of Everyday Antiblackness*. Boston: MIT Press, 2023.

Keevak, Michael. *Becoming Yellow: A Short History of Racial Thinking*. Princeton, NJ: Princeton University Press, 2011.

Kelley, Robin D.G. *Race Rebels: Culture, Politics and the Black Working Class*. New York: Free Press, 1994.

———. *Freedom Dreams: The Black Radical Imagination Revised and Expanded*. Boston: Beacon Press, 2022.

———. "Making History, Making Worlds." *American Quarterly*, 75, no. 2 (2023): 383–90.

Kelly, Casey Ryan. "Whiteness, Repressive Victimhood, and the Foil of the Intolerant Left." *First Amendment Studies* 55, no. 1 (2021): 59–76.

Kendi, Ibram X. *Stamped from the Beginning: The Definitive History of Racist Ideas in America*. New York: Nation Books, 2016.

Kennedy, Dane. *Islands of White: Settler Society and Culture in Kenya and Southern Rhodesia, 1890–1939*. Durham, NC: Duke University Press, 1987.

Khoury, Rana B. "Western Sahara and Palestine: A Comparative Study of Colonialisms, Occupations, and Nationalisms." *New Middle Eastern Studies* 1 (2011).

Kiernan, Ben. *The Pol Pot Regime: Race, Power, and Genocide in Cambodia under the Khmer Rouge.* New Haven, CT: Yale University Press, 1996.

Kim, Claire Jean. "The Racial Triangulation of Asian Americans." *Politics & Society* 27, no. 1 (1999): 105–38.

———. "Asian Americans and Anti-Blackness." *Politics, Groups, and Identities* 10, no. 3 (2022): 503–10.

———. *Asian Americans in an Anti-Black World.* Cambridge: Cambridge University Press, 2023.

Kim, Dorothy. "White Supremacists Have Weaponized an Imaginary Viking Past." *Time*, April 15, 2019. https://time.com/5569399/viking-history-white-nationalists/.

Kim, Jae Kyun, and Moon-Kie Jung. "'Not to be Slaves of Others': Antiblackness in Precolonial Korea." In *Anti-Blackness,* edited by Joao H. Costa Vargas and Moon-Kie Jung, 143–67. Durham, NC: Duke University Press, 2021.

Kim, Joong Won. "The Racialization of the Cultural Toolkit and the Racial Positions of Asia and Asian America." *Social Currents* 11, no. 3 (2024): 259–73.

Kim, Nadia Y. "Critical Thoughts on Asian American Assimilation in the Whitening Literature." *Social Forces* 86, no. 2 (2007): 561–74.

———. *Imperial Citizens: Koreans and Race from Seoul to LA.* Stanford, CA: Stanford University Press, 2008.

Kimari, Wangui, and Henrik Ernstson. "Imperial Remains and Imperial Invitations: Centering Race within the Contemporary Large-Scale Infrastructures of East Africa." *Antipode* 52, no. 3 (2020): 825–46.

King, Martin Luther. "A Time to Break Silence." In *A Testament of Hope: The Essential Writings and Speeches of Martin Luther King Jr.*, edited by James M. Washington, 231–44. San Francisco: HarperCollins, 1986.

King, Stephen. J. "Black Arabs and African Migrants: Between Slavery and Racism in North Arica." *Journal of North African Studies* 26, no. 1 (2021): 8–50.

King, Tiffany Lethabo, Jenell Navarro, and Andrea Smith. "Introduction: Beyond Incommensurability: Toward an Otherwise Stance on Black and Indigenous Relationality." In *Otherwise Worlds: Against Settler Colonialism and Anti-Blackness,* edited by Tiffany Lethabo King, Jenell Navarro, and Andrea Smith, 1–23. Durham, NC: Duke University Press, 2020.

Kirby, Jen. "'Black Lives Matter' Has Become a Global Rallying Cry against Racism and Police Brutality." *Vox*, June 12, 2020. https://www.vox.com/2020/6/12/21285244/black-lives-matter-global-protests-george-floyd-uk-belgium.

Koekkoek, René, Anne-Isabelle Richard, and Arthur Weststeijn. "Visions of Dutch Empire: Towards a Long-Term Global Perspective." *Low Countries Historical Review* 132, no. 2 (2017): 79–96.

Kokkindis, Tasos. "The 'Lost Antetokounmpos' of Greece." *Greek Reporter*, September 6, 2022. https://greekreporter.com/2022/09/06/antetokounmpo-undocumented-children-citizenship-greece/.

Kowner, Rotem. "Race and Racism." In *Routledge Handbook of Modern Japanese History*, 92–102. New York: Routledge, 2017.

Kowner, Rotem, and Walter Demel, eds. *Race and Racism in Modern East Asia: Interactions, Nationalism, Gender and Lineage.* Boston: Brill, 2015.

Kozol, Jonathan. *The Shame of the Nation: The Restoration of Apartheid Schooling in America.* New York: Crown, 2005.

Kraidy, Marwan M., and Omar Al-Ghazzi. "Neo-Ottoman Cool: Turkish Popular Culture in the Arab Public Sphere." *Popular Communication* 11, no. 1 (2013): 17–29.

Kramer, P.A. "Shades of Sovereignty: Racialized Power, the United States and the World." In *Explaining the History of American Foreign Relations,* edited by Frank Costigliola and Michael J. Hogan, 245–70. Cambridge: Cambridge University Press, 2016.

Krivonos, Daria. "Racial Capitalism and the Production of Difference in Helsinki and Warsaw." *Journal of Ethnic and Migration Studies* 49, no. 6 (2023): 1500–516.

Kumar, Krishnan. *Visions of Empire: How Five Imperial Regimes Shaped the World.* Princeton, NJ: Princeton University Press, 2017.

Kusumaryati, Veronika. "#Papuanlivesmatter: Black Consciousness and Political Movements in West Papua." *Critical Asian Studies* 53, no. 4 (2021): 453–75.

Labelle Jr., Maurice M. "Tensions of Decolonization: Lebanon, West Africans, and a Color Line within a Global Color Line." *Radical History Review* 131 (2018): 36–57.

Labib, Tahar. *Imagining the Arab Other: How Arabs and Non-Arabs View Each Other.* London: I.B. Tauris Press, 2009.

Ladner, Joyce, ed. *The Death of White Sociology: Essays on Race and Culture.* Baltimore: Black Classic Press, 1998.

Laforteza, Elaine Marie Carbonell. *The Somatechnics of Whiteness and Race: Colonialism and Mestiza Privilege.* Farnham: Ashgate, 2015.

Lake, Marilyn, and Henry Reynolds. *Drawing the Global Colour Line: White Men's Countries and the International Challenge of Racial Equality.* Cambridge: Cambridge University Press, 2008.

Lanzano, Cristiano. "Italian Fascists Quote Samora Machel and Sankara."*Africa Is a Country,* September 9, 2018. https://africasacountry.com/2018/09/twisting-pan-africanism-to-promote-anti-africanism.

Laruelle, Marlene. "Central Asian Labor Migrants in Russia: The Diasporization of the Central Asian States?" *China and Eurasia Forum Quarterly* 5, no. 3 (2007): 101–19.

Law, Ian. *Red Racisms: Racisms in Communist and Post-Communist Contexts.* New York: Palgrave Macmillan, 2012.

———. *Mediterranean Racisms: Connections and Complexities in the Racialization of the Mediterranean Region.* New York: Palgrave Macmillan, 2014.

Lawton, Sophie. "Tucker Carlson's Embrace of Foreign Authoritarian Leaders." *Media Matters,* August 3, 2022. https://www.mediamatters.org/tucker-carlson/tucker-carlsons-embrace-foreign-authoritarian-leaders.

Le Renard, Amélie. *Western Privilege: Work, Intimacy and Postcolonial Hierarchies in Dubai.* Palo Alto, CA: Stanford University Press, 2021.

Le Renard, Amélie, and Neha Vora. "Interrogating Race in Gulf Studies." In *Racial Formations in Africa and the Middle East: A Transregional Approach,* 96–101. Project on African Social Research, 2022.

Lee, Erika. "The 'Yellow Peril' and Asian Exclusion in the Americas." *Pacific Historical Review* 76, no. 4 (2007): 537–62.
Lee, Joseph Tse-Hei, and Satish Kolluri, eds. *Hong Kong and Bollywood: Globalization of Asian Cinemas*. Springer, 2016.
Lee, Robert G. *Orientals*. Philadelphia: Temple University Press, 1999.
Lefkaditou, Ageliki. "Observations on Race and Racism in Greece." *Journal of Anthropological Sciences* 95 (2017): 329–38.
———. "Blood Affairs: Racial Blood Group Research and Nation Building in Greece, 1920s–1940s." *Perspectives on Science* 30, no. 1 (2022): 47–76.
Leibman, Laura Arnold, and Sam May. "Making Jews: Race, Gender and Identity in Barbados in the Age of Emancipation." *American Jewish History* 99, no. 1 (2015): 1–26.
Lentin, Alana. "Replacing 'Race,' Historicizing 'Culture' in Multiculturalism." *Patterns of Prejudice* 39, no. 4 (2005): 379–96.
———. "Europe and the Silence about Race." *European Journal of Social Theory* 11, no. 4 (2008): 487–503.
———. "Post-Race, Post Politics: The Paradoxical Rise of Culture after Multiculturalism." *Ethnic and Racial Studies* 37, no. 8 (2014): 4–21.
———. "Beyond Denial: 'Not Racism' as Racist Violence." *Continuum Journal of Media & Cultural Studies* 32 (2018): 400–414.
———. *Why Race Still Matters*. Cambridge: Polity, 2020.
Lentin, Alana, and Gavan Titley. *The Crises of Multiculturalism: Racism in a Neoliberal Age*. London: Bloomsbury, 2011.
Lentin, Ronit. *Traces of Racial Exception: Racializing Israeli Settler Colonialism*. London: Bloomsbury Academic, 2018.
Lesser, Jeffrey. *Immigration, Ethnicity, and National Identity in Brazil, 1808 to the Present*. Cambridge: Cambridge University Press, 2013.
Levine-Rasky, C., ed. *Working through Whiteness: International Perspectives*. Albany: State University of New York Press, 2002.
Lewis, Jovan Scott. *Scammer's Yard: The Crime of Black Repair in Jamaica*. Minneapolis: University of Minnesota Press, 2020.
Lewicki, Aleksandra. "East–West Inequalities and the Ambiguous Racialisation of 'Eastern Europeans.'" *Journal of Ethnic and Migration Studies* 49, no. 6 (2023): 1481–99.
Lincoln, David. "Labour Migration in the Global Division of Labour: Migrant Workers in Mauritius." *International Migration* 47, no. 4 (2009): 129–56.
Lindner, Ulrike. "Contested Concepts of 'White'/'Native' and Mixed Marriages in German South West Africa and The Cape Colony 1900–1914: A Histoire Croiseé." *Journal of Namibian Studies* 6 (2009): 57–79.
Lipsitz, George. *The Possessive Investment in Whiteness: How White People Profit from Identity Politics*. Philadelphia: Temple University Press, 2006.
———. "Rejecting the Racial Contract: Charles Mills and Critical Race Theory." *Race Ethnicity and Education* 26, no. 4 (2023): 533–52.
Loftsdóttir, Kristín, and Lars Jensen. 2012. "Nordic Exceptionalism and the Nordic Others." In *Whiteness and Postcolonialism in the Nordic Region: Exceptionalism, Mi-*

grant Others and National Identities, edited by Kristin Loftdóttir and Lars Jensen, 1–12. Burlington: Ashgate, 2012.

Lombardi-Diop, Cristina. "Postracial/Postcolonial Italy." In *Postcolonial Italy: Challenging National Homogeneity*, edited by Cristina Lombardi-Diop and Caterina Romeo, 175–90. New York: Palgrave Macmillan, 2012.

Long, Edward. *History of Jamaica*. Montreal: McGill University Press, [1774] 2002.

Longley, Kyle. *Sparrow and the Hawk: Costa Rica and the United States during the Rise of José Figueres*. Tuscaloosa: University of Alabama Press, 1997.

Lopez, Ian Haney. *White by Law: The Legal Construction of Race*. New York: New York University Press, 2006.

Lori, Noora. "Who Counts as 'People of the Gulf'? Disputes over the Arab Status of Zanzibaris in the UAE." In *Racial Formations in Africa and the Middle East: A Transregional Approach*, 107–14. Project on African Social Research, 2021.

Lorimer, Douglas A. *Science, Race Relations, and Resistance: Britain, 1870–1914*. Manchester: Manchester University Press, 2013.

Loveman, Mara. *National Colors: Racial Classification and the State in Latin America*. New York: Oxford University Press, 2014.

Lowe, Lisa. *The Intimacies of Four Continents*. Durham, NC: Duke University Press, 2015.

Ltifi, Afifa. "Disarticulating Blackness or the Semantics of Anti(Blackness) in Tunisia." In *Racial Formations in Africa and the Middle East: A Transregional Approach*, 55–60. Project on African Social Research, 2021.

Lu, Amy Shirong. "The Many Faces of Internationalization in Japanese Anime." *Animation* 3, no. 2 (2008): 169–87.

Lubkemann, S.C. "Unsettling the Metropole: Race and Settler Reincorporation in Postcolonial Portugal." In *Settler Colonialism in the Twentieth Century*, edited by C. Elkins and S. Pedersen, 271–84. New York: Routledge, 2012.

Luttikhuis, Bart. "Beyond Race: Constructions of 'Europeanness' in Late-Colonial Legal Practice in the Dutch East Indies." *European Review of History* 20, no. 4 (2013): 539–58.

"Lynching in America: Confronting the Legacy of Racial Terror." Montgomery, AL: Equal Justice Initiative, 2017. https://lynchinginamerica.eji.org/report/.

MacLean, Ken. "The Rohingya Crisis and the Practices of Erasure." *Journal of Genocide Research* 21, no. 1 (2019): 83–95.

MacPherson, Cluny. *Reinventing the Nation: Building a Bicultural Future from a Monocultural Past in Aotearoa/New Zealand*. New York: Routledge, 2005.

Madley, Benjamin. "From Africa to Auschwitz: How German South West Africa Incubated Ideas and Methods Adopted and Developed by the Nazis in Eastern Europe." *European History Quarterly* 35, no. 3 (2005): 429–64.

Maghbouleh, Neda. *The Limits of Whiteness: Iranian Americans and Everyday Politics of Race*. Palo Alto, CA: Stanford University Press, 2017.

Magubane, Zine. "American Sociology's Racial Ontology: Remembering Slavery, Deconstructing Modernity, and Chartering the Future of Global Historical Sociology." *Cultural Sociology* 10, no. 3 (2016): 369–84.

Mahler, Anne Garland. "Beyond the Color Curtain: The Metonymic Color Politics of the

Tricontinental and the (New) Global South." In *The Global South Atlantic*, edited by K. Bystrom and J.R. Slaughter, 99–123. New York: Fordham University Press, 2017.

———. *From the Tricontinental to the Global South: Race, Radicalism, and Transnational Solidarity.* Durham, NC: Duke University Press, 2018.

Maldonado-Torres, Nelson. "On the Coloniality of Being." *Cultural Studies* 21, no. 2/3 (2007): 240–70.

Mama, Amina. "Challenging Subjects: Gender and Power in African Contexts." *African Sociological Review* 5, no. 2 (2001): 63–73.

———. *Beyond the Masks: Race, Gender and Subjectivity.* New York: Routledge, 2002.

Mamdani, Mahmood. "Race and Ethnicity as Political Identities in the African Context." In *Keywords: Identity, For a Different Kind of Globalization*, 1–23. New York: Other Press, 2004.

Manrique, Linnete. "Dreaming of A Cosmic Race: José Vasconcelos and the Politics of Race in Mexico, 1920–1930s." *Cogent Arts & Humanities* 3, no. 1 (2016): 1218–316.

Marable, Manning. "Introduction." *Transnational Blackness Navigating the Global Color Line*, edited by M. Marable, 1–8. New York: Palgrave Macmillan, 2008.

Marchand, Iris. "Being Dogla: Hybridity and Ethnicity in Post-Colonial Suriname." PhD diss., University of Edinburgh, 2014.

Marczuk, Karina Paulina. "Origins of Immigration to Australia, 1787–1914." *Arhivele Olteniei* 31 (2017): 39–50.

Mariscal, George. "The Role of Spain in Contemporary Race Theory." *Arizona Journal of Hispanic Cultural Studies* 2 (1998): 7–22.

Marrison, Erica, "Canada's "Freedom Convoy" Trucker Protests Aren't about Freedom." *Teen Vogue*, February 10, 2022. https://www.teenvogue.com/story/canada-freedom-convoy.

Massey, Douglas, and Nancy Denton. *American Apartheid: Segregation and the Making of the Underclass.* Cambridge, MA: Harvard University Press, 1993.

Matereke, Kudzai. "Space Matters: Rethinking Spatiality in Discourses of Colonial and Postcolonial Boundaries." In *Bondage of Boundaries and Identity Politics in Postcolonial Africa: the 'Northern Problem' and Ethno-Futures*, edited by Sabelo J. Ndlovu-Gatsheni and Brilliant Mhlanga, 24–44. Braamfontein: African Books, 2013.

Mathias, Christopher. "This Is Why You're Seeing the Confederate Flag across Europe." *Huffington Post*, July 14, 2017. https://www.huffpost.com/entry/confederate-flag-europe-trump-poland_n_5968a317e4b017418626ab5e.

Matsuda, Mari. "We Will Not Be Used." *Asian Pacific American Law Journal* 1 (1993): 79.

———. "Planet Asian America." *Asian Law Journal* 8 (2001): 169.

Matsuoka, Manami. "Unveiling Race and Japanese Identity through Kokusai Kekkon." MA thesis, Minnesota State University, Mankato, 2021.

Matthewson, Amy. "Satirising Imperial Anxiety in Victorian Britain: Representing Japan in Punch Magazine, 1852–1893." *Contemporary Japan* 33, no. 2 (2021): 201–24.

Mattos, Hebe. "'Pretos' and 'Pardos' between the Cross and the Sword: Racial Categories in Seventeenth-Century Brazil." *European Review of Latin American and Caribbean Studies* (2006): 43–55.

Mays, Kyle T. *An Afro-Indigenous History of United States*. New York: Beacon Press, 2021.
Mayorga-Gallo, Sarah. "The White-Centering Logic of Diversity Ideology." *American Behavioral Scientist* 63, no. 13 (2019): 1789–809.
Mbaria, John, and Mordecai Ogada. *Big Conservation Lie: The Untold Story of Wildlife Conservation in Kenya*. Seattle: Lens & Pens, 2016.
Mbembe, Achille. *Critique of Black Reason*. Durham, NC: Duke University Press, 2017.
McClintock, Anne. *Imperial Leather: Race, Gender, and Sexuality in the Colonial Context*. New York: Routledge, 1995.
McKay, Dwanna L. "Masking Legitimized Racism: Indigeneity, Colorblindness, and the Sociology of Race." In *Seeing Race Again: Countering Colorblindness Across the Disciplines*, edited by Kimberlé Williams Crenshaw. Berkeley: University of California Press, 2019.
McKittrick, Katherine. "'Their Blood Is There, and They Can't Throw It Out.': Honoring Black Canadian Geographies." *Topia: Canadian Journal of Cultural Studies* 7 (2002): 27–37.
———. "Wait Canada Anticipate Black." *CLR James Journal* 20, no. 1/2 (2014): 243–50.
———. *Dear Science and Other Stories*. Durham, NC: Duke University Press, 2020.
McMichael, Philip, and Heloise Weber. *Development and Social Change a Global Perspective, Seventh Edition*. London: Sage, 2022.
McMillan Cottom, Tressie. *Thick*. New York: New Press, 2019.
Meer, Nasar. "The Wreckage of White Supremacy." *Identities* 26, no. 5 (2019): 501–9.
———. *The Cruel Optimism of Racial Justice*. Bristol: Policy Press, 2022.
Meer, Nasar, and Anoop Nayak. "Race Ends Where? Race, Racism and Contemporary Sociology." *Sociology* 49, no. 6 (2015): NP3–NP20.
Meghji, Ali. "Toward a Theoretical Synergy: Critical Race Theory and Decolonial Thought in Trumpamerica and Brexit Britain." *Current Sociology* 70, no. 5 (2022): 647–64.
———. *The Racialized Social System*. Cambridge: Polity, 2022.
Mehrotra, Karishma. "Israel Turns to Indian Workers as Gaza War Worsens Labor Shortage." *Washington Post*, January 24, 2024. https://www.washingtonpost.com/world/2024/01/24/israel-india-migrant-workers/.
Meier, Anna. "The Idea of Terror: White Supremacist Violence and the Making of Counterterrorism." PhD diss., University of Wisconsin-Madison, 2021.
Melamed, Jodi. *Represent and Destroy: Rationalizing Violence in the New Racial Capitalism*. Minneapolis: University of Minnesota Press, 2011.
Mellino, Miguel. "De-Provincializing Italy: Notes on Race, Racialization, and Italy's Coloniality." In *Postcolonial Italy: Challenging National Homogeneity*, edited by Christina Lombardi-Diop and Caterina Romeo, 83–101. New York: Palgrave Macmillan, 2012.
Memmi, Albert. *The Colonizer and the Colonized*. Boston: Beacon Press, [1957] 1965.
Merrill, Lisa. "Exhibiting Race 'Under the World's Huge Glass Case': William and Ellen Craft and William Wells Brown at the Great Exhibition in Crystal Palace, London 1851." *Slavery & Abolition* 33, no. 2 (2012): 321–36.
Mgbeoji, Ikechi. *Global Biopiracy: Patents, Plants, and Indigenous Knowledge*. Vancouver: UBC Press, 2007.

Michel, Noémi. "Sheepology: The Postcolonial Politics of Raceless Racism in Switzerland." *Postcolonial Studies* 18, no. 4 (2015): 410–26.

Mignolo, Walter D. "The Role of BRICS Countries in the Becoming World Order: Humanity, Colonial/Imperial Differences, and the Racial Distribution of Capital and Knowledge." Paper presented and discussed at the Meeting of the Academy of Latinity and Tsinghua University, Beijing, 2012.

Milazzo, Marzia. "The Rhetorics of Racial Power: Enforcing Colorblindness in Post-Apartheid Scholarship on Race." *Journal of International and Intercultural Communication* 1 (2015): 7–26.

———. "On the Transportability, Malleability, and Longevity of Colorblindness: Reproducing White Supremacy in Brazil and South Africa." In *Seeing Race Again: Countering Colorblindness across the Disciplines*, edited by Kimberlé Williams Crenshaw, 105–27. Berkeley: University of California Press, 2019.

———. *Colorblind Tools: Global Technologies of Racial Power*. Chicago: Northwestern University Press, 2022.

Mills, Charles. *The Racial Contract*. Ithaca, NY: Cornell University Press, 1997.

———. *From Class to Race: Essays in White Marxism and Black Radicalism*. Lanham, MD: Rowman & Littlefield, 2003.

———. *Black Rights/White Wrongs: The Critique of Racial Liberalism*. Oxford: Oxford University Press, 2017.

———. "The Illumination of Blackness." In *Anti-Blackness*, edited by Joao H. Costa Vargas and Moon-Kie Jung, 17–36. Durham, NC: Duke University Press, 2021.

Milner-Thornton, Juliette. "Measuring Mixedness in Zambia: Creating and Erasing Coloureds in Zambia's Colonial and Post-Colonial Census, 1921–2010." In *The Palgrave International Handbook of Mixed Racial and Ethnic Classification*, edited by Zarine L. Rocha and Peter J. Aspinall. Springer International, 2020.

Mogilner, Marina. "When Race Is Language and Empire Is a Context." *Slavic Review* 80, no. 2 (2021): 207–15.

Molina, Natalia, Daniel Martinez HoSang, and Ramón A. Gutiérrez, eds. *Relational Formations of Race: Theory, Method, and Practice*. Berkeley: University of California Press, 2019.

Moll, Yasmin. "Narrating Nubia: Between Sentimentalism and Solidarity." In *Racial Formations in Africa and the Middle East: A Transregional Approach*, 81–86. Project on African Social Research, 2021.

Mollett, Sharlene. "The Power to Plunder: Rethinking Land Grabbing in Latin America." *Antipode* 48, no. 2 (2016): 412–32.

Monaville, Pedro. "The Politics of Elegance: An Interview with Daniel Tödt." *Africa Is a Country*, January 21, 2022. https://africasacountry.com/2022/01/the-politics-of-elegance.

Mondesire, Zachary. 2021. "Race after Revolution: Imagining Blackness and Africanity in the 'New Sudan.'" In *Racial Formations in Africa and the Middle East: A Transregional Approach*, 87–91. Project on African Social Research, 2021.

Mondon, Aurelien, and Aaron Winter. 2020. "Racist Movements, the Far Right and

Mainstreaming." In *The Routledge International Handbook of Contemporary Racism*, edited by John Solomos, 147–59. Abingdon: Routledge, 2020.

Monsour, Anne. "Undesirable Alien to Good Citizen: Syrian/Lebanese in 'White' Australia." *Journal of Middle East and North African Migration* 3, no. 1 (2015): 130–56.

Monteiro, Lyra D. "Race Conscious Casting and the Erasure of the Black Past in Lin-Manuel Miranda's *Hamilton*." *Public Historian* 38, no. 1 (2016): 89–98.

Moore, Wendy Leo. *Reproducing Racism: White Space, Elite Law Schools, and Racial Inequality*. Lanham, MD: Rowman & Littlefield, 2008.

Moreton-Robinson, Aileen. *The White Possessive: Property, Power, and Indigenous Sovereignty*. Minneapolis: University of Minnesota Press, 2015.

Moreton-Robinson, Aileen, Maryrose Casey, and Fiona Nicoll, eds. *Transnational Whiteness Matters*. Lanham, MD: Lexington Books, 2008.

Morning, Ann. "Ethnic Classification in Global Perspective: A Cross-National Survey of the 2000 Census Round." *Population Research Policy Review* 27 (2008): 239–72.

Morning, Ann, and Marcello Maneri. *An Ugly Word: Rethinking Race in Italy and the United States*. New York: Russell Sage Foundation, 2022.

Morris, Wesley. "Music." In *The 1619 Project*, edited by Nikole Hannah-Jones, Caitlin Roper, Ilena Silverman, and Jake Silverstein, 358–79. New York: One World, 2021.

Morrison, Matthew D. "The Sound(s) of Subjection: Constructing American Popular Music and Racial Identity through Blacksound." *Women & Performance: A Journal of Feminist Theory* 27, no. 1 (2017): 13–24.

Morrison, Toni. *Playing in the Dark: Whiteness and the Literary Imagination*. New York: Vintage, 1992.

———. "On the Backs of Blacks." In *Toni Morrison: What Moves at the Margin*. Edited by Carolyn C. Denard. Jackson: University Press of Mississippi, 2008.

Morton, Samuel George. *Crania Americana: A Comparative View of the Skulls of Various Aboriginal Nations of North and South America*. Philadelphia: John Pennington, 1839.

Mosse, George L. *Toward a Final Solution: A History of European Racism*. Howard Fettig, 1978.

Motadel, David. "Iran and the Aryan Myth." In *Perceptions of Iran: History, Myths and Nationalism from Medieval Persia to the Islamic Republic*, edited by Ali M. Ansari, 119–46. London: Bloomsbury, 2014.

Moulton, Alex A. "Towards the Arboreal Side-Effects of Marronage: Black Geographies and Ecologies of the Jamaican Forest." *Nature and Space E* 6, no. 1 (2022): 3–23.

Muckle, Adrian. "The Presumption of Indigeneity: Colonial Administration, the Community of Race and the Category of Indigène in New Caledonia, 1887–1946." *Journal of Pacific History* 47, no. 3 (2012): 309–28.

Mueller, Jennifer C. "Racial Ideology or Racial Ignorance? An Alternative Theory of Racial Cognition." *Sociological Theory* 38, no. 2 (2020): 142–69.

Muhammad, Khalil Gibran. *The Condemnation of Blackness: Race, Crime, and the Making of Modern Urban America*. Cambridge, MA: Harvard University Press, 2019.

Mukherjee, Kunal. "Race Relations and Ethnic Minorities in Contemporary Myanmar."

In *Routledge Handbook of Race and Ethnicity in Asia*, edited by Michael Weiner, 108–25. London: Routledge, 2021.

Müller, Ulrike Anne. "Far Away So Close: Race, Whiteness, and German Identity." *Identities* 18, no. 6 (2011): 620–45.

Mullings, Leith. "Interrogating Racism: Toward an Antiracist Anthropology." *Annual Review of Anthropology* 34 (2005): 667–93.

Nadhiri, Aman Y. *Saracens and Franks in 12th–15th Century European and Near Eastern Literature: Perceptions of Self and Other*. New York: Routledge, 2017.

Nagel, Joane. *Race, Ethnicity and Sexuality. Intimate Intersections, Forbidden Frontiers*. New York: Oxford University Press, 2003.

Najar, José. "The Privileges of Positivist Whiteness: The Syrian-Lebanese of Sao Paulo, Brazil (1888–1939)." PhD diss., Indiana University, 2012.

Narkowicz, Kasia. "White Enough, Not White Enough: Racism and Racialisation among Poles in the UK." *Journal of Ethnic and Migration Studies* 49, no. 6 (2023): 1534–51.

Nathan, Dev, and Sandip Sarkar. "Blood on Your Mobile Phone? Capturing the Gains for Artisanal Miners, Poor Workers, and Women." *Capturing the Gains*, February 2011.

Navarro, Tami. *Virgin Capital: Race, Gender, and Financialization in the U.S. Virgin Islands*. New York: State University of New York Press, 2021.

Ndlovu-Gatsheni, Sabelo J. *Empire, Global Coloniality and African Subjectivity*. New York: Berghahn, 2013.

———. "Ali A. Mazrui on the Invention of Africa and Postcolonial Predicaments: 'My Life Is One Long Debate.'" *Third World Quarterly* 36, no. 2 (2015): 205–22.

———. "The Cognitive Empire, Politics of Knowledge and African Intellectual Productions: Reflections on Struggles for Epistemic Freedom and Resurgence of Decolonisation in the Twenty-First Century." *Third World Quarterly* 42, no. 5 (2021): 882–901.

Ndlovu-Gatsheni, Sabelo and Brilliant Mhlanga, eds. *Bondage of Boundaries and Identity Politics in Postcolonial Africa: The Northern Problem and Ethno-Futures*. Africa Institute of South Africa, 2013.

Nevola, Luca. "'Black People, White Hearts': Origin, Race, and Colour in Contemporary Yemen." *Anthropologia* 7, no. 1 (2020): 93–115.

Newman, Brooke N. *Dark Inheritance: Blood, Race, and Sex in Colonial Jamaica*. New Haven, CT: Yale University Press, 2018.

Ng'weno, Bettina, and Lok Siu. "Comparative Raciality: Erasure and Hypervisibility of Asian and Afro Mexicans." In *Global Raciality: Empire, PostColoniality, DeColoniality*, edited by P. Bacchetta, S. Maira, and H. Winant, 62–81. London: Routledge, 2019.

Niang, Mame-Fatou. "Innocence, Ignorance et Arrogance: Les Trois Grâces de l'Anti-Noirité en France." *Contemporary French and Francophone Studies* 26, no. 4/5 (2022): 361–74.

Nicoll, Fiona. "Consuming Pathologies: The Australian against Indigenous Sovereignties." In *Transnational Whiteness Matters*, edited by Aileen Moreton Robinson, Maryrose Casey, and Fiona Nicoll, 57–89. Lanham, MD: Lexington Books, 2008.

Nonini, Donald M., and Aihwa Ong. "Chinese Transnationals as Alternative Modernity." In *Ungrounded Empires: The Cultural Politics of Modern Chinese Transnationalism*, edited by Aihwa Ong and Donald Nonini, 3–14. London: Routledge, 1996.

Novati, Anita Calchi. "The Battle for the *Jus Soli*." *A Path for Europe*, May 11, 2021. https://pathforeurope.eu/the-battle-for-the-jus-soli/.

O'Connor, P.S. "Keeping New Zealand White, 1908–1920." *New Zealand Journal of History* 1, no. 3 (1967): 41–65.

Oh, Chuyun. "Performing Post-Racial Asianness: K-Pop's Appropriation of Hip-Hop Culture." *Congress on Research in Dance Conference Proceedings* (2014): 121–25.

Oliver, Melvin, and Thomas Shapiro. *Black Wealth / White Wealth: A New Perspective on Racial Inequality*. New York: Routledge, 2013.

Olivieri, Sergio, Francesc Ortega, Ana Rivadeneira, and Eliana Carranza. "The Labour Market Effects of Venezuelan Migration in Ecuador." *Journal of Development Studies* 58, no. 4 (2022): 713–29.

Omi, Michael, and Howard Winant. *Racial Formation in the United States*, 3rd ed. New York: Routledge, 2015.

Owens, Christina D. "Traveling Yellow Peril: Race, Gender, and Empire in Japan's English Teaching Industry." *American Studies* 55, no. 4 (2017): 29–49.

Oxfam Briefing Paper. "Fueling Conflict: Analyzing the Human Impact of War in Yemen." January 2023. https://policy-practice.oxfam.org/resources/fueling-conflict-analyzing-the-human-impact-of-the-war-in-yemen-621478/.

Painter, Nell. *The History of White People*. New York: W.W. Norton, 2010.

Pallister-Wilkins, Polly. "Saving the Souls of White Folk: Humanitarianism as White Supremacy." *Security Dialogue* 52, no. 1 (2021): 98–106.

Parikh, Shreya. "The Limits of Confronting Racial Discrimination in Tunisia with Law 50." *Middle East Report* 299 (Summer 2021).

Parker, B.A., Gene Demby, Courtney Stein, and Dalia Mortada. "From 'Fight the Power' to Advertising for the Power: Hip-Hop Turns 50." *Code Switch*, August 9, 2023. https://www.npr.org/2023/07/28/1190798156/from-fight-the-power-to-advertising-for-the-power-hip-hop-turns-50.

Parreñas, Rhacel Salazar. *Unfree: Migrant Domestic Work in Arab States*. Palo Alto, CA: Stanford University Press, 2021.

Paschel, Tianna S. "From Colombia to the U.S. Black Lives Have Always Mattered." *NACLA Report on the Americas* 49, no. 1 (2017): 27–29.

Patel, Ian Sanjay. "How Imperial Hopes for the Commonwealth Led to British Citizenship Being Redefined along Racial Lines." *LSE British Politics and Policy*, May 20, 2021. https://blogs.lse.ac.uk/politicsandpolicy/commonwealth-hostile-environment/.

Patil, Vrushali. *Webbed Connectivities: The Imperial Sociology of Sex, Gender, and Sexuality*. Minneapolis: University of Minnesota Press, 2022.

Patil, Vrushali, and Bandana Purkayastha. "The Transnational Assemblage of Indian Rape Culture." *Ethnic and Racial Studies* 41, no. 11 (2018): 1952–70.

Pérez, Elizabeth. "The Ontology of Twerk: from 'Sexy' Black Movement Style to Afro-Diasporic Sacred Dance." *African and Black Diaspora* 9, no. 1 (2016): 16–31.

Pérez, Lisandro. "Cuba." In *The New Americans, A Guide to Immigration since 1965*, edited by Mary C. Waters and Reed Ueda, 386–98. Cambridge, MA: Harvard University Press, 2007.

Peréz, Raúl. *The Souls of White Jokes: How Racist Humor Fuels White Supremacy*. Palo Alto, CA: Stanford University Press, 2022.

Pergher, Roberta. "The Allure of Citizenship: Subjects, Citizens, and Special Citizens in the Fascist Empire." In *Citizens and Subjects of the Italian Colonies: Legal Constructions and Social Practice*, edited by Simona Berhe and Olindo de Napoli, 47–67. New York: Routledge, 2021.

Perry, Imani. "Of Desi, J. Lo and Color Matters: Law, Critical Race Theory, the Architecture of Race." *Cleveland State Law Review* 52, no. 1/2 (2004): 139–54.

———. *South to America: A Journey below the Mason-Dixon to Understand the Soul of a Nation*. New York: HarperCollins, 2022.

Perry, Keisha-Khan. *Black Women against the Land Grab: The Fight for Racial Justice in Brazil*. Minneapolis: University of Minnesota Press, 2013.

———. "The Resurgent Far Right and the Black Feminist Struggle for Social Democracy in Brazil." *American Anthropologist* 122, no. 1 (2019): 157–62.

Perry, Marc D. "Global Black Self-Fashioning: Hip Hop as Diasporic Space." *Identities* 15, no. 6 (2008): 635–64.

Pesarini, Angelica, and Guido Tintori. "Mixed Identities in Italy: A Country in Denial." In *The Palgrave International Handbook of Mixed Racial and Ethnic Classification*, edited by Zarine L. Rocha and Peter J. Aspinall, 349–65. Springer International, 2020.

Phelps, Nicole M. "Scientific Racism and Self-Determination: The Case of Austria-Hungary." *White House Studies* 10, no. 4 (2011): 407–24.

Philpott, Simon. "Fear of the Dark: Indonesia and the Australian National Imagination." *Australian Journal of International Affairs* 55, no. 3 (2001): 371–88.

Pierce, Lori. "Creating a Racial Paradise: Citizenship and Sociology in Hawai'i." In *Race and Nation*, edited by Paul Spickard, 69–86. New York: Routledge, 2005.

Pierre, Jemima. *The Predicament of Blackness: Postcolonial Ghana and the Politics of Race*. Chicago: University of Chicago Press, 2012.

———. "Race in Africa Today: A Commentary." *American Anthropological Association* 28, no. 3 (2013): 547–51.

———. "The Racial Vernaculars of Development: A View from West Africa." *American Anthropologist* 122, no. 1 (2020): 86–98.

Ponce, Aaron. "A Genealogy of Islamophobia in a Global Critical Race Framework: Religion, Whiteness, and Controlling Rationality." *Ethnic and Racial Studies* (2024). DOI: 10.1080/01419870.2024.2317953.

powell, john. "Race: Power of an Illusion, Episode Three: The House We Live in." Transcript. https://newsreel.org/transcripts/race3.htm.

———. "Post-Racialism or Targeted Universalism." *Denver University Law Review* 86 (2008): 785.

Power, Marcus. "Anti-Racism, Deconstruction, and 'Overdevelopment.'" *Progress in Development Studies* 6, no. 1 (2006): 24–36.

Prashad, Vijay. *The Karma of Brown Folk*. Minneapolis: University of Minnesota Press, 2000.

———. *The Darker Nations: A People's History of the Third World*. New York: New Press, 2007.

Pryke, Jonathan. "The Risks of China's Ambitions in the South Pacific." *Brookings*, July 20, 2020. https://www.brookings.edu/articles/the-risks-of-chinas-ambitions-in-the-south-pacific/.

Pulido, Laura. *Black, Brown, Yellow & Left: Radical Activism in Los Angeles*. Berkeley: University of California Press, 2006.

Purtschert, Patricia, Francesca Falk, and Barbara Lüthi. "Switzerland and Colonialism without Colonies." *Interventions: International Journal of Postcolonial Studies* 18, no. 2 (2016): 286–302.

Quijano, Aníbal. "Coloniality of Power and Eurocentrism in Latin America." *International Sociology* 15, no. 2 (2000): 215–32.

———. "Questioning 'Race.'" *Socialism and Democracy* 21, no. 1 (2007): 45–53.

Quince, Vanessa E. "Racism by Design: The Role of Race and Ethnicity in the Design of International Trade Agreements." PhD diss., University of Washington, 2018.

Quinn, Josephine Crawley. *In Search of the Phoenicians*. Princeton, NJ: Princeton University Press, 2018.

Quisumbing King, Katrina. "Recentering US Empire: A Structural Perspective on the Color Line." *Sociology of Race and Ethnicity* 5, no. 1 (2019): 11–25.

Raghuram, Parvati. "New Racism or New Asia: What Exactly Is New and How Does Race Matter?" *Ethnic and Racial Studies* 45, no. 4 (2022): 778–88.

Rahman, Rhea. "White-Adjacent Muslim Development: Racializing British Muslim Aid in Mali." *Africa* 93, no. 2 (2023): 256–72.

Rai, Rohini. "From Colonial 'Mongoloid' to Neoliberal 'Northeastern': Theorising 'Race', Racialization and Racism in Contemporary India." *Asian Ethnicity* 23, no. 3 (2022): 442–62.

Raj-Reichert, Gale. "The Role of Transnational First Tier Suppliers in GVC Governance." In *Handbook on Global Value Chains*, edited by Stefano Ponte, Gary Gereffi, and Gale Raj-Reichert, 354–69. Cheltenham: Elgar, 2019.

Ramsey, Guthrie. *Race Music: Black Cultures from Bebop to Hip-Hop*. Berkeley: University of California Press, 2003.

Rana, Junaid. *Terrifying Muslims: Race and Labor in the South Asian Diaspora*. Durham, NC: Duke University Press, 2011.

Ransby, Barbara. *Making All Black Lives Matter: Reimagining Freedom in the 21st Century*. Berkeley: University of California Press, 2018.

Ravindran, Tathagatan. "What Undecidability Does: Enduring Racism in the Context of Indigenous Resurgence in Bolivia." *Ethnic and Racial Studies* 43, no. 6 (2020): 976–94.

———. 2021. "The Power of Phenotype: Toward an Ethnography of Pigmentocracy in Andean Bolivia." *Journal of Latin American and Caribbean Anthropology* 26, no. 2 (2021): 219–36.

Razack, Sherene. "A Catastrophically Damaged Gene Pool: Law, White Supremacy, and the Muslim Psyche." In *With Stones in Our Hands: Writings on Muslims, Racism, and Empire*, edited by Sohail Daulatzai and Junaid Rana, 183–200. Minneapolis: University of Minnesota Press, 2018.

Rêgo, Cacilda M., and Antonio C. La Pastina. "Brazil and the Globalization of Telenovelas." In *Media On the Move*, edited by Daya Kishan Thussu, 89–103. New York: Routledge, 2006.

Remers, Isabel. "Voluntourism in Sub-Saharan Africa Is Expiation by the West, but Only Creates Further Dependency on the West." *Glocality* 5, no. 1 (2022).

Repinecz, Martin. "Unearthing Spanish Racism, Then and Now: A Conversation with Tomás Calvo Buezas." *International Journal of Iberian Studies* 34, no. 2 (2021): 171–77.

Richards, Bedelia Nicola, Hugo Ceron-Anaya, Susan A. Dumais, Jennifer C. Mueller, Patricia Sánchez-Connally, and Derron Wallace. "What's Race Got to Do with It? Disrupting Whiteness in Cultural Capital Research." *Sociology of Race and Ethnicity* (2023): 1–16.

Rifai-Hasan, P.A. "Development, Power, and the Mining Industry in Papua: A Study of Freeport Indonesia." *Journal of Business Ethics* 89 (2009): 129–43.

Rigby, Jennifer, and James Crisp. "Fortress Europe." *The Telegraph*. https://www.telegraph.co.uk/global-health/fortress-europe-borders-wall-fence-controls-eu-countries-migrants-crisis/.

Rivadeneyra, Rocío. "Gender and Race Portrayals on Spanish Language Television." *Sex Roles* 65: (2011): 208–22.

Rivera-Rideau, Petra R. *Remixing Reggaetón: The Cultural Politics of Race in Puerto Rico*. Durham, NC: Duke University Press, 2015.

Rivera-Rideau, Petra, and Jericko Torres-Lescnik. "The Colors and Flavors of My Puerto Rico: Mapping 'Despacito's' Crossovers." *Journal of Popular Music Studies* 31, no. 1 (2019): 87–108.

Roberts, Dorothy. *Fatal Invention: How Science, Politics, and Big Business Re-Create Race in the Twenty-First Century*. New York: New Press, 2011.

Roberts, Peder. "The White (Supremacist) Continent: Antarctica and Fantasies of Nazi Survival." In *Antarctica and the Humanities*, edited by Peter Roberts, Lize Marie van der Watt, and Adrian Howkins, 105–24. New York: Palgrave Macmillan, 2016.

Robinson, Cedric J. *Black Marxism: The Making of the Black Radical Tradition*. Chapel Hill: University of North Carolina Press, [1983] 2000.

Rocha, Jorge. "Race and Society in Portugal: Two Notes and a Remark." *Journal of Anthropological Sciences* 95 (2017): 339–43.

Rocha, Zarine L., and Peter J. Aspinall. "Introduction: Africa, the Middle East, and Central Asia and the Caucasus." In *The Palgrave International Handbook of Mixed Racial and Ethnic Classification*, edited by Zarine L. Rocha and Peter J. Aspinall, 407–24. Springer International, 2020.

Roediger, David. *Wages of Whiteness: Race and the Making of the American Working Class*. London: Verso, 1991.

Rodney, Walter. *How Europe Underdeveloped Africa*. Washington, DC: Howard University Press, 1982.

Rodríguez-García, Dan. "The Persistence of Racial Constructs in Spain: Bringing Race and Colorblindness into the Debate on Interculturalism." *Social Sciences* 11, no. 13 (2022): 1–25.

Roithmayr, Daria. *Reproducing Racism: How Everyday Choices Lock in White Advantage*. New York: New York University Press, 2014.

Roitman, Jessica. "Mediating Multiculturalism: Jews, Blacks, and Curacao, 1825–1970." In *The Sephardic Atlantic: Colonial Histories and Postcolonial Perspectives*, edited by Sina Rauschenbach and Jonathan Schorsch. Springer International, 2019.

Roitman, Karem. *Race, Ethnicity, and Power in Ecuador: The Manipulation of Mestizaje*. Boulder, CO: First Forum Press, 2009.

Romero, Mary. *Maid in the USA*. London: Psychology Press, 2002.

———. *Introducing Intersectionality*. Hoboken, NJ: John Wiley & Sons, 2017.

Roper, Danielle. "Blackface at the Andean Fiesta: Performing Blackness in the Danza de Caporales." *Latin American Research Review* 54, no. 2 (2019): 381–97.

Roque, Ricardo. "The Colonial Ethnological Line: Timor and the Racial Geography of the Malay Archipelago." *Journal of Southeast Asian Studies* 49, no. 3 (2018): 387–409.

———. "Transnational Isolates: Portuguese Colonial Race Science and the Foreign World." *Perspectives on Science* 30, no. 1 (2022): 108–36.

Roth, Wendy D. *Race Migrations: Latinos and the Cultural Transformation of Race*. Palo Alto, CA: Stanford University Press. 2012.

Roth-Gordon, Jennifer, Jessica Harris, and Stephanie Zamora. "'Producing White Comfort through 'Corporate Cool': Linguistic Appropriation, Social Media, and @BrandsSayingBae." *International Journal of the Sociology of Language*, no. 265 (2020): 107–28.

Rouighi, Ramzi. "Race on the Mind: When Europeans Colonized North Africa, They Imposed Their Preoccupation with Race onto Its Diverse Peoples and Deep Past." *Aeon*, September 18, 2019. https://aeon.co/essays/how-the-west-made-arabs-and-berbers-into-races.

Rouleau, Brian. "In the Wake of Jim Crow." *Common Place* 12, no. 4 (2012). https://commonplace.online/article/wake-jim-crow/.

Rucker-Chang, Sunnie, and Chelsi West Ohueri. "A Moment of Reckoning: Transcending Bias, Engaging Race and Racial Formations in Slavic and East European Studies." *Slavic Review* 80, no. 2 (2021): 216–23.

Russell, John. "Race and Reflexivity: The Black Other in Contemporary Japanese Mass Culture." *Cultural Anthropology* 6, no. 1 (1991): 3–25.

Sabbagh-Khoury, Areej. *Colonizing Palestine: The Zionist Left and the Making of the Palestinian Nakba*. Palo Alto, CA: Stanford University Press, 2023.

Sadeghi, Sahar. "Racial Boundaries, Stigma, and the Re-Emergence of 'Always Being Foreigners': Iranians and the Refugee Crisis in Germany." *Ethnic and Racial Studies* 42, no. 10 (2019): 1613–31.

Said, Edward. *Orientalism*. New York: Vintage Books, [1978] 1996.

Samaras, Georgios. "The End of Golden Dawn: Has Greece Shown Us How to Deal with Neo-Nazis." *The Conversation*, November 26, 2020. https://theconversation.com/the-end-of-golden-dawn-has-greece-shown-us-how-to-deal-with-neo-nazis-150239.

Sand, Peter H. "Diego Garcia: British–American Legal Black Hole in the Indian Ocean?" *Journal of Environmental Law* 21, no. 1 (2009): 113–37.

Sartre, Jean-Paul. "Introduction." In *The Colonizer and the Colonized*, by Albert Memmi, xxi–xxix. Boston: Beacon Press, [1957] 1965.

Savell, Stephanie. "How Death Outlives War: The Reverberating Impact of the Post-9/11 Wars on Human Health." Watson Institute, International & Public Affairs. Brown University. May 15, 2023.

Sebring, Serena. "Reproductive Citizenship: Women of Color and Coercive Sterilization in North Carolina, 1950–1980." PhD diss., Duke University, 2012.

Selod, Saher. *Forever Suspect: Racialized Surveillance of Muslim Americans in the War on Terror*. New Brunswick, NJ: Rutgers University Press, 2018.

Selod, Saher, Inaash Islam, and Steve Garner. *A Global Racial Enemy: Muslims in the 21st Century Racism*. Cambridge: Polity, 2024.

Shahin, Saif, Junki Nakahara, and Mariana Sánchez. "Black Lives Matter Goes Global: Connective Action Meets Cultural Hybridity in Brazil, India, and Japan." *New Media & Society* 26, no. 1 (2021).

Shahjahan, Riyad A., and Kirsten E. Edwards. "Whiteness as Futurity and Globalization of Higher Education." *Higher Education* (2021): 1–18.

Sharkey, Heather J. "Arab Identity and Ideology in Sudan: The Politics of Language, Ethnicity, and Race." *African Affairs* 107, no. 426 (2008): 21–43.

Sharma, Jayeeta. *Empire's Garden: Assam and the Making of India*. Durham, NC: Duke University Press, 2011.

Sharma, Nandita, and Cynthia Wright. "Decolonizing Resistance, Challenging Colonial States." *Social Justice* 35, no. 3 (2008–09): 120–38.

Sharma, Nitasha Tamar. *Hawai'i Is My Haven: Race and Indigeneity in the Black Pacific*. Durham, NC: Duke University Press, 2021.

Sharpe, Christina. *In the Wake: On Blackness and Being*. Durham, NC: Duke University Press, 2016.

Sharf, Zack. "Taraji P. Henson Broke Down in Tears When Asked about Quitting Acting, Says She's Still Not Paid Fairly: 'Enough Is Enough! This Industry Will Steal Your Soul.'" *Variety*, December 20, 2023. https://variety.com/2023/film/news/taraji-p-henson-cries-quitting-acting-pay-disparity-hollywood-1235847420/.

Shaw, Carolyn Martin. *Colonial Inscriptions: Race, Sex and Class in Kenya*. Minneapolis: University of Minnesota Press, 1995.

Sheller, Mimi. *Consuming the Caribbean: from Arawaks to Zombies*. New York: Routledge, 2003.

Shohat, Ella. "The Specter of the Blackamoor: Figuring Africa and the Orient." *The Comparatist* 42 (2018): 158–88.

Shome, Raka. "Whiteness and the Politics of Location: Postcolonial Reflections." In *Whiteness and Communication of Social Identity*, edited by T.K. Nakayama and J.N. Martin, 109–28. Thousand Oaks, CA: Sage, 1999.

Sidaway, James D., and Marcus Power. "'The Tears of Portugal': Empire, Identity, 'Race' and Destiny in Portuguese Geopolitical Narratives." *Environment and Planning D: Society and Space* 23, no. 4 (2005): 527–54.

Silverstein, Paul. "The Racial Politics of the Amazigh Revival in North Africa and Beyond." In *Racial Formations in Africa and the Middle East: A Transregional Approach*, 49–54. Project on African Social Research, 2021.

Silverstein, Shayna, and Darci Sprengel. "An (Un)Marked Foreigner: Race-Making in Egyptian, Syrian and German Popular Cultures." *Lateral* 10, no. 1 (2021).

Simpson, Brad. "'Illegally and Beautifully': The United States, the Indonesian Invasion of East Timor and the International Community, 1974–76." *Cold War History* 5, no. 3 (2005): 281–315.

Slate, Nico. "Introduction: The Borders of Black Power." In *Black Power beyond Borders: The Global Dimensions of the Black Power Movement*, edited by Nico Slate, 1–10. New York: Palgrave Macmillan, 2012.

———. "The Dalit Panthers: Race, Caste and Black Power in India." In *Black Power beyond Borders: The Global Dimensions of the Black Power Movement*, edited by Nico Slate, 127–43. New York: Palgrave Macmillan, 2012.

Small, Stephen. "Theorizing Visibility and Vulnerability in Black Europe and the African Diaspora." *Ethnic and Racial Studies* 41, no. 6 (2018): 1182–1197.

Smalls, James. "'Race' as Spectacle in Late 19th Century French Art." *French Historical Studies* 26, no. 2 (2003): 351–82.

Smedley, Audrey, and Brian D. Smedley. *Race in North America: The Origin and Evolution of a Worldview*. 4th ed. Boulder, CO: Westview Press, 2012.

Smith, Danyel. *Shine Bright: A Very Personal History of Black Women in Pop*. New York: Roc Lit, 2022.

Smith, Emma. "What's Behind the Deaths at Morocco's Land Border with EU." New Humanitarian, September 8, 2022. https://www.thenewhumanitarian.org/analysis/2022/09/08/Migrant-crisis-Morocco-Spain-border.

Snoek, Kartia. "Empire, Race, Naturalisation: The Naturalisation Act 1903." *Melbourne Historical Journal* 40, no. 1 (2012): 103–29.

Solomos, John, and Les Back. *Racism and Society*. London: Macmillan Press, 1996.

Spangler, Eve. *Understanding Israel/Palestine: Race, Nation, and Human Rights in the Conflict*. Leiden: Brill, 2019.

"Spanish King Praises Conquistadors Who Turned Puerto Rico in 'Model of Colonialism.'" *The Telegraph*, January 26, 2022.

Steinmetz, George. *The Devil's Handwriting: Precoloniality and the German Colonial State in Qingdao, Samoa, and Southwest Africa*. Chicago: University of Chicago Press, 2007.

———. "The Sociology of Empires, Colonies and Postcolonies." *Annual Review of Sociology* 40 (2014): 77–103.

———. "Social Fields, Subfields, and Social Spaces at the Scale of Empires: Explaining the Colonial State and Colonial Sociology." *Sociological Review Monographs* 64, no. 2 (2016): 98–123.

Stelkia, Krista. "Police Brutality in Canada: A Symptom of Structural Racism and Colonial Violence." *Yellowhead Institute* 72 (2020).

Steyn, Melissa, and Don Foster. "Repertoires for Talking White: Resistant Whiteness in Post-Apartheid South Africa." *Ethnic and Racial Studies* 31, no. 1 (2008): 25–51.

Stoddard, Lothrop. *The Rising Tide of Color against White World-Supremacy*. New York: Scribner, 1920.

Stoever, Jennifer Lynn. *The Sonic Color Line: Race and the Cultural Politics of Listening*. New York: New York University Press, 2016.

Stoler, Ann Laura. *Race and the Education of Desire: Foucault's History of Sexuality and the Colonial Order of Things*. Durham, NC: Duke University Press, 1995.

———. *Carnal Knowledge and Imperial Power: Race and the Intimate in Colonial Rule*. Berkeley: University of California Press, 2002.

———, ed. *Haunted by Empire: Geographies of Intimacy in North American History*. Durham, NC: Duke University Press, 2006.

Streets, Heather. *Martial Races*. Manchester: Manchester University Press, 2004.

Strings, Sabrina. *Fearing the Black Body: The Racial Origins of Fat Phobia*. New York: New York University Press, 2019.

Strmic-Pawl, Hephzibah V., Brandon A. Jackson, and Steve Garner. "Race Counts: Racial and Ethnic Data on the US Census and the Implications for Tracking Inequality." *Sociology of Race and Ethnicity* 4, no. 1 (2018): 1–13.

Su, Christine. "Becoming Cambodian: Ethnicity and the Vietnamese in Kampuchea." In *Race and Nation: Ethnic Systems in the Modern World*, edited by Paul Spickard, 273. New York: Routledge, 2005.

Sue, Christina A. *Land of the Cosmic Race: Race, Mixture, Racism, and Blackness in Mexico*. New York: Oxford University Press, 2013.

———. "Is Mexico beyond Mestizaje? Blackness, Race Mixture and Discrimination." *Latin American and Caribbean Ethnic Studies* 18, no. 1 (2023): 47–74.

Sugino, Corinne Mitsuye. "Multicultural Redemption: *Crazy Rich Asians* and the Politics of Representation." *Lateral* 8, no. 2 (2019).

Suljagić, Emir. "The Role of Croatia in Bosnia and Herzegovina." *Insight Turkey* 21, no. 2 (2019): 23–36.

Suzuki, Kazuko. "Empire and Racialization: Reinterpreting Japan's Pan-Asianism from a Du Boisian Perspective." *Global Historical Sociology of Race and Racism* 38 (2021): 23–54.

Swan, Quito. *Pasifika Black: Oceania, Anti-Colonialism and the African World*. New York: New York University Press, 2022.

Sysling, Fenneke. *Racial Science and Human Diversity in Colonial Indonesia*. Singapore: NUS Press, 2017.

Tahrir Institute for Middle East Policy. "Egypt's Racial Nationalism: Neo-Pharaonism as a Tool of the State." September 20, 2023. https://timep.org/2023/09/20/egypts-racial-nationalism-neo-pharaonism-as-a-tool-of-the-state/.

Táíwò, Olúfẹ́mi O. *Reconsidering Reparations*. Oxford: Oxford University Press, 2022.

———. *Elite Capture: How the Powerful Took over Identity Politics (and Everything Else)*. Chicago: Haymarket Books, 2022.

Tamale, Sylvia. *Decolonization and Afro-Feminism*. Ottawa: Daraja Press, 2020.

Tan, Rhe-Anne. "We Are Not Red and White, We Are Morning Star: Internal Colonialization, Indigenous Identity, and the Idea of Indonesia." *Journal of International Affairs* 73, no. 2 (2020): 270–84.

Tate, Merze. "The War Aims of World War I and World War II and Their Relation to the Darker Peoples of the World." *Journal of Negro Education* 12, no. 3 (1943): 521–32.

Tate, Shirley Anne. "'I Do Not See Myself as Anything Else than White': Black Resistance to Racial Cosplay Blackfishing." In *The Routledge Companion to Beauty Politics*, edited by Maxine Leeds Craig, 205–14. New York: Routledge, 2021.

Tate, Shirley Anne, and Ian Law. *Caribbean Racisms: Connections and Complexities in the Racialization of the Caribbean Region.* New York: Palgrave Macmillan, 2015.

Tayeb, Leila. "What Is Whiteness in North Africa?" *Lateral* 10, no. 1 (2021).

Taylor, Keeanga-Yamahtta. *Race for Profit: How Banks and the Real Estate Industry Undermined Black Homeownership.* Chapel Hill: University of North Carolina Press, 2019.

———. *From #BlackLivesMatter to Black Liberation.* Chicago: Haymarket Books, 2016.

———. "Forward." In *Scenes of Subjection: Terror, Slavery, and Self-Making in Nineteenth-Century America,* by Saidiya Hartman, xiii–xxxviii. New York: W.W. Norton, [1997] 2022.

Tehranian, John. "Compulsory Whiteness: Towards a Middle Eastern Legal Scholarship." *Indiana Law Review* 82 (2007): 1.

Telles, Edward. "Race and Ethnicity and Latin America's United Nations Millennium Development Goals." *Latin American and Caribbean Ethnic Studies* 2, no. 2 (2007): 185–200.

Telles, Edward, and René Flores. "Not Just Color: Whiteness, Nation, and Status in Latin America." *Hispanic American Historical Review* 93, no. 3 (2013): 411–49.

Terreblanche, Sampie. *Western Empires, Christianity, and the Inequalities between the West and the Rest, 1500–2010.* Johannesburg: Penguin Books, 2014.

———. "A Wealth Tax for South Africa." Johannesburg: SCIS, Wits University. SCIS Working Paper Number 1, 2018.

The Red Nation. *The Red Deal: Indigenous Action to Save Our Earth.* Commons Notion, 2021.

Thelwell, Chinua. *Exporting Jim Crow: Blackface Minstrelsy in South Africa and Beyond.* Amherst: University of Massachusetts Press, 2020.

Thomas, Chantal. "Race as a Technology of Global Economic Governance." *UCLA Law Review* 67, no. 6 (April 2021): 1860–96.

Thomas, Deborah A. *Modern Blackness: Nationalism, Globalization, and the Politics of Culture in Jamaica.* Durham, NC: Duke University Press, 2004.

Thomas, Deborah A., and M. Kamari Clark. "Globalization and Race: Structures of Inequality, New Sovereignties, and Citizenship in a Neoliberal Era." *Annual Review of Anthropology* 42 (2013): 305–25.

Thompson, Debra. "Through, Against and Beyond the Racial State: The Transnational Stratum of Race." *Cambridge Review of International Affairs* 26, no. 1 (2013): 133–151.

———. *The Schematic State: Race, Transnationalism, and the Politics of the Census.* Cambridge: Cambridge University Press, 2016.

———. "Democratic Hauntings: Michael Hanchard's the Spectre of Race and the Challenge of Comparison." *Ethnic and Racial Studies* 42, no. 8 (2019): 1313–20.

Thompson, Elizabeth. *Colonial Citizens Republic Rights, Paternal Privilege and Gender in French Syria and Lebanon*. New York: Colombia University Press, 2000.

Thomson, Andrew. *Outsourced Empire: How Militias, Mercenaries and Contractors Support US Statecraft*. London: Pluto, 2018.

Tilley, Virginia Q. "Mestizaje and the 'Ethnicization' of Race in Latin America." *Race and Nation*, edited by Paul Spickard, 67–82. New York: Routledge, 2005.

Titley, Gavan. "On 'Are We All Postracial Yet?'" *Ethnic and Racial Studies* 39, no. 13 (2016): 2269–77.

Todorova, Miglena. "Race Travels: Whiteness and Modernity across National Borders." PhD diss., University of Minnesota, 2006.

———. *Unequal under Socialism: Race, Women, and Transnationalism in Bulgaria*. Toronto: University of Toronto Press, 2021.

Tofiño-Quesada, Ignacio. "Spanish Orientalism: Uses of the Past in Spain's Colonization of Africa." *Comparative Studies of South Asia, Africa, and the Middle East* 23, no. 1 (2003): 141–48.

Tondo, Lorenzo, and Marta Bellingreri. "Tunisian Cemeteries Fill Up as Hundreds of Dead Refugees Wash Up on Coast." *The Guardian*, April 30, 2023. https://www.theguardian.com/world/2023/apr/30/tunisian-cemeteries-fill-up-as-hundreds-of-dead-refugees-wash-up-on-coast.

Törngren, Sayaka Osanami. "Does Race Matter in Sweden? Challenging Colorblindness in Sweden." *Sophia Journal of European Studies* 7 (2015): 125–37.

Trenta, Luca. "Remote Killing? Remoteness, Covertness, and the US Government's Involvement in Assassination." *Defense Studies* 21, no. 4 (2021): 468–488.

Troutt Powell, Eve. *A Different Shade of Colonialism: Egypt, Great Britain, and the Mastery of Sudan*. Berkeley: University of California Press, 2003.

Tsika, Noah A. *Nollywood Stars*. Bloomington: Indiana University Press, 2015.

Ture, Kwame, and Charles Hamilton. *Black Power: The Politics of Liberation*. New York: Vintage Books, [1967] 1992.

Twine, France Winddance. *Racism in a Racial Democracy: The Maintenance of White Supremacy in Brazil*. New Brunswick, NJ: Rutgers University Press, 1998.

Twinam, Ann. "Purchasing Whiteness: Conversations on the Essence of Pardo-ness and Mulatto-ness at the End of Empire." In *Imperial Subjects: Race and Identity in Colonial Latin America*, edited by Andrew B. Fisher and Matthew D. O'Hara, 141–65. Durham, NC: Duke University Press, 2009.

———. *Purchasing Whiteness: Pardos, Mulattos, and the Quest for Social Mobility in the Spanish Indies*. Palo Alto, CA: Stanford University Press, 2015.

United Nations Conference on Trade and Development. *World Investment Report 2022*. International Tax Reforms and Sustainable Investment.

United Nations Department of Economic and Social Affairs. *World Social Report 2020: Inequality in a Rapidly Changing World*. https://www.un.org/development/desa/dspd/wp-content/uploads/sites/22/2020/02/World-Social-Report2020-FullReport.pdf.

United Nations High Commission for Refugees. *Statistics of Foreigners in Israel, 2013*.

https://www.unhcr.org/il/wp-content/uploads/sites/6/2020/07/PIBA-2016-Summary-English-stats.pdf.

United States Commission on Civil Rights. *Micronesians in Hawaii: Migrant Group Faces Barriers to Equal Opportunity*. A Report of the Hawaii Advisory Committee to the U.S. Commission on Civil Rights, March 2019. https://www.usccr.gov/files/pubs/2019/08-13-Hawaii-Micronesian-Report.pdf.

Uzuegbunam, Chikezie E. "Oppositional Gaze or Revenge? A Critical Ideological Analysis of Foreignness and Foreign Identities in Nollywood Feature Films." *Catalan Journal of Communication & Cultural Studies* 13, no. 1 (2021): 121–39.

Valdes, Francisco, and Sumi Cho. "Critical Race Materialism: Theorizing Justice in the Wake of Global Neoliberalism." *Connecticut Law Review* 43, no. 5 (2011): 1513–72.

Valluvan, Sivamohan. "What Is 'Post-Race' and What Does It Reveal about Contemporary Racisms?" *Ethnic and Racial Studies* 39, no. 13 (2016): 2241–51.

Van der Watt, Lize-Marié and Sandra Swart. "The Whiteness of Antarctica: Race and South Africa's Antarctic History." In *Antarctica and the Humanities*, edited by Peter Roberts, Lize Marie van der Watt, and Adrian Howkins, 125–56. New York: Palgrave Macmillan, 2016.

Van Hooste, Emma. "Metis in the Belgian Congo: An Archival Research on the Racial Categorisation and Colonial Treatment of Metis." PhD diss., Ghent University, 2020.

Van Houtum, Henk. "Human Blacklisting: The Global Apartheid of the EU's External Border Regime." In *Geographies of Privilege*, edited by France Winddance Twine and Bradley Gardener, 161–87. New York: Routledge, 2013.

Van Zyl-Hermann, and Jacob Boersema. "Introduction: The Politics of Whiteness in Africa." *Africa* 87, no. 4 (2017): 651–61.

Vasconcelos, José. *The Cosmic Race, La Raza Cósmica*. Baltimore: Johns Hopkins University Press, [1925] 1997.

Velasquez-Manoff, Moises. "Want to Be Less Racist? Move to Hawaii." *New York Times*, June 28, 2019. https://www.nytimes.com/2019/06/28/opinion/sunday/racism-hawaii.html.

Velayutham, Selvaraj. "Everyday Racism in Singapore." In *Everyday Multiculuralism*, edited by A. Wise and S. Velayutham, 255–73. London: Palgrave Macmillan, 2009.

———. "Races without Racism?: Everyday Race Relations in Singapore." *Identities* 24, no. 4 (2017): 455–73.

Villafranca, Richard. *Costa Rica: The Gem of American Republics*. Sackett & Wilhelms Litho, 1895.

Villén-Pérez, Sara, Paulo Moutinho, Caroline Corrêa Nóbrega, and Paulo De Marco Jr. "Brazilian Amazon Gold: Indigenous Land Rights under Risk." *Elementa: Science of the Anthropocene* 8 (2020): 31.

Vine, David. *Base Nation: How U.S. Military Bases Abroad Harm America and the World*. New York: Metropolitan Books, 2015.

Vink, Wieke. *Creole Jews: Negotiating Community in Colonial Suriname*. Leiden: Brill, 2008.

Vinson III, Ben. *Before Mestizaje: The Frontiers of Race and Caste in Colonial Mexico*. New York: Cambridge University Press, 2018.

Virdee, Satnam, and Brendan McGeever. "Racism, Crisis, Brexit." *Ethnic and Racial Studies* 41, no. 10 (2018): 1802–19.
Vitalis, Robert. *America's Kingdom: Mythmaking on the Saudi Oil Frontier.* Palo Alto, CA: Stanford University Press, 2007.
———. *White World Order, Black Power Politics.* Ithaca, NY: Cornell University Press, 2016.
———. "The Midnight Ride of Kwame Nkrumah and Other Fables of Bandung (Bandoong)." *Humanity: An International Journal of Human Rights, Humanitarianism, and Development* 4, no. 2 (2013): 261–88.
Vowles, Jack, and Matthew Gibbons. "Representation, Identity and Indigeneity: Changes in Māori Roll Choice in Aotearoa-New Zealand." *New Zealand Journal of Social Sciences* 18, no. 1 (2023): 64–84.
Wacquant, Loïc. *Racial Domination.* Cambridge: Polity, 2024.
Wade, Peter. *Race and Ethnicity in Latin America.* London: Pluto Press, 1997.
Wakenge, Claude Iguma. "'Referees Become Players': Accessing Coltan Mines in the Eastern Democratic Republic of Congo." *Extractive Industries and Society* 5, no. 1 (2018): 66–72.
Walker, David. "Appeal to the Coloured Citizens of the World, but in Particular, and Very Expressly, to Those of the United States." 1829.
Walker, Shaun, and Flora Garamvolgyi. "Victor Orbán Sparks Outrage with Attack on 'Race Mixing' in Europe." *The Guardian*, July 24, 2022.
Wallerstein, Immanuel. "The Ideological Tensions of Capitalism: Universalism versus Racism and Sexism." In *Race, Nation, Class Ambiguous Identities*, 29–36. London: Verso, 1991.
Warren, Jonathan W. *Racial Revolutions: Antiracism and Indian Resurgence in Brazil.* Durham, NC: Duke University Press, 2001.
Webby, Elizabeth. "Images of Europe in Two Nineteenth-Century Australian Illustrated Magazines." *Victorian Periodicals Review* 37, no. 4 (2004): 10–24.
Weiner, Melissa F. "Towards a Critical Global Race Theory." *Sociology Compass* 6, no. 4 (2012): 332–50.
———. "The Ideologically Colonized Metropole: Dutch Racism and Racist Denial." *Sociology Compass* 8, no. 6 (2014): 731–44.
Weinstein, Barbara. *The Color of Modernity: São Paulo and the Making of Race and Nation in Brazil.* Durham, NC: Duke University Press, 2015.
Wekker, Gloria. *White Innocence: Paradoxes of Colonialism and Race.* Durham, NC: Duke University Press, 2016.
Wells-Barnett, Ida B. *On Lynchings.* New York: Humanity Books, [1892] 2002.
Wesseling, Elisabeth, and Jacques Dane. "Are 'the Natives' Educable?" *Journal of Educational Media, Memory & Society* 10, no. 1 (2019): 28–43.
White, Abbey. "Use of Blackface to Portray Kendrick Lamar, Beyoncé in Polish TV Impersonation Competition under Investigation, Says Spokesperson." *Hollywood Reporter*, September 12, 2023. https://www.hollywoodreporter.com/tv/tv-news/poland-your-face-sounds-familiar-condenmed-blackface-n-word-1235588322/.
White, Charles. *An Account of The Regular Gradation in Man, and In Different Animals*

and Vegetables and From the Former to the Latter. London: Printed for C. Dilly, In The Poultry, 1799.

Wildenthal, Lora. "Race, Gender, and Citizenship in the German Colonial Empire." In *Tensions of Empire: Colonial Cultures in a Bourgeois World*, edited by Frederic Cooper and Ann Laura Stoler, 263–84. Berkeley: University of California Press, 1997.

Wilcox, Vanda. *The Italian Empire and the Great War*. Oxford: Oxford University Press, 2021.

Williams, Eric. *Capitalism and Slavery, Third Edition*. Chapel Hill: University of North Carolina Press, 2021.

Williams, Erica Lorraine. *Sex Tourism in Bahia: Ambiguous Entanglements*. Urbana: University of Illinois Press, 2013.

Williams, Susan. *White Malice: The CIA and the Covert Recolonization of Africa*. New York: Public Affairs, 2021.

Wilson, Kalpana. *Race, Racism and Development: Interrogating History, Discourse and Practice*. London: Bloomsbury, 2013.

Winant, Howard. *The World Is a Ghetto: Race and Democracy since World War II*. New York: Basic Books, 2001.

Woldemikael, Tekle M. "Eritrea's Identity as a Cultural Crossroads." In *Race and Nation*, edited by Paul Spickard, 351–68. New York: Routledge, 2005.

Wolfe, Patrick. "Land, Labor, and Difference: Elementary Structures of Race." *American Historical Review* 106, no. 3 (June 2001): 866–905.

———. "Race and Racialisation: Some Thoughts." *Postcolonial Studies: Culture, Politics, Economy* 5, no. 1 (2002): 51–62.

———. *Traces of History: Elementary Structures of Race*. New York: Verso, 2016.

Wood, Bryan. "Could Bolivia's Current Politics Be Fueling Indigenous Discrimination?" *PBS News Hour*, November 25, 2019. https://www.pbs.org/newshour/world/could-bolivias-current-politics-be-fueling-indigenous-discrimination.

Woolford, Andrew. "Discipline, Territory and the Colonial Mesh: Indigenous Boarding School in the United States and Canada." In *Colonial Genocide in Indigenous North America*, edited by Andrew Woolford, Jeff Benvenuto, and Alexander Laban Hinton. Durham, NC: Duke University Press, 2014.

Woolford, Andrew, and Jeff Benvenuto. "Canada and Colonial Genocide." *Journal of Genocide Research* 17, no. 4 (2015): 373–90.

Woolford, Andrew, Jeff Benvenuto, and Alexander Laban Hinton, eds. *Colonial Genocide in Indigenous North America*. Durham, NC: Duke University Press, 2014.

Wong, Diane. "The Future Is Ours to Build: Asian American Abolitionist Counterstories for Black Liberation." *Politics, Groups, and Identities* 10, no. 3 (2022): 493–502.

World Social Report 2020: Inequality in a Rapidly Changing World. United Nations Report. Department of Economic and Social Affairs.

Worrell, Rodney. "George Padmore Engaged Pan-African Activist and Theorist: The Relevance of His Political Praxis and Theorization on Pan-Africanism." *Contemporary Journal of African Studies* 8, no. 1 (2021): 10–20.

Wright, Richard. *The Color Curtain: A Report on the Bandung Conference*. Cleveland: The World, 1956.

Wu, Grace, and Kevin Edmonds. "Trump and the Continent of American Empire in Haiti." In *The Future of U.S. Empire in the Americas,* edited by Tim Gill, 208–31. New York: Routledge, 2020.

Wu, Frank. *Yellow: Race in America beyond Black and White.* New York: Basic Books, 2002.

Wynter, Sylvia. "1492: A New World View." In *Race, Discourse and the Origins of the Americas,* edited by Vera Lawrence Hyatt and Rex Nettleford, 1–57. Washington, DC: Smithsonian Institution Press, 1995.

Yancy, George. "When Heaven and Earth Are Shaken to Their Foundation." In *Unveiling Whiteness in the Twenty-First Century: Global Manifestations, Transdisciplinary Interventions,* edited by Veronica Watson, et al., 195–210. Lanham, MD: Lexington Books, 2014.

Yaron, Hadas, Nurit Hashimshony-Yaffe, and John Campbell. " 'Infiltrators' or Refugees? An Analysis of Israel's Policy towards African Asylum-Seekers." *International Migration* (2013): 1–14.

Yerushalmi, Yosef Hayim. "Between Amsterdam and New Amsterdam: The Place of Curaçao and the Caribbean in Early Modern Jewish History." *American Jewish History* 72, no. 2 (1982): 172–92.

Yonezawa, Miyuki. "Memories of Japanese Identity and Racial Hierarchy." In *Race and Nation,* edited by Paul Spickard, 129–46. New York: Routledge, 2005.

Young, Robert Alexander. *The Ethiopian Manifesto: Issued in Defence of the Black Man's Rights in the Scale of Universal Freedom,* 1829.

Yusuf, Hakeem O., and Tanzil Chowdhury. "The Persistence of Colonial Constitutionalism in British Overseas Territories." *Global Constitutionalism* 8, no. 1 (2019): 157–90.

Yusupova, Marina. "The Invisibility of Race in Sociological Research on Contemporary Russia: A Decolonial Intervention." *Slavic Review* 80, no. 2 (2021): 224–33.

Zakaria, Rafia. "White Russian Empire: The Racist Myths behind Vladimir Putin's Power Grabs." *The Forum,* March 10, 2022.

Zakharov, Nikolay. *Race and Racism in Russia.* New York: Springer, 2015.

Zang, Xiaowei. *Ethnicity in China: A Critical Introduction.* Hoboken, NJ: John Wiley & Sons, 2015.

Zaragoza-Cristiani, Jonathan. "Containing the Refugee Crisis: How the EU Turned the Balkans and Turkey into an EU Borderland." *International Spectator* 52, no. 4 (2017): 59–75.

Železný, Jan. "More than Just Hedging? The Reactions of Cambodia and Vietnam to the Power Struggle between the United States and China in Times of Obama's 'Pivot to Asia.'" *Asian Politics & Policy* 14, no. 2 (2022): 216–48.

Zhang, Chenchen. "Race, Gender, and Occidentalism in Global Reactionary Discourses." *Review of International Studies* (2024): 1–23. https://doi.org/10.1017/S02602 10524000299.

Zia-Ebrahimi, Reza. "Self-Orientalization and Dislocation: The Uses and Abuses of the 'Aryan' Discourse in Iran." *Iranian Studies* 44, no. 4 (2011): 445–72.

———. " 'Arab Invasion' and Decline, or the Import of European Racial Thought by Iranian Nationalists." *Ethnic and Racial Studies* 37, no. 6 (2014): 1043–61.

Zuberi, Tukufu. 2000. *Thicker than Blood: How Racial Statistics Lie.* Minneapolis: University of Minnesota Press, 2001.

———. "Sociology and the African Diaspora Experience." In *A Companion to African-American Studies*, edited by Jane Anna Gordon and Lewis Gordon, 246–64. Hoboken, NJ: John Wiley & Sons, 2006.

Index

Page numbers in italics denote tables and figures. Endnotes are indicated by "n" followed by the endnote number.

abolition democracy, 202, 203
"Aborigine" designation, 32
An Account of the Regular Gradation in Man (White), *10*, 14
accumulation by dispossession, 59
Achiume, E. Tandayi, 55
Adams, Romanzo, 174, 249n169
The Adventures of Two Dutch Dolls and a Golliwog (Upton), 23
advertising, 23
Afghanistan, 54, 70, 72
Africa: African migrants in China, 107; asylum seekers from, 73–74; atomic weapons testing in, 67; conservation initiatives as land grabs, 61–62; counterterrorism in, 68; enslavement as "social institution," 34–35; enslavement in liberal discourse, 8; entangled racial zones in, *90*, 110–11, 115–19; forced labor, 35; German and Italian imperialism, 49–51, 139; in global field of whiteness, 122, *123*; group racial mobility in, 135; imperial racial categorization, 32, *42*, 47–48; multiculturalism in, *156*, 164, 167–68; Nollywood (Nigerian cinema), 81–82; organized resistance, 197; petitions for whiteness in, 130–31; Portuguese colonial settlement, 98; "predicament of Blackness," *156*, 180, 181; Russian resource extraction in, 71; "Scramble for Africa," 37–38. *See also* transatlantic slave trade
African Times and Orient Review, 191
Africa Orientale Italiana (AOI), 51
Afrocriollo movement, 191
afterlife of slavery, 138
Agassiz, Louis, *11*, 14, 21, 146
agency. *See* resistance
Ahmed, Patricia, 146

307

Ahmed, Sara, 55, 121
Albania, *149*
Alexander, Michelle, 195
Algeria, *42*, 48, 49, 99, 116–17
Algerian National Liberation Front, 67
Alien Land Law (1913; United States), 39
All African People's Conference (1958), 191
allochtoon ("originating abroad"), 99–100, 137
Althusser, Louis, 208n13
Alves, Jaime, 95
Amin, Samir, 208n13
Áñez, Jeanine, 171
Angola, *42*, 44, 136, 181
anime, internationalization of, 81
Anne of Denmark, Queen of England, 1, 21
Anquetil-Duperron, Abraham Hyacinthe, 15
Antarctica, 29–30, 219n29
antemurale myth, 150
Antetokounmpo, Giannis, 234n107
anti-Asian sentiment: anti-Chinese spectacle, 22; current racial order and, 104–5, 106–7; "Yellow Peril" discourse, 38–39, 64, 106–7, 135, 141
anti-Blackness: in Arab regions, 114–16; Black enslavement and, 34–36; Chinese presence in Africa and, 64; criminalization of asylum seekers, 75; cultural theft and, 76–80; in EU designations, 150; global anti-Black imaginary, xiii, 6; global field of whiteness, 122–25, *123*; as hierarchical location, xiii–xiv, 211n44; imperial racial categorization and, 138–39; imperial weaponization of, 135–36; inequality and, 55; "interest convergence" and, 85–86; nationalism through commodification of, 22; paternalism, 172; "predicament of Blackness," xix, 156, 180–83; "social blackness," 115; Soviet position on, 234n119; systemic racism,

Latin America, 94–95. *See also* Blackness; white supremacy
Anti-Caste journal, 191
anti-Jewish sentiment, 2, 16, 144
anti-Muslim racialization, 110–11, 113–15, 151, 159, 160, 166, 169
anti/postracialism. *See* post/antiracialism
"anti-woke" campaigns, 187, 193–94, 252n249
appropriation, cultural, 23–24, 78–80
"Arab" identity, 69–70, 99, 111–16, 119, 134, 142–44, 151
Arab/Islamic slavery (AIS) scholarship, 213n25
Arab Spring uprising, 111, 116
ARAMCO (oil producer), 113
Arawak people, 3
Argentina, 22, *90*, 92, 94, 145, 146
Armenia, 103, 130
Aryanism, 15–16, 47, 50, 70, 134, 142, 177–79
Ashutosh, Ishan, 187
al-Assad, Bashar, 71
"assimilado" ("assimilated") designation, 136
asylum seekers, criminalization of, 73–75
asymmetrical racialization, 159
atig ("liberated by"), 116
Atlantic Monthly magazine, 19
atomic weapons, 66–67, 72
Australia: anti-Asian policies, 39; atomic weapons testing in, 67; contemporary racial order, 89–90, *90*, 104–10; current colonial governance, 87, 231n18; diasporic communities in, 134; distribution of inequality and, 54; externalized border control, 73; far right conservatism, 186; forced labor, 35, 36; indigenous child removals, 138; minstrel spectacle, 22; multiculturalism in, *156*, 164, 167–68; racial social commentary, 19; settler colonial whitening project, 141; white legal petition cases, 130–31

Austria, *149*, 160
autochtoon (indigenous, authentic "Dutch"), 99
Avrutim, Eugene, 103
Azerbaijan, 103

Baartman, Saartjie "Sara," 20–21
Bair, Jennifer, 57
Baker, Catherine, 102
Baker, Ella, 199
Bakic'-Hayden, Milica, 101
Balibar, Étienne, 208n13
Bandelj, Nina, 125
Bandung Conference (1955), 190, 192
Barder, Alexander, 7
Barskanmaz, Cengiz, 161
Bashir, Haroon, 213n25, 214n71
Bashi Treitler, Vilna, xix, 155, 210n31
Bauman, Zygmunt, 6
Beaman, Jean, xiv, 158, 188, 197
"Becoming Black of the World," 196
Belarus, 180
Belgium, 38, 61, 66, 136–37, *149*
Bell, Derrick, 85, 86, 194
Bengalee Baboo (minstrel show), 22
Benjamin, Ruha, 201
Benoit, P. J., 133
"Berbers" designation, 49
Berlin Conference (1884–85), 27, 38
Bernier, François, *10*, 12
Beyoncé, 77
Bharatiya Janata Party (BJP), 178
Bhattacharyya, Gargi, 225n23
Bikini Atoll, 72
Biko, Steve, 196
binarism, advancement of, 1
The Birth of a Nation (1915), 21
"blackamoors," 1–2, 21, 23
Black Diaspora, 78, 117–18, 181
blackface performance, 1, 21–22, 23, 76–77, 79
Black Lives Matter movement, xiv, 185, 193–94, 196–99, 229n177, 254n62

Blackness: within "Arabness," 114–16; colonial racial categorizations of, 32–33, 44, 47–48; duality of, 181; indigeneity and, 31, 211n45, 212n22, 254n68; intersection with other markers, 111; "predicament" of, xix, *156*, 180–83; in seventeenth-century liberal discourse, 7–8; Soviet position on, 234n119; "tropes of blackness," 1. *See also* anti-Blackness; whiteness; white supremacy
Black Panthers, 198
"Black Peril" of Black male sexuality, 38
Black Power Movement, 198
"Blacksound," commodification of, 78–79, 80, 229n171
blanqueamiento (whitening) policies, 120–21, 144–47
Bledsoe, Adam, 52, 59
Blumenbach, Johann Friedrich, *10*, 13, 17, 126
Boatcă, Manuela, 64
Bolivia, 171
Bollywood industry, 81
Bolsonaro, Jair, 174, 185
Bonaparte, Napoleon, 48
Bonilla-Silva, Eduardo, xi, 238n16
border management, 73–75, 148–49
Böröcz, József, 101, 148
Bosnia and Herzegovina, *149*
Bourdieu, Pierre, 208n9, 238n18, 239n23
BP (oil and gas company), 60
Bracey, Glenn, 210n31
Brand, Dionne, xvi, 95–96
Brazil: anti-Asian policies, 39; enslaved peoples in, 33; enslaved runaway communities, 37; as entangled racial zone, *90*, 94–95, 232n60; far right conservatism, 186, 187; group racial mobility in, 133, 134, 135; hypersexualization of women in media, 82; imperial racial categorization, *42*; organized resistance, 197; racial democracy, 173–74; as semi-peripheral economic state, 63; whitening immigration policies, 145

Breen, Damian, 166
Bretton Woods system, 65
Brexit (2016), 151, 167
BRICS (Brazil, Russia, India, China, and South Africa), 63, 226n59
Britain: among competing racial empires, 29; anti-Jewish sentiment, 2; atomic weapons testing, 67; counterterrorism, 68; cultural appropriation, 23; England as entangled racial zone, 103–4, 108, 113; first imperial formation and, 27; forced labor and racialization, 35; imperial racial categorization, 40, *42, 45*–48, 119, 135–36, 137; imperial whitening policy, 129; multiculturalism in, *156,* 164, 166–67, 247n91; private military contractors, 72; racial commentary and spectacle, 1, 19, 20, 21; transatlantic slave trade, 33. *See also* United Kingdom
British Balfour Declaration (1917), 111
British Indian Ocean Territory (BIOT), 72
British Nationality Act (1948), 104
Brown, Karida, 6
Brown and Root (industrial services company), 71
Brussels World's Fair (1958), 20
BTS (musical group), 229n177
Buck v. Bell, 18
Buffon, Georges-Louis Leclerc, *10, 12,* 13
Bulgaria, 143, *149*
Bulletin magazine, 19
Bumiputera people (ethnic Malays), 169
Bunche, Ralph, 15, 18, 52
Burkina Faso, 68
Burma, 108, 130
"burnt cork nationalism," 22

Cabral, Amílcar, 192, 201
Cabrera, Miguel, 222n123
Calderón, Tego, 79–80
Cambodia, 107–8
Canada: anti-Asian policies, 39; contemporary racial order, 89–90, *90,* 95–96; far right conservatism, 186; imperial racial classifications, 46; indigenous child removals, 138; multiculturalism in, *156,* 164, 165; residential school system, 31; settler colonial whitening policies, 141; sterilization programs, 18
Canary Islands, 3, 30
capitalism: commodification of "Black-sound," 78–79, 80, 229n171; commodification of racist spectacle, 20–23; disaster capitalism, 93; expropriated space, 59–63; free trade and imperialism, 27; global production networks, 56–57; within global racial system, xi; justifying white racial advancement, 8, 14; labor exploitation, 57–59; racist products and advertising, 23–24; sexual commodification, 58; transatlantic slave trade commodities, 3, 34; "unjust enrichment," 55; white capital protection, 65–66. *See also* racial capitalism
care (as form of resistance), xix, 196, 198, 201
Caribbean: Dutch colonialism, 27, 31; early usage of "white" classification, 127; as entangled racial zone, *90,* 92–93; EU designations, 150; global economic inequities and, 54; Jewish expulsion from, 133; legal petitions for whiteness, 129, 134; maroon settlements in, 37; *mestizaje* and racial democracy, 169–70, 171–72; ongoing colonial governance, 87, 160; "predicament of Blackness," 180, 182; racial classification, 46; racial enslavement, 33–34; Spanish colonialism, 3, 132
Caribbean CARICOM project, 202
Caribbean mestizaje, 172
Carlson, Tucker, 185–86
Carrera, Magali, 222n123

Carson, A. D., 80
cartography, racial knowledge and, 6–7
casta designations, 44, 92, 128, 222n123
Castillo, Roberto, 64
Catholic Church: anxieties over Muslim rule, 2; imperial identity-policing, 41, 44; as measure of whiteness, 132; missionary orphanages, 138; transatlantic slave trade and, 2–4. *See also* Christianity
Central African Republic, 71
Central American Free Trade Agreement, 91
Césaire, Aimé, 41
Chagossian people, 72
Chatterjee, Partha, 27
Cheng, Yinghong, 107
Cherokee people, 31
Chevron Corporation, 60, 113
Chicago World's Fair (1893), 20
Chickasaw people, 31
Children's books, 23
Chile, *90*, 92, 94
China: anti-Chinese spectacle, 22; anti-Muslim campaign, 68–69; "anti-woke" narratives, 187; atomic weapons testing, 67; contemporary racial order, 104–10; ethnic dominance, 17, 176, 177; foreign direct investment, 65; group racial mobility, 135; "Huallywood" cinema, 81; petitions for whiteness from, 130; resource extraction, 60; as semi-peripheral economic state, 63, 64; "Yellow Peril" discourse and, 38–39, 64, 106–7
Chinese Exclusion Act (1882; United States), 39
Chinese Head Tax (1885; Canada), 39
Chinese Immigration Act (1923; Canada), 39
Chisholm, Amanda, 71
Cho, Michelle, 79
Cho, Sumi, 157

Choctaw people, 31
Christianity: antemurale myth, 150; "Arab" designation and, 112–13; within emerging racist modernity, 5; imperial racial categorization and, 49, 51; as measure of whiteness, 131, 132, 134, 136, 137, 163. *See also* Catholic Church
Christmas Island, 73
cimarrones (enslaved runaway communities), 37
cinema, 21, 81–83
citational practice, xvi
Citizenship Law (1982; Burma), 108
Civil Rights movement, 85, 194
Claremont Institute, 185, 252n249
Clarno, Andy, 69
Clelland, Donald A., 226n59
climate justice, 202
climate theory of degeneration, 9, 13
"coalition of consciousness," 196
Code Noir (Black Code) decree (1685–1848), 48
"co-ethnic racialization," 106
Cold War period, 64, 66, 72, 85–86, 111, 230n8
Collins, Patricia Hill, 196
Colombia, 92, 94, 95, 128
colonialism: centrality of racial categorization in, 40–41; centrality of violence in, 30, 66, 67; colonial exhibits and spectacle, 20; "colonialism without colonies," 160; contemporary inequities and, 55, 60, 61–62, 65; contemporary racialization and, x, xiii, 85–89, 92–93, 117, 118–19, 207n1; global whitening processes and, 121, 123–24, 127; group racial mobility within, 133–39; imperial whitening policies, 128–30, 137, 144–45; indigenous genocide and categorization, 30–32; legacy of colonial militarism, 66–67; "linguistic *détournement*," 97–98; *luso-tropicalism* ideology and, 163–64, 173; *mestizaje*

colonialism (*cont.*)
  ideology and, 170; neocolonialism, 194; "racial pragmatism," 39; racial scientific language, 13–14, 215n92; "rule of colonial difference," 27; "Scramble for Africa," 38; settler colonial whitening projects, 140–42, 144; "white supremacy" in early colonialism, 28. *See also* entangled racial zones; imperialism
color quebrado (broken color), 44
coltan mining, 60–61
Columbus, Christopher, 3, 30, 171
Commander, Michelle, 87, 118, 191, 203
commodification. *See under* capitalism
Commonwealth Immigrants Act (1968), 104
communism, 86, 92
concentration camps, 50
Confederate iconography, 186
conflict minerals, 61
Confucianism, 107
consciousness, racial, 195–200
conservation initiatives, as land grabs, 61–62
conservative right, 156, 183–88, 193–94
Cook, James, 219n29
"coolies," 35
Cooper, Anna Julia, 24, 52
"cosmic race," 171
Costa Rica, *90*, 92, 94, 120–21, 187
Costa Rica (Villafranca), 120
Cost of War project, 70
cotton production, 34
counterknowledges as resistance, xix, 24–25. *See also* resistance
counterterrorism, 68–70
COVID-19 pandemic, 107, 188, 193
Cox, Oliver, 208n13
Crania Americana; Crania Aegyptiaca (Morton), *10*, 126–27
Creek peoples, 31
Crenshaw, Kimberlé, 194
Crimea, 71

critical race theory: attacks on, 185, 193–94, 253n29; author's approach, x, 207n7, 208n9; on "interest convergence," 85–86; on legal coercion and ideology, 239n37
Croatia, *149*, 150
cruel optimism, 194
Cuba, 33, 90, *90*, 92, 128, 145, 172
Cugoano, Quobna Ottobah, 24
Cullors, Patrisse, 197
culture: anti-Black representation and cultural theft, 23–24, 78–80; counternarratives and resistance, 24–25; cultural codes of whiteness, 122, 124, 127; global racial cultural production, 75–76; liberalism and racist modernity, 7–9; racist spectacle, 18–24, 185–86; regional cultural products, 80–83; traveling racism and, xi, 55, 56, 83–84. *See also* politicultures
"culture of taste," 23
Curington, Celeste, 98
Cuvier, Georges, 21
Cyprus, *149*
Czechia, *149*

Dark Princess (Du Bois), 192
Darwin, Charles, 14, 215n96
Da Silva, Denise Ferreira, 95
Daulatzai, Sohail, 68
Davenport, Charles, 18
Davis, Angela, 182
Davis, John, 219n29
Dear Science (McKittrick), xvi
deep whiteness, 56, 63, 66, 83. *See also* traveling racism
De las Casas, Bartolomé, 3, 212n22
Delatolla, Andrew, 88
Democratic Republic of Congo, 60–61, 66–67
De Napoli, Olindo, 51
Denmark, 33, 103, 129, *149*, 160, 161, 231n18
deportation sites, 73–75

de-racialized cultural representation, 81
"development" discourse, 58, 65–66, 180
Dial magazine, 19
Diego Garcia (British atoll), 72
Dikötter, Frank, 17, 88
dime novels, 19
"Dinaric race," 102
disaster capitalism, 93
Diversity, Equity & Inclusion (DEI), 165–66, 252n249
diversity ideology, 164
Doctrine of Discovery, 30
Dominican Republic, 93–94, 171, 172
Douglass, Frederick, 24, 37
"duality" of Blackness, 181
Du Bois, W.E.B.: at 1900 *Exposition Universelle*, 216n142; "abolition democracy," 203; on Black enslavement, 34; on the color line, 52, 154, 192, 244n2; global mechanisms of race, x, 207n1, 208n13; on Japanese imperialism, 221n107; on racial modernity, 6; on resistance and counterknowledges, 24, 191
Dumont d'Urville, Jules-Sébastien-César, 110
Dunaway, Wilma A., 226n59
Dutch East India Company (VOC), 33, 45
"Dutchification" policy, 45
Dutch West India Company (WIC), 33–34, 45, 133
Dvornikovic, Vladimir, 102
DynCorp (private military contractor), 71

East Timor, *42*, 44, 109
Edmund Burke Foundation, 185
Edwards, Erika Denise, 129, 140
Edwards, Kirsten, 121
Egypt, 22, 68, 115–17
Ekwenchi, Ogochukwu C., 82
Elmina Castle (Ghana), 118
El-Tayeb, Fatima, 198
Emigh, Rebecca, 146

England. *See* Britain
entangled racial zones: Australia, New Zealand and China, 104–10; characterized, 88–91, *90*; within global racial system, xii, 118–19, 210n31; Israel, 110–18; persistence of colonial governance, 85–89; United States, 91–96; western Europe and Russia, 96–104
entertainment: anti-Black representation and cultural theft, 23–24, 76–80; cultural spectacle as, 1, 18–23; regional cultural products, 80–83. *See also* culture
"entrepreneurial" discourse, 58
Eritrea, *42*, 74
Ernston, Henrik, 63
Essay on the Inequality of Human Races (Gobineau), *11*
Essed, Philomena, 99, 100, 207n7
Estatutos de Pureza de Sangue (Purity of Blood Statutes), 44
Estonia, *149*, 180
ethnic dominance: Aryan mythologies, 177–79; as colorblind politiculture, xix, 156, *156*, 175–76, 249n175; East Asia national essences, 176–77; "Slavic" whiteness, 179–80
Ethridge, Robbie, 30
Eugenical News, 18
eugenics, 15, 17–18, 141, 145, 170
"Europeans" as racial category, 48
European Union, 147–51, *149*, 167
"*évolué*" ("evolved") designation, 136–37
exceptionalism, 159–61, 188–89
Exhibition of Women's Work (1898), 20
Export Processing Zones (EPZs), 65
Exposition Universelle (1855), 20, 216n142
expropriation of space, 59–63
extraction economies, 59–61, 66, 71
ExxonMobil Corporation, 60, 113

Fanon, Frantz, 89, 121, 208n13
far right conservatism, 183–88, 193–94

fascism, 161–62, 163, 183
fear-based law and policy, 36–39
Fees Must Fall movement, 197
feminism, 159, 185, 197, 198, 203
feminized racialized labor, 58
fetishization, 77, 158, 180
Fiji, 36, 110, 141
film, 21, 81–83
Finland, 103, *149*, 160, 161
First Universal Races Congress (1911), 191
Five Star Movement (M5S), 162
Fleming, Crystal, 158, 159
Floyd, George, 165, 193
Footit and *Chocolate* clown team, 22
forced labor, 35–36, 50
foreign direct investment (FDI), 64, 65
"Fortress Europe," 148
Fox News Channel, 185
France: 2023 anticolonial protests, 198; atomic weapons testing, 67; contemporary racial order, 99, 107–8, 113; counterterrorism in Mali, 68; cultural appropriation, 23; current colonial governance, 87, 231n18; EU designation, *149*; far right conservatism, *156*; first imperial formation and, 27; Haitian Revolution and, 37; imperial racial categorization, 40, *43*, 48–49, 136, 138–39; imperial whitening policies, 129–30; New Phoenicianism ideology, 143; post/antiracialism, *156*, 157, 158–59; private military contractors, 72; racial spectacle, 20, 21, 22; resource extraction, 60; transatlantic slave trade, 33
Franco, Francisco, 98, 163
Franco, Marielle, 187
Fraser, Nancy, 59, 225n23
Frederick VI, King of Denmark, 129
freedom: defying imperialism, 51–53; enslaved resistance, 36–38, 52–53, 94; freedom dreams, 196; individual freedoms, 168, 183; in liberal discourse, 8; twentieth-century liberation movements, 190–95. *See also* resistance
"Freedom Convoy" protest (2022), 96
Freeport-McMoran Copper and Gold Inc., 60
French Indochina, 20, *43*, 49, 135, 138
Freyre, Gilberto, 163–64, 173
FRONTEX border agency, 73, 74
frontierism, 19
"frozen racism," 157
Fukuzawa Yukichi, 16–17
"Fundamental British Values" (FBV), 166

Galton, Francis, *11*, 15, 215n96, 217n146
Garciá-Peña, Lorgia, 93
Garner, Steve, 68
Garrigus, John, 129
Garza, Alicia, 197
Garza, Joyhanna Yoo, 79
Gayles, Prisca, 173
Gaza Strip occupation, 111, 112
Gazetteer of the Persian Gulf, Oman, and Central Arabia (Lorimer), 113
Gazprom (energy corporation), 60
gender: Brazilian racial democracy and, 173–74; feminized racialized labor, 52–53, 58; hypersexualization of women in media, 82; in racial science, 12; racist gendered spectacle, 20–21; sexual exploitation and, 73
General Agreement on Trade in Services (GATS), 65
genocide: of European Jews, xlv, 18, 50, 100, 161; of indigenous peoples, 3, 30, 32, 91, 93, 96, 202; under Italian fascism, 51; Rwandan, 111; Southwest Africa, 161
Gentleman's Agreement (1907–8; United States), 39
geography: ethnic identity and, 175; geographical racial knowledge, 6–7; geographic boundaries of whiteness, 126–27; racial ideological production

and, 31–32, 40; span of global racial empires, 29–30
Georgia, 103, *149*
German exceptionalism, 161
Germany: current racial order, 100; EU designation, *149*; far right conservatism, 186; imperial racial categorization, 40, *43*, 49–50; imperial whitening policies, 139; post/antiracialism, *156*, 157, 161; "Scramble for Africa," 38; sterilization programs, 18
Ghana, 3, 118, 191
Al-Ghazzi, Omar, 83
Ghebremariam Tesfau', Mackda, 162, 184
Gillam, Reighan, 82–83
Gilman, Sander, 212n6
Gilmore, Ruth Wilson, 203
Gliddon, George, *11*, 14
global anti-Black imaginary, xiii, 6
global colorblindness: colorblind politicultures, 97, 155–57, *156*; conservative right, 183–88; contemporary anti-Black representation, 77; ethnic dominance, 175–80; within global racial system, xii, xiv–xv; *mestizaje* and racial democracy, 169–75; multiculturalism, 164–69; post/antiracialism, 157–64; "predicament of Blackness," 180–83; "problem" of Black subjectivity, 154; racial exceptionalism, 188–89; of traveling racial practices, 56
global commons, 201, 203
"A Global Critical Race and Racism Framework" (Christian), x
globalization, economic, 65–66
"global Muslim racialization," 68
global racial system: author's approach, xv–xviii, 207n7, 208n9; domino effect of, 55–56; foundational inflection points, 1–5; as framework, xi–xv; global racial imaginary, 6–7; imperialism within, xi, 26–30; "intimacies" within, 26; racism as, x–xi, xv,

208n9, 208n13, 209n15; text overview, xviii–xix. *See also* entangled racial zones; global colorblindness; global whitening; imperialism; modernity; resistance; traveling racism
Global War on Terror, xiv, 67, 68–70, 71, 72, 91, 111
global whitening: ambiguous whiteness, 132–35; dubious categorical prestige, 135–37; endeavors for whiteness, 120–21; European Union expansion, 147–51, *149*; global field of whiteness, xii–xiii, 122–25, *123*, 238n18; group racial mobility, 131; institutionalized whitening, 139–40; legal petitions for whiteness, 128–31, 239n37; multiracial uncertainties, 137–39; settler colonial whitening projects, 140–42; states on the margins, 142–44; unstable racial movement, 126–28, 151–53; whitening immigration policies, 144–47
Gobineau, Joseph-Arthur de, *11*
Goldberg, David Theo: author's approach and, 207n7; on colonial racialization, 223n155; on indigeneity, 212n22; on justifications for imperialism, 28; on liberalism, 7; on post/antiracialism, 157; on "racist exclusions," 210n31; on "Trufism," 193
Golden Dawn political party, 100, 101
Gómez, Laura, 140
Google, 178
Gramsci, Antonio, 208n13
Grant, Madison, 141
Great Exhibition (1851), 20
Greece, 100–101, *149*, 234n107
Greenland, 103, 161
Griffith, D. W., 21
Grosfoguel, Ramón, 89
Gross-Wyrtzen, Leslie, 181
Gualtieri, Sarah, 134
Guatemala, 128, 171
Gubara, Dahlia, 213n25

Guinea, 136
Gurkha soldiers, 71

Habasha (Orthodox Christians), 51
Hage, Ghassan, 141, 167, 238n18
Haiti: as entangled racial zone, 90, *90*, 93–94; global inequities and, 54; imperial racial categorization, *42*, 48; legal petitions for whiteness from, 129–30; "predicament of Blackness," *156*, 180, 182
Haitian Revolution (1791–1804), 37–38, 48
Hall, Bruce, 181, 251n221
Hall, Kim, 1
Hall, Stuart, 57, 75, 186, 208n13, 233n81
Halliburton (energy services company), 70–71
Hamilton: An American Musical (2015), 166
Hamlet (Shakespeare), 1
Hannaford, Ivan, 208n9
Harlem Renaissance movement, 191
Harper's Magazine, 19
Harris, Cheryl, 8, 123
Harrison, Olivia, 97–98
Hartman, Saidiya, xv, 7, 19, 34, 35, 52, 77
Harvey, David, 59
Hawaii, 72, 110, 130, *156*, 174–75, 249n170
Hawthorne, Camilla, 100
"hemispheric Orientalism," 38–39
Hereditary Genius (Galton), *11*
Heritage Foundation, 185, 252n249
Hernández, Tanya, 92, 172
Hesse, Barnor, 5, 6
hierarchies, racial: among competing empires, 28–29; within "Arabness," 113–16; Black enslavement and, 34–35; emergence of racial subjectivities, 6; entangled racial zones, 88–91, *90*; global field of whiteness, 122–25, *123*, 238n18; global racial state hierarchy, 118–19; within global racial system, xiii–xiv, 211n44; racial classifications by region, 41–51, *42–43*; racial formations as control, 39–41, 135; racialization of indigenous peoples, 30–33; racial science and, 9–18, *10–11*; semiperipheral economic states and, 63–64; translation of Arabic works and, 214n71; War on Terror and, 69–70
Hindu Aryans, 47
Hindutva (Hindu nationalism), 177–78
hip-hop, appropriation of, 78–79, 80
Hiroshima bombing, 66
Histoire Naturelle (Leclerc), *10*
History of Jamaica (Long), *10*, 13, 14
Hitler, Adolf, 162
Holly, James Theodore, 37
Holocaust, xiv, 18, 50, 100, 144, 161
Honduras, 128
Hooker, Juliet, 146, 173
Hopkins, Pauline, 24
Horne, Gerald, 30, 45, 86, 221n107
"Hottentot Venus," 20–21
Houthi rebels, 69, 115
Howard, John, 73
Howard School of International Relations, 52
Huang Zunxian, 17
Hübinette, Tobias, 165
Hume, David, 8, 14
Hungary, 101, *149*, *156*, 185, 187
Hunter, Marcus, 34, 52, 197
Hurwitz, Edith, 129
Hurwitz, Samuel, 129
Husain, Atiya, 67

Ibn Khaldūn, 214n71
Iceland, 29, 160, 161
Ignatiev, Noel, 199
"ilustrados" ("enlightened ones") designation, 138
"immatriculé" ("registered") designation, 137
immigration. *See* migration
Immigration Act (1924; United States), 39

Immigration Act (1971; England), 104
Immigration Restriction Act (1901; Australia), 39, 141
imperialism: cultural appropriation, 23–24; "durabilities and invitations," 63; enslavement and forced labor, 33–36; within global racist system, xi, 26–30; imperial whitening policies, 128–30, 137, 144–45; indigenous genocide and racialization, xii, 30–33; knowing and defying, 51–53; manufactured fears, 36–39; post-racial, xv; racial classifications by region, 41–51, *42–43*; racial formations as control, 39–41; racial science in, 16; racist modernity and, 3–4. *See also* colonialism
Imre, Anikó, 175
indentured labor, 35–36, 50
India: anticolonial resistance, 191; Bollywood industry, 81; as entangled racial zone, *90*; ethnic dominance, *156*, 177–78; imperial racial categorization, *42*, 44, 46–47, 136; minstrel performance, 22; racialized labor, 35; as semi-peripheral economic state, 63
"Indian" designation, 32
Indian Mutiny (1857), 47
"*indigène*" designation, 32, 40, 49, 136
indigenous peoples: Blackness and indigeneity, 211n45, 212n22, 254n68; Canadian multicultural ethos and, 165; child removals and enforced whiteness, 138; in entangled racial zones, 93, 95–96, 105–6; historical group whitening, 131; imperial racialization and genocide, 30–33; *mestizaje* ideology, 170–72; models for reparations and liberation, 202; under Spanish and Portuguese imperialism, 3; theft of indigenous knowledge, 66; under US settler colonialism, 141
Indochina, 20, *43*, 49, 135, 138
"*indo-mestizaje*," 170

Indonesia, 35, 99, 107, 109, 137, 164, 165, 190
Industrial Revolution, 34
inequality: colonial legacies of, 55, 60, 61–62; geographical distribution of, 54–55; global colorblindness and, 56; legal protections of whiteness, 65–66; wealth inequities, United States, 91
"institutionalized whitening," 140
interest convergence, 85–86
International Federation of Eugenics Organizations (IFEO), 18
International Labour Organization, 54
International League Against Racism and Anti-Semitism, 159
international lending, 65
International Monetary Fund (IMF), 65
International Organization for Migration, 148–50
intersectionality, 40, 58, 88, 195
Inuit people, 31
Iran: Aryan concept and, 15, *156*, 179; blackface performances, 77; enslavement and anti-Blackness, 35; as entangled racial zone, *90*; global militarism and, 70; legal petitions for whiteness and, 131; national whitening campaign, 142
Iraq, 70, 72
Ireland, 132, 142, *149*
Islam. *See* Muslims
Islam, Inaash, 68
Islamophobia, 68–70
Israel, 68, 69, 73–74, 89–90, *90*, 110–18, 143–44
Israel Defense Forces (IDF), 112
Italian East Africa, 51
Italy: among competing racial empires, 29; contemporary racial order, 100–101; EU designation, *149*; imperial racial categorization, 40, *43*, 49–51; imperial whitening policies, 139; post/antiracialism, *156*, 157, 161–62
Itzigsohn, José, 6

Jackson, Lauren Michele, 77
Jamaica, *42*, 46, 104, 129, 182
James, C.L.R., 24, 38, 52
Japan: among competing racial empires, 29, 218n23; anti-Asian policies and, 38, 39, 221n107; co-ethnic racialization, 106; consumption of racist spectacle, 23; de-racialized anime characters, 81; ethnic nationalism, 16–17, 176; racial mobility strategies, 135, 142
Jefferson, Thomas, *10*, 13, 14, 21, 31
Jensen, Lars, 160–61
Jewish National Fund Law (1953), 112
Jews: anti-Jewish sentiment, 2, 16, 144; contemporary racial order and, 111–12; Libyan racial categorizations and, 51; racial mobility and, 132–34, 143–44. *See also* anti-Jewish sentiment
Johnson-Reed Act (1942; United States), 141
Jones, Claudia, 52
Jordan, 112, 113, 114
Journey Law (1908; Canada), 39
"jungle films," 21
jus sanguini (right of blood), 100

Kaatje Kekkelbek (minstrel show), 22
Kachin people, 108
Kalmar, Ivan, 101, 148, 152, 187
Kanak Melanesians, 49
Kant, Immanuel, 8, *10*, 13
Karen people, 108, 109
Kaufmann, Eric, 251n240
Kawai, Yuko, 176
Kazakhstan, 67
Keane, Augustus, 20, 127
Keaton, Trica, 158
Kelley, Robin, 196
Kenya, 61–62, 67
Khmer people, 49
Khmer Rouge movement, 107–8
Khoikhoi people, 20–21, 32, 45, 49–50, 217n146

Khoisan peoples, 45
Kim, Claire Jean, 122, 238n11
Kim, Nadia, xii, 177, 238n16
Kimari, Wangui, 63
King, Martin Luther, Jr., 66, 195
King, Tiffany Lethabo, 254n68
Kinh people, 49
Klopse Carnival Troupes, 22
knowledge production: author's approach, xvi; colorblindness and, 155; counter-knowledges, 24–25; geographical racial knowledge, 6–7; theft of indigenous knowledge, 66. *See also* global color-blindness; resistance
Knox, Robert, 15
Kosovo, *149*
K-Pop, 79–80, 229n177
Kraidy, Marwan, 83
Ku Klux Klan, 21
Kumar, Krishan, 218n20
Kung Fu films, 81

labor: 1980s deregulation policies, 65; exploitation, 57–59; feminized racialized labor, 52–53, 58; forced, 35–36, 50; racial mobility and, 131; rise in non-standard forms of, 54; US racialized labor projects, 146. *See also* slavery; transatlantic slave trade
Laforteza, Elaine, 137–38
La Isla Española (Hispaniola) colony, 3
Lamar, Kendrick, 77
Lamarckism, 18
Land and Freedom Movement, 67
land grabbing, 61
language: adoption of "race" as term, 12; "Aryan" concept, 15–16; author's approach, xvi–xvii; coining of "Latin America," 170–71; current "Non-Self-Governing Territories," 87; denoting slave ancestry, 116, 129; elimination of "race" terms, 157–58, 161, 162, 165, 244n17; imperial racial formations,

31–33, 39–41, *42–43*; "linguistic *détournement*," 97–98; racial scientific language, 14, 126; racial terms, seventeenth-century, 2; reifying colonial knowledge, xvi; "terrorist" as colonial construct, 67
Laos, 107
La Raza Cósmica (Vasconcelos), 171
Latin America: coining of, 170–71; as entangled racial zone, *90*, 91–96; legal petitions for whiteness, 134; neo-Lamarckian theories, 18; ongoing colonial governance, 87; organized resistance, 197; racial mobility, 146; racist cultural production, 23
latino-mestizaje, 170
Latvia, *149*
Law, Ian, 51, 132, 172, 182
Law of Absentees' Property (1950; Israel), 112
League of Nations Mandate System, 29
Lebanon, 112, 114, 134, 143
Leclerc, Georges-Louis, *10*, 12, 13
Lee, Erica, 38
legal petitions for whiteness, 128–31, 239n37
Lentin, Alana, 157, 159, 207n7
Leopold II, King of Belgium, 137
Leyenda Blanca (White Legend) of Costa Rica, 121
LGBTQ communities, 185, 193, 197
Liang Qichao, 17
liberalism, in racist modernity, 4, 7–9, 24, 25
Libya, *42*, 50–51, 70, 74
"linguistic *détournement*," 97–98
Linnaeus, Carl, *10*, 12, 13, 31, 126
Lipsitz, George, 200
literacy, racial, 195–200
Lithuania, *149*, 180
Living Races of Mankind (Keane), 20
Locke, Alain, 52
Locke, John, 8

Loftsdóttir, Kristín, 160–61
Long, Edward, *10*, 13–14
Lorde, Audre, 201
Lorimer, John Gordon, 113
Louisiana Purchase (1803), 37
Louisiana Purchase Exposition (1904), 20
Lowe, Lisa, 7, 23, 26
Ltifi, Afifa, 115
Lu, Amy Shirong, 81
Lula da Silva, Luiz Inácio, 94
Lumumba, Patrice, 67
Lundström, Catrin, 165
luso-tropicalism ideology, 163–64, 173, 181
Luxembourg, *149*
lynching, as spectacle, 21

Maasai people, 32
Macron, Emmanuel, 159
Madagascar, 71
Madrid Forum, 185
Maduro, Nicolás, 92
Maghbouleh, Neda, 125, 179
mainstreaming, of far-right ideology, 184–86
Malay people, 32, 169
Malaysia, 169
Mali, 68
Malta, *149*
Mamdani, Mahmood, 47, 223n155, 251n221
Mandela, Nelson, 85
Maneri, Marcello, 162
Māori people, 105, 219n29
Mao Zedong, 107
marielitos (nonwhite Cubans), 92
maroon settlements, 36–37, 52
marriage, interracial, 44, 50, 137, 139
Marshall Islands, 66–67, 72
Martin, Trayvon, 197
The Masque of Blackness (Jonson), 1
Matsuda, Mari, 199
Matsuoka, Manami, 106
Mau Mau rebellion (1952–1960), 67

Mauritania, 116
Mauritius, 72, 74
May, Theresa, 104
Mbembe, Achille, 6, 52, 158, 181, 196
McClintock, Anne, 22
McKittrick, Katherine, xvi, 25
McMichael, Philip, 65
media, 19–20, 24–25, 184–86
Meer, Nasar, 166, 194
Meghji, Ali, 207n7
Melanesia: as entangled racial zone, 90, *90*, 110; forced labor, 35, 36; geographical distribution of inequality and, 54; "Melanesian" designation, 32; "predicament of Blackness," *156*, 182–83
Meloni, Georgia, 162
Memmi, Albert, 41, 221n116
Merzouk, Nahel, 198
mestizaje ideology, xix, 80, 92, 145, 156, *156*, 169–75
"*mestizo*" designation, 59, 137–38, 170, 171
Metaxas, Ioannis, 100
"*meticci*" designation, 51
Métis groups, 31, 138
Mexican-American War (1848), 170
Mexico: anti-Chinese sentiment, 39; as entangled racial zone, *90*, 92; externalized border management and, 74; *mestizaje* ideology and, 170–71; petitions for whiteness from, 130; racial democracy and *mestizaje*, 169; sterilization programs, 18; US annexation of, 140
Michel, Noémi, 160
"*Michling*" designation, 50
"Middle East," as entangled racial zone, 97, 110, 113–14, 117
Mignolo, Walter D., 226n59
migration: 2015 "migrant crisis," 97, 151; anti-Asian sentiment and, 91, 96; anti-immigrant sentiment, UK, 104; border management and security, 73–75, 148–50; far right conservatism and, 185; group racial mobility and, 132–35; migrant workers, 58–59, 114; whitening immigration policies, 120–21, 144–47
militarism: building worlds without, 200–203; colonial antecedents, 66–67; externalized border management, 73–75; Global War on Terror, xiv, 67, 68–70, 71, 72, 91, 111; military contractors and sacrifice zones, 70–73; in postwar decolonial policies, 86; traveling racism and, xi, 55, 56
Mill, John Stuart, 8
Miller, Stephen, 251n240
Mills, Charles, x, 7, 207n1, 207n7
mining industry, 60–61
minjok ideology, 177
"minstrel diplomacy," 23
minstrel shows, 1, 21–22, 23, 78
minzoku (Japanese ethnic group), 17, 176
miscegenation, 137–39, 169–70
mobility, racial. *See* racial mobility
Mobutu Sese Seko, 67
"modern Blackness" aesthetics, 182
modernity: characterized, xi; emerging subjectivities and geographies, 5–7; foundational and counterknowledges, 24–25; foundational inflection points, 1–5; liberalism, 7–9; science, 9–18, *10–11*; spectacle, 18–24
"modernizing" discourse, 58, 65
Mogilner, Marina, 16
Moldova, *149*
Mollett, Sharlene, 61
Mondon, Aurelien, 184
"Mongolians" designation, *10–11*, 13, 16
monogenesis, 9, *10*
Monroe Doctrine (1823), 91
Montenegro, *149*
"Moors," 1–2, 3, 77, 162, 212n6
Morales Ayma, Evo, 171
Moreton-Robinson, Aileen, 8
Morning, Ann, 162
Morocco, 74, 75, 99, 116

Morris, Wesley, 77
Morrison, Matthew, 78
Morrison, Toni, x, xvi, 142
Morton, Samuel, *10*, 14, 126–27
Mozambique, 71, 136
Muhamasheen Yemenis ("marginalized ones"), 69, 115
multiculturalism: attacks on, 166–67; as colorblind politiculture, xix, 156, *156*, 164–66; paranoia around, 167–68; as state policy, 169
Multiculturalism Policy of Canada (1985), 165
"multiple modernities" perspective, 208n9
Muñoz-Muñoz, Marianela, 173
Muslims: Arab/Islamic slavery scholarship, 213n25; European racial order and, 101, 103; global colorblindness and, 159, 160, 166; Global War on Terror and, 68–70; Libyan racial categorizations and, 51; "Middle East" as entangled racial zone, 110–11, 113–15; in racial mobility discourse, 133–34, 142, 151; as religious "Others," 1–2, 3; Rohingya people, violence against, 108–9; Turkish soap operas and, 83; work of Ibn Khaldūn, 214n71
Mwasi Collective (Afrofeminist group), 159
Myanmar, 107, 108

Nagasaki bombing, 66
Nakba (catastrophe), 112
Namaganda, Assumpta, 201
Nama people, 50, 139
National Front political party, 159
nationalism: ethnic dominance and, 175, 249n175; *Hindutva* (Hindu nationalism), 177–78; "institutionalized whitening," 139–40; in nineteenth-century media, 19; racial science and, 15, 16–17; settler colonial whitening projects, 140–42; states on the margins of whiteness, 142–44; through commodified anti-Blackness, 22; whitening immigration policies, 144–47. *See also* entangled racial zones; ethnic dominance
"national security," 67, 71, 73–75. *See also* militarism
"Native" designation, 32, 40
Naturalization Act (1903; Australia), 141
Naturalization Law (1790; United States), 140
Nauru, 73
Nazi Germany, 18
Ndlovu-Gatsheni, Sabelo, xvi, 117, 202
negative eugenics, 17
Negritude movement, 191
neocolonialism, 194
neo-Lamarckism, 18
neoliberalism, xiv, 56, 57, 65, 168, 172–73
"Neo-Ottoman Cool," 83
neo-Pharaonism, 116
neoteric Pan-Africanism, 203
Nepal, 29
nested Orientalism, 101
Netherlands: among competing racial empires, 29; colonial exhibits, 20; consumption of anti-Black representation, 77; contemporary racial order, 99–100, 109; current colonial governance, 87, 231n18; EU designation, *149*; European "culture of taste," 23, 218n176; far right conservatism, *156*, 185; first imperial formation and, 27; imperial group racial mobility, 133; imperial racial categorizations, 40, *42*, 45–46, 137; imperial "welfare" practices, 138; multiculturalism in, 164; post/antiracialism in, 159–61; transatlantic slave trade, 33
New Caledonia, 36, 48, 49, 110
A New Division of the Earth (Bernier), *10*
New Guinea, 110
Ne Win (Burmese army general), 108

New Laws of the Indies (1542), 3
Newman, Brooke, 129
New Mexico, 66
New Phoenicianism, 134, 143
New Zealand: contemporary racial order, 89–90, *90*, 104–5, 107, 110; current colonial governance, 231n18; far right conservatism, 187; global inequities and, 54; imperial racial classifications, 46; multiculturalism in, *156*, 164; settler colonial whitening project, 141
NGOs (non-governmental organizations), 66, 94
Niang, Mame-Fatou, 158
Nicaragua, 94
Niger, 68
Nigeria, 135
Nihonjin ("Japanese people"), 176
Nkrumah, Kwame, 191, 194
"No Borders" political project, 203
Nollywood (Nigerian cinema), 81–82
Nonini, Donald, 64
Nordic exceptionalism, 159–61
Norse symbolism, 186
North Africa, *90*, 110, 115–17, 181, 197
North American Free Trade Agreement (NAFTA), 91
North Korea, 176, 177
North Macedonia, *149*
Norway, 18, 160, 187, 231n18
Notes on the State of Virginia (Jefferson), *10*, 13, 14
Nott, Josiah, *11*, 14
Nubia, 116
Nueva España, 42
Nyansapo Festival, 159

O'Connor, P. S., 141
Of National Characters (Hume), 8
Of the Different Human Races (Kant), *10*
Oh, Chuyun, 79
Ong, Aiwha, 64
On the Natural Variety of Mankind (Blumenbach), *10*, 13

On the Origin of Species (Darwin), 14
Operation Barkhane (2014), 68
Operation Serval (2013), 68
Operation Sovereign Borders, 73
Orbán, Viktor, 185, 187
Orientalism, 38–39, 101, 178
Osman 'Abd al-Basit (minstrel show), 22
Ottoman empire, 29, 50, 113, 131, 143, 144, 151, 179
Ovaherero people, 50

Pacific Island Labourers Act (1901), 141
Pacífico, Maria Bernadete, 187
Padmore, George, 52, 191
Page Law (1875; United States), 38–39
Painter, Nell, 9
Pākehā people (European New Zealanders), 105
Pakistan, 70
Palestine, 69, 90, *90*, 111–12, 144
Pan African Association, 191
Panama, 128
Pan American Eugenics Organization, 18
Pancasila ideology (Indonesia), 109
Papua New Guinea, 73, 110
paternalism, 172
Pérez, Lucrecia, 99
Perry, Keisha-Khan, 95, 232n60
Peru, 39, 128
PetroChina Company Limited, 60
Petts, Amy, xiv
Philippines, 42, 72, 130, 137–38
Phoenician myth, 134, 143
Picker, Giovanni, 162, 184
Pierre, Jemima, 124, 180–81, 209n15
Playing in the Dark (Morrison), xvi
Poland, 101, *149*, 234n114
"political quilting," 199
politicultures: characterized, xix, 210n31; conservative right, 183–88; ethnic dominance, 175–80; global colorblindness and, 155–57, *156*; multiculturalism, 164–69; post/antiracialism, 157–64; "predicament of Blackness," 180–83;

racial democracy and *mestizaje*, 169–75. See also global colorblindness
Pol Pot, 107–8
polygenism, 9, *10–11*, 14
Polynesia, 110
"polyracism" perspective, 208n9
Portugal: colonial exhibits, 20; contemporary racial order, 98; EU designation, *149*; first imperial formation and, 27; forced labor, 35; group racial mobility, 132; imperial racial categorization, 40, 41, *42*, 44, 136; *mestizaje* ideology and, 170, 173; post/antiracialism, 163–64; transatlantic slave trade, 2–3, 33
Portuguese Colonial Act (1930), 136
positive eugenics, 17, 145
Post and Telegraph Act (1901), 141
post/antiracialism: as colorblind politiculture, xix, 156, *156*, 157–58; fascist hauntings, 161–64; French "raceblind Republicanism," 158–59; Nordic exceptionalism, 159–61; post-racial imperialism, xv
powell, john, 56
"predicament of Blackness," xix, 156, 180–83
Présence Africaine journal, 191
Prevention of Infiltration Law (Israel), 74
Principles of Biology; Descriptive Sociology (Spencer), *11*
Private Military Contractors (PMCs), 70–72
privatization, economic, 65–66
production networks, global, 56–57
Protestantism, 46
PT Freeport Indonesia (mining company), 60
Puerto Rico, 72, 79–80, 93, 146, 172
Pulido, Laura, 199
Punch magazine, 19
Putin, Vladimir, 71, 102, 187

"queer impossible subjects," 198
quilombo (enslaved runaway communities), 37

raceblind Republicanism, 158
"race critical" vs. "critical race," 207n7
"race music," 229n171
"race relations," 86
The Races of Europe (Ripley), 15
Races of Man (Knox), 15
racial capitalism: author's usage, 225n23; building worlds without, 200–203; coining of, 208n13; commodification of racist spectacle, 20–23; expropriated space, 59–63; labor exploitation, 57–59; replication of, 63–64; as "unjust enrichment," 55; white capital protection, 65–66. See also capitalism
racial degeneration, 9, 13, 15, 17–18
racial democracy and *mestizaje*: Brazil, 173–74; as colorblind politiculture, xix, 156, *156*, 169–73; Hawaii, 174–75
racial Europeanization, 157
racial exceptionalism, 188–89
racial gaslighting, 188
racial hinges and loopholes, 125, 151–53
"racial innocence," entreaties of, 172
racialized geographies, 6–7
racial mobility: group mobility, 131–39; instabilities in, 126–31, 151–53; national strategies, 139–47
racial pragmatism, 39
racism. See entangled racial zones; global colorblindness; global whitening; imperialism; modernity; resistance; traveling racism
racist erasure, 155
Rai, Rohini, 177
Rana, Junaid, 68, 209n15
Ransby, Barbara, 199
Rassengefühl (racial feeling), 50
Ravindran, Tathagatan, 95
raza designation, 44
"The Red Deal: Indigenous Action to Save Our Earth," 202
"reform conflicts," 61
"reform-retrenchment," 194
refusal, as resistance, xv, xix, 203, 205

reggaetón phenomenon, 79–80
Rehobothers ethnic group, 49–50, 139
religion. *See* Catholic Church; Christianity; Muslims
reparations, 202
repressive victimhood, 183, 251n240
reproductive labor, 58
resistance: building new worlds, 200–203; counterknowledges as, xix, 24–25; defying imperialism, 51–53; by enslaved peoples, 36–38, 52; to know, feel, and move, 203–4; "modern Blackness" aesthetics, 182; as ongoing and ever-present, 193–95; "predicament of Blackness" and, 181; racial consciousness, literacy and solidarity, 195–200; refusal as, xv, xix; twentieth-century activism, 190–92
resource extraction, 60, 66, 71
Rhaman, Rhea, 66
Rhodes Must Fall movement, 197
Right of Conquest, 30
Right of Return (1950), 112
right-wing conservatism, 183–88, 193–94
Riley, Dylan, 146
Ripley, William, 15
Rising Tide of Color (Stoddard), 38
Risley, Sir Herbert, 47
Rivera-Rideau, Petra, 79
Robinson, Cedric, 208n13, 212n23
Robinson, Zandria, 52
Rodney, Walter, 37, 208n13
Rohingya people, 108–9
Romania, *149*
Roma people, 98, 143
Ronald Reagan Ballistic Missile Defense, 72
Rouighi, Ramzi, 214n71
Royal Pragmatic decree, 44
Rufo, Christopher, 193
"rule of colonial difference," 27
"rules of representation," xvi
Runnymede Trust Commission, 166

Russia: anti-Asian policies, 39; contemporary racial order, 89–90, *90*, 96, 101, 102–3; counterterrorism in Mali, 68; ethnic whiteness, 179–80; far right conservatism, *156*, 187; private military contractors, 71, 72; resource extraction, 60; scientific racial logics, 16; as semi-peripheral economic state, 63
Rwanda, 74, 111

Sabbagh-Khoury, Areej, 144
sacrifice zones, 70–73
"safari" tourism, 61–62
Saied, Kais, 75
Salazar, António de Oliveira, 98, 164, 173
Samoa, *42*, 49, 110
São Tomé Island, 3
"Saracens" (Muslim populations), 1–2, 3
Sarmiento, Domingo Faustino, 146
Sartre, Jean-Paul, 27
Saudi Arabia, 69, 70, 113, 114, 115
"scavenger" qualities of racism, 210n27
science: racial, 9–18, 50, 101–2, 106, 126, 138, 170, 176; racist spectacle and, 21; scientific multiculturalism, 165
Scotland, 167
Scott, Jovan, 182
"Scramble for Africa," 37–38
"secondhand blackness," 77
Second Treatise on Government (Locke), 8
"*seikou toutei*" (Japanese notion), 106
Selod, Saher, 68
Seminole people, 31
September 11th attacks, 111
Sepulveda, Juan Ginés, 212n22
Serbia, *149*
Seven Years' War (1756–63), 129
sexual commodification and exploitation, 58, 73
Shahjahan, Riyad, 121
Shakespeare, William, 1
Sharma, Nandita, 254n68
Sharma, Nitasha, 199

"shatter zones" of colonial contact, 30
Shell (oil and gas company), 60
Singapore, 106, *156*, 164, 169
Sketch of the Natural Provinces of the Animal World (Agassiz), *11*
slavery: "afterlife of slavery," 138; Arab/Islamic slavery scholarship, 213n25; contemporary racial order and, 91, 93; enslaved resistance, 36–38, 52–53, 94; imperial France and, 48; indentured labor, 35–36; indigenous enslavement, 30–31, 33; labels denoting slave ancestry, 116; in racial science discourse, 13–14; seventeenth-century liberalism and, 8; as "social institution," 34–35; systemic anti-Blackness, Brazil, 95. *See also* transatlantic slave trade
"Slavic" whiteness, 101–2, 179–80
Slovakia, *149*
Slovenia, *149*, 150
Small, Stephen, 40, 97
Smith, Danyel, 78
"social blackness," 115
Social Darwinism, 14–17, 38, 49
social protections, disinvestment in, 65–66
Sociology of Race and Ethnicity (journal), ix–x
soldiering, racial construction of, 71
solidarity-building, 195–200
Somalia, 70
Song, Daniel, 130–31
sound, racialization of, 78–79, 80
South Africa: as entangled racial zone, *90*; forced labor, 35; minstrel performances, 22; multiculturalism, *156*, 167–68; petitions for whiteness from, 130–31; as semi-peripheral economic state, 63–64
South African Apartheid (1948–94), 85, 99, 100, 117, 135, 157, 168
South Korea: adoption of racial hierarchies, 17; appropriation of hip-hop, 78–80, 229n177; consumption of racist spectacle, 23; current racial order, 106; ethnic dominance, 176–77
South Sudan, 119
Southwest Africa, *42*, 44, 49
Soviet Union, 67, 86, 102, 103, 234n119
space expropriation, 59–63
Spain: among competing racial empires, 28–29, 147; contemporary racial order, 98–99; enslaved runaway communities, 37; EU designation, *149*; first imperial formation and, 27; imperial whitening policies, 128–29, 130, 145; *mestizaje* ideology and, 170; Muslim rule in, 1–2; post/antiracialism, *156*, 157, 162–63; racial categorization, 40, 41, *42*, 44, 92, 137; transatlantic slave trade, 2–3, 33
Spanish-American War (1898), 170
Special Economic Zones, 65
spectacle, 18–24, 185–86
Spencer, Herbert, *11*, 14, 15
Stalin, Joseph, 234n119
Standing Up for Racial Justice (SURJ), 199
St. Domingue. *See* Haiti
Steinmetz, George, 27, 238n18
sterilization programs, 18
Stewart, Maria W., 25
Stoddard, Lothrop, 38, 141
Stoever, Jennifer Lynn, 78
Stoler, Ann, 28
Strings, Sabrina, 12
structural adjustment policies (SAPs), 65, 82, 111, 194
subjectivity: of Black resistance, 191; codification of Blackness, 34–35; generated by racist modernity, 5–7; imperialist racial formations, xii, 30–33, 39–41, *42*–*43*; indigeneity and Blackness, 31, 211n45, 212n22, 254n68; "problem" of Black subjectivity, 154; through racist spectacle, 18–19. *See also* hierarchies, racial

sub-Saharan Africa: colonial naming of, xvi; as entangled racial zone, 90, *90*, 110; geographical distribution of inequality and, 55; imperial racial categorization, 48; Russian resource extraction in, 71; transatlantic slave trade, 3
Sudan, 116, 119
sugarcane industry, 34
Suharto (Indonesian general), 109
Sun Yat-sen, 177
Suriname, 34, *42*, 45, 99, 133
Suzuki, Kazuko, 176, 218n23
Sweden, 18, *149*, 160, 164, 165, 186
Swiss People's Party, 160
Switzerland, 18, 157, 159–61
Syria: 2015 "migrant crisis," 151; as entangled racial zone, 90, *90*, 100, 114; impact of militarism on, 70, 71, 72; petitions for whiteness from, 130; racial mobility and, 134, 143, 152
Syrian civil war, 111, 152
Systema Naturae (Linnaeus), *10*, 13, 126

Tacky's Slave Revolt (1760), 129
Taíno people, 172
Taiwan, 64
Táíwò, Olúfẹ́mi, 88, 201, 202
Tamale, Sylvia, 203
Tanzanian school of radical scholars, 208n13
taste, culture of, 23
Tate, Merze, 52, 53
Tate, Shirley, 80, 132, 171–72, 182
Tatlıtuğ, Kıvanç, 83
taxonomy, racial, 9–18, *10–11*. See also hierarchies, racial
Tayeb, Leila, 115, 122
television series, 82–83
Terreblanche, Sampie, 28, 55
terrorism, 67, 68–70. See also War on Terror
Texaco, Inc., 113

Thailand, 29
Thelwell, Chinua, 22
"third country" agreements, 73–74
Thomas, Deborah, 182
Tilley, Virginia, 170
Todorova, Miglena, 143, 198
Tometi, Ayọ, 197
Torres-Leschnik, Jericko, 79
Torres Strait Islanders, 105–6
TotalEnergies (oil and gas company), 60
tourism industry, 58, 61–62
Trade-Related Intellectual Property Rights (TRIPs), 65
Trade-Related Investment Measures (TRIMs), 65–66
transatlantic slave trade: development of, 31, 33–35; eras of imperial formation and, 27; as foundational to racist modernity, 2–4, 212n22; maroon settlements and resistance, 36–38, 52–53. See also slavery
"transnational Black resistant subjectivity," 191
traveling racism: anti-Black representation and cultural theft, 76–80; "Aryan" concept, 15–16; cascading effects of, 55–56; characterized, xi–xii, 83–84; expropriated space, 59–63; externalized border management, 73–75; global inequality, 54–55; global production networks, 56–57; labor exploitation, 57–59; legacies of colonial militarism, 66–67; military contractors and sacrifice zones, 70–73; racial cultural production, 75–76; regional cultural products, 80–83; replicating global racial capitalism, 63–64; "terrorist" containment, 68–70; white capital protection, 65–66
"travestied emancipation," 35
Treaty of Alcáçovas (1479), 2–3
Treaty of Guadalupe (1848), 140
Treaty of Waitangi (1840), 105

Tricontinental Conference (1966), 192
Trienekens, Sandra, 100
Trinidad and Tobago, 182
"tropes of blackness," 1
Troutt Powell, Eve, 115
"Trufism," 193
Trump, Donald, 186, 188
Tsika, Noah, 82
Tunisia, 74, 75, 99, 116–17
Turkey: Aryan mythologies, *156*, 178–79; as entangled racial zone, *90*, 99, 100; EU designation, *149*, 150–51; "Neo-Ottoman Cool," 83
Turkic Muslims, 69
Twinam, Ann, 128
Types of Mankind (Nott and Gliddon), 14

ubuntu philosophy, 203
Uganda, 74
Ukraine, 71, *149*, 180
"unequal marriages," 44
UNESCO (United Nation's Educational Scientific and Cultural Organization), 173
United Fruit Company, 91
United Kingdom: contemporary racial order, 103–4; current colonial governance, 87, 231n18; externalized border control, 74; resource extraction, 60. *See also* Britain
United Nations, 71, 87
United Nations Partition Plan for Palestine (1947), 144
United States: anti-Asian policies, 38–39; atomic weapons testing, 66–67; attacks on critical race theory, 185, 253n29; Black solidarity in, 198, 199; Cold War-era relations with China, 64; colonial exhibits, 20; contemporary racial order, 89–96, *90*; corporate racism, 113; current colonial governance, 87, 231n18; eugenics programs, 18; far right conservatism, *156*, 185–86,

187; in global field of whiteness, 122, *123*; imperial expansion, Hawaii, 174; imperial racial classifications, 46; indigenous child removals, 138; investments in antiterrorism, 68; Italian immigration to, 50; Louisiana Purchase, 37; *mestizaje* ideology and, 170–71, 172; minstrel spectacle, 22; multiculturalism in, *156*, 164, 165–66, 247n86; post/antiracialism, 157; postwar geopolitical policies, 86, 230n8; private military contractors, 71–72; racial commentary in popular press, 19; racialized labor projects, 146; racial mobility in, 134; resource extraction, 60; settler colonial whitening project, 140–42; support for Israel, 69; transatlantic slave trade, 33, 34; US-Haiti relations, 182; white legal petition cases, 130–31
"unjust enrichment/impoverishment," 55, 65
Upton, Florence Kate, 23
Uruguay, 22, 145
Uyghur people, 69, 107

Vanuatu, 110
Vasconcelos, José, 171
Venezuela, 92, 94, 128
Vietnam, 35, 48, 107–8, 138–39
Villafranca, Richard, 120
Vine, David, 72
Viral Justice (Benjamin), 201
Vox political party (Spain), 163
voyeurism, 21

Wacquant, Loïc, 208n9
Wakenge, Claude, 61
Walker, David, 24, 37
Wallerstein, Immanuel, 208n13
War on Terror, xiv, 67, 68–70, 71, 72, 91, 111
Weiner, Melissa, 207n7
Wekker, Gloria, 99, 160

welfare systems, disinvestment in, 65
Wells-Barnett, Ida B., 24
Werner, Marion, 57
West Bank occupation, 111, 112
West Indies, xvi, 14, 46, 129
West Papua, 60, 109
Wherry, Frederick, 125
White, Charles, *10*, 14, 31
whiteness: deep whiteness, 56, 63, 66, 83; as emerging racial subjectivity, 6–7; European Union expansion and, 147–51, *149*; as form of inheritance, 55; global field of, 122–25, *123*; global "possessive investment" in, 56; within global racial hierarchy, xiv, 28–29; imperial racial designations of, 40–41; legal petitions for, 128–31; legal protection of, 65–66; in regional cultural products, 81, 82, 83; "Slavic" whiteness, 101–2, 179–80; Swedish "white melancholy," 165; used herein, xvii; white fears, 36–39; white innocence, 160; white paranoia, 167–68; "white personhood" in liberal discourse, 7–8; white possessive, 8; white saviorism, 117–18. *See also* Blackness; global colorblindness; global whitening
"Whiteness as Property" (Harris), 8
white racist sedimentation, 55
white supremacy: Black scholarship on, 52; building consciousness about, 195–200; colorblindness and, 154–55; early colonial conceptualization of, 28; foundational inflection points, 1–5; as global system, x; "interest convergence" and, 85–86; repressive victimhood, 183–84; white fears and, 36–39. *See also* entangled racial zones; global colorblindness; global whitening; imperialism; modernity; resistance; traveling racism
Williams, Eric, 52
Williams, Henry Sylvester, 191
Wilson, Woodrow, 101
Winant, Howard, 6, 209n15
Winter, Aaron, 184
Witbooi people, 50
Wolfe, Patrick, 26, 30
Wong, Diane, 196
Workers' Party (Brazil), 174
World Bank, 65, 172
World Inequality Lab, 54
The World's Peoples (Keane), 127
World Trade Organization (WTO), 65
World War I, 27, 29, 38, 101
World War II, 27–28, 39, 46, 53, 66, 161–62
Wright, Cynthia, 254n68
Wright, Jamaal, 59
Wright, Richard, 190
Wynter, Sylvia, xvi, 5

X, Malcolm, 192

Yan Fu, 17
"Yellow Peril" discourse, 38–39, 64, 106–7, 135, 141
Yemen, 54, 69, 70, 114–15
Young, Robert Alexander, 24
youth culture, 78
Yugoslavia, 101, 102

Zakaria, Rafia, 71
Zia-Ebrahimi, Reza, 142
Zuberi, Tukufu, 24, 52
Zwarte Piet (Black Pete), 77